New Plays from Chicago

The Sara Lee Foundation is honored and excited to be the exclusive sponsor of Chicago Dramatists' inaugural publication NEW PLAYS FROM CHICAGO.

The national distribution of this anthology increases access and awareness of the premier works developed by Chicago Dramatists' Resident Playwrights and produced by some of Chicago's leading theatre companies.

We congratulate Chicago Dramatists and all of its Resident Playwrights on this inaugural publication, and hope that you and many others enjoy these rich and diverse new plays from Chicago.

Sara Lee Foundation

New Plays from Chicago

Edited by Russ Tutterow and Ann Filmer

CHICAGO
DRAMATISTS

THE PLAYWRIGHTS' THEATRE

A Chicago Dramatists Press Book
Published by Chicago Dramatists Press
1105 W. Chicago Avenue, Chicago, IL 60622

Copyright 2005 by Chicago Dramatists Press
All rights reserved

Manufactured in the United States of America

Cover photography by Johnny Knight

First Edition: July 2005

ALL INQUIRIES CONCERNING RIGHTS, INCLUDING AMATEUR RIGHTS, SHOULD BE ADDRESSED TO:
Russ Tutterow, Artistic Director, Chicago Dramatists, 1105 W. Chicago Avenue, Chicago, IL, 60622
Email: rtutterow@chicagodramatists.org; Phone (312) 633-0630

Contents

Acknowledgements

Thanks to the following persons for their invaluable assistance in compiling this volume of plays:

Keith Huff

Johnny Knight

Brian Loevner

Kathleen Powers

Dave Stanley

Deborah Stewart

FOREWORD by Rebecca Gilman

The plays in this collection reflect the landscape in which they were written. People who live outside the Midwest are under the mistaken impression that our part of the country is flat. But ask anyone who has ever ridden a bike across Iowa, or climbed the sand dunes of Michigan, and she will tell you that the terrain rises and falls dramatically. Even the flatness of Chicago is deceptive. Jog Chicago's lakefront, or walk down Michigan Avenue in the dead of winter, and see how long it takes for the wind to knock you sideways. That's what these plays do. They knock you sideways with their insight, their humor and their revelations.

The plays in this collection are alike in some ways. Many are about family; either those we are born into, or, as in Susan Lieberman's *Arrangement for Two Violas*, those we choose. And many are about the healing of wounds. Some, like Robert Koon's *Vintage Red and the Dust of the Road*, explore the struggle to salve old wounds newly re-opened. Others, like Brett Neveu's *Drawing War*, describe those who deny their hurt at all costs. And at least two of the plays - David Barr's *The Face of Emmett Till*, and Joel Drake Johnson's *The End of the Tour* - successfully argue that there are some wounds that should never be healed.

But these plays are also completely different from one another. The voices represented here are strong and distinctive; their world views clear and surprising. And the surprises are often stunning. An affair strengthens a marriage in John Green's *The Liquid Moon*. Self-reliance is taught through utter dependence in Mia McCullough's *Taking Care*. And in Marsha Estell's *Heat*, a family's curse is transformed into a blessing.

So take a journey across the landscape of these plays, across their hard climbs and breathtaking falls. I guarantee you'll enjoy the ride.

Rebecca Gilman
Resident Playwright Alumna, Chicago Dramatists

REBECCA GILMAN's plays include *Spinning Into Butter, Boy Gets Girl, The Glory of Living, The Heart is a Lonely Hunter* and *Dollhouse*. She joined Chicago Dramatists as a Resident Playwright in 1995, and currently serves on its Artistic Advisory Board.

INTRODUCTION by Russ Tutterow

Well, look what's happened. We finally turned Chicago into a great town for playwrights – or at least a damn good one.

One day, back in the 1980s, I remember feeling badly for a young playwright who told me that he had moved to Chicago because he heard it was a playwrights' town. I guess Chicago got that reputation for about two months because of the success David Mamet had here in the 1970s and early 1980s – before he left. My home theatre, Chicago Dramatists, was founded in 1979 by a small group of playwrights who just wanted a place to work. They certainly weren't finding it at any other theatre, so in the best Chicago theatre tradition they decided to do it themselves.

From the time I started working in professional theatre here in the mid-1970s, through sometime in the mid-1990s, a new play was either a play that had premiered in New York City but hadn't played Chicago yet or, in the rare instance that it actually was a brand new play with a playwright sitting there writing and rewriting it, it was a novelty for a theatre's season of shows.

The "renaissance" in Chicago theatre, as we used to call it, began for different people at different times. For us Baby Boomers, it was the mid-1970s. The most significant thing we brought to the movement was a staggering number of college graduates with theatre degrees. There weren't enough theatres to hire us all, New York was becoming harsh and expensive, and we discovered this great new thing called "not-for-profit." (I know not-for-profit had been around for some time, but hey, all history began with the Baby Boomers.) In large part, the theatres that started up here in the 1970s and 1980s were formed by graduates of nearby colleges who decided to stay on and make work for themselves. We also brought something of a hippie sensibility, I think, which included a respect for art and a joy for the theatre.

But something was missing: playwrights – and a regard for the importance of new work and the knowledge and skill to make it. I fault our colleges at the time for paying no attention whatsoever to playwrights and new work. (This has now changed.) So what shows did we produce? We produced what we knew: Shakespeare, Williams, Terry, Shakespeare, Guare, Shepard, Bullins, Shakespeare, Norman, Albee, Fugard, Shakespeare, and Shakespeare. Despite our theatrical daring in other ways, I think we had a sort of nutty fear of new plays, of the unknown. I remember talking to the young artistic director of a respected storefront theatre back in the 1980s, and asking him why they never produced new work. He said they could not afford to do it because nobody would come to see a new play. So what were they producing next? Some obscure Bulgarian play by some obscure Bulgarian playwright. His audiences weren't scared of new plays, he was. Also, it was just sort of understood that all new work came from New York.

By the mid-1990s, all this had started to change. Lots of talented young playwrights were moving here, greatly enlarging the pool of writers. The press (notably Richard Christiansen at the Chicago Tribune) started giving priority to reviewing new plays (they were probably the first to weary of seeing the same plays again and again). Theatre artists just got tired of doing the same old plays. And, most importantly, once they got a taste of the joys of developing and producing a brand new play in collaboration with a living, breathing playwright, theatre artists finally saw the light. I would like to think that they finally learned that, though your show only lasts (in Chicago) for five or six weeks, if it's a new play, there's a chance your work could live on and become part of the national repertory.

And one more thing. The growth of institutional new play development (something, from time to time, bemoaned in other parts of the U.S., but not here) has played a major role in turning this town into the center for new plays that it is today. Serious credit must be given to Victory Gardens Theater, which focused on new work by native authors since its founding in 1974; and in the early-to-mid-1990s, it was the initiatives of our two biggest theatres, the Goodman and Steppenwolf, which really sent a signal throughout our theatre community. Both institutions created new staff positions in new play development that led by example. I am, of course, eager to cite here the persistent, excellent work done by my own theatre, Chicago Dramatists, which since 1979 has been solely devoted to developing new plays and providing a safe but challenging home to countless writers. The large numbers of playwrights we work with (annual membership now over 200), and the large numbers of successful plays we develop (we counted 624 productions, awards, commissions, readings, and other honors for our plays and playwrights, just in the last year alone) are what distinguish Chicago Dramatists from all other theatres in the region.

Today, it's hard to find a Chicago theatre that does not produce a new work at some time during its season. Several more theatres now specialize in new work: Stage Left, Terrapin, Live Bait, ETA, Prop, Visions & Voices, Factory, Curious Theatre Branch (there are more). From the smallest storefront playhouse to the largest institution, there are now countless opportunities for playwrights in this town. Many theatres produce new play festivals in various formats, and they take them seriously too. The Goodman and Steppenwolf continue to lead by example and new initiatives.

I am proud of the role that Chicago Dramatists has played in this history, transforming Chicago from a city more or less barren of new plays thirty years ago, to what is now a national center for new play development and production.

It's a damn good town for playwrights.

* * *

I am especially proud to offer to the rest of the country this collection of great new plays. There have been many efforts over the years to publish such an anthology, and—with the generous and visionary support of the Sara Lee Foundation—Chicago Dramatists has finally done it! Thanks and credit must be extended to several people for their commitment, perseverance, and guidance in the publication of this book: Chicago Dramatists' Resident Playwright Keith Huff, Managing Director Brian Loevner, former Development Director Deborah Stewart, and our Co-Editor Ann Filmer, who initiated the entire project.

Our main goal for this publication is to give theatres, theatre artists, colleges, and their future audiences around the country the opportunity to experience these singularly Chicago voices. You will find here a great variety of style and subject matter. All of the plays have been developed, at least in part, at Chicago Dramatists and successfully produced here in Chicago in the last four years. Every one of these writers is a Resident Playwright at Chicago Dramatists (where you may contact them), and is someone you should know.

Are these the "best" new Chicago plays? Well, sure. But at Chicago Dramatists, every one of our (presently) twenty-six Resident Playwrights has at least another two or three plays each that we could not squeeze into this book, many of which have not yet been produced and all of which are just as exciting and worthy of your attention. Potential producers can search through all of our plays and order reading copies through our online New Play Catalog at Chicago Dramatists' web site (www.chicagodramatists.org).

I hope you, your theatre, and your audiences will enjoy some of the best new plays Chicago has to offer.

Russ Tutterow
Co-Editor
Artistic Director, Chicago Dramatists

RUSS TUTTEROW, Artistic Director of Chicago Dramatists since 1986, has directed countless new play readings and nurtured the art and careers of hundreds of playwrights. He received the League of Chicago Theatre's Artistic Leadership Award in 2005, currently serves on the First Look Council for Steppenwolf Theatre, and has directed, managed or taught for such Chicago theatres as the Goodman, Victory Gardens, Royal George, Mercury, Briar Street, Prop, Zebra Crossing, and Igloo, as well as Café LaMama/Hollywood.

EDITOR'S NOTES by Ann Filmer

When I first joined Chicago Dramatists as its Producing Director in 2000, it was a personal goal of mine to publish an anthology of plays by Chicago playwrights.

After all, Broadway, off-Broadway, and even off-off Broadway have their publications. The California Theatre Council published "West Coast Plays" beginning in 1977. And of course we all are familiar with Actors' Theatre of Louisville's many editions of "Plays from the Humana Festival."

As a young director, I would scour the shelves at the old Act One Bookstore searching for that gem of a play that I could bring to life. Anthologies were ideal because I could get six, seven, eight, or more plays for under twenty bucks. I bought them up like crazy. I bought the new ones to find that play that no one (in Chicago at least) had discovered. I bought the old ones to find that obscure play, long forgotten, but ready for a revival. Even when not finding one to produce myself or pitch to another theatre company, I came in touch with the work of living playwrights, with the living theatre.

So why didn't Chicago publish an anthology of its plays? After all, Chicago is home to over 200 theatre companies. Look through the Chicago Reader in any given week, and one will find over 200 productions. Out of those, often a large percentage are world premieres, many by Chicago's own playwrights. Now, quantity does not equal quality, but in order to create those gems, the pool must be deep. And Chicago's pool certainly is, and has been, very deep.

So why were our plays not written down? A play exists for the time that it performs for an audience. But if it is not written down and recorded, does it cease to exist? Well, not necessarily, but who in the future will know about it? If play seekers don't know about, or don't have access to that new gem of a play, it may as well not exist. So where were Chicago's records of our theatrical history? And aren't our playwrights the keepers of that history?

Richard Christiansen, former chief critic of the Chicago Tribune, was certainly asking the same questions when he sat down to pen "A Theater of Our Own." Finally we have our book! But where are our plays? Many plays that moved on to Broadway or off-Broadway have been recorded. Yet Chicago's thousands of other plays exist only by name in his book, in critic's reviews, and in our memories. But do they really live on?

We are publishing these eight plays so that they may live on. So they may receive second, third, and fourth productions. So they may remain in the American theatrical cannon for years to come.

So a young director somewhere in the country has the opportunity to pick up "New Plays from Chicago", hoping to find that gem of a play they can bring to life.

Ann Filmer
Co-Editor

ANN FILMER as a young director moved to Chicago in 1993. She co-founded and was the Artistic Director of The Aardvark (producing and directing plays by Chicago playwrights) before becoming the Producing Director of Chicago Dramatists from 2000–2004. She was awarded the Goodman Theatre's 2004-05 Michael Maggio Directing Fellowship and continues to work as a freelance director, in addition to producing and directing Chicago's bi-annual *Estrogen Fest*.

Drawing War

by Brett Neveu

ORIGINALLY PRODUCED by Chicago Dramatists

Founded in 1979
1105 W. Chicago Ave., Chicago, IL 60622
www.chicagodramatist.org

Russ Tutterow, Artistic Director
Brian Loevner, Managing Director

Chicago Dramatists' mission is to develop and advance the new plays and playwrights that will contribute to the American theatre repertory. Supporting the whole writer, rather than isolated projects, it forms long-term associations with playwrights in order to develop "voices," careers, and ever-maturing bodies of plays. The range and depth of its writer-driven new play development programming is unduplicated by any other theatre in the region.

Chicago Dramatists has played a major role in transforming Chicago from a city nearly barren of original work in the 1970s to an important, national center for the discovery and development of new plays and playwrights. It has grown from a small, grassroots playwrights' collective to a company serving over 500 playwrights annually, with a professional staff headed by Russ Tutterow, Artistic Director since 1986.

Since 1979, literally thousands of playwrights have found Chicago Dramatists a challenging but safe home in the theatre—writers like Rebecca Gilman *(The Glory of Living, Spinning Into Butter, Boy Gets Girl)*, Rick Cleveland *(The West Wing, Six Feet Under)*, Tina Fey *(Saturday Night Live)*, Lydia R. Diamond *(The Gift Horse)*, Roger Rueff *(The Big Kahuna)*, Carson Grace Becker *(A Mislaid Heaven)*, Jim Henry *(The Angels of Lemnos)*, Keith Huff *(Birdsend, Dog Stories)*, Jenny Laird *(Sky Girls)*, Evan Guilford-Blake *(Nighthawks)*, David Rush *(Leander Stillwell, Police Deaf Near Far)*, and the playwrights in this anthology, to mention only a few.

In 2003/2004 alone, Chicago Dramatists' playwrights earned 624 productions, awards or other honors—a two-fold increase in just four years—including 64 professional productions in Chicago, 76 across the nation, and 7 internationally.

Chicago Dramatists provides its playwrights with dramaturgical services, career guidance, networking opportunities, artistic support, script referrals, and marketing services, including its online New Play Catalog. It accomplishes this through two membership programs: The Resident Playwright Program (annual submission deadline, April 1) and The Playwrights' Network (open year-round to all playwrights in the nation).

Among Chicago Dramatists' principal programs is its Readings & Workshops, which encompass The Saturday Series, The Studio Project, the Monday Night and First Draft Series, the 10-Minute Workshop, and public panel discussions. It produces two world premieres each season, offers professional playwriting and screenwriting classes, and conducts outreach to young writers in the Chicago Public Schools.

* * *

Brett Neveu has been a Resident Playwright with Chicago Dramatists now for, must be about seven years. In that time, I have watched him become probably the most familiar and frequently produced Chicago playwright. His is, I think, a distinctive and important voice and will, in my opinion, make a major contribution to the American theatre. Raised in Iowa, Brett's voice is as Midwestern as Pinter's is East End. In fact, these two playwrights have much stylistically in common. Directing *Drawing War* was very much like my experiences directing Pinter, except, notably, Brett seemed to be writing about all the people, attitudes, longings, regrets, and suppressed emotions I grew up with in Indiana. Like all of his plays, *Drawing War* is alternately hilarious and searing, with layers upon layers of emotions hidden deeply in what seems to be the simplest of everyday conversation. With teenage and domestic violence continuously on the news and in our minds, Brett's plays are a mirror to our times. The Chicago critics have been universally respectful and enthusiastic about all of his many plays produced here, including this one. Here's how we described *Drawing War* in the publicity materials for our Chicago Dramatists' world premiere:

Through his minimalist and darkly comic style, playwright Brett Neveu draws a fractured portrait of a disintegrating Midwestern family. Neither snow nor guilt nor jail nor violent death will keep the Brauns' from delivering their Christmas cookies.

Russ Tutterow
Artistic Director, Chicago Dramatists

BIOGRAPHY

Born in California and raised in Iowa, current productions include *4 Murders* with A Red Orchid Theatre (Chicago) in April 2005, and *Eric LaRue* with Royal Shakespeare Company (Stratford) in October 2005. Past production credits include *American Dead* with American Theatre Company (Chicago), *the go* with Terrapin Theatre Company (Chicago), *Eric LaRue* with A Red Orchid Theatre (Chicago), *Empty* with Stage Left

Theatre (Chicago), *Eagle Hills, Eagle Ridge, Eagle Landing* and *twentyone* with Spring Theatreworks (New York), *Drawing War* with Chicago Dramatists and *The Last Barbecue* with the Asylum Theatre (Las Vegas), The Aardvark (Chicago), and 29th Street Rep (New York). He has also worked with various play development groups such as The Playwright's Center in Minneapolis, No Shame Theatre in Iowa City and Chicago, The New Group and The 42nd Street Workshop in New York. He is currently a Resident Playwright at Chicago Dramatists as well as a proud ensemble member of A Red Orchid Theatre. Brett has been commissioned twice by Steppenwolf Theatre Company for their New Play Initiative and was given Goodman Theatre's Ofner Prize for New Work for which he wrote *Heritage,* featured in the 2004 Goodman Theatre's New Stages Series. Brett also teaches playwriting with Steppenwolf's Crosstown teen program and lives in Chicago with his wife, artist Kristen Neveu.

DEVELOPMENTAL HISTORY
Drawing War was developed with the ROOM 41 Reading Series and with Chicago Dramatists.

ORIGINAL PRODUCTION
Drawing War premiered at Chicago Dramatists on March 23, 2001. It was directed by Artistic Director Russ Tutterow with the following cast:

MR. BRAUN . . . . .Robert W. Behr
CHAD UDELHOVEN. . . . . .Justin Cholewa
GRANDMA FANDER . . . . .Kate Winters
JEFF BRAUN . . . . .Philip Dawkins
MRS. BRAUN . . . . .Suellen Burton

and the following production staff:

Set Designer. . . . . .Ann Davis
Lighting Designer. . . . . .Jeff Pines
Sound Designer . . . . .Chris J. Johnson
Costume Designer . . . . .Michelle Lynette Bush
Stage Manager . . . . .Barbara Walk

CHARACTERS

CHAD UDELHOVEN: male, 13

MR. BRAUN: male, 40s

MRS. BRAUN: female, 40s

JEFF BRAUN: male, 17

GRANDMA FANDER: female, 70s

TIME & PLACE

The present. Outside a church, a jail cell, a nursing home, the Braun home, a fast food restaurant, a holding area at a courthouse, a cemetery, the Uldelhoven home—all located in a small, Midwestern town.

Suellen Burton (left) as Mrs. Braun and Philip Dawkins as Jeff Braun in Chicago Dramatists' 2001 production of *Drawing War* by Brett Neveu, directed by Russ Tutterow.
Photo by Jeff Pines

Drawing War

ACT I

SCENE 1

Lights up. Christmas Eve. Mr. Braun stands alone. He wears a long, heavy coat. Chad enters slowly. He holds an umbrella over his head. He stares at Mr. Braun for a few beats.

CHAD: Merry Christmas, Mr. Braun.

MR. BRAUN: Hello, Chad.

CHAD: Merry Christmas.

MR. BRAUN: Merry Christmas.

CHAD: It's pretty bad weather.

MR. BRAUN: It sure is bad. Maybe it will snow later.

CHAD: It's still pretty slick.

MR. BRAUN: How's school?

CHAD: Fine. *(Pause.)* My mom and I are just waiting for my dad to come pick us up.

MR. BRAUN: I hope it isn't too slick to drive.

CHAD: Me, too. *(Pause.)* We're going to look at lights on houses after this. If it's not too slick.

MR. BRAUN: Let's hope it's not. *(Pause.)* Seems strange tomorrow is already Jesus' birthday.

CHAD: Yeah.

MR. BRAUN: What did they say about Jesus' birthday in Sunday school?

CHAD: Tonight?

MR. BRAUN: Yes.

CHAD: They don't have Sunday school on Christmas Eve.

MR. BRAUN: Oh.

CHAD: We just came for service.

MR. BRAUN: I don't know why I would have thought they would have had Sunday school tonight. I thought I remembered Matt going to Sunday school on Christmas Eve. Probably not, though.

CHAD: I don't go to Sunday school anymore.

MR. BRAUN: You don't?

CHAD: We don't come to church that much.

MR. BRAUN: You don't?

CHAD: We stopped going every Sunday.

MR. BRAUN: I haven't been in a while, either.

CHAD: Oh.

MR. BRAUN: Things have been a little hectic at home, so it's hard to get out on the weekends. Jeff is visiting Grandma Fander at the nursing home tonight, and we're picking Mrs. Braun up at the courthouse tomorrow.

CHAD: Oh.

MR. BRAUN: They're letting her out on Christmas.

CHAD: Good.

MR. BRAUN: I don't know if they did that on purpose, or it just worked out that way.

(Pause.)

MR. BRAUN: It's bad weather for Jesus tonight.

CHAD: Yeah.

MR. BRAUN: Well, bye.

CHAD: Bye.

(Mr. Braun exits. Chad stands alone holding his umbrella. Lights fade.)

SCENE 2

A nursing home. Jeff and Grandma sit at a round, folding table. Grandma smiles blankly and has dirty teeth. Grandma smoothes out the placemat in front of her. Both Jeff and Grandma have a piece of peppermint pie in front of them. There is a Christmas present on the table.

GRANDMA: It was cold. Cold in the. Shucka shucka shucka shucka shucka shucka...

JEFF: Uh-huh.

GRANDMA: She wasn't going to tell me, she wasn't going to tell me, she was leaving—

JEFF: Do you want some pie, Grandma?

(Grandma smiles and looks at Jeff. Jeff puts a fork in Grandma's hand. Jeff and

Grandma eat the peppermint pie. Grandma eats big pieces of her pie fast, while Jeff stops eating after his first bite.)

JEFF: Eew. Peppermint pie.

(Grandma continues to eat her peppermint pie. Grandma finishes her pie.)

JEFF: It's freezing rain outside. *(Long pause.)* Do you want to open your Christmas present?

(Jeff tries to hand the present to Grandma.)

GRANDMA: No, no, no, no.

(Grandma attempts to smooth out the paper on the present.)

JEFF: Here. I'll start it.

(Jeff rips a little bit of the paper, then puts Grandma's hand on the package. Grandma attempts to smooth the paper back down. Jeff rips more of the paper. Grandma tries to smooth. Jeff rips. Grandma smoothes. Jeff tears off all of the paper.)

JEFF: I'll open the box.

(Jeff takes the present out of the box, which is wrapped in tissue paper. Removing the tissue paper, Jeff reveals a wind-up, twirling, mirrored, circular box topped by a mirror-covered angel.)

JEFF: What the hell is this? Do you like this?

GRANDMA: I don't like it.

JEFF: This can't go in your room.

GRANDMA: You're going to take, yes, shucka, shucka, shucka *(some clicking sounds)*—

(Jeff winds up the music box.)

JEFF: "Memory?" It plays "Memory" from "Cats?"

GRANDMA: Oh yes, I like it.

JEFF: Shit. Merry Christmas, Grandma.

(Grandma smoothes out both placemats. She piles them on top of each other, then begins to eat Jeff's peppermint pie. Lights fade.)

SCENE 3

Mrs. Braun sits alone in her jail cell.

MRS. BRAUN: There was this house that my family used to live in, in New Mexico. This house had been nearly abandoned, but we didn't have any money, so we rented it and fixed it up a little. It had a sunken tub in the back. The house had previously been owned by a Korean couple that had just moved to the United States. They had gotten married right when they came to America, and they were happy. I think there might have been something about the woman's family not approving of the marriage. I'm not sure, I can't remember. Anyhow, the young man was then drafted in the war and the woman was left alone. He was then killed in battle. The young woman was so upset by the news of his death that she went to the kitchen of this house and took a butcher knife out of a drawer and killed herself. When we lived there, my family heard strange noises all of the time. Sometimes late at night, you could hear the drawers in the kitchen opening and the silverware rattling around. You could hear footsteps walking in the upstairs hall. There was a room in the house that was always kept locked, that had the dead young woman's things in it. The door to this room would open and shut by itself. Objects would move around in the house-they would change places. One night, when I was twelve, I was sleeping and something woke me. I looked toward the doorway of my room, and a white figure stood floating above the floor. I watched it for a moment, then I pulled the covers over my face and froze. I prayed to God to make it go away. I prayed for what seemed like hours. I must have fallen asleep because when I woke up, it was morning. Our family didn't stay in the house much longer. My mother felt the woman's presence once, but she never saw her.

(Lights fade.)

SCENE 4

Christmas music. Christmas morning. Opened boxes and ripped wrapping paper litter the floor. Jeff wears a robe and sits in a large, comfortable chair. He has a sweatshirt draped over him as if to see how it will look when on. Mr. Braun sits in a chair opposite, smiling at Jeff. A few beats. A doorbell rings. Mr. Braun gets up and exits. Muffled voices are heard offstage. Mr. Braun reenters, followed by Chad. Chad wears a coat, gloves, boots, and a stocking cap. Chad holds a paper plate of Christmas cookies wrapped in clear plastic. A beat.

CHAD: Hey, Jeff.

MR. BRAUN: Chad came over with a plate of cookies for us.

CHAD: Merry Christmas.

MR. BRAUN: Are you having a nice Christmas, Chad?

CHAD: We already opened our presents.

MR. BRAUN: I hope you got something you liked.

CHAD: Yeah.

MR. BRAUN: We were just opening our presents.

JEFF: I'll be right back.

(Jeff exits.)

MR. BRAUN: What did you get?

CHAD: A sweater.

MR. BRAUN: I got a new belt.

CHAD: Me, too.

MR. BRAUN: Hm.

CHAD: It was in my stocking.

(The Christmas music is suddenly turned off. A beat. Jeff reenters. He has a plate of cookies that looks a lot like the one Chad brought, except Jeff's is wrapped in green cellophane.)

MR. BRAUN: Here's a plate of cookies for your family. Jeff and I made those. Here. Jeff?

(Jeff unwraps the green cellophane and begins to eat the cookies.)

MR. BRAUN: Oh.

CHAD: My mom just wanted me to stop by with some cookies for your family.

MR. BRAUN: Tell your mom, "thank you."

CHAD: Okay.

MR. BRAUN: Did you need a ride back home?

CHAD: No. I walked.

MR. BRAUN: That's too far of a walk. Let me give you a ride back.

CHAD: That's okay.

MR. BRAUN: I'll drop you off on my way to the nursing home. You remember Matt's grandma, Grandma Fander?

CHAD: Yes.

MR. BRAUN: When was the last time you saw her?

CHAD: With Matt.

MR. BRAUN: You guys were visiting her?

CHAD: Our music class was doing a holiday play at the nursing home and she was there.

MR. BRAUN: You were doing a Christmas play?

CHAD: A holiday play.

MR. BRAUN: Wow. Maybe we could stop at the nursing home first so that you could say "hi" to her. We need to make a quick stop and take some presents over there. Maybe you can do some of your Christmas play for her?

JEFF: We're taking Chad to the nursing home with us?

MR. BRAUN: It's on the way.

JEFF: You could have gone last night.

MR. BRAUN: I was at church.

CHAD: I wouldn't mind seeing her.

MR. BRAUN: Great!

(A beat. Mr. Braun exits. Jeff and Chad look at each other. Mr. Braun reenters with a huge, plastic garbage bag and begins to stuff it full of the paper and boxes that are scattered on the floor. Lights fade.)

SCENE 5

Mrs. Braun sits in her jail cell.

MRS. BRAUN: Right after my father died, I could smell electric shave. Also, my cousin had a strange thing happen to him. When he was young, he had this habit of climbing one of my father's peach trees, and eating peaches from its branches. Whenever my father would catch him, he would always say, "Kevin, get out of that tree!" then my father would whistle real loud. Kevin would always climb from the tree and run all the way home. About two weeks after my father died, my cousin was still into the habit of climbing that peach tree and eating peaches in the branches. He was sitting on a branch in the middle of the day eating a peach when he heard, "Kevin, get out of that tree!" and that same loud whistle. Kevin was so scared he fell out of the tree and nearly broke his leg, and almost choked to death on a peach. Only recently, about three years ago, did Kevin tell me that story. He says it still frightens him to think about it.

(Lights fade.)

SCENE 6

Mr. Braun, Jeff, Grandma, and Chad sit at a table at the nursing home. They each have a plastic glass in front of them, which is filled with eggnog. Grandma wears a wrinkled sweat suit. Mr. Braun has three gifts in a large, paper bag.

MR. BRAUN: Merry Christmas, Margaret.

JEFF: Merry Christmas.

CHAD: Merry Christmas.

MR. BRAUN: Hey, Margaret. We brought you the rest of your presents.

(Mr. Braun takes the presents from the bag.)

MR BRAUN: This one's from Steve and Shelly, and this one's from us, and this one's from Steve and Shelly, too.

GRANDMA: No, she was going to leave and she didn't want it. No, she didn't shucka shucka shucka shucka—

MR. BRAUN: Uh-huh.

(Grandma smoothes out the wrapping paper on the presents.)

MR. BRAUN: Do you want to open the presents?

(Mr. Braun takes Grandma's hand.)

MR. BRAUN: Here. Tear here. It's already started.

JEFF: Dad, did you see what Joel got her?

MR. BRAUN: No.

JEFF: He got her a music box. It's got some strange angel on top of it.

MR. BRAUN: An angel?

JEFF: When you wind it up it plays the song "Memory" from "Cats."

MR. BRAUN: It does?

JEFF: Yes.

MR. BRAUN: I'm sure they didn't mean anything. *(Pause.)* It has glass on it?

JEFF: I guess.

MR. BRAUN: She really can't have that in her room.

(Grandma points at, then touches Chad's face. Chad is startled. Mr. Braun moves Grandma's hands from Chad's face.)

GRANDMA: She didn't know, you see, something better was something better...*(clicking sounds)*—

MR. BRAUN: We should open her other presents.

(Mr. Braun unwraps one of the presents. It's a sweatshirt. The sweatshirt is like the one she is wearing, but new.)

MR. BRAUN: That's a nice sweatshirt. Who's that from, again?

(Mr. Braun shows the sweatshirt to Grandma. She smoothes the sweatshirt out on the

table.)

MR. BRAUN: Where's our present?

JEFF: Here.

(Jeff opens her present. The present is some slippers.)

JEFF: Slippers.

(Grandma picks up her eggnog and begins to drink it.)

MR. BRAUN: I hope we got the right size.

(Jeff opens her other present.)

JEFF: Sweat bottoms.

MR. BRAUN: They go with the top. Here, Margaret. See?

(Mr. Braun shows her the sweat bottoms. Grandma finishes her eggnog.)

MR. BRAUN: She really likes eggnog.

(Mr. Braun laughs.)

JEFF: Have mine, Grandma.

MR. BRAUN: She doesn't need more eggnog.

JEFF: She wants more.

(Grandma begins to drink Jeff's eggnog.)

MR. BRAUN: *(To Chad.)* She's probably a little different than the last time you were here.

CHAD: Yeah.

MR. BRAUN: We should get you home, Chad.

(Mr. Braun cleans up all the wrapping paper and exits with the loose pile.)

GRANDMA: Yes, yes, yes, yes.

(Grandma touches Chad's face again. Chad does not move. He sits still, staring at Jeff. A few beats. Mr. Braun reenters and moves Grandma's hand from Chad's face.)

MR. BRAUN: Everybody ready?

JEFF: I'll take her back to her room.

(Jeff helps Grandma out of her chair. Jeff and Grandma exit.)

MR. BRAUN: When do you go back to school, Chad?

CHAD: Soon.

MR. BRAUN: What date do you go back?

CHAD: January 6th.

MR. BRAUN: That's still a long ways away.

CHAD: They give us two and a half weeks.

MR. BRAUN: Your folks probably think you got lost with those cookies.

CHAD: Yeah.

(Lights fade.)

SCENE 7

Grandma sits. She has a blanket over her.

GRANDMA: And there she was, there she was. We were all there and there she was. I tried to see her, but no. No no no. *(Long pause.)* We went up, you see, we went up, and she wasn't there. I wanted to see her, but she wasn't there. No, she wasn't there. That's what she wasn't there no no. We were all there, she wasn't going to go. She told them she wasn't going to go, and she she she was going, no no no. Shucka shucka shucka shucka shucka... It's the *(Muffled sounds.)*, it's the... He didn't know, he didn't know. She was down, down. I didn't tell them. I didn't tell them any of what they were saying. That's not what she wanted. No, no. She didn't want it, she left then. It was out of the window, you could see the flowers. They were there, and then down the driveway. You could see the yellow flowers then down the driveway. She was there, and she saw flowers. I wanted to get flowers, I wanted to get them but she wasn't there. I'd like to go, I'd like to go out there. Yes? I'd like to go out there and see it. I'd like to see it. She was laughing, she was laughing and then yes yes, then she was going. No, no...

(Grandma carefully stands, then exits very slowly. Lights fade.)

SCENE 8

Chad and Mr. Braun sit at a fast food restaurant. They both have bags of fast food in front of them, as well as sodas.

MR. BRAUN: I can't believe they're open.

CHAD: Yeah.

MR. BRAUN: I can't usually eat this, but today it's Christmas so I don't care.

CHAD: Oh.

MR. BRAUN: It usually messes up my stomach.

CHAD: Thanks for lunch.

MR. BRAUN: Thanks for letting me drive all the way out to the courthouse so that I could drop Jeff off.

CHAD: Are you going to visit Matt at the cemetery today?

MR. BRAUN: When Mrs. Braun gets home. We forgot to do some of your holiday play at the nursing home.

CHAD: That's okay.

MR. BRAUN: That was for music class?

CHAD: Yes. In fifth grade.

MR. BRAUN: What part did Matt play?

CHAD: He was a present.

MR. BRAUN: I don't think I got to see it.

CHAD: He was a big present.

MR. BRAUN: A big present?

CHAD: There were five or six big presents in the play. The people that were presents all wore big cardboard boxes that were wrapped with gift wrap. Their heads stuck out of the top, and their arms came out of the sides. They had bows on top of their heads.

MR. BRAUN: Oh.

CHAD: I played the judge. I wore a judge's robe.

(Chad and Mr. Braun quietly open their bags, unwrap their food, and begin to eat.)

MR. BRAUN: Did you know that Mrs. Braun had gotten in trouble?

CHAD: Yes.

MR. BRAUN: Did you see her in the newspaper?

CHAD: Yes.

MR. BRAUN: The whole thing really wasn't as bad as the article made it sound.

CHAD: I just saw the picture of her.

MR. BRAUN: It was a bad picture.

CHAD: Oh.

MR. BRAUN: Did you want some ketchup?

(Chad pulls about fifteen packets of ketchup from his bag. Mr. Braun laughs hard. Pause.)

MR. BRAUN: I really don't eat here often. My stomach.

CHAD: I used to come here with my parents.

MR. BRAUN: I haven't been here in years.

CHAD: We used to come here for lunch after church.

MR. BRAUN: You did?

CHAD: I guess not every time.

MR. BRAUN: Jeff is picking up Mrs. Braun's car at the station house.

CHAD: Oh.

MR. BRAUN: They impounded her car along with the other folks' cars that were outside. The people she was with had parked their cars a couple of blocks away because they were ordered not to come within thirty feet of the clinic or the doctor or any of the women. Then they just walked over there anyway and stood blocking the entrance. Afterwards, the police got the license numbers of the cars and impounded them. Jeff is going to pick her up so that she doesn't have to drive herself. They should be back when I get home.

CHAD: That's good.

MR. BRAUN: She has had a tough time. They offered her a chance to come home earlier, but she told them she wanted to carry out her sentence. During the arrest, the newspaper took that picture of her and then they wrote that article. Even though the article only mentioned her name one time, that picture made it look like the whole thing was about her. Mrs. Braun believes very strongly in what she is doing, and there have been a lot of people calling to tell me they're praying for her.

CHAD: Good.

MR. BRAUN: A lot of people have told me that they can understand and see her point of view.

CHAD: I can understand her point of view.

MR. BRAUN: You can?

CHAD: I guess I can.

MR. BRAUN: I can, too. *(Pause.)* How is school going?

CHAD: Fine.

MR. BRAUN: You're in high school next year.

CHAD: Yeah.

MR. BRAUN: Are you ready? You'll be a freshman.

CHAD: I guess I'm ready.

MR. BRAUN: It'll be pretty different at the high school.

CHAD: It shouldn't be that bad.

MR. BRAUN: No.

CHAD: I'm looking forward to it.

MR. BRAUN: The science classes will be harder. But maybe you can do a science project, like you and Matt did. Maybe you can be in the science fair. You and Matt had a great science fair project.

CHAD: It wasn't very good.

MR. BRAUN: You and Matt showed how blood flows in the body by using celery stalks. You guys had a microscope set up and had magnified a vein from the celery.

CHAD: It wasn't a very good project.

MR. BRAUN: You guys worked hard on it.

CHAD: We got a "C−."

MR. BRAUN: You did?

CHAD: Yes.

MR. BRAUN: I don't remember what grade you and Matt got.

CHAD: We got a "C-."

MR. BRAUN: I remember you and Matt doing the blood flow project for the science fair.

CHAD: Marci Ringer's project won. She got an "A."

MR. BRAUN: I don't remember that. What else happened at the science fair?

CHAD: Nothing, really.

MR. BRAUN: Did you guys have fun?

CHAD: Yes.

MR. BRAUN: I can't believe you guys got a "C−."

CHAD: I know. Oh, well.

> (Pause. Chad and Mr. Braun eat. Lights fade.)

SCENE 9

> Lights up on Mrs. Braun. She is in a waiting area of the jail.

MRS. BRAUN: I've seen a picture of a ghost. The name of the ghost is "The Brown Lady." The picture was probably taken in the 1920s or the 1930s, and it's of a long staircase.

In the picture, you can see wooden stairs with a center runner, and at the bottom you can see the end of the stair's railing. In the center of the picture is a form of some kind. The form is white and transparent and floats just above the ground, as if it were floating down the steps.

(Jeff enters quietly behind Mrs. Braun. She does not notice him come in.)

MRS. BRAUN: The form clearly has the shape of a woman. If you look closely, you can see her face and arms, but her bottom half fades down into the steps. I don't know the history of "The Brown Lady," or where the picture was taken, but the photo has been examined by experts. No one doubts that it is a true picture of a ghost. And the ghost is beautiful. She was once a very beautiful woman who had walked down this long, dark stairway. She is graceful and elegant. "The Brown Lady" walks down that stairway eternally, living and moving forever.

JEFF: Merry Christmas, Mom.

MRS. BRAUN: *(Pause.)* Jeff. Did you get the car?

JEFF: You have to sign for it at the lot.

MRS. BRAUN: Did they give you the keys?

JEFF: Yes.

MRS. BRAUN: I'm ready, then.

(Mrs. Braun exits. A pause. Jeff exits. Lights fade.)

SCENE 10

Mr. Braun and Chad sit at the Braun home. Chad is eating a sugar cookie.

MR. BRAUN: They should be home any minute now.

CHAD: Great.

MR. BRAUN: I know that Mrs. Braun would like very much to say "hi" to you, and thank you for the plate of cookies you brought over. It'll just be a few minutes then I'll drive you on home.

CHAD: It would be nice to see her.

MR. BRAUN: She'll be happy to be home.

CHAD: Yeah.

MR. BRAUN: Chad?

CHAD: Yeah?

MR. BRAUN: Do you want another cookie?

CHAD: That's okay.

MR. BRAUN: You can have some of the ones you brought.

CHAD: We have lots still at home.

MR. BRAUN: Cookies are good.

(Long pause.)

MR. BRAUN: When did you and Matt do that science fair project?

CHAD: It was seventh grade science class. It was the first semester of last year.

MR. BRAUN: You guys were lab partners?

CHAD: Mr. Polastrini split the class up using opposite ends of the alphabet.

MR. BRAUN: What was your teacher's name?

CHAD: Mr. Polastrini.

MR. BRAUN: Last year. Seventh grade.

CHAD: The first semester of seventh grade.

MR. BRAUN: It seemed like you were lab partners for longer than that.

CHAD: Mr. Polastrini's class was hard.

MR. BRAUN: It was?

CHAD: He made us dissect things. Most people don't have to dissect anything until eighth grade.

MR. BRAUN: Oh.

CHAD: We had lab assignments and everything.

MR. BRAUN: That seems early to be dissecting.

CHAD: Mr. Polastrini wanted to see if we could do it.

MR. BRAUN: You and Matt dissected things together?

CHAD: If you were in the class, you had to dissect or you would get an "F."

MR. BRAUN: I don't remember him saying he had to do that.

CHAD: We dissected a worm, a frog, and a goldfish.

MR. BRAUN: You guys dissected all of those?

CHAD: Yes.

MR. BRAUN: Did you like it?

CHAD: This year we dissected a fetal pig.

MR. BRAUN: Jeff dissected a fetal pig in eighth grade.

CHAD: Hm.

MR. BRAUN: I remember he said that he had to be very careful not to cut the pig's veins or arteries because they had to examine them separately later for the lab assignment.

CHAD: We didn't have to do that.

MR. BRAUN: Matt would have liked to dissect a fetal pig.

CHAD: My lab partner ate part of the ear off of his pig.

(Pause.)

MR. BRAUN: You should probably get home.

CHAD: It's okay. I don't mind waiting to say "hi" to Mrs. Braun.

MR. BRAUN: Maybe her car wouldn't start. It's been sitting in that lot for a while.

CHAD: I don't mind waiting.

MR. BRAUN: Maybe I should drive back over there. They might need a ride.

CHAD: Maybe.

MR. BRAUN: I hope the car didn't conk out on their way back. Ah, I'm sure they're fine.

CHAD: Yeah.

MR. BRAUN: You want to wait?

CHAD: I don't mind.

(A beat. Lights fade.)

SCENE 11

Mrs. Braun and Jeff are with Grandma in the nursing home. Grandma wanders as Mrs. Braun attempts to have her sit in a chair.

MRS. BRAUN: Why don't you sit?

GRANDMA: I told her that was shucka shucka shucka—

MRS. BRAUN: Sit, Mom. Just sit down right here so we can talk.

(Mrs. Braun helps Grandma into the chair.)

MRS. BRAUN: *(To Jeff.)* Where is the music box?

JEFF: It's not really a music box. There's no box part.

MRS. BRAUN: She can't have something like that in here. It could break.

JEFF: I put it in her room in a drawer.

MRS. BRAUN: I don't know why Joel sent that to her. He knows Mom can't have something like that here.

JEFF: It plays "Memory" from "Cats."

MRS. BRAUN: I'm sure that was a mistake. They probably didn't listen to it first.

JEFF: Steve and Shelly got her a sweatshirt.

MRS. BRAUN: Good.

(Grandma stands and begins to walk away from her chair.)

MRS. BRAUN: Mom, sit so we can talk.

JEFF: Dad's home by now, after he dropped Chad Udelhoven off.

MRS. BRAUN: That was nice of the Udelhovens to bring over those cookies. *(To Grandma.)* Mom, sit.

JEFF: Who were you talking to?

MRS. BRAUN: When?

JEFF: When I came in to get you at the courthouse.

MRS. BRAUN: I wasn't talking to anyone.

JEFF: Yes, you were.

MRS. BRAUN: It's none of your business.

JEFF: What do you mean?

MRS. BRAUN: It's none of your business.

JEFF: Why not?

MRS. BRAUN: Jeff. I want to spend some time with my mother on Christmas.

JEFF: Go ahead.

MRS. BRAUN: Go and get that music box for me out of her room.

(Jeff exits. Mrs. Braun walks to Grandma and helps her into the chair again.)

MRS. BRAUN: There you go, Mom.

GRANDMA: She was here and then she went down down and I was here I don't and then she was laughing laughing, and then she was gone and then she left and was going and and here I was here she was laughing I was and I didn't know yeah yeah—

MRS. BRAUN: She was laughing?

(Mrs. Braun sits with Grandma. Pause. Jeff enters, holding the music box.)

JEFF: Here.

(Jeff hands Mrs. Braun the music box. A pause.)

MRS. BRAUN: Oh boy! *(Laughs hard.)*

JEFF: Look.

(Jeff winds up the music box. The angel spins while playing the song "Memory" from the musical "Cats." Mrs. Braun continues to laugh. Mrs. Braun slowly stops laughing. Lights fade.)

SCENE 12

The Braun house. Chad sits in the same chair he was sitting in previously. A few beats. Mr. Braun enters quickly with a large, cardboard box.

MR. BRAUN: Here it is. It should be in here.

(Mr. Braun begins to look in the box. It is filled with notebook papers and folders.)

MR. BRAUN: He sure had a lot of school work.

CHAD: Yeah.

MR. BRAUN: More work than I remember having when I was in school.

CHAD: Yeah.

MR. BRAUN: Jeff didn't have this much. This is too much.

(Mr. Braun again rummages through the box.)

MR. BRAUN: Here it is. *(Mr. Braun pulls out a red folder. Reading.)* "Earth Science." *(Mr. Braun opens the folder and looks through it.)* I don't see it. What was the name of the project?

CHAD: I don't remember what we named it.

(Mr. Braun pulls something from the folder.)

MR. BRAUN: What's this?

(Mr. Braun looks carefully at a piece of notebook paper. There are small drawings on the paper of stick men in a battle. He holds it up for Chad to see.)

MR. BRAUN: Is this Matt's?

CHAD: Probably.

MR. BRAUN: He drew this? What is it?

CHAD: He was just drawing war. Lots of guys in seventh grade used to draw war.

MR. BRAUN: Is this blood?

CHAD: We had red pens for science class, so the ones anyone drew in science had a lot of blood.

MR. BRAUN: These people are all broken apart.

CHAD: Sometimes you would start one and the other guy would finish it.

MR. BRAUN: This is Matt's?

CHAD: Nobody draws those anymore.

MR. BRAUN: He drew these people?

CHAD: They're stick men. *(Pause.)* Lots of guys drew war.

MR. BRAUN: The drawings all looked like this?

CHAD: Mostly.

MR. BRAUN: This is his?

CHAD: Probably.

(A beat. Mr. Braun closes the box and exits with it. Pause. Mr. Braun enters without the box. He sits. A beat.)

MR. BRAUN: I should get you back home.

CHAD: I don't mind waiting.

MR. BRAUN: Maybe we'll see them on the way. We can look for them as we go.

CHAD: That's okay.

MR. BRAUN: I'll drive for a while and if we see her we'll stop. If we don't, then I'll drive you on home.

CHAD: Okay.

MR. BRAUN: The roads shouldn't be too slick.

(Lights fade.)

SCENE 13

Jeff and Mrs. Braun at the fast food restaurant. They sit eating some fast food.

MRS. BRAUN: I'm surprised they're open on Christmas.

JEFF: Me, too.

MRS. BRAUN: We should probably hurry so we can all go to the cemetery later. I just was getting the shakes from being so hungry. *(Pause.)* When does school start again?

JEFF: January 10th.

MRS. BRAUN: That's a ways away.

JEFF: I guess.

MRS. BRAUN: They give you quite a break.

JEFF: Yeah.

MRS. BRAUN: Did Mrs. Kenworthy call?

JEFF: Yes.

MRS. BRAUN: She was setting up the next event.

JEFF: She called with the information, but I told her you'd call her back.

MRS. BRAUN: Good.

JEFF: You've got her phone number, so I didn't write it down.

MRS. BRAUN: I'm doing this for the children, Jeff.

JEFF: I know.

MRS. BRAUN: I don't want you to worry.

JEFF: I'm not worried.

MRS. BRAUN: That's good.

JEFF: Dad got me a sweatshirt.

MRS. BRAUN: I'll have to take care of Christmas this week. What did you get your dad for Christmas?

JEFF: I got him a CD.

MRS. BRAUN: Did he listen to it yet?

JEFF: I don't know.

MRS. BRAUN: I'm sure he'll like it.

JEFF: Yeah.

MRS. BRAUN: I'm done eating.

JEFF: Okay.

MRS. BRAUN: Are you almost finished?

JEFF: Almost.

MRS. BRAUN: Are you doing anything interesting in school?

JEFF: I did okay on my finals.

MRS. BRAUN: That's great.

(Pause. Mrs. Braun stands and puts her coat on, then sits back in her chair. Jeff eats semi-quickly. Lights fade.)

SCENE 14

Chad and Mr. Braun are at a cemetery, standing in front of a small, snow covered grave. The gravestone is inserted into the ground and looks more like an enlarged marble plaque than a headstone.

MR. BRAUN: I was going to stop later. I was waiting for Mrs. Braun and we were all going to stop together for Christmas.

CHAD: I haven't been here since Matt's funeral.

MR. BRAUN: It was on the way. I'll run you home afterwards.

CHAD: Okay.

MR. BRAUN: I haven't been here in a while.

(They stand in silence for a few beats.)

MR. BRAUN: I'll come back later. Are you ready, Chad?

CHAD: No.

MR. BRAUN: I should probably get you back home.

CHAD: I have to tell you something, Mr. Braun.

MR. BRAUN: You do?

CHAD: Yes.

MR. BRAUN: What is it?

CHAD: I feel really bad.

MR. BRAUN: What is it?

CHAD: I feel so bad about it.

MR. BRAUN: Can you tell me in the car?

CHAD: About six months before Matt died I was at this party over at Amy Hartman's house and Matt was there. It was in the basement of her house and mostly we just stood around and ate. Later, we decided to play light as a feather. Matt was the person who was dead so we turned off the lights and he laid down on the floor. The floor was concrete and it was really cold, I don't know how he just laid there. We all put our fingers under Matt and then someone started the story about how Matt had become dead. It was about a car accident and at the beginning people were goofing around and laughing and then as the story went on and it was so dark and all you could do was hear the people talking and Matt breathing real low and each of us spoke. The story went around the circle twice and then we got to the end and Matt was dead. So we all said that he was as light as a feather three times, he's as light as a feather, he's as light as a feather, he's as light as a feather, and we all picked him up with our fingers and he was. He was as light as a feather and we all picked him up into the air. We were holding him in the air for a while. He was as light as a feather. Then we put him down. It was really silent. It was really cold.

MR. BRAUN: Do you think that game has something to do with Matt's death?

CHAD: I don't know.

MR. BRAUN: You've got to be stupid.

CHAD: I thought God was watching us.

MR. BRAUN: Are you stupid?

CHAD: I don't know.

MR. BRAUN: Matt's death was an accident. You must be stupid to think that this crap had anything to do with Matt's death. Matt was accidentally shot in the head, Chad.

CHAD: I know.

MR. BRAUN: It was a goddamn accident.

CHAD: I know.

MR. BRAUN: I've got to get home.

CHAD: No.

MR. BRAUN: Let's go.

CHAD: I feel so bad!

MR. BRAUN: Come on, or I'm leaving you!

CHAD: I just wanted to tell you! I knew you'd be upset!

MR. BRAUN: Some stupid party game didn't do anything to Matt.

CHAD: I'm so sorry, Mr. Braun!

MR. BRAUN: It was a goddamn accident, Chad!

(*Mr. Braun exits. Pause. Chad sits on the ground near the grave. Lights fade.*)

END OF ACT I

ACT II

SCENE 1

The Braun's home. Mrs. Braun sits in a chair, with a Christmas present on her lap. Mr. Braun stands next to Mrs. Braun's chair. Jeff sits in the other chair.

MRS. BRAUN: This is a present from Tom.

(Mrs. Braun unwraps the present. It's a bath pillow. Jeff quickly takes a photo.)

MRS. BRAUN: This will be nice.

(Mrs. Braun hands the pillow to Jeff.)

JEFF: A bath pillow.

MRS. BRAUN: That should be nice in the tub. It has terry cloth on it. It's from Tom.

(Jeff attempts to hand the pillow to Mr. Braun. Mr. Braun doesn't notice. Jeff nudges Mr. Braun.)

MR. BRAUN: Oh.

JEFF: Here.

(Jeff hands the pillow to Mr. Braun.)

MR. BRAUN: This is nice.

MRS. BRAUN: I like it. *(Pause.)* Are there any more presents?

JEFF: No.

MRS. BRAUN: Okay. *(Pause.)* I would really like all of us to go out to the nursing home, then we should go to the cemetery afterwards.

JEFF: I've already been to the nursing home twice today.

MRS. BRAUN: I think we should all go together.

JEFF: Dad and I went this morning.

MRS. BRAUN: I know.

JEFF: We already gave her her presents.

MRS. BRAUN: I just thought it would be good if all of us went to see her.

MR. BRAUN: You two go ahead. I need to do a few things around here.

MRS. BRAUN: I want the three of us to go.

MR. BRAUN: I've already been to the nursing home today.

JEFF: *(To Mrs. Braun.)* Don't you want to stay home for a while?

MRS. BRAUN: Yes, but it wouldn't take a long time just to go out to see Mom.

MR. BRAUN: We don't have to run around all day.

MRS. BRAUN: I'm not running around.

MR. BRAUN: I have to put gas in my car.

MRS. BRAUN: That's fine. Jeff and I will take my car and meet you at the nursing home in the lobby. Then we can all see her together.

(Pause.)

MR. BRAUN: I'll get my coat.

MRS. BRAUN: This will be nice for Mom.

JEFF: I was just at the nursing home.

(Lights fade.)

SCENE 2

The nursing home. Grandma sits, looking worn. Chad sits next to her with his coat on. He shivers slightly.

GRANDMA: He didn't know, he didn't know. She was down, down. I didn't tell them. I didn't tell them any of what they were saying. Yes, yes. Shucka shucka shucka... Yes? Yes?

(Chad tries to put Grandma's hand on his face, but Grandma lets it drop to the table.)

GRANDMA: Oh, no. That's not what she wanted. She was going she was going. She said that no one was going to tell her, and then she didn't come. She didn't want to do that. No, no. She didn't want it. I'd like to go, I'd like to go out there. Yes? I'd like to go out there and see it. I'd like to see it.

(Grandma smoothes out a wrinkle in Chad's coat. A few beats. Jeff, Mrs. Braun, and Mr. Braun enter. They all are wearing coats.)

MRS. BRAUN: Hello?

JEFF: Chad?

MRS. BRAUN: Chad Udelhoven? What are you doing here?

MR. BRAUN: Hello.

MRS. BRAUN: What happened? Are you okay?

JEFF: Chad? What are you doing?

MR. BRAUN: Let me get you home.

CHAD: *(To Mr. Braun.)* I'm sorry.

MR. BRAUN: Let's go.

MRS. BRAUN: Why are you sorry?

CHAD: *(To Mr. Braun.)* I didn't mean to make you mad.

JEFF: What are you doing here?

CHAD: I got cold.

JEFF: You got cold?

MRS. BRAUN: *(To Mr. Braun.)* Why don't you drive him home.

MR. BRAUN: Okay.

JEFF: I can drive him.

MRS. BRAUN: You shouldn't stay outside and get so cold, Chad.

JEFF: Let's go, Chad. I'll drive you home.

MR. BRAUN: I'll drive him.

MRS. BRAUN: Let Jeff do it.

MR. BRAUN: Okay.

JEFF: Let's go, Chad.

CHAD: Goodbye, Mrs. Fander.

(Grandma stares at Chad. Grandma tries to stand.)

MRS. BRAUN: No, Mom, you sit.

MR. BRAUN: Goodbye, Chad.

MRS. BRAUN: It was nice to see you. Tell your mother thank you for the cookie plate.

CHAD: Bye.

JEFF: I'll take Mom's car, then I'll meet you back at home.

MRS. BRAUN: Okay.

(Chad and Jeff exit. Pause.)

MRS. BRAUN: Hi, Mom. Merry Christmas.

(Lights fade.)

SCENE 3

Chad and Jeff are at the fast food restaurant. Jeff is eating. Chad sucks on a straw attached to a pop.

JEFF: Do you want some fries?

CHAD: No.

JEFF: I'll buy.

CHAD: No, thank you.

JEFF: Are you okay?

CHAD: Yes.

JEFF: Why were you at the nursing home?

CHAD: It was close and I was cold.

JEFF: Close to where?

CHAD: Nowhere.

JEFF: Did my dad drop you off at your house before?

CHAD: Yes.

JEFF: Bullshit.

CHAD: What?

JEFF: I said bullshit.

CHAD: I just was walking around after I went home.

JEFF: What did you do?

CHAD: Walked around.

JEFF: It's too cold to walk around.

CHAD: I know.

JEFF: Where did you go?

CHAD: I was just walking around.

JEFF: Listen, Chad. Tell me why the hell you were at the nursing home.

CHAD: I did tell you. I got cold, so I went there.

JEFF: My dad didn't drop you off at your house, did he?

CHAD: I don't know.

JEFF: Goddamn tell me what happened or I'll beat the crap of you right here. He didn't drop you off at your house.

CHAD: *(Pause.)* No, he didn't drop me off.

JEFF: Where did you go?

CHAD: To the cemetery to see Matt.

JEFF: You did?

CHAD: Yes.

JEFF: What did you do?

CHAD: Talked.

JEFF: About what?

CHAD: I told him something about Matt.

JEFF: What was it?

CHAD: That he played light as a feather.

JEFF: Oh.

CHAD: I should go home.

JEFF: Let me go get you some fries.

CHAD: That's okay.

JEFF: Then wait until I'm finished.

CHAD: Okay.

JEFF: Then he just left you out there in the cemetery?

CHAD: Yes.

JEFF: *(Pause.)* Hm.

CHAD: I hadn't been there since Matt's funeral.

JEFF: Drink your pop.

(Chad drinks his pop. Lights fade.)

SCENE 4

Mr. Braun sits alone at the nursing home, looking at the piece of paper with Matt's drawing on it. The picture looks as if it has been folded up. Mrs. Braun enters. Mr. Braun quickly puts the piece of paper away.

MRS. BRAUN: I can't find her new slippers. We gave them to her today and now they're gone already.

MR. BRAUN: This place is nuts.

MRS. BRAUN: Mom's room is so dark. I hate leaving her in there by herself. *(Pause.)* I would like to go out to the cemetery.

MR. BRAUN: Okay.

MRS. BRAUN: We need to pick up Jeff at home first.

MR. BRAUN: Okay.

MRS. BRAUN: It's nice to be out of prison.

(Pause. Mr. Braun slowly pulls Matt's drawing from his pocket. He unfolds it and looks at it for a moment.)

MR. BRAUN: Have you ever seen this before?

(Mr. Braun shows Mrs. Braun Matt's drawing.)

MRS. BRAUN: No.

MR. BRAUN: It's a drawing of stick people having a war.

MRS. BRAUN: Why are you showing me this?

MR. BRAUN: I was looking through some of Matt's papers from school, his science class folder, and I found it. I asked Chad Udelhoven about it, and he said Matt drew these things all the time.

MRS. BRAUN: Boys draw pictures like that.

MR. BRAUN: Not all of them.

MRS. BRAUN: My brother used to draw pages of strange things.

MR. BRAUN: These stick men are bleeding to death. There are pools of blood under them.

MRS. BRAUN: You should put it back where you found it.

MR. BRAUN: There are probably more of them in the folder.

MRS. BRAUN: I'm ready to go.

MR. BRAUN: There are tanks exploding and airplanes breaking apart. Men breaking in half, bleeding. Arms blown off of bodies.

MRS. BRAUN: I'm ready to go.

MR. BRAUN: Okay.

MRS. BRAUN: I need to get Mom some new slippers.

MR. BRAUN: We can stop by the cemetery on the way back.

MRS. BRAUN: I'd like to go home.

MR. BRAUN: Okay.

MRS. BRAUN: I want to stop somewhere and get some slippers so I can bring them by tomorrow morning.

MR. BRAUN: It's Christmas. Everything's closed.

MRS. BRAUN: I would like to enjoy the holiday.

MR. BRAUN: I know.

MRS. BRAUN: I want to go home now. We can go to the cemetery to see Matt later with Jeff. Later, the three of us can go together.

MR. BRAUN: Okay.

(Mrs. Braun exits. Mr. Braun folds the paper and puts it in his pocket. Mr. Braun exits. Lights fade.)

SCENE 5

Jeff and Chad are at the cemetery. They stand over Matt's grave.

JEFF: Hey. Your footprints.

CHAD: Yeah.

JEFF: And you were sitting right over here?

(Jeff points to an area on the ground.)

CHAD: Yeah.

(Pause. Jeff sits where Chad was sitting.)

JEFF: *(To grave.)* Hey, Matt.

CHAD: That's not funny.

JEFF: Are you kidding?

CHAD: I don't think that's very funny.

JEFF: You suddenly care?

CHAD: I just feel bad.

JEFF: Don't.

CHAD: He was a friend of mine.

JEFF: No, he wasn't. He was your goddamn lab partner for one semester in seventh grade.

CHAD: We were also in a holiday play together.

JEFF: *(To Chad.)* Pussy.

CHAD: He was in my class.

JEFF: Shut-up.

> *(Long pause. Jeff stands. Chad is startled. Pause.)*

JEFF: You're scared of me.

CHAD: No, I'm not.

JEFF: Yes.

CHAD: No.

JEFF: Everyone from Matt's grade is scared of me.

CHAD: I don't know.

JEFF: You are.

CHAD: I need to get home.

JEFF: You'll go home in a minute.

CHAD: I want to go.

> *(Pause.)*

JEFF: Did you know that Matt shot himself with my dad's gun?

CHAD: Yes.

JEFF: Did you know Matt died right in front of me?

CHAD: Those were in the newspaper.

JEFF: What kind of news is that?

CHAD: I don't know.

JEFF: That's not news. *(Pause.)* How is 8th grade going?

CHAD: Fine.

JEFF: I remember 8th grade.

CHAD: It's not that bad.

JEFF: Wait until high school.

CHAD: I'm going to the car.

> *(Pause. Chad starts to walk away.)*

JEFF: Say bye to your best friend Matt.

(Chad exits.)

JEFF: (To grave.) Merry Christmas.

(Lights fade.)

SCENE 6

Mr. Braun and Mrs. Braun are at their home. They sit.

MRS. BRAUN: Ah, it's nice to be home.

MR. BRAUN: I think I'm going to go for a walk.

MRS. BRAUN: It's cold out there.

MR. BRAUN: It's not too bad.

MRS. BRAUN: Well, go ahead. It'll give me a chance to call Mrs. Kenworthy and find out when the next event is.

MR. BRAUN: You just got home.

MRS. BRAUN: I'm not going anywhere. I'm just making a phone call.

MR. BRAUN: I know.

MRS. BRAUN: I want to tell her I'm home and I'm fine.

MR. BRAUN: I know. *(Pause.)* I understand your point of view.

MRS. BRAUN: I'm doing this for the children.

MR. BRAUN: I know.

MRS. BRAUN: Go ahead on your walk. We can go to the cemetery later. Jeff should be home any minute.

MR. BRAUN: Okay.

(Mr. Braun exits. A few beats. Mr. Braun enters wearing his coat, gloves, and hat.)

MR. BRAUN: I'm going for a walk now.

MRS. BRAUN: Okay. I might go out later.

MR. BRAUN: Okay. I'll be right back after my walk.

MRS. BRAUN: Okay.

(A beat. Mr. Braun exits towards the kitchen. He returns with a plate of cookies. Mr. Braun exits to go outside. Lights fade.)

Scene 7

Chad's house. Chad and Jeff sit near a small coffee table.

JEFF: Do you have a pop?

(Chad exits. Pause. Chad enters holding a pop.)

CHAD: Here.

JEFF: Thanks.

CHAD: I don't know where my parents went to. They should be home.

JEFF: Oh.

CHAD: They are probably at my aunt's.

JEFF: Did you get some good Christmas presents?

CHAD: Yes.

JEFF: What did you get?

CHAD: I don't know. A sweater.

JEFF: Hm. What else?

CHAD: A belt.

JEFF: My dad got a belt.

CHAD: It was an okay Christmas.

JEFF: Do you think my mom's crazy?

CHAD: No.

JEFF: You don't?

CHAD: No.

JEFF: She was in jail for a month.

CHAD: I know.

JEFF: She was talking to herself in jail.

CHAD: Hm.

JEFF: I walked in and she was talking about a ghost.

CHAD: I understand her point of view.

JEFF: What?

CHAD: I understand her point of view.

JEFF: What the hell does that mean?

CHAD: I just understand it.

JEFF: You do?

CHAD: Yes.

JEFF: What is it then?

CHAD: She cares about children.

JEFF: Who doesn't?

CHAD: She cares about other things.

JEFF: That's crap.

CHAD: I don't know.

JEFF: I think that my mom's crazy.

CHAD: Hm.

JEFF: I think that she misses Matt.

CHAD: She's Matt's mom.

JEFF: No kidding.

CHAD: I'm sorry I made your dad mad.

JEFF: You didn't make him mad.

CHAD: I told him—

JEFF: It doesn't matter what you told him.

CHAD: I'm sorry.

JEFF: I should hit you in the face or something.

CHAD: My parents should be right home.

JEFF: My mom was talking to the wall and she said it wasn't any of my business.

>*(Pause.)*

CHAD: I'm going to call over to my aunt's and see if my parents are there.

JEFF: Go ahead.

>*(Pause.)*

CHAD: I'll be right back.

>*(Chad exits. Jeff drinks his pop. Lights fade.)*

Scene 8

The nursing home. Mrs. Braun sits with Grandma.

MRS. BRAUN: This past summer I was sitting outside in our backyard and I saw what I thought was a squirrel. It was near evening, so I really didn't know what shadows belonged with what objects, when I noticed some movement near the top of the back fence. I really didn't pay that much attention to it. I relaxed my eyes for a moment, and when I opened them again, the shape had moved to the lawn. It also had seemed to grow slightly. I stood to look at it and noticed that it was vibrating. It was shaking like a hummingbird and gave off a dull buzzing sound. The sound grew as the shape's size grew until it was about size of a small dog. I tried to go inside, but I couldn't. I was frozen staring at this spot, watching this thing grow. I realized I was watching something very strange. I was seeing something that was sent for me to see. I was experiencing this moment, this happening, and, Mom, something like a key entered me and turned, unlocking something. Then the shaking, buzzing thing on my lawn was gone. It had left nothing for me. Nothing had been unlocked, there had been no key. The shape was gone. It was getting dark, so I finished my dinner and went inside. Then it was nighttime.

(Pause.)

GRANDMA: He didn't know, he didn't know. She was down, down. I didn't tell them. I didn't tell them any of what they were saying. Yes, yes. Shucka shucka shucka… Yes? Yes?

(Lights fade.)

SCENE 9

Chad's house. Chad sits in a chair looking at a sweater and a belt. There is knock at the door offstage. Chad gets up and exits. A beat. Mr. Braun, holding a plate of cookies, enters. Chad enters following.

MR. BRAUN: I thought I should drop these off.

CHAD: Thanks.

MR. BRAUN: I wanted to talk to you more.

CHAD: My parents should be home any minute. You can give them the cookies.

MR. BRAUN: I want to know about Matt.

CHAD: I told you already.

MR. BRAUN: I don't mean about what happened at some party. I want to know about him and his classes.

CHAD: The only classes I had with him were science and music.

MR. BRAUN: Tell me about science class.

CHAD: I did already.

MR. BRAUN: No, you didn't.

CHAD: I don't know what you want me to tell you about.

MR. BRAUN: Tell me more about the class.

CHAD: It was hard.

MR. BRAUN: What did you do?

CHAD: I told you.

MR. BRAUN: Dissections. What else?

CHAD: We had to make a bug collection.

MR. BRAUN: I remember that.

CHAD: We had to kill bugs and pin them to a board. One guy didn't kill his bugs all the way, and they were flapping on his desk with pins stuck through them.

MR. BRAUN: Matt was there?

CHAD: Yes.

MR. BRAUN: What was the person's name who did that?

CHAD: It might have been Steve Cotton.

MR. BRAUN: And you drew pictures of war in that class, too?

CHAD: Yes.

MR. BRAUN: When?

CHAD: Before class started.

MR. BRAUN: Tell me about Matt and these pictures.

CHAD: I already did.

MR. BRAUN: Tell me more.

CHAD: I don't understand what you mean.

MR. BRAUN: Why was he drawing these?

CHAD: I already told you. Everyone was drawing them.

MR. BRAUN: Everyone in the class was doing this?

CHAD: Just the boys.

MR. BRAUN: Did Matt say anything to you about the drawings?

CHAD: No.

MR. BRAUN: What did you guys talk about?

CHAD: He said he was crazy.

MR. BRAUN: He said he was what?

CHAD: He said he was crazy.

MR. BRAUN: Why would he say that?

CHAD: He was joking.

MR. BRAUN: What do you mean he was joking?

CHAD: I said he was weird, and he said that he wasn't weird that he was crazy.

MR. BRAUN: He wasn't weird.

CHAD: It was a joke. He was kidding.

MR. BRAUN: Was everyone calling him weird?

CHAD: No. I don't know. There were other weird people in the class.

MR. BRAUN: I'm not asking about other people.

CHAD: David Juvis stepped on a guppy in that class. That was weird.

MR. BRAUN: I don't care about David Juvis!

CHAD: I know, but I'm trying to tell you it was a joke!

MR. BRAUN: Do you see that it's not?

CHAD: Matt was just kidding.

MR. BRAUN: You shouldn't have been picking on Matt.

CHAD: I wasn't.

MR. BRAUN: You guys did that project for the science fair, and you went around calling him names.

CHAD: I didn't.

MR. BRAUN: He wasn't crazy.

CHAD: I know.

MR. BRAUN: You know, that was my gun that Matt shot himself with.

CHAD: I know.

MR. BRAUN: I should tell your parents what you did to Matt.

CHAD: I didn't do anything.

MR. BRAUN: You can't really tell me anything at all, can you?

CHAD: What do you want me to tell you?

MR. BRAUN: This is unbelievable. I am really upset. *(Pause.)* When did Jeff drop you off?

CHAD: He just left.

MR. BRAUN: He just left now?

CHAD: Yes.

(Pause.)

MR. BRAUN: Tell your parents Merry Christmas.

(Mr. Braun exits. Chad sits. A long pause. A quick knocking is heard offstage. Chad continues to sit. More knocks. Chad remains seated. Jeff enters.)

JEFF: What did my dad want?

CHAD: You can't just walk into someone's house.

JEFF: What was he telling you?

CHAD: My parents are on their way home, and I really think you should go.

JEFF: After I left I saw my dad coming into your house.

CHAD: He wanted to drop off a plate of cookies.

JEFF: What did he say?

CHAD: He was dropping off cookies, see?

(Chad points at the cookies. A beat.)

JEFF: Was he asking you about Matt?

CHAD: Yes.

JEFF: What did he want to know?

CHAD: Nothing.

JEFF: Tell me.

CHAD: He wanted to know what Matt did in school.

JEFF: When?

CHAD: In science class.

JEFF: Why?

(Pause. Chad sits silently.)

JEFF: Chad?

CHAD: What.

JEFF: Do you want to know something about Matt?

CHAD: No.

JEFF: Something that nobody in your class, or anyone at school, knows?

CHAD: No.

JEFF: I'll tell you anyway.

CHAD: I don't want to know anything.

JEFF: I shot him.

CHAD: Please, go home.

JEFF: Matt and I were home by ourselves playing war in the basement, and Matt had my dad's gun. We were playing for a while, then we heard my mom upstairs opening the front door. We both started running around picking up stuff so it looked like we weren't doing anything, and then I had the gun and I pointed it at Matt's head and I shot him and he fell over. My mom was at the top of the stairs and saw the whole thing. Later, my mom told the police and my dad that Matt had done it himself on accident so that no one would think it was my fault, but it was. I shot Matt.

CHAD: I heard that story before.

JEFF: What?

CHAD: I had heard that story before.

JEFF: Where did you hear that?

CHAD: At school.

JEFF: You did?

CHAD: Someone told me that.

JEFF: It's the truth.

CHAD: I also heard that Matt killed himself.

JEFF: That's a lie.

CHAD: I heard that he put the gun in his mouth and pulled the trigger.

JEFF: That's not true.

CHAD: I heard that at school.

JEFF: That's not true. The bullet went into Matt's head and put a hole right there by his ear. Then the bullet came out the other side of his head and made a huge hole, and his brains and pieces of his skull went flying all over the couch and the carpet and the wall. Blood came out of his head and went all over and Matt's mouth was hanging open and he fell down. When he landed on the floor, more blood came out of his head and more brains went all over the couch. He was bleeding and my mom saw it happen and it was my fault. I was the one that did it.

CHAD: That's a lie. You're lying. *(Long pause.)* You should go.

JEFF: Ask my mom if you don't believe me. *(Pause.)* I'm not ready to go.

CHAD: Just go.

(A beat. Jeff exits.)

SCENE 10

Mr. Braun and Jeff are at the Braun home. Christmas music plays offstage.

MR. BRAUN: Are you hungry?

JEFF: Yes.

MR. BRAUN: What should we have for dinner?

JEFF: I don't know.

MR. BRAUN: I'll check the freezer and see what we have.

JEFF: I think there might be a pie in the freezer.

MR. BRAUN: We should listen to that CD you got me for Christmas.

JEFF: Okay.

MR. BRAUN: Your mother should be home any minute. *(Pause.)* It was cold for Jesus' birthday today. But it didn't snow.

(Lights fade to black.)

END OF PLAY

Vintage Red and the Dust of the Road

by Robert Koon

ORIGINALLY PRODUCED by Visions & Voices Theatre Co.

Founded in 2001
2007 W. Argyle #3, Chicago, IL 60625
www.visionandvoices.org

Brian Alan Hill, Artistic Director
John S. Beckman, Managing Director
David Scott Hay, Literary Director

It's hard to sit down and write a coherent statement on why anyone starts and continues to run a theatre company that produces new works. Let me put it simply. Theatre will die unless we support new voices in American Theatre. *Death of a Salesman* wasn't "*Death of a Salesman*" when it first opened. But for many people, new works equal risk.

The works that we produced that are featured in this anthology were strong works of theatre because they embraced theatricality. They also, and most importantly, adhered to these very simple elements: clear story, compelling characters, and dynamic language. The playwrights took a risk on a young company and for that I am grateful that they trusted us with their words.

* * *

Visions & Voices had just produced its first show and needed a show for the fall. Literary Director, David Scott Hay, remembered a play he had seen during Chicago Dramatists' Saturday Series and thought it might be a good fit for the company. He called up the author, got a copy of the script, and gave it to me to read. Two days later, I told Dave to make an offer. When Dave called Rob about producing *Vintage Red and the Dust of the Road*, Rob paused and replied, "But I'm folding laundry."

Well, needless to say, the laundry got folded that day and we were given permission to produce this beautiful family story. The circumstances are different than my family but I responded to the quandaries and hurts that Rob put on the page. We were blessed during the process to have incredible designers, actors, and direction, but the words were the great foundation that propelled that production. *Vintage Red and the Dust of the Road* is special to me not because of the accolades and good reviews. The show is special because every night a completely different group of people walked away from that show deeply impacted the way I had been. They too recognized their own families there on the stage. That's pretty powerful stuff.

Brian Alan Hill
Artistic Director, Visions & Voices Theatre Co.

BIOGRAPHY

Robert Koon is a Resident Playwright at Chicago Dramatists and the director of its affiliated writer's program, The Playwrights' Network. Mr. Koon's play, *Odin's Horse*, was the winner at the first Ecodrama Playwrights Festival in California in 2004. His other work includes *St. Colm's Inch*, *Inpainting*, *The Leverage of Affection*, *Changing Attire*, *The Point of Honor*, and *Looking West from Firá*. Mr. Koon also teaches playwriting at Chicago

Dramatists and in the Chicago Public Schools through the theatre's educational outreach program. He has been a featured presenter for the Indiana Theatre Association and the William Inge Theatre Festival. Mr. Koon is a member of the Dramatists Guild of America and The Playwrights Collective. Mr. Koon has received critical praise as a director and for his work as scenic and lighting designer, and his acting work includes appearances at regional venues as well as several theatres in the Chicago area. He received his Master of Fine Arts degree from the University of California at Davis and currently resides in Chicago with his wife, Jean Marie, and daughter, Kelsey.

DEVELOPMENTAL HISTORY

Vintage Red and the Dust of the Road was developed through private and public readings at Chicago Dramatists and American Theater Company. It was presented as part of FutureFest at the Dayton Playhouse in 2002.

AWARDS AND HONORS

Vintage Red and the Dust of the Road received a Joseph Jefferson Awards Citation for New Work and was nominated for the American Theatre Critics Association Steinberg Award.

ORIGINAL PRODUCTION

Vintage Red and the Dust of the Road premiered at Strawdog Theatre, Chicago in a Visions & Voices Theatre Co. production on November 10, 2002. It was directed by Anna C. Bahow with the following cast:

TED WILK . . . . Kelly Van Kirk
NIAMH O'NEILL . . . . Lisa Stevens
VAN WILK . . . . Paul Noble
KAREN WILK . . . . Elizabeth Rich
DANA MALONE . . . . Michelle Courvais

and the following production staff:

Set Designer . . . . Ryan Hall
Lighting Designer . . . . Carrie Hill
Sound Designer . . . . Joshua Horvath
Costume Designer. . . . . Joyce Croft
Stage Manager. . . . . Nichole A. Shuman

CHARACTERS

NIAMH O'NEILL: 24, lives with Ted. Irish, from Galway.

TED WILK: 42, a photographer, formerly in charge of the family winery.

VAN WILK: 41, Ted's brother. An ex-Marine, he is physically disabled, with a twisted right arm and a patch on one eye.

KAREN WILK: 35, Ted's sister, currently in charge of the winery.

DANA MALONE: 35, Ted's ex-wife.

TIME & PLACE

The present; summer. A Chicago loft shared by Ted and Niamh and the cooperage of the Wolf Creek Winery in the Napa Valley. The two settings exist together, with the cooperage extending around and over the loft.

Kelly Van Kirk (left) as Ted, Paul Noble as Van and Elizabeth Rich as Karen in Vision & Voices Theatre Co.'s 2002 production of *Vintage Red and the Dust of the Road* by Robert Koon, directed by Anna C. Bahow. Photo by Anna C. Bahow

Vintage Red
and the Dust of the Road

ACT I

The stage contains two distinct areas, the Chicago loft shared by Ted and Niamh, and the cooperage of the Wolf Creek Winery in the hills above the Napa Valley. The loft takes up a corner of the stage, while the cooperage extends around it, racks of barrels around the loft space. The cooperage is lit by lamps hung from a high ceiling, which cast shadows among the barrels. At rise, Ted, a man in his early 40s, is sitting on the floor of the cooperage, his back against the barrels, dimly lit. Niamh, a beautiful young woman in her early 20s, makes her way in between the racks of barrels. Neither she nor Ted acknowledges the other's presence. Niamh is Irish, with the accent of her home in Galway.

NIAMH: Oisín was the son of a giant, the great hero, Finn MacCool, who built the Giants' Causeway in County Antrim in the North. He was a poet, and what we know of the deeds of Finn MacCool we know from the words of Oisín, his son. The Fianna, his people, were the greatest in Ireland in the days before St. Patrick, Oisín no less than the rest. But it is no easy thing to be the son of a giant. One day, Oisín was hunting on the shores of a great lake, and he saw a beautiful woman riding toward him on the back of a handsome white horse that ran across the waves. She was a princess from the land of Tir na Nóg, where youth is eternal and time is unknown, and she was called Niamh, Niamh of the Golden Hair. She had watched Oisín from afar and fallen in love with the sight of him, and with his fine words, and she asked him if he would come back to the land of Tir na Nóg and be her husband, and of course you know that he said that he would. And he swung up onto the fine white horse that ran across the waves, and in a flash like the sun on the water they were gone. Now, the seasons pass in the land of Tir na Nóg, though time does not exist, and Oisín dwelt there happily with his love until one day, perhaps in the summer, perhaps on a fine day with the sun in the sky and the wind in the trees, perhaps with a memory of hunting, Oisín began to think of his home, and brothers, and his father.

(As Ted speaks, light comes up around him so that we see the cooperage more clearly. Barrels are stacked in racks around him, and at the rear of the stage there are two large wooden vats, each perhaps ten feet high.)

TED: Seventy-three years old. That's a good, long life, I guess. Still, it's hard to believe, you know?

NIAMH: Oisín went to his love and said, "If you'll lend me that fine horse that brought us here, I would like to go back to see my father and my brothers." But his love begged him not to go, not to think of Ireland and the past; but finally, sadly, she allowed him to borrow the great horse that ran over the waves. As he swung up into the saddle, she clung to him and told him not to leave the back of the horse, not to let his feet touch the ground, lest he become lost and unable to return to her. He kissed her and he promised he would do as she said, and away he rode.

TED: I could make the drive from the airport in my sleep. Into St. Helena, left turn, up the hill...the wall of heat when you step out of the air-conditioned car...the dust in the air. Dry. Gritty...and the sun drying you out...

NIAMH: When Oisín arrived, he found the roads overgrown and the fields gone wild. No one knew of his father, Finn, or his brothers, for although Oisín had seen only three turns of the seasons, in truth it had been three hundred years since he had departed. The people laughed when he told them stories of his family, and he looked for a way to prove the truth of what he said. From the back of the great white horse he saw ten men trying to move a large boulder. He said "If I move that stone for you, will you believe me?" And he rode over to the stone, and, leaning down from the saddle, careful not to touch the ground, he took hold of it and began to lift.

TED: *(Gestures at the walls of the cooperage.)* Stone. All native stone. Cool, even when it's ungodly hot outside. Not a bad place to live. Wine, it's alive...breathes, just like we do...ages...matures. One hopes. All of this...all of these... *(Gestures at the barrels.)* Sometimes I used to come in here, and I would swear that I could hear them all struggling for breath. Inside the wood. Waiting. The years stenciled on the heads of the barrels. Like headstones. My father used to say this was really a nursery, but I tell you, some days this place started to feel more like a crypt than anything.

(Lights dim, except on Niamh.)

NIAMH: As the people looked on in amazement, the stone began to move. But the girth of the saddle did not have Oisín's strength, and as he lifted the stone, the girth broke under the strain, and Oisín fell to the ground. As he touched the earth, the weight of the three hundred years fell down on him in an instant, and he was turned into a withered, blind, old man. All the people were astonished, as they looked down at Oisín, lying in the dust of the road. Then the great horse reared, turned, and was gone so quickly that they could hardly believe that it had ever been there at all.

(Lights fade on Niamh and go out. Lights come back up in the empty loft. Ted comes in, carrying an overnight bag and a garment bag. It is nighttime. He drops his bags on the floor, turns and locks the door.)

NIAMH: *(Offstage.)* Ted? Ted, is that you, then?

TED: Yeah.

(Niamh comes in from the bedroom, wearing the oversized t-shirt that serves as her nightgown. She runs over to Ted and hugs him.)

NIAMH: Oh, Lord, I was wondering if you'd ever come home.

TED: God, if I never have another flight like that one…

NIAMH: I kept calling the airline and they kept telling me that you were delayed. Then they said you had left, and then that you were in Kansas City. Why in God's name were you in Kansas City?

TED: Because there wasn't a gate available in Hell. Was the weather really that bad here?

NIAMH: Awful. There was a tornado near here, they said on the news. And we lost our electricity. It just came back on an hour ago.

TED: *(Looks at his watch.)* Thirteen hours. Jesus. When it rains at O'Hare, birds don't fly.

NIAMH: Sit down.

TED: Jesus, I've been sitting down for thirteen hours. I don't want to sit down. I don't have anything tomorrow, do I?

NIAMH: Two actors for their headshots.

TED: Oh, God.

NIAMH: Should I call and cancel them?

TED: No. Too late. Might as well get right back to work, I guess.

(Niamh hugs him.)

NIAMH: Can I fix you anything?

TED: No. I'm fine.

NIAMH: I could put the kettle on.

TED: That's okay. I don't need anything. This is nice, though.

(They stand, holding onto each other for a long time, then kiss.)

NIAMH: Ah. You've something stronger than tea in mind, then?

TED: Yeah, but I'd like a drink first.

(Niamh laughs, hugs him, and then leaves. Light slowly comes up in the cooperage.)

TED: Two hours in the terminal in San Francisco. Board and taxi, then wait. Another hour. Back to the gate. Sit for another hour before we finally take off, and we wind up in Kansas City. Two more hours. Then, finally, to Chicago, where there are no gates and we sit for another hour. I swear to God, it was like "Voyage of the Damned." All because of rain. Rain in the summertime. I'm still not used that. For me, summer means hot and dry. Heat and dust.

(Light is up full in the cooperage. Van is there. He is slightly shorter than Ted, but his bearing gives the impression that he is taller. His right eye is covered by a patch, and his right arm seems twisted and a little shorter than his left. Aside from that, he

appears to be extremely fit.)

VAN: And how old is she, exactly?

TED: What?

VAN: On the phone she sounds about twelve. I thought, "Damn, he's got kids. I didn't think he'd been gone that long."

TED: She's twenty-four.

VAN: Wow. Some guys.

TED: She'll be twenty-five in September.

VAN: Oh, well, that makes all the difference then.

TED: Knock it off.

VAN: Twenty-four?

TED: Yeah.

VAN: Well, hoo-rah. That accent for real?

TED: She says she'll lose it as soon as she goes home. Says in Galway I'll be the one with the accent. She speaks it, too. Irish.

VAN: No kidding. So you're studying a foreign tongue.

TED: Fuck you.

VAN: How'd you find her?

TED: Her uncle owns a bar on Clark Street, up by Wrigley. I'd go in every now and then. Got these pictures up on the wall, landscape stuff, really good. One day I asked who took them, he introduced me to Niamh. She came over to work for him about three years ago. All the kids in her family did it for a while. They come over, go back. Niamh's the first one to stay more than a year or so. I guess they get homesick. Their family's pretty tight.

VAN: Oh. Well. So, ever been there? Ireland?

TED: No.

VAN: I hear it's pretty country.

TED: Yeah. Well, I've seen the pictures. She's got a good eye.

VAN: Well, you'd know. It's your business.

TED: She's pretty good in the darkroom, too.

VAN: I'll bet she is.

TED: Fuck you.

(Pause.)

VAN: Okay, you've been down here for five minutes. Need a bucket yet?

TED: No. I'm okay.

VAN: Want to go sit in the office?

TED: No.

VAN: Go back up to the house?

TED: Not yet.

VAN: Sit in here for a while?

TED: Whatever.

VAN: Got a six-pack back in the fridge.

TED: That'd be all right.

VAN: Be right back.

(Van leaves. Niamh returns, wearing a pair of baggy plaid shorts along with her t-shirt. She is carrying two beers, hands one to Ted.)

TED: It was strange to be back. I mean, it was all familiar, but it was really strange at the same time. New buildings, that's all that's different. Nothing else, really.

NIAMH: The people?

TED: Older. Everyone's...older. I mean, that's expected, but it's still a surprise. An expected surprise. Like when you handed me the phone and said, "It's your brother." My first thought was "Who died?" I expected it, but still...

(Van returns, carrying a six-pack of beer. One of the beers has been removed. He takes another out and opens it.)

VAN: I thought you were pretty matter-of-fact, that first time I called.

TED: Stunned. Surprised. Surprised you were calling, and surprised...

VAN: Yeah. I guess. Me, too. Must have been late there. Wasn't thinking about the time difference.

TED: No, I was awake. Letterman.

VAN: Oh, yeah.

(They drink.)

TED: Like going back in time. *(An old password.)* Beers in the basement.

VAN: *(The countersign.)* Lords of the Underworld.

(They give each other a small, ritualized salute.)

TED: Summertime, work all day in the heat, knock off and sit down in the cool and dark and have a cold one. *(Pause.)* Half expect the old man to come walking in and chew us out.

VAN: Know what you mean. It's only two days. I'm still looking for him too.

TED: Yeah. *(Raises his beer.)* This pissed him off.

VAN: Nah, he didn't mind.

TED: Sure he did. "Beer drinkers take money out of our pocket." Like Bud drinkers would be drinking our stuff instead.

VAN: He didn't mind. Just when we left the cans.

TED: You ever have a beer with him down here?

VAN: No.

TED: Well? It pissed him off.

NIAMH: *(From the loft.)* Was there a wake?

TED: I always heard about it from him.

NIAMH: Was there a wake?

TED: Wakes really aren't a big thing here.

VAN: Another one?

TED: Jesus, give me a minute.

NIAMH: And how was your ma?

TED: Okay. She held up great. She has lots of friends, and there was always someone around.

NIAMH: She was happy you came, I'm sure.

TED: Oh, yes. I guess.

NIAMH: It's been how many years?

TED: Five. I told you.

NIAMH: Of course, you did. I was just asking to see if you remembered.

TED: I thought I told you.

VAN: Long time.

TED: Yeah.

NIAMH: What?

TED: It's a long time.

NIAMH: And isn't it, though? It's only three years for me, and if feels like ages since I was home.

TED: You talk to them once a month on the phone, letters, e-mail from your sister…how do you feel like you've ever left?

NIAMH: I don't see them.

TED: Whenever you want to visit—

NIAMH: When would you like to go? *(Pause.)* Well, then.

(Ted speaks to Van.)

TED: She's the youngest of five kids. Got a brother about your age. Dad drives a cab, a "hackney," she calls it. Mom has a store. Tourist stuff. They all live upstairs. I can't picture going back there.

VAN: Different world.

TED: I can't picture it.

(Karen enters, wearing jeans, work boots, and a cotton shirt with the sleeves rolled up to her elbows. She is 35, but has the weathered look of someone who has spent long hours in the sun.)

KAREN: *(To Ted.)* When did you get in?

TED: Just now.

KAREN: Well. Didn't take long to have a meeting of the boy's club.

(Ted stands up, Karen does not come over to him.)

TED: Kay.

KAREN: Where are you staying?

TED: I was going to get a room, but...

KAREN: Mom's made up a room for you up at the house.

TED: I know. She didn't have to do that.

KAREN: That's what I told her. How long are you staying?

TED: Day after tomorrow.

KAREN: Why are you in here?

TED: Just where we wound up.

VAN: Having a beer. Want one?

KAREN: Have you been up to the house?

VAN: Yeah. Ida Sandoval and a couple of the ladies are up there.

TED: Ida hasn't changed.

KAREN: Mom expects us all for dinner.

VAN: I know.

KAREN: Don't leave the cans in here.

VAN: Aye-aye.

KAREN: Van, could I talk to you, please?

(He nods.)

KAREN: Outside.

VAN: Yes, ma'am.

NIAMH: How was your sister?

TED: Like I said, five years older. Running the place. Only one of us with a formal education in winemaking. Enology. UC Davis.

NIAMH: You never studied it?

TED: Nope. My winemaking education was strictly on-the-job. But Kay...she's got a flair for it. She loves it. Always did. She always wanted to go out and work with me. Even when she was a kid. The old man, he didn't think that girls were supposed to do that kind of work, but Kay always wanted to go along, so I took her whenever I could. She'd be so excited. We had fun. Now...now it's her place, I guess.

NIAMH: Yours, too, isn't it?

TED: No. I sold my interest in the place before I moved. I needed the cash. So I'm clear of that business, at least.

(Van returns.)

TED: You in the dog house?

VAN: Bow-wow-wow. We're supposed to stay up at the house, not come down here and get drunk. Want that other one now?

TED: Get you in trouble.

VAN: Kay doesn't run everything around here. Just thinks she does. (He hands Ted a beer.) Gunny told me once, he said, "No offense, sir, but the hard part of my job is making you think that everything I do is your idea."

TED: The place does look good.

VAN: Well, that's Kay. She keeps things wired pretty tight.

TED: Yeah. What does she let you do?

VAN: Got the office all to myself.

TED: Oh, she dumped the paperwork on you. You go to all the meetings, too?

VAN: Not all the ones I'm supposed to.

TED: I hated those meetings. Vintners Association. Board of Supervisors. And all the god-damn paperwork. Never felt like I was getting anything done. How do you handle it?

VAN: Marine Corps training, son.

TED: What, you set fire to it?

VAN: You know what is just about the most important skill for a professional military officer to have? You've got to know how to type. Hell, if you're an enlisted man and you know how to type, you'll never see combat. Half the job's just moving paper sometimes. Beggars can't be choosers, you know?

(Niamh comes down to Ted in the cooperage.)

NIAMH: You hate paperwork. That's why you have me around.

TED: Beggars can't be choosers.

NIAMH: Go on. You're lucky to have me.

VAN: Lucky to have something, you know?

TED: Yeah. Some people have all the luck.

NIAMH: Well, why don't you try it yourself, then?

TED: *(Back to Niamh.)* What?

NIAMH: "Some people have all the luck."

TED: What are you—

NIAMH: If it occurs to you, you might say "thank you" occasionally. You'd do as much for a clerk.

(She turns and goes back into the loft. Ted follows.)

TED: I'm sorry, I wasn't...I mean, I do appreciate—

NIAMH: I've been sitting here worried, now, haven't I? With the weather. A tornado, for the love of God. And, of course, you couldn't think to phone.

TED: I was on a plane.

NIAMH: On the plane, were you? For two days? And, of course, I'm not to go at all.

TED: It was not the time. *(Pause.)* I'm sorry I didn't call. I wasn't thinking, okay? I've had other things on my mind, you know?

NIAMH: I was worried.

TED: I'm sorry.

NIAMH: You're still miles away.

TED: Yeah. I was thinking about my brother, back home doing paperwork. Sitting behind a desk.

NIAMH: It's all right.

TED: It's not.

NIAMH: What's he like? Your brother.

TED: Van?

NIAMH: Van, yes. The mysterious Van. You know, you might have told me his name. When he called, the other night, and he said "Van," I thought he meant delivery van and I asked him what delivery, at that hour. Didn't I feel foolish.

TED: I told you his name.

NIAMH: You didn't. You would think you had, I mean you know the names of all my brothers and sisters, you know my Uncle Sean and my cousin Ciaran at the bar, you would think you'd at least have said, "Ciaran? I have a sister named Karen."

TED: A guy Ciaran's size, you don't say "Hey, you've got the same name as my sister."

NIAMH: Well, you might have thought to say it to me. You know, I was thinking it was odd…I've never seen a picture of your family. That's odd, I think, you being a photographer and all.

TED: Sure you have.

NIAMH: Sure and I haven't. I've looked.

(Ted turns to Niamh.)

NIAMH: Don't give me that face-you leave me for two days and, of course, I'm going to look. But, of course, it's no use. I've still no faces to put with anyone. Karen. The mysterious Van.

TED: Van's his middle name. Part of it. Barton Van Fleet Wilk. We call him Van. Better than Bart.

NIAMH: A very high-sounding name.

TED: Embarrasses the hell out of him. Don't ever call him that.

NIAMH: And when would I have the occasion?

TED: You'll meet him. Someday.

NIAMH: I won't be holding my breath. "Barton Van Fleet Wilk." And you just poor Theodore.

TED: Theodore Roosevelt Junior Wilk.

NIAMH: Dear Lord.

TED: Do you know who Teddy Roosevelt was?

NIAMH: I do. I'm not illiterate. Do you know who Michael Collins was?

TED: Sure. He was an astronaut. Apollo 11. Couldn't have named us Bill and George.

NIAMH: So you're named for the President?

TED: The President's son. He was a general in the Army in World War II. My dad's unit. General Barton, Colonel Van Fleet, them too. On D-Day. 4th Infantry Division.

NIAMH: A soldier.

TED: Yeah. Ran away from home, lied about his age, and joined the Army so that we could be free to give our children God-awful names so that they could get teased unmercifully in school and have a legacy, goddamnit.

NIAMH: At least you were never named for a fairy tale.

TED: What?

NIAMH: I was named for a fairy tale. "Niamh of the Golden Hair." I told you once.

TED: Oh, yeah. The one with the horse.

NIAMH: Couldn't they just name me Rapunzel and be done with it?

TED: Yeah, well, no one expected you to join the fairies.

NIAMH: And were you? Expected to join the fairies?

TED: Don't even joke. Dad was always, you know, "a man's not a man until he's served his country, doesn't know what he's made of," that sort of thing. Van, he went for it. Joined the Marines. Ate up the whole line of fucking John Wayne bullshit. Wound up commanding an infantry company, finally. Dad was in hog heaven.

NIAMH: That's colorful.

TED: Yeah, well, you Irish don't have a monopoly on colorful sayings.

NIAMH: And how could we aspire to the poetry of "hog heaven?" *(Pause.)* Do you not like John Wayne, then? I only ask because when you come to Ireland—if you come, I should say—I'll need to know if I should take you on "The Quiet Man" tour or not.

(Pause. Ted does not respond.)

NIAMH: It's quite the thing for the tourists.

(No response.)

NIAMH: It's a lovely film. John Wayne plays an American prizefighter, and he—

TED: I know, I know. I know the movie, okay? I just really don't give a shit about John Wayne.

NIAMH: Well, that's off the list, then. *(Pause.)* So, where are these well—hidden pictures of your family?

TED: Okay, Jesus. They're in the filing cabinet. Bottom drawer. In the back.

NIAMH: Of course. If they're in the filing cabinet, then, of course, they're in the bottom drawer, and if they're in the bottom drawer, then, of course, they're in the back. Come from an ugly family do you? *(Pulls out a file folder.)* These, then? Well, these are normal enough. No serious deformities. *(She holds up a photo.)* Your ma and your da? I can see it well enough. Dead alike, you are, you and your father. Your mother's a handsome woman.

TED: I'll pass that along.

NIAMH: I'll be holding my breath. Your brother and sister? Well, of course, who else would they be? Your brother's a handsome man. Takes after your ma. Your sister looks like you, but we all have our cross to bear. We should have these up.

TED: No.

NIAMH: We have pictures of my family, we should have pictures of your family.

TED: I know what they look like. I don't need to put up a picture.

(She holds up the photo of Van and Karen.)

NIAMH: This is a beautiful place. Where is it?

TED: Lake Berryessa. It's in the hills, just east of the Valley. We used to go up there to water-ski. Van liked to water-ski. Van was the athlete.

NIAMH: He looks it. Not that I'm ogling your brother, now, but he does look very fit.

TED: It's an old picture.

NIAMH: He's gone to seed now, has he?

TED: That was before he went overseas. Persian Gulf.

NIAMH: He was in the war?

TED: He won the Silver Star. *(To Van.)* Ever get up to Berryessa?

VAN: Oh, yeah. Water-skiing every weekend. No. Not really. I don't drive, you know? State of California has a little problem with a one-eyed man driving. Used to ride my bike up there now and then. Rigged up an extender for my arm. Works pretty well.

TED: Man.

VAN: Got to have some way of getting around town.

TED: I guess. Keeps you in shape, too. Over the hills.

VAN: Yeah. That and running.

TED: Still running?

VAN: Nothing wrong with my legs. *(Van gets up and starts out.)* Well, I've got to hit the head.

TED: Two beers?

VAN: Age. You know the feeling.

TED: Not me. Got the bladder of a twenty-two year old.

VAN: Thought she was twenty-four.

TED: Funny man. Be sure to wash your hands.

(Van goes out.)

NIAMH: You were all proud of him, I'm sure.

TED: Oh, yes. We all were. They all came home and had parades and everyone was proud. Then they went to Somalia. Gigantic…I forget what he called it. "Cluster fuck."

NIAMH: Should I put that down next to "hog heaven?"

TED: Came home from that, too. Got promoted, even. And then he was overseas some-where. Guam? I don't remember. And he and this other guy were having a race. Last one to the Officer's Club buys the beer. Van could always run. He ran right through the sliding glass door, which was closed. He never saw it.

NIAMH: Oh, Jesus.

TED: Glass. Lost his right eye. Cut up his right arm pretty deep. 500-something stitches, some ungodly number. Had something like four operations, but they never could fix it. Some kind of nerve damage.

NIAMH: Oh, that's awful.

TED: And the Marines, well, if you can't be an infantryman, you can't be a Marine. So they cut him loose. Silver Star, doesn't matter. Adios. He's officially disabled. "Physically incapable," that's the term.

NIAMH: After all that. All that fighting…

TED: Yeah. Ironic. You appreciate irony, don't you?

NIAMH: I'm Irish.

TED: Yeah. So he comes home and he's all messed up, and Dad doesn't want to tell anyone about how it happened. It's embarrassing, I guess. If he'd been wounded in battle, well, that would have been something different, but to run through a sliding glass door...Not heroic, you see. Just careless. I mean, John Wayne never would have...Shit, if Van hadn't bought into all the John Wayne bullshit, he'd... probably be coaching high school football somewhere. Wife and a couple of kids.

NIAMH: He's not married?

TED: No.

NIAMH: Too bad.

TED: Yeah.

(Niamh goes back to the folder, pulls out another photo.)

NIAMH: And here's one of all of you...except for you, of course. You're not in any of them, I see.

TED: I took them.

NIAMH: And you're too proud to use the timer.

TED: Well, you know me. Things only make sense when I'm looking through the viewfinder. So I'm not in the picture. So sue me.

NIAMH: Is this your house?

TED: Mom's house. The winery's her family's.

(Pause.)

NIAMH: And who is this?

TED: Guess.

NIAMH: Is this your wife, then?

TED: Yes. That's Dana.

NIAMH: Ah.

TED: Still think we should have it out? Really brighten up the room, wouldn't it? Lovely photo of the ex-wife?

NIAMH: I thought she was just a friend. With her arm around your sister and all.

TED: She and Karen were friends. All through school.

NIAMH: She's pretty.

TED: Yes. Dana's a beautiful woman. It always kind of took me by surprise. Dana's looks.

NIAMH: She was evil, though, wasn't she?

TED: Yes. A real witch. Sacrificed small animals in the living room.

NIAMH: Go on with you.

DANA *(Offstage.)* Van?

TED: Dana was…is…probably one of the nicest people I have ever met in my life.

DANA *(Offstage.)* Van, are you—

> *(Dana enters the cooperage. She is an attractive woman of about thirty-five, who has clearly not spent a lot of time in the fields. She is dressed in clothes that look casual but clearly cost more than most people's dress clothes, and she is carrying a large artist's folio. When she sees Ted, she stops short.)*

DANA: Oh. Hi.

TED: Hi.

DANA: This is a surprise.

TED: Yeah.

DANA: You came.

TED: Yeah, of course, I did.

DANA: Well, good. How've you been?

TED: Getting along. You?

DANA: Getting along. They told me Van was in here.

TED: He'll be right back.

DANA: Beers in the basement.

TED: Lords of the Underworld.

> *(Dana mimics their salute.)*

TED: Want one?

DANA: No. Thanks. When did you get in?

TED: Just now.

DANA: Have you been up to the house?

TED: Yeah. Ida Sandoval and the ladies. There's a house full.

DANA: I was wondering how your mother was doing.

TED: Fine, I guess. Staying busy. Plans. Arrangements. Like when Grandpa died, you know.

DANA: I remember. Are you staying up there?

TED: I guess. She made up a room for me, so I guess I'll be there.

DANA: Tell her if there's anything she needs…

TED: I will. Thanks.

NIAMH: How long were you married?

TED: Six years.

DANA: Five years.

TED: Huh? Oh, yeah. Time flies.

DANA: *(She gestures at his hair.)* The gray is nice. Makes you look kind of intellectual.

TED: Kind of what I'm going for. Passage of time.

DANA: I know. Me, too.

TED: Really?

DANA: Pay good money to hide it.

TED: Wouldn't have known.

NIAMH: Did you see her when you went back?

TED: I did. She… she was at the funeral. My father liked her. Thought she hung the moon. Everyone likes Dana.

(Van reenters.)

VAN: Oh. Hi.

DANA: They told me you were in here.

VAN: Who?

DANA: What's-his-name. The new guy.

VAN: Eric? I told him to go home.

DANA: He had some books out. I guess he was studying. I see the bar is open.

VAN: Want one?

DANA: Sure. Just like old times.

(Van opens a beer and hands it to Dana.)

VAN: The good old days.

DANA: Well, the old days, anyway.

VAN: *(Points to folio.)* I was going to bring those down.

DANA: You've been busy.

VAN: Yeah. Thanks. They're really nice. I stuck a Post-It on a couple of them, just to—

DANA: I'll take a look at them. It was a shock to hear about your dad. Thanks for the call.

VAN: No problem. Figured you'd want to know.

DANA: When's the service?

VAN: The viewing starts at one. Service is at four, and then I guess everyone's coming up to the house afterward. Ida said that the ladies are cooking, and you know what that means.

DANA: Is there anything I can do?

VAN: No. Thanks.

DANA: How's Kay?

VAN: Who knows? She's been off all day. Truck had been up at Hilltop since Dad's heart attack...you know, just sitting up there...it had run out of gas. She took a can up, drove it back down, then went back out somewhere.

DANA: Oh. Well, tell her I came by.

VAN: Sure.

DANA: Well. I guess I'd better get going. Maybe Ida's left me a message, telling me to bring something.

TED: You're one of "the ladies" now?

DANA: Sometimes. I'll see you tomorrow, then.

TED: Yeah. See you tomorrow.

VAN: I'll walk you out.

DANA: No need.

VAN: My good deed for the day.

(Karen enters.)

KAREN: Van, are you going to...Oh, hi.

DANA: Hi.

KAREN: What brings you up here?

(Dana gestures to folio.)

KAREN: Ah. I forgot we had those.

DANA: Understandable.

KAREN: Sorry.

DANA: It's okay. How are you?

KAREN: I'm okay.

DANA: Need anything?

KAREN: No. You might check up at the house, though. Ida's there.

DANA: Yeah, Van said.

KAREN: She might know.

DANA: I'll call her. Tell your mom I—

KAREN: Yeah. I will. Thanks.

DANA: We should get together.

KAREN: Yeah. We should.

DANA: Call me.

KAREN: Yeah. Okay.

DANA: Well. I'll see you tomorrow.

KAREN: You're coming?

DANA: Of course.

KAREN: Well, I'll see you then.

(Dana and Van go out. Ted and Karen look at each other but don't speak.)

NIAMH: How did you meet?

TED: What?

(Karen turns and goes. Niamh comes down to Ted.)

NIAMH: Your wife. How did you meet?

TED: We didn't "meet." She was my sister's best friend. I've known her since she was eight. Dana...Danny. Danny Malone.

NIAMH: So you've a weakness for Irish women, have you?

TED: Yeah. I have a soft spot in my head for them. She's second generation, though. Her family were coopers. I think her grandfather or somebody worked for Guinness, back in Ireland, making barrels. They had barrels, we had wine.

NIAMH: A marriage of convenience.

TED: No. Maybe. She still lives in the house. Her parents bought us this house when we got married. Beautiful house in St. Helena. My folks furnished it. I can't begin to guess who spent more. Decorated…I came home one day and there was this photographer taking pictures in my house for this magazine. This other photographer, taking pictures in my house.

NIAMH: That's what you get for not marking your territory.

TED: It didn't piss me off until later. I mean, it never felt like my house. I always felt like company. A guest. And then, every so often, I'd catch a glimpse of this beautiful woman around the house, and honest to God my first thought would always be "who's that?" And then after a second I'd realize that it was Danny, that it was that little gap-toothed girl who was always hanging around with my stupid sister. My wife. It was always…it felt…it never seemed real.

NIAMH: So, what happened to the two of you?

(Long pause.)

TED: Hard to hold onto something that doesn't seem real.

(Karen returns, with a glass and a wine thief, a long pipelike instrument used for extracting wine from a barrel. She also carries a notebook and an empty coffee can.)

KAREN: You're still here.

TED: Just waiting for Van. *(He crosses down toward Karen.)* Odd moment, there.

KAREN: Why?

TED: I didn't expect—

KAREN: You think because you left she can't still be friends with us?

TED: No.

KAREN: She was my friend first. She's still my friend. She does the labels because I ask her to.

TED: She always did the labels.

KAREN: She stopped for a couple of years. But I asked her to, so she does.

TED: Okay.

KAREN: We use them for the calendar, too. We use reproductions of the old labels. Sells a lot better than the old ones. With the photographs.

TED: Well, good.

(Niamh is holding a calendar, with the reproductions of the labels.)

NIAMH: She's talented.

TED: She's talented.

KAREN: You're damn right she is.

TED: Looks like she's doing well.

KAREN: Never better.

TED: Probably.

(Pause. Karen goes over to one of the barrels.)

KAREN: How long are you staying?

TED: Day after tomorrow. Though maybe I could change it and fly out after the service tomorrow. If you prefer.

KAREN: Stay as long as you like. *(Pause.)* Mom's probably waiting for you.

TED: Soon as Van comes back.

(Karen takes a lockback knife from her pocket and uses it to extract the bung from the barrel. She inserts the thief and draws out a sample of the wine, which she pours into the glass.)

TED: What is that?

KAREN: Last year's Cab. From Hilltop.

TED: Hilltop. Finally getting something from Hilltop.

KAREN: We've been getting something from Hilltop for a couple of years now.

TED: How much?

KAREN: A bit. Ten thousand liters.

TED: Ten thousand? How much did you plant?

KAREN: Enough. You didn't think we could.

TED: I never said that.

KAREN: Yes, you did.

TED: I said that it would be hard to—

KAREN: Well, we did.

TED: I said that I didn't know if it would pay off.

KAREN: It will. *(She swirls the wine in the glass, holding it up to the light.)* This, we are figuring at a hundred forty, hundred fifty dollars a bottle. Say, sixteen hundred dollars a case, times…well, you're the expert, you tell me if it'll pay off.

TED: How'd you solve the water problem? Reservoir?

KAREN: Yeah.

TED: I thought there'd be a lot of digging.

KAREN: Yes, we did some digging.

TED: Ten thousand, you did a lot of digging.

KAREN: We did some digging.

TED: Big investment. Take a while to pay off, even at that rate. Even if the market holds.

KAREN: We sell out before release now. If we need to, we'll bump the price.

TED: Okay, fine. I hope it works out.

(*Karen tastes the wine, sniffing it in the glass, swirling it around in her mouth, then spits it back into the coffee can.*)

TED: How is it?

KAREN: Fine.

TED: Get a taste?

KAREN: You're not old enough.

TED: Come on, Kay. Just a taste.

KAREN: No.

TED: Okay, I was just curious.

KAREN: You'll live.

TED: You let Van taste it?

KAREN: Yes.

TED: Van doesn't know what he's tasting.

KAREN: Van works here. The public doesn't get to taste it until it's ready.

TED: You know, I have done this before.

KAREN: Yeah, you're an expert, aren't you? Well, you used to be.

TED: I think I remember a thing or two. I think I can still taste something at a year and know where it will be in five.

KAREN: Well, I think you don't know a damn thing about it. I planted this vineyard, I was there at the harvest, and I have been here every damn day. I know where it's been, I know where it's going to be. You don't know a damn thing about it.

TED: Oh, please. I'm sure it's fine.

KAREN: Oh, thank you. That means so much to me. The Ted Wilk seal of approval. I can rest easy at last. The five gold medals we won last year didn't mean a damn thing to me, I was waiting for my big brother's okay. I'm glad to know that it was his boundless confidence in me that allowed him to—

TED: I do have confidence—

KAREN: I don't need your fucking approval.

TED: I know.

KAREN: Well, I'm glad we've got that straight.

TED: I was just curious.

KAREN: Oh, you were just curious. Well, then, that makes all the difference in the world. When did you get curious? When did you start to wonder? Just now? In here? You got curious to see what I did with what you left me. A lot. A hell of a lot. Whether you admit it or not. You left, it's mine now, and I don't have to show you a goddamn thing until I'm good and ready.

TED: Fine. Okay.

KAREN: I'm surprised you can even stand to be down here. All this wine, all around you. The smell of it. Doesn't it make you gag? Break out in a cold sweat? Give you the shakes? How can you stand it down here, all by yourself?

TED: Kay—

KAREN: Oh, is it okay now? Are you all better? Well, maybe I should give you a taste, then.

(She quickly draws another taste with the thief, and pours it into the glass, splashing some of the wine.)

TED: Kay, it's not—

KAREN: No, no, I insist. *(She slams the bung back into the barrel, smacking it with the heel of her hand. She picks up the glass and holds it out to him.)* Go on. Have a taste.

(He doesn't take it.)

KAREN: What gives you the right to come in here and look over my shoulder? What gives you the right?

(He doesn't answer. She puts the glass down on top of a barrel.)

KAREN: You just be sure you fucking finish it.

(Karen exits. After a moment, Ted picks up the glass of wine. He does not drink it.)

NIAMH: *(Niamh also has a glass.)* It's rarely I see you drink the stuff.

TED: Yeah. Guess I had my fill.

NIAMH: I can't picture you as a farmer.

TED: Neither could I, eventually.

NIAMH: You're one of those experts, then, who can taste a wine and tell you where it's from?

TED: No. Maybe Napa wine, but—

NIAMH: This is Napa wine.

TED: I don't think it is.

NIAMH: It is. Look for yourself.

(She produces a bottle.)

TED: It's not.

NIAMH: It says—

TED: I know what it says. The winery's Napa Valley. Rutherford. Right on the side of the highway. I know the people who run it. They used to sell real estate in L.A. Now they sell wine, and t-shirts, and corkscrews, and napkin rings, and pretzels, and sixteen different kinds of mustard. It's a tourist trap. Most of them are tourist traps. And the grapes they use are not from Napa. If the grapes were from Napa, it would say "Napa Valley Cabernet Sauvignon," and it would cost three times as much, and you wouldn't be able to find it at the White Hen.

NIAMH: I'm sorry, I wanted to—

TED: No, no, it's okay. It's all bullshit, anyway. The wine crap. Most people don't know the difference. Drink what you like. Don't overpay for the label. But you see, that's why I don't drink wine much. It's always my first thought. Someone takes out a bottle of wine. "How much did it cost?" How much a bottle equals how much a case, and what's the markup and…and it's all overpriced.

NIAMH: It's the merchant in you.

TED: Yeah. So I usually just go get a beer and try to forget about it.

NIAMH: I wanted to buy a proper bottle of wine for you.

TED: It's proper. I mean, it's fine. Don't worry about it.

NIAMH: Well, it was part of your life for—

TED: Was. Was part of. This is my life now, okay?

NIAMH: Well, I think it's fascinating.

TED: Oh, yeah. Riveting.

NIAMH: It is, to me. I've learned more about you this night than in the six months I've lived with you, and it's about time, too. Go on. More.

(Ted shakes his head.)

NIAMH: Are you afraid I'll get bored without the mystery?

TED: There's no great mystery.

NIAMH: You know all my life story.

TED: You're twenty-four.

NIAMH: So? *(Pause.)* So you're to know all of mine and I'm to know none of yours? Sure, that's fair enough.

TED: I can't do this tonight. I'm tired.

NIAMH: Oh, then let's just go to bed and forget about it, shall we?

(Pause.)

TED: You go ahead.

NIAMH: Ted, love, I know about working for your family. I used to work in my ma's shop.

TED: Yeah, I know.

NIAMH: I know it's hard sometimes. When you live upstairs and you can never get away.

TED: And you left when you were twenty-one. I worked at the winery from when I was twelve until I went to college, but I only went to college thirty miles away so I was always home to help with things when I was called. Then I came home and I worked at the winery until I was thirty-six. Twelve to thirty-six. Even when I was a kid, family vacations were to France, or to Italy. It was all around this stuff.

(He swirls the glass, but doesn't drink. Through this next section, the lights slowly fade to a spot on Ted, Niamh and the surroundings fading into darkness.)

TED: There's this great American myth about working the land. "All a man needs is a good piece of fertile ground to earn his living by the sweat of his brow, and come home to his loving wife and watch his little children playing about his feet." A myth. Working the land. Like you're doing something to it. Like things wouldn't grow if we didn't make them, like things hadn't been growing out of the ground for millions of years, all by themselves. "Working the land." The only people who believe that are people who don't try to do it. People who, the closest they come to agriculture is the produce section of the Jewel. That's what they think of when they think of "working the land," all the nice neat rows of fruits and vegetables, with the misters coming on every five minutes to make sure everything stays cool and crisp, everything right there for them when they want it. All clean and sparkling. They don't think about dirt. They don't think about how your life turns around the weather report every day. Too wet, too dry, too cold, too hot. How you have to be on the lookout for this fungus, or that insect, or some unknown kind of rot that's just waiting to wipe you out. How it's every single fucking day and it never stops, before dawn to after dark. "Working the land." The land. It's the land that's working you, and that's the truth of it. But we live like the myth is the truth, get up and work and go home, and marry a pretty girl you've known all your life because it seems like the thing to do at the time, you take over the family business when your dad supposedly retires, and you work and not only do you have to make this stuff, you have to go sell it, and because the only people who know about you are wine snobs who don't shop at Super Wham-O Cut-Rate Liquor Stores you don't make the ten-thousand case sale, you have to make a thousand ten-case sales, which is hard enough but if you only make nine hundred of those sales, I mean 90% is pretty damn good in most things, but if you only make nine hundred of those sales you come home knowing that your dad is going to come in and say we're down 10% in sales and it's your fault, that this place, this place your great-grandfather built with his own two hands, is going under because you're not good enough to keep it going. *(He takes a deep breath, in and out.)* And if you worked for someone else, they'd just do the humane thing and fire you. But your family…doesn't fire you. *(Another breath. He wipes his forehead.)* And then you go home, to your lovely house that your parents bought for you and the pretty girl you've known all your life. And she's tied to the social life of the valley, and I mean, you can't be a recluse, you have to make appearances. You go home and you get dressed and you go out, and you serve on this committee, or that board, because you have to be active in the community, and you drag yourself home and your pretty wife starts again about how she's not getting any younger and you should start your family soon, which is what you've been hearing from your parents and hers, I mean she's an only child and her parents want it, and your parents, well, your brother is a cripple and your sister hasn't shown any inclination to settle down and breed, so you're it. And you think about having kids and it all starts to look like another crop to you, more produce, more plowing and tending and feeding and worrying about things that are completely out of your hands, and only hearing about the things you do wrong. *(Pause. Breathing.)* One night we were…we were doing this benefit, we were part of this tasting. It was at this theater in Berkeley, and they were having this tasting and a reception after the play, and we were…part of it. And we went down to see the play. It was Shakespeare. Richard the Third. I didn't know it then, but I know it now. *(Another breath.)* There's this scene…where this guy is killed…they drown him in a barrel of wine. He's been talking about how frightened he is of drowning…and they drown him in a barrel of wine. And I was sitting there, and I started…God, look at me, I'm starting now…sweating. Panting like a dog, couldn't get any air, trying to keep from jumping up and running out…I didn't go back for the second act, told them I had to help get things set up for…and then, we're doing the tasting and I've gotten myself back together and all and we get to the part where you…get your nose inside the glass and breathe in the…bouquet…and I looked down and I saw this wine and I took a breath and all I could smell was… *(He sets the glass down, spilling some.)* Stupid. *(He wipes his forehead.)* Somehow…I made it to the men's room. Threw up until there was nothing left to throw up. And all the way home I heard about how I'd embarrassed everyone by leaving. *(Pause.)* God, I'd have embarrassed them more if I hadn't. *(Pause. He is a little calmer.)* And every so often I'd have one of these…things. Sweats, no air…and the smell or the taste just made me…and then they started happening more often, and, well…There were only two ways out, it felt like, two ways, and one was feet first, and I wasn't going that way…well, I thought about it but then I thought "no, they'll cremate me and scatter me over the vineyard." So the next thing I know Dana and I are signing papers in a lawyer's office and I'm packing up my car and shaking my brother's hand because he was the only one who came to say good-bye, and driving two thousand miles so I could do temp work until this little waste-of-time hobby of mine, that's what Dad said about photography, the thing I did for me, the thing that mattered to me, just a stupid-little waste-of-time hobby…began to make me a living. And I started to be okay. Little by little, a day at a time…time goes by, and…it gets to be okay. I can even have an occasional glass of wine now.

(He swirls the glass, sticks his nose into it and breathes, looks at it, sets it down on top of a barrel without drinking. Lights out.)

END OF ACT I

Act II

The glass of wine sits on the barrel where it was left at the end of Act I. Karen enters, dressed in a dark suit, jacket and slacks. She picks up the wine and comes downstage. Ted is upstage, in the loft area.

KAREN: My father used to say that this was a taste of the past. When I was a little girl, we'd go out at night and look at the stars, and he would tell me that the light we were seeing had been traveling for thousands of years, just to get to us, so we were really seeing them as they were thousands of years ago. It was like looking back in time, he said. But it didn't mean anything to me. If the star looked like that a thousand years ago or five minutes ago, it didn't make any difference to me. It was just a little light, like any other little light in the sky. And then, later, when I was older and heard him giving the tours, I heard him say that each barrel of wine contained the past, a taste of the past. And that meant something to me. This is something you can see, and touch, and smell, and taste. It's real, not just a light in the sky. And when you taste it, you remember that year, that time. It comes alive for you again. What you were doing. Who you were with. Things-people-who aren't around anymore. That's why, though this is a sad day, I can't feel like my father is gone forever. For me, he will always be very close, and very real.

(Van enters, also dressed in a dark suit. He is not wearing his eye patch, but is apparently wearing a prosthetic eye. Karen hands him the glass of wine.)

VAN: A taste of the past. Dad also said that this represents faith in the future, that when you are making wine you are always thinking about what it's going to be. Most of you have heard the story-he loved to tell it-about how he was wounded, and while he was recuperating in that little French town he saw the people going out to their little vineyards, putting away wine even though the war was still on. Faith in the future. I didn't know what that could mean to him, back then. Never could picture him as a scared 17-year-old kid in a combat zone-I mean, my dad? Come on. Then I saw my first action, and I realized how important it was, that faith in the future, that belief that-in spite of everything-you are going to get through it and things will be okay. I mean, you don't have that…well, you're probably not going to get through it. When I came home, the first time I shook my father's hand, I knew that we had something in common, that we understood things that no one else in our family could know. And I was proud of that.

(Van stops. He holds out the glass of wine as if waiting for someone to take it. He waits a long time. Karen finally comes up and takes Van's arm, and they go off.)

TED: *(After they are gone.)* Van was looking right at me. He wanted me to have a chance to say something, too. A couple of people turned around to see if I was going to go up there. I mean, we'd already had the guy from the American Legion, and the woman from the VA hospital, and the guy from the Vintner's Association, and Sam Sandoval and Van and Kay…what did people expect me to add? They all knew what had happened—it's a small town. What did they expect me to say? He was my hero. My dad. The war hero. D-Day. Purple Heart. Worked his way across country, wound up here and became a pillar of the community. Did everything, and I mean…Jesus, everything. Conscience of the industry, they said that, "conscience of the industry," all those old guys who fought him all the time. Friend to many, respected by everyone else. He was my hero. For a long, long time. Do I get up and say that? With people sitting there, thinking, "Yeah? So how come you did what you did?" And all I can say to that is, maybe it was easy to be his friend. Easy, when you can go home. Try being his son.

(Van comes back into the cooperage, carrying a paper bag. He reaches in and pulls out a beer. Van is once again wearing his eye patch.)

VAN: You look like you need one.

TED: *(Moves from loft to cooperage.)* Wouldn't say no. Took it out, huh?

VAN: What, the big marble? Yeah. It's not real comfortable.

TED: Really?

VAN: Yeah. I don't know what's wrong. I think it's the wrong size. It just bothers me. Besides, the patch looks dashing, doesn't it? Mom says it looks dashing. Like a pirate. *(Holds up his right arm.)* I should get a hook, too, huh? Hear the one about the pirate in the bar? Pirate's in this bar, you know, hook, eyepatch, all that, and this guy sits next to him, and after a couple of drinks he asks the pirate how he got the hook. Pirate says, "We were boarding a Spanish man-o-war, a fine prize she was, and I was fighting her captain, him with his sword and me with me cutlass, and he cut off me hand as I slit his gizzard with me trusty blade." Guy says, "Wow. That's some story. How'd you get the patch?" Pirate says, "A seagull shit in me eye." *(Beat.)* "It was the first day I had the hook."

(Ted laughs. Pause. They drink.)

VAN: Dad always wanted me to wear it. I figured I'd wear it today.

(Ted nods. They drink.)

TED: Nice service.

(Van nods.)

TED: That was nice, what you said. You and Kay.

VAN: Thanks.

TED: Mom held up real well.

VAN: Yeah. She's a champ.

TED: I was thinking I'd look after her, but I didn't really have the chance.

VAN: Yeah. "The ladies." They kind of swarm.

TED: I'm kind of glad they're up there with her now. I wasn't really looking forward to the whole post-burial social thing. Not without my camera.

VAN: Oh, yeah, there's some pictures you really want to see.

TED: I know. It's just…you know, photography got me through more social events than I care to count. Great thing about being the photographer, you always have something to do. You don't have to stand around, making conversation…But you're right. Funerals aren't that kind of event. No one wants to get out the funeral album, no one wants to look at the funeral video. Photographer at a funeral…pretty fucking useless, right? And if you're one of the family at a funeral, people are always trying to keep you from having to do anything, anyway. You just sit there and they all come up to you.

VAN: Everybody seemed happy to see you.

TED: Oh, yeah, they were fine…then they'd be off in a group, watching me and talking to each other.

VAN: What, you think everyone was talking about you?

TED: No. I overheard some of the old guys. They were talking business. This going to hurt the price?

VAN: Dad dying?

TED: Yeah. Market's funny about things like that. You guys going to be okay?

VAN: I think so. Probably. Price on this stuff should actually go up. You know, John Lennon dies and his albums sell like crazy. Took a hit when you left, though.

TED: Why?

VAN: Guy running the place leaves because the smell of wine makes him puke, kind of raises a question about quality, you know? People talk. Market's funny about things like that.

TED: Kay said you sell out before release now.

VAN: Yeah. Money in a bottle.

TED: Kay should have been doing this all along, you know? I mean…she's great at this. Right after she got out of Davis. Right here, in charge…she should have been.

VAN: What, they should have fired you?

TED: Yes. Jesus. Fire me, hire Kay. That would have made sense.

(Niamh comes into the loft area, to the place where she was at the end of Act I.)

VAN: Dad wouldn't have fired you.

TED: No. And he wouldn't have hired Kay if he'd had a choice.

VAN: *(Opens another beer.)* Man's world.

TED: Fuckin' A. All that. I remember Grandpa telling me when I was a kid, "I was so happy when your father came along because then I had a son to pass my business to." I mean, he had a daughter, but he never thought of that. Automatically, it goes from son to son.

VAN: What, you didn't want it?

TED: No.

VAN: You acted like you did.

TED: I was supposed to, wasn't I?

NIAMH: And that was the only reason?

TED: Don't you want to do what you're supposed to do? Make your parents proud? I was supposed to take over the family business. Van was supposed to serve his country. Kay was supposed to…I don't know, go have babies or something.

NIAMH: So it's all your father's fault?

TED: No, it's my fault. *(To Van.)* Our fault. We swallowed the bullshit. We swallowed it all. He fed it to us and we lined up and swallowed it. Thank God I got out before I had to start eating any more of it.

(Karen comes into the cooperage. Neither Ted nor Van see her.)

TED: Somebody had to break the chain. And thank God. Kay's got a great reputation. You're selling out before release. None of that would've happened if we'd just kept on doing what we were supposed to do.

KAREN: Well, once again, I see I have you to thank for everything.

TED: I'm not looking for thanks, Kay.

KAREN: No, I don't want to be ungrateful. Thank you for leaving. It was the best thing you could have ever done for everyone.

VAN: Knock it off, Kay.

KAREN: I only want to—

VAN: Just stow it.

KAREN: No, I think I should—

VAN: I think you should SHUT THE FUCK UP. No one needs this shit right now. It's completely fucking pointless and I'm not going to spend one more goddamn minute on it, is that clear?

KAREN: I'm not—

VAN: IS THAT CLEAR?

(No one moves.)

VAN: Jesus fucking Christ. *(He drinks.)* One fucking day. Just one goddamn day. Can we have just one goddamn day? Today? I mean, Jesus, today? *(He drinks. Pause. He reaches into the bag and pulls out a beer. He offers it to Karen.)* Here.

KAREN: No.

VAN: Have one.

KAREN: I'm going back up to the house.

VAN: Bullshit. You're not going up there any more than we are.

KAREN: You should. The family should be there. You should be there for Mom.

VAN: There are eighty people up there for Mom. Our mother has friends around her three deep right now. She hasn't even noticed that we're not there.

KAREN: How do you know—

VAN: Has she asked for us?

(Karen does not answer.)

VAN: All those people are going to leave soon. That's when we need to be there for Mom. And that's when we'll all go back up there. Now have a beer.

(She doesn't take it.)

VAN: Come on. Sit down and have a beer.

KAREN: I don't want a beer.

VAN: Come on. You were always bitching and moaning about how you were never invited to have a beer with us. You're being invited.

KAREN: I don't—

TED: *(Takes the beer from Van, holds it out to Karen.)* Kay. Come on. Would it kill you?

(Karen takes the beer. Pause.)

TED: I was just telling Van that I liked what you guys said at the service. It was really nice.

KAREN: Thanks.

TED: Dad would have liked that. The taste of the past thing. That's good. And what Van said. He'd have liked that, too.

KAREN: Why didn't you say anything?

TED: You guys were fine.

(He drinks. No one speaks.)

TED: You said it all better than I would've. There wasn't much left for me to say.

KAREN: At your father's funeral.

TED: You guys were fine.

(Niamh comes into the cooperage, but stays at the edge.)

NIAMH: And you didn't have a wake at all?

TED: Couple of beers with my brother. Does that count? Me and my brother and sister. Wakes aren't really big here. I can't really picture anyone I know throwing a big party with a dead body as a centerpiece.

NIAMH: That's not what it is.

TED: I wouldn't know. I've never been to one. All you ever hear about is a lot of drinking and crying and singing and…what have you. Goes on for days.

NIAMH: Well, its not the first fable I've heard about Ireland since I've been here.

TED: *(Goes up to Niamh.)* So what goes on? At a real wake?

NIAMH: Well, there is some drinking, and perhaps someone will tell a joke or you'll have a favorite song or some such. In the old days they might have said that they were trying to convince the dead man to stay with them a while by recalling all the good times they had together. And perhaps someone will cry because it's a sad thing after all, and in the old days they might have said that the dead man should take pity on the women's tears and stay a while. And, of course, you'd have the body there because that would be the last time you'd see the face of the dead man. But that's perhaps what they did in the old days. Now, it's a time to remember all the good times you had with them, and share your sadness at their passing, and to say good-bye.

TED: Yeah. Well, like I said, they aren't a real big thing over here. *(Pause. Back to Van and Karen.)* So, Sam's at Silverhill now?

VAN: Assistant vineyard manager. Silverhill, you know, they've got all that corporate money. Made him an offer he couldn't refuse and we couldn't match.

TED: Good for him. Looks like it agrees with him.

KAREN: Yeah, I guess.

TED: Be weird around here without Sam.

VAN: Yeah. Ida still comes up, couple times a week to see Mom. Sit out on the porch and drink iced tea all afternoon.

TED: Hundred and five degrees?

VAN: You know it. "Oh, it's not that bad."

TED: Mom and her porch.

VAN: Getting about time to rebuild it again.

TED: Have fun.

VAN: Come on. You can help, can't you? Go crawl around in the dust under there. Bet there aren't too many snakes down there.

TED: Fucking snakes. Thought I was going to fucking die.

KAREN: It was just a little snake. It wasn't any big thing.

TED: Oh, yeah, right. What were you then, five? Six?

VAN: Not like it was some damn man-eater or anything.

TED: No, just a cute little timber rattler. Sweet little thing with adorable little fangs and dainty little poison. Shit. And where were you that day? Why weren't you there to go crawling under the porch?

VAN: I don't know. Off riding bikes with my buddies, I guess.

TED: Shit. You're riding bikes and she's playing Barbies and I'm crawling around under the porch trying not to get bit by a fucking rattlesnake.

VAN: Dad said that he thought you had been bit, the way you came flying out of there.

TED: Jesus. And, of course, Sam was there, the big kid, must have just gotten out of high school, and he dives under there and comes out a minute later holding this snake. And the son of a bitch throws the goddamn thing at me.

KAREN: It was dead.

TED: You can get bit by a dead snake. It's just reflex. There's still poison there.

KAREN: Not with its head cut off.

TED: Well, I didn't know he'd cut its head off. I didn't get a chance to examine the goddamn thing.

VAN: Scream like a girl? Dad said "He screamed like a little girl."

TED: Oh, yeah, and then he orders me back under the fucking porch. Back under the fucking porch, and I don't know if there's another snake under there or not. Sam said he'd go back under there and, I don't remember what we were doing under there, cutting out the joists or what, but he said he would do it and Dad said, "No, he's got to do it. He's got to learn how to be a man and do a job and not just leave it to everyone else."

KAREN: There's an idea.

TED: Fucking thirteen-year-old kid. "Get back under there, boy." Like I had to get bit to prove myself to him.

VAN: Well, you didn't get bit.

TED: I'll bet he was so disappointed.

(Pause.)

KAREN: Well, it's probably best that you didn't say anything at the service. That's just too heartwarming for words.

TED: Yeah, that probably was a little harsh, wasn't it. For the day.

KAREN: You feel how you feel.

VAN: Hey, you know the old man, right? "If everybody always loves you it's because you spend half your time lying to them."

TED: Yeah, well, he was a pretty truthful guy.

KAREN: And still, look at all those people today.

VAN: That was respect.

KAREN: Yeah. They respected him.

TED: Tough not to.

VAN: Another one?

(Ted nods, Van hands him another beer.)

KAREN: Put the empties in the bag, okay? I don't want to find a bunch of shit down here tomorrow morning.

VAN: We packed it in, we'll pack it out. It'll be lighter then.

KAREN: Yeah, you've got most of it inside you.

VAN: Not for long. Getting ready to go lighten the load. Got to lighten the load. Lay your burden down. Travel light, brothers and sisters. If you keep hanging onto stuff, pretty soon you can't move. You're just kind of dragging ass. You go through life dragging ass, you know what you get?

TED: What?

VAN: Hole in the seat of your pants. Then your ass is in the wind, and you know what you have to do then? Cover your ass. 'Cause if you don't cover your ass, you know what happens? You lose your ass. You lose your ass and you're shit out of luck, son.

TED: Words of wisdom.

VAN: 'Oo-rah. Your basic ass management protocol. Don't you forget it. *(He starts out.)* You two behave yourselves while I'm gone. No fighting.

TED: Neutral corners.

VAN: Good. Or I might have to kick your ass. *(He laughs and goes, weaving slightly.)*

TED: *(To Niamh.)* There was a bit of drinking. Reminiscing. I guess it would qualify as a wake. Don't know if we'd have convinced anyone to stay around, though.

NIAMH: *(Drawing Ted back toward the loft.)* They never stay. They've already gone. They don't come back. It's just sometimes, when you ask them and they say, "no, I'm off," it helps you to say "all right, I'll just go on, then." It helps you to go on with your life.

TED: Well, I said my good-byes a long time ago, and I've gone on with my life, so maybe it was just all lost on me.

NIAMH: Yes, and that's you, then. You've not had your da for five years now. But there's your ma, and your brother, and your sister. It's all new for them, now, isn't it?

(They stop their cross.)

TED: Mom's fine. I mean, I guess. She stays up at the house like always, her friends come up like they have her whole life. She grew up in that house, it's her thing, it's her place. As long as she can live there she'll be fine. Van…God knows he's had to adjust to enough already. Karen, well, you know, she works. She just…I mean, it wasn't enough for me, but for her maybe… *(Pause. To Karen.)* So. You, uh, seeing anyone?

KAREN: What?

TED: *(Leaves Niamh, crossing back toward Karen.)* Just making conversation. You seeing anyone?

KAREN: No.

TED: No?

KAREN: No. No, I am not seeing anyone. No. I don't have time. I have a place to run. This takes up all my time. I don't have time to "see anyone."

TED: Whatever happened with that guy over at—

KAREN: I really don't want to talk about my social life with you.

TED: Okay.

(Van returns.)

VAN: You two behaving?

TED: We're fine. Having a good time not talking about Kay's social life.

VAN: Not much to not talk about. Sister Kay. Our Lady of the Vineyards. Surprised she never tried to join the Christian Brothers. *(He sits, takes another beer out of the bag.)* Whoo. Running low. So, Reverend Mother, how are things in the convent?

KAREN: I don't have to take this shit from either of you.

TED: Forget it. *(To Van.)* So, how about you? You seeing anyone?

KAREN: Yeah, Van, who are you seeing?

VAN: Knock it off, Kay.

KAREN: Come on.

VAN: I'm not seeing anyone, and I haven't been seeing anyone.

KAREN: That's not what I hear.

TED: You got a girlfriend?

VAN: No-

KAREN: Listen, Ted's concerned about us. That's nice, isn't it? That he's so concerned? After all this time?

VAN: Just can it. Now.

KAREN: Why don't we just tell him all about our lives, so then he can go back and rest easy knowing that I'm taking care of this place while you take care of—

VAN: Shut up before I—

KAREN: What? Shut me up? It would take both arms for that.

TED: *(Shocked.)* Kay. *(Pause.)* Guys, we are not going to do this today. Not today. So both of you just drop it. Let it go.

(Pause. Neither Van nor Karen speaks.)

TED: Come on, Van, let's go up to the house.

KAREN: No. No, you two just stay here and have your little boys club. Your little frat-boy beer club. Make your little jokes about Sister Karen joining the Christian Brothers. I don't care. I'll go up to the house and I'll take care of things. I'll take care of things because that's what I do. Whether you're here or not. *(Karen turns and goes.)*

TED: What the fuck was that all about?

VAN: Nothing. Nothing you need to worry about.

TED: Okay.

VAN: She's just…it's just malicious bullshit. All for my benefit.

TED: Yeah?

VAN: It's nothing.

TED: Malicious nothing.

VAN: Yeah.

(Pause.)

TED: Does it involve me?

VAN: No. Not…no. No, it doesn't involve you.

(Pause.)

TED: How does it involve me?

VAN: It's nothing.

TED: The more you say it's nothing—

VAN: Okay. Look. It is nothing. Dana and I have lunch once a week or so. (Pause.) That's it.

TED: Okay.

VAN: Kay saw us once, and now she's convinced we're having this thing.

TED: Oh.

VAN: We're not.

TED: Okay.

VAN: I mean it.

TED: And you told Kay this? Just like you told me?

VAN: Yes.

TED: So now she's convinced you're sleeping together.

VAN: We're not. (Pause.) I mean it.

TED: Van—

VAN: That's the thing. That's the big secret. That's what she meant.

TED: Okay. (Pause.) You know, it's not that I don't…it's not why I left. Not because I didn't like Dana. Not just—

VAN: I know.

TED: So it's okay you're friends. It's not like, what-disloyal? It's…it's not. I don't think you really need my approval or anything, but…I don't have this big thing about it.

VAN: It's not anything. Soft-shell tacos down at the La Nita.

TED: Okay. (Pause.) Margaritas?

VAN: Yeah. (Pause.) She drives me places sometimes. Meetings, you know. State of California kind of frowns on a one-eyed man driving.

TED: That's good.

VAN: That's it. (Pause.) Kay's got a big thing about it, though. She didn't talk to me for two weeks after she saw us.

TED: Jesus, what were you doing?

VAN: Talking. We were just—she told this joke, and we were laughing, and I looked up and there was Kay. She turned around and took off and didn't talk to me for two weeks.

TED: Wow.

VAN: We were just talking.

TED: Van, she's my ex-wife. Ex-wife, okay? Until yesterday I hadn't seen or spoken to her in five years. It's not like I'm going to fight you for her or anything.

VAN: Okay. *(Pause.)* Good thing 'cause I'd just have to kick your ass.

(They laugh. It dies. They drink. Pause.)

VAN: She's seeing someone.

TED: Who? Kay?

VAN: Dana. She's seeing some guy in the City.

TED: Well. Good for her.

VAN: I don't think he's twenty-four, though.

TED: I imagine she's doing okay, anyway.

VAN: Oh, yeah. *(Pause.)* I've missed you, man.

TED: I've missed you, too.

VAN: How come you never call?

TED: How come you never call? *(Pause.)* Five years goes by in a hurry.

VAN: Time flies when you're fucking a teenager, huh?

TED: Time flies when you're having to work your ass off while you watch your bank account hemorrhage cash like it's got a sucking chest wound.

VAN: I know.

TED: I mean, I've got my place and all, but it took a lot of what I had when I went out there, and photography's fucking expensive. Couple of bad months and my loft turns into a cardboard box in the park.

VAN: Yeah.

TED: So I have to keep going all the time. And time…goes by fast when you're busy.

VAN: It does.

TED: Every year, Christmastime, it's "God, where did the year go?" Winter. Jesus. There are days, let me tell you, when the temperature really drops, I start thinking about California.

VAN: Yeah?

TED: Fucking A, yeah.

VAN: So how come you don't come out?

TED: Didn't think I'd be welcome.

VAN: What the fuck is that?

TED: Hey, I didn't know how welcome I'd be coming out here now.

VAN: That's bullshit.

TED: Well, Kay hasn't exactly been Miss Welcome Home.

VAN: So?

TED: And Ida Sandoval? Last night when we went up to the house she was basically treating me like a live grenade. I've known Ida all my life.

VAN: She was worried about Mom.

TED: And Mom…Jesus. She's like…nothing's happened at all. Just like always. Whatever happened, whatever went on, the house was always separate from everything. And she's fixed up my old room? "Welcome home, honey." Like I've been away at camp for five years.

VAN: Well, you know Mom. People come and people go, but the house goes on forever.

TED: People come and people go. Like furniture.

VAN: Be nice if the furniture called once in a while.

TED: I did call.

VAN: When?

TED: When I first moved out there. I called. Four times. Got the old man every time. Called to give my address, my phone number. "Why would we need those?" One-word answers. "Yes." "No." "Fine." Last time was when I moved into the loft. "Yeah, well, good for you." I sent Christmas cards the first couple of years. Never got one. Figured the message was "Fuck off, Ted."

VAN: You never called *me*.

TED: You were still living at the house when I left. You had just…you were doing that rehab…I didn't have a number for you until two days ago. *(Pause.)* You never called *me*.

VAN: I didn't think you wanted a call. Did you?

TED: I don't know. I got used to it. I figured that someday we'd…well. Five years goes by in a hurry.

VAN: Yeah. I didn't get used to it. The whole brotherhood thing…some people take it seriously.

TED: Yeah, I guess after the whole Marine thing—

VAN: Fuck the Marines. Fuck them. Bullshit. "You're part of a brotherhood." Fuck. "You are a Marine forever." You're a Marine forever, until they tell you you're not, anymore. "Sorry. You're broken. You're no good to us now. Shove off, here's a pension, don't let the door hit you in the ass on your way out." Out the door and gone. Fuck them. But you know, anyplace that decides to take you can decide to get rid of you. That's just the facts, and you've got to live with that. There's places that talk about brotherhood, and then there's your brother. No comparison. *(Pause.)* I've missed you, man.

TED: I'm sorry. I couldn't get past the old man.

VAN: He was rough on you, but he was okay. You think he was a bastard, fine. He could be a bastard sometimes, but he did it for a reason, okay? He thought this—*(Takes in the cooperage.)*—was important. You didn't think it was important, fine. You left. But just because you left doesn't mean that he stopped thinking it was important.

TED: Well, I guess I just couldn't take it, then.

VAN: Because you didn't want it.

TED: I didn't want it.

VAN: The thing he thought was most important, you didn't want it. What did you expect from him? A slap on the back? "Way to go, buddy?"

TED: I didn't expect his approval. I never got it, so I never expected it.

VAN: So? What, you call four times, he doesn't change, so that's it? You're done? You call that making an effort? You left people. You left people behind. Four fucking phone calls? That's your fucking gesture? Let me tell you that is pretty goddamn weak, mister.

TED: So I was supposed to what, keep putting up with it?

VAN: You haven't had to put up with shit, all right? You haven't had to put up with shit, so shut the fuck up about it. Just shut the fuck up. Just... *(Van is starting to cry. He moves away from Ted.)* Fuck...

(Van tries to control himself. Ted remains still, uncertain of what to do.)

VAN: Shit. My fucking brother. You should have called.

TED: I'm sorry. You're right. I'm sorry.

VAN: Shit.

(They are silent for a long time, not looking at each other. Niamh comes down to Ted.)

TED: It's not something I'm...I was in the middle of it, and when you're in the middle you can't see. I know it shook people up. I wish...

NIAMH: If wishes were horses, then beggars would ride.

TED: You want everybody to be okay. I mean, eventually. You don't want to think you've fucked people up, I mean, then you think you shouldn't have...and you know you had to do something, so...I don't regret where I am. And they're better off. Really. But the way everything happened, I...I wish it hadn't been so fucked up.

NIAMH: That's a great comfort to your family, I'm sure.

DANA *(Offstage.)* Hello?

NIAMH: And your wife? You just left her?

TED: Yeah.

NIAMH: Did you not love her at all?

TED: Jesus, Niamh.

NIAMH: It's a simple question.

DANA: *(Entering.)* Everything okay, here?

TED: Simple. You're twenty-four. Call me when you're thirty-four.

DANA: Are you guys—

TED: We're fine. Thanks.

DANA: I just wanted to let you know that things were breaking up, up at the house, and if you guys were heading back up there...

TED: Okay, yeah, we'll head on up then.

DANA: Sure you're okay?

TED: Yeah.

DANA: Van? You okay?

VAN: Yeah. I'm fine. I'm okay. Thanks.

DANA: Is Karen here? Her truck's still outside.

TED: She was here. I guess she's around somewhere.

VAN: She's probably in the office. I'll go get her.

DANA: No, I can just—

VAN: No, I'll get her. Hang on. *(Van leaves.)*

DANA: Is he okay?

TED: I guess. I don't know. It's a bad day all around.

DANA: Yes. It's all so sudden. Your mom's doing well, though.

TED: I don't think it's sunk in yet.

DANA: Probably not. Too soon.

TED: I'm worried about her.

DANA: She'll be okay.

(Ted doesn't answer.)

DANA: I remember when your grandfather died, my mom and dad were worried about her. I'd hear them talking. She did fine, though, didn't she?

TED: She still had Dad.

DANA: And she still has you guys. *(Pause.)* Van and Karen. They're still around. It's not like she's going to be all alone.

TED: I guess.

DANA: I'll stop by, too, every once and a while.

TED: Well…good.

DANA: I've been coming up here as long as I can remember. It would feel weird not to.

TED: Yeah. I guess. So. How are your folks?

DANA: Oh, they're fine.

TED: The flowers looked nice. The ones they sent.

DANA: They were sorry they couldn't get up here.

TED: Yeah, Van told me they moved to…Arizona?

DANA: Yeah. Scottsdale. Playing a lot of golf.

TED: Always liked the golf.

DANA: Yes.

TED: You still playing?

DANA: Couple of times a week.

TED: Well, good. *(Pause. To Niamh.)* First time I kissed Dana was in the cooperage. My hideout. We had always had this mock-flirty thing going on. My little sister's friend. One day she was home from Stanford, and I guess she came by looking for Kay and found me. And all of a sudden the mock-flirty thing wasn't. For either of us.

DANA: What?

TED: Just thinking.

DANA: Yeah. I know. *(Pause.)* Wonder what happened to Van and Karen?

TED: I could go look.

DANA: No. I'm not in a hurry.

TED: Want a beer? I think Van's had about enough.

DANA: Sure, I'll have one.

(He gets two beers out of the bag, hands one to Dana. Niamh goes back into the loft.)

DANA: Just like old times.

TED: Better days.

DANA: Things are okay now.

TED: Good. I'm glad.

DANA: (Laughs.) You haven't really been up late worrying, have you?

TED: There have been some "What have I done?" nights.

DANA: Well. Good. I would hope so.

TED: Well, there were.

DANA: Good. That makes me feel better.

TED: Well, I'm glad.

(Pause. They drink.)

DANA: I had some, too. Nights.

TED: You didn't do anything.

DANA: I know. You know, I kind of wish I had. Done something. I think you have fewer "what have I done?" nights when you've actually done something. When you've actually done something, you can answer the question. Then you go on to "why did I do that?" And you can answer that question, whatever reason you had. And if you had terrible reasons, you can just say, "well, I sure won't do that again." And then you can get to sleep. Otherwise, you sit up late and do a lot of snacking. I gained twenty-five pounds.

TED: Can't tell.

DANA: I lost it.

TED: You look like you're doing well, now, though.

DANA: Oh, yes. I'm doing fine.

TED: Van tells me you're seeing someone.

DANA: You two discuss my love life?

TED: It just came up. Kay tried to convince me that you two, you and Van, were having a thing.

DANA: A thing?

TED: She insinuated.

DANA: We have lunch once a week.

TED: I know. Van told me. Kay was just being—

DANA: You know, she's the one I'm worried about. Mad at the world all the time.

TED: I thought it was just me.

DANA: No. She's gotten really tough to be around. Really…remote, I guess. I don't know how to say it. We barely speak anymore.

TED: I don't know what to tell you. She's been as mad as hell at me, but I can understand that. I don't have the faintest idea why she's mad at you. She asked you to do the labels, didn't she?

DANA: Yes. And she never looks at them. Van does.

TED: I don't know, Danny. She won't talk to me. She's more interested in beating me up right now. Kind of what I expected from you.

DANA: Missed your chance. You should have come back a couple of years ago. I'd have kicked your ass from here to Calistoga.

TED: Why not now?

DANA: Wearing my good shoes. Don't want to scuff them up.

TED: Can I say for the record that I'm sorry?

DANA: Can I say for the record that, that sounds pretty pathetic? And that if you say it again I'm going to throw this beer at you? I'm over it, okay? It's over, and I've spent enough of my emotional capital on you, and I'm not going to spend any more, all right? It's not worth it anymore. Not to me. It takes too much energy. *(Pause.)* But I will admit that when I saw you yesterday the first thing that came to my mind was "why did you leave me?" Which is kind of pathetic, too, I think. So maybe I'm full of it. Maybe I'm not as over it as I'd like to think. I should call my therapist and ask for my money back.

TED: I appreciate all you've done today. For Mom.

DANA: I love your mom. And your dad. Mom and Dad Wilk. All those years.

TED: They always thought a lot of you.

DANA: I guess. I guess so. I missed them.

TED: Sorry.

(She cocks her arm holding the beer. Ted ducks.)

DANA: I mean it. I never want to hear that come out of your mouth again. That was the last word you said to me, and I never want to think about that again. Do you have any idea how empty that sounds? After everything?

TED: I guess.

DANA: I should go.

TED: Okay.

DANA: Jesus, why...Why? Why would you ever think that I would want to hear that from you?

TED: I didn't think you wanted to hear it. I just wanted to say it.

DANA: Feel better?

TED: Not at the moment.

DANA: Okay, then.

TED: I was talking about Mom and Dad. You said you missed them.

DANA: Yes, I did miss them.

TED: That's what I was talking about.

DANA: Okay.

TED: Though this is a little more what I expected.

DANA: Well, I wouldn't want you to be disappointed. *(Pause. She picks up her beer and drinks.)* So much for maturity. Jesus. You know, I was really proud of myself for a while, there. "Aren't we being civil?" Rising above it. Aren't I wonderful? Cool and indifferent. Above it, over it, whatever. Over it. I had myself all talked into that. But right now I'm not. And it pisses me off. *(Pause.)* It's sad. It's a sad day.

TED: Yeah.

DANA: Lots of memories.

TED: Yes.

DANA: Some of them...some of them are good.

TED: Good. Good. I hope so.

(Pause.)

DANA: I've always kind of thought that maybe I should have apologized to you.

TED: What? Why?

DANA: I mean, you were really unhappy.

TED: It wasn't—

DANA: More than any of us imagined. And I sure didn't do anything to help.

TED: No, no, don't you start—

DANA: I've thought about this. Give me some credit. I've tried to understand—

TED: Your husband just went nuts, okay? He went nuts, and you got through it, and it's better now, right?

(Pause.)

DANA: You never asked me to come with you.

TED: What?

DANA: You never even asked.

TED: I never thought…If I had, would you have?

DANA: No. No. I've been happy here. I have never wanted to leave.

TED: That's what I thought. I—

DANA: You still could have asked. Just to be nice.

(Pause.)

TED: I was pretty nuts when I left.

DANA: Better now, though.

TED: Better, yeah, I guess.

DANA: You can come down here. I remember when just the smell—

TED: Yeah, well, it's been okay.

DANA: So time has, what, transformed you? Your state?

TED: Yeah. One hopes.

DANA: You'd do it all differently, now?

TED: I don't know, Danny. Maybe. Better, maybe. If there is a "better."

DANA: Well, that's good to know. *(Pause.)* Long time since you called me Danny.

TED: Habit. I wasn't thinking.

DANA: I don't mind. *(Pause.)* But you're okay, now.

TED: I guess.

DANA: Good. *(Pause.)* Sometimes love doesn't conquer all, does it?

TED: No. Can I be sorry about that without you throwing that beer at me?

DANA: Doesn't matter. *(She looks at her beer, sets it down.)* It's all gone.

(She turns away. Ted speaks to Niamh.)

TED: Did I love her? I can't…it's all wrapped up in everything that was going on when I left. I couldn't separate Dana from all of that…But seeing her…apart from all the crap…you wonder… *(Pause.)* Amicable divorce. I hate that phrase. It's so fucking unreal. All the dreams, the hopes for the future, just trashed. Turned into politeness. What a fucking waste.

(Van returns.)

VAN: I can't find her. I looked all over.

DANA: It's okay. I'll see her around. You guys get up to the house, now.

TED: Yes, ma'am.

DANA: When are you leaving?

TED: Tomorrow morning.

DANA: Well, have a good flight.

TED: Thanks. Take care.

DANA: You, too.

(They hug. Dana goes to hug Van.)

DANA: Up to the house with you.

VAN: Aye-aye.

DANA: Good-bye.

(She is gone. Van begins to pick up the empties.)

VAN: Nice of her to come.

TED: Yeah.

VAN: *(Indicates Ted's beer.)* So. You done?

TED: I can be.

VAN: Okay, then.

(Karen returns, with her tasting equipment. She stops short when she sees the two of them.)

KAREN: Didn't know you two were still here.

TED: Just heading out. Dana was just here.

KAREN: Oh?

(Pause.)

VAN: *(With the bag of empties.)* I'm going to take these out. *(To Ted.)* Meet you at the car.

(Van exits. Pause.)

TED: So. You really need to do that today?

KAREN: Every day. It doesn't stop just because we do.

TED: You're the one who said that there's no reason that she can't still be friends with you guys.

KAREN: That's right.

TED: So they can go out for lunch if they like.

KAREN: No one's stopping anybody.

TED: Okay. *(Pause.)* We're heading up to the house. You coming?

KAREN: Yeah.

TED: Okay, then.

KAREN: Don't I get to go out for lunch sometimes?

TED: Whenever you want.

KAREN: No, I don't have time. I have things to do. I have things to take care of.

TED: Don't give me that. I used to do what you do, remember? Don't give me the "I don't have any time" crap. Doesn't fool me. If you want to go, go. Go to lunch. Go to Bay Meadows and bet on the horses. Go up to Calistoga and take a mud bath. Whatever you want. It's not Van's fault if you don't.

KAREN: No. It's not Van's fault. I've been working every single day with Dad since you left. Every day. He never took a day off. Seventy years old. How do I take a day off? I take a day off, I go to lunch with Dana, and he works? No. So I stayed here with him and we worked. And it was okay. I like this work. I liked working with him.

TED: Well, take some time now.

KAREN: Sure. I've got all the time in the world now.

TED: Hire someone.

KAREN: We will.

TED: You can get another set of hands.

KAREN: Thanks. Thanks for reminding me. I hadn't gotten around to thinking of replacing Dad yet.

TED: Jesus, I'm not saying—

KAREN: No. You're right. I've got to think about that now.

TED: Kay—

KAREN: Forget it. Just forget I said anything. It's all water under the bridge now, anyway.

TED: You're the one saying that.

KAREN: It's not really important.

TED: If you—

KAREN: It's not important. I mean, you're leaving tomorrow, right? *(Pause.)* Okay. So, if you'll excuse me, I have work to do. Some things you need to taste every day, and some things are hardly worth opening up. (*Karen turns and goes.*)

TED: Hardly worth opening up.

NIAMH: I'm glad you told me.

TED: I'm sure it was real pleasant.

NIAMH: Does it have to be pleasant to be good? Just…hearing it, it feels…closer? It feels that way, doesn't it? And that's good, I think. Isn't it?

(Pause. Ted looks at Niamh.)

NIAMH: What is it?

TED: Feeling old. Old enough to be your dad.

NIAMH: Well, you're not. My father happens to be fifty-seven. You're not even close.

(Ted does not react.)

NIAMH: I don't look at you that way.

TED: Twenty-four. Long way between me and twenty-four.

NIAMH: It's not so far.

TED: You have no idea. No idea, the stuff between me and twenty-four.

NIAMH: God, Ted, I love you but I swear if you mention my age one more time, I'll grab you and shake you until your brains rattle.

TED: Yeah, I know, if someone told me this when I was twenty-four I'd have been pissed off, too, but all the same, it's experience. Age and experience.

NIAMH: Well, that's fine, then. You go on, you listen to your experience. With experience as vast as yours, why should you bother to take the word of anyone else about anything? I'm astonished, though, that with such a vast supply of experience on your back you're able to move at all. I'm amazed that it doesn't crush you down into the dust of the road.

(Pause.)

TED: Me, too.

(Pause.)

NIAMH: Come to Ireland with me, love. Let's go away for a while. We can manage it. We can go away for a while, and take long walks in the day, and sit and watch the sun go down on Galway Bay, and let the world go skip a while without us. Please. Let's just go.

TED: Sounds nice.

NIAMH: Please.

TED: Someday.

NIAMH: Please, love.

TED: I'm not ready to meet your family.

NIAMH: I've not seen them in three years.

TED: Well, you should go. I mean, absolutely. You should. Just because I can't is no reason... *(Pause.)* If you want to go, there's no reason you shouldn't.

(Pause.)

NIAMH: Well, then.

TED: I mean, no reason.

NIAMH: Well, then, I'll think on that a while.

TED: Just, well...

NIAMH: I'll think on it. It's late. Are you coming to bed?

TED: You go ahead.

(She starts to leave.)

TED: Niamh. I'm...

NIAMH: Yes?

TED: That, you know, "twenty-four" stuff. It sounded like I think you're stupid or something. I don't mean that.

NIAMH: All right, then.

TED: Really. *(Pause.)* So, you'll come back, won't you? When you go?

(Pause.)

NIAMH: Of course. Good night.

(Niamh goes. Ted is alone in the loft. He picks up the folder with his family pictures. He takes out the picture of the whole family.)

TED: I remember this day. The wine auction. Van home on leave, Kay-wearing a dress, my God-Mom and Dad...Dana. *(Holds up picture, points at Dana.)* Dana. Twenty-four. The happy family. Who wouldn't want to be a part of this family?

(A light comes up on Niamh upstage, as at the beginning of the play.)

NIAMH: And perhaps on a fine day, with the sun in the sky and the wind in the trees, he began to think of his home, and his brothers, and his father...

TED: *(Looks at the picture.)* The frozen moment. People just stuck in time, like this. Then you see them later and you see all this time has passed and you go, "what happened?" Time goes by, and everyone's...different. Better? Maybe? One hopes.

NIAMH: And he saw ten men trying to move a large stone, and he said "If I move that stone, will you believe what I have told you?"

TED: But it's gone. The frozen moment. Everyone moves on. Everyone. Whether you're in the picture or not.

NIAMH: He leaned over in the saddle and took hold of the stone and began to lift...

TED: But, just when you start to think that way, something brings you back. You feel it all over again. Something small, like a trick of the light, something familiar...like the smell of red wine in oak, or the taste of dust in your mouth...

NIAMH: All the people were astonished as they looked down at Oisín, lying in the dust of the road. Then the great horse reared, turned, and was gone in an instant... so quickly that they could hardly believe that it had ever been there at all.

(Ted looks back at Niamh. Lights fade.)

END OF PLAY

The End of the Tour

by Joel Drake Johnson

For my parents Henrietta Drake and Raymond Ross Johnson

and Larry B. Salzman

with special thanks to Sandy Shinner and Marc Silvia

ALL INQUIRIES CONCERNING RIGHTS, INCLUDING AMATEUR RIGHTS, SHOULD BE ADDRESSED TO:
Russ Tutterow, Artistic Director, Chicago Dramatists, 1105 W. Chicago Avenue, Chicago, IL, 60622
Email: rtutterow@chicagodramatists.org; Phone (312) 633-0630 or Joel Drake Johnson, Email: burwellchi@aol.com

ORIGINALLY PRODUCED by Victory Gardens Theater

Founded in 1974
2257 N. Lincoln Ave., Chicago, IL 60614
www.victorygardens.org

Dennis Zacek, Artistic Director
Marcelle McVay, Managing Director

Victory Gardens, home to more world premiere mainstage productions than any other Chicago theatre, has remained true to an undeniably challenging mission since 1974—developing and producing new plays with an emphasis on Chicago writers and its own 12-member Playwrights Ensemble. With the receipt of the 2001 Regional Theater Tony Award, the American Theater Critics Association and the Tony Committee recognized Victory Gardens for its "continuous level of artistic achievement contributing to the growth of theatre nationally." Victory Gardens is the first theatre dedicated solely to new work and one of the few mid-sized theatres in the country to receive this significant award. The Wall Street Journal recognizes Victory Gardens as "the nation's most important incubator of new playwrights." Victory Gardens has almost 6,000 subscribers and continues to expand its artistic, financial and institutional boundaries under the guidance of Artistic Director **Dennis Zacek**, Managing Director **Marcelle McVay**, Director of Institutional Advancement **Robert Alpaugh**, Associate Artistic Director **Sandy Shinner**, and a dedicated staff and Board of Directors.

*   *   *

I first worked with Joel in 1998 when Victory Gardens premiered his emotional and funny *Before My Eyes*. It was an experience that immediately created a "family" of the cast and Joel began to hear their voices for *The End of the Tour*. During the process of many readings and rewriting, Joel detoured into a dark new play, *The Fall to Earth*. After he wrestled to expand that initial half-hour script to a full-length, he came back to *Tour* with a new structure and Victory Gardens produced the world premiere in 2003. The complex emotional territory of the play walked the line exquisitely between laughter and tears. Audiences were passionate about the play, its politics and, as always, its insight into relationships.

Joel creates indelible characters in all of his plays. They are outrageously funny and painfully human. Joel's carefully crafted spare dialogue can make an audience howl with laughter and, in the next moment, gasp at the ferocity of the truths being revealed. Actors salivate to play roles that all of us recognize in some way: parent; child; lover; sibling; friend. In *The End of the Tour*, a lot of unintentional emotional damage has been done, but it is clear that this playwright loves all his characters…and so do we.

Sandy Shinner
Associate Artistic Director, Victory Gardens Theater

BIOGRAPHY

Joel Drake Johnson is a Resident Playwright with Chicago Dramatists. He got his start as a writer with the critically acclaimed Econo-Art Theatre where *Beautiful Dreamer*, *A Slim and Crooked Genius*, and three other plays were produced. *Beautiful Dreamer* was later produced at the Stonehill Theatre and the Ensemble Studio Theatre in NYC. *As the Beaver*, a critical hit for Chicago's Zebra Crossing Theatre in 1994, was moved to the Theatre Building for an extended run and later played at the Burbage Theatre in L.A. and the Vortex Theatre in Austin, TX. In 1998, the Tony Award Winning Victory Gardens Theater produced *Before My Eyes*, which was

nominated for best new play by the Joseph Jefferson Committee. The play was subsequently staged at The Neighborhood Playhouse in Atlanta. Other plays have been produced at the New Playwrights' Theatre in Ashland, Oregon; the Haunted Space in L.A.; the West Bank Theatre in NYC, and the Milwaukee Repertory Theatre. Johnson won an Illinois Arts Council grant in 1990 for *Blind Hearts* and, once again, in 2002 for *A Blue Moon*. *A Blue Moon* was produced at Chicago Dramatists in March/April of 2002, at the Woodstock Theatre in Woodstock, NY, in August/September of 2002, and at the Steele Beam Theatre in St. Charles, IL, in January/February of 2003. In the fall of 2002, *A Blue Moon* was nominated for best new play by the Joseph Jefferson Committee. Victory Gardens produced the 2003 Jeff nominated *The End of the Tour*. In the spring of 2004, *The Fall to Earth* was produced by Steppenwolf Theatre in an extended run. Along with Victory Gardens' playwright-in-residence, John Logan, he was nominated for an Emmy Award for the teleplay, *Moment of Rage*. Currently, Johnson is working on *A Blameless Life* and *Final Days*, two plays commissioned by Steppenwolf Theatre. He is a member of The Dramatists Guild.

DEVELOPMENTAL HISTORY

The End of the Tour was developed through a series of staged readings at Victory Gardens Theater, Chicago Dramatists, and Steppenwolf Theatre, from 1999 – 2001.

ORIGINAL PRODUCTION

The End of the Tour premiered at Victory Gardens Theater, Chicago, May 23, 2003. It was directed by Sandy Shinner with the following cast:

JAN (MORRIS) WILLIAMSON . . . . Annabel Armour
ANDREW MORRIS . . . . Tim Hendrickson
MAE (MORRIS) PIERCE . . . . .Mary Ann Thebus
CHUCK WILLIAMSON. . . . . .Rob Riley
DAVID SABIN . . . . .Andrew Rothenberg
TOMMY JOHNS. . . . . .Marc Silvia
NORMA. . . . . .Kitty Taber

and the following production staff:

Set Designer. . . . . .Jeff Bauer
Lighting Designer . . . . .Rita Pietraszek
Sound Designers . . . . .Andre Pluess and Ben Sussman
Costume Designer . . . . .Judith Lundberg
Properties Designer. . . . . .Katie Vandehey
Stage Manager. . . . . .Tina M. Jach

CHARACTERS

JAN (MORRIS) WILLIAMSON: 48-50
ANDREW MORRIS: 37-40, her younger brother
MAE (MORRIS) PIERCE: 68-70, her mother
CHUCK WILLIAMSON: 50-51, Jan's husband
DAVID SABIN: 35-38, Andrew's boyfriend
TOMMY JOHNS: 48-50 a friend of Chuck's
NORMA, ancient, a patient

TIME & PLACE

Various locations in Dixon, a small Illinois town. All scenes (with the exception of Scene 1) take place in a one hour time period. It is a spring day shortly before the death of Ronald Reagan.

Andrew Rothenberg (left) as David and Tim Hendrickson as Andrew in Victory Gardens Theater's 2003 production of *The End of the Tour* by Joel Drake Johnson, directed by Sandy Shinner. Photo by Liz Lauren

The End of the Tour

A spot comes up on Jan who is standing by a phone. Beat. Jan picks up the phone and dials. She hangs up. Beat. Jan dials again. She hangs up. She paces and then picks up the phone to dial. A phone rings in another spot. Andrew stumbles to answer it.

ANDREW*: (As the lights come up.)* Hello.

JAN: Andrew? It's Jan.

ANDREW: Who?

DAVID: Who is it?

ANDREW: I don't know.

JAN: It's Jan. Your sister

ANDREW: Did Mom die?

JAN: No.

DAVID: *(Overlapping.)* What time is it?

JAN: Did you get my messages? I left you—

ANDREW: I got your messages. I got all your messages.

DAVID: Who is it?

ANDREW: My sister.

JAN: I'm sorry to call so late. I couldn't sleep. I was pacing—

ANDREW: You woke me up.

JAN: Are you coming?

DAVID: *(Overlapping.)* Why is she calling so late? Is your mom dead?

ANDREW: *(Overlapping.)* We hadn't planned on coming, no. *(To David.)* She wants to know if we're coming.

JAN: Who are you talking to?

DAVID: *(Overlapping.)* Did your mom die?

ANDREW: David.

JAN: What?

ANDREW: It's David. His name is David.

JAN: Another boyfriend?

ANDREW: I beg your pardon—

JAN: I'm sorry. I wasn't—

ANDREW: If this isn't an emergency—even if it is an emergency—

JAN: Mom's depressed. She's in a nursing home—

ANDREW: I know all this—

JAN: Then why haven't you—it's been close to a month—

ANDREW: Do you know what time it is? This is really upsetting me.

DAVID: *(Into phone.)* Don't upset my boyfriend.

ANDREW: I'm not coming home. I'd have to take a day off work—it's not—

JAN: I've taken days off—

ANDREW: And I can't drive—

JAN: You can drive—

ANDREW: I lost my driver's license—

JAN: How did you—

ANDREW: I flunked the test and I refuse to go back—

JAN: You should have a driver's license—

ANDREW: No, I shouldn't—fuck this—

JAN: What did I do to you? What did I ever do to you?

ANDREW: It's after midnight—

JAN: I would like to know. I was always supportive of you. I was always protective—

ANDREW: *(He hands phone to David.)* I can't talk to her. You talk to her.

JAN: *(Overlapping.)* What did I ever do?

DAVID: *(Overlapping.)* I don't know her. I've never met her—

JAN: *(Overlapping.)* Hello? Andy? Andrew?

DAVID: Hello. He's upset. You've upset him.

JAN: Can you get him back on the phone?

DAVID: I don't want you to upset him. He'll never get to sleep now. Never. You shouldn't have done this—

JAN: I just want him to come home—

ANDREW: *(Overlapping.)* Hang up, okay? Just hang up.

DAVID: *(Overlapping.)* He doesn't want to come home— *(To Andrew.)* You come over here and hang up.

JAN: Do I sound like I want to hurt him? What has he said—

ANDREW: *(Overlapping.)* What is she saying?

DAVID: *(To Andrew.)* Shhhh.

ANDREW: Don't shush me!

DAVID: *(To Andrew.)* Will you come back to the phone?

ANDREW: No, I will not come back to the phone—

DAVID: He won't come back—

JAN: I heard him.

DAVID: Sorry.

ANDREW: Don't apologize for me.

DAVID: I'm not.

JAN: He really needs to deal with this.

ANDREW: What's she saying?

DAVID: Well...

JAN: I'm sorry. Maybe you can convince him.

DAVID: He's a hard sell—

ANDREW: What is she saying?

JAN: But maybe you could. He shouldn't let this go like that. David? Is that your name? David?

DAVID: David, yes. Nice to meet you.

JAN: Do you love him, David?

ANDREW: What is—

DAVID: *(To Andrew.)* Shhh. *(To Jan.)* Yes. Yes, I do.

JAN: Me, too. I love him, too.

DAVID: Oh...Hold on a second. *(To Andrew.)* I think we should go.

(Andrew drops his head. Beat.)

DAVID: Andrew?

ANDREW: What?!

(David holds phone out to Andrew. Beat.)

DAVID: Take the phone.

ANDREW: *(Overlapping.)* Don't tell me what to do. Don't tell me what to do.

DAVID: *(Overlapping.)* Take the phone. Take the phone.

(Andrew comes to the phone.)

ANDREW: Jan.

JAN: Yes?

ANDREW: It's Andrew.

JAN: I—

ANDREW: *(Quickly.)* And okay. We'll come. Tomorrow. *(To David.)* Tomorrow's okay?

DAVID: Tomorrow's fine.

ANDREW: *(To Jan.)* Tomorrow?

JAN: Okay.

ANDREW: Alright.

JAN: She's in the Lee County Nursing Home.

ANDREW: You'll be there?

JAN: I'll be there.

ANDREW: Chuck?

JAN: No, no Chuck.

ANDREW: Okay, then. Sometime tomorrow...ummm, it's good to hear from you—

JAN: It is?

ANDREW: Good night.

JAN: Good night.

(She hangs up. As she pauses at phone, Andrew and David stare at one another.)

ANDREW: This is not something I want to do. This is not something—I want to forget this shit—I do not want to—

DAVID: I'll be with you, Andrew.

ANDREW: I'll have to make a couple of calls in the morning.

DAVID: Me, too.

ANDREW: I have a couple of appointments—A couple of interviews. A class to teach—

DAVID: Sure.

ANDREW: I suppose Margaret can take it.

(Andrew puts his head in his hands. David comes to Andrew and holds him.)

DAVID: You can give me the tour of beautiful Dixon, Illinois.

ANDREW: I'll give you the tour.

DAVID: I want to go through Reagan's house.

ANDREW: It's boring.

DAVID: I want to leave droppings. Please?

ANDREW: Yeh.

DAVID: And introduce me to the old lady?

ANDREW: God. Promise to still like me—

DAVID: What?

ANDREW: Promise. No matter what. To still like me. Still like me.

DAVID: Boy Scout Honor.

ANDREW: Okay.

Music. The lights crossfade to Tommy and Chuck who are in the kitchen of his home. They sit at table. There is a beer bottle in front of Tommy and Chuck. It's morning.

TOMMY: So I get called at two in the morning! Two in the morning. And it's Lorna Utter asking me to come right over "to the Reagan House". The pipes have burst and the basement is flooding—

CHUCK: Jesus Christ.

TOMMY: Exactly what I'm thinking—and so I say in this fog I'm in, I say—Lorna, what the hell are you doing at the Reagan Home at two in the morning and what in God's name are you doing in the basement? She tells me she always goes there when she can't sleep and she does touch up painting on the rooms. She's painting around the front door in the hall and she hears water running. Turns out it's a broken pipe and can I get right over because it's "an historical emergency." I'm telling you I should have never volunteered to work the place. Never. I love the man, but what does he know anymore? What he does know? So I get out of bed and go on over and get the water turned off and get back to bed at three. I was not polite to Lorna.

CHUCK: I'm glad you came over.

TOMMY: Why wouldn't I come over, Chuck?

CHUCK: I got all wound up.

TOMMY: *(Looking into box.)* So he's not doing so well?

CHUCK: What do you think his problem is?

TOMMY: He's tired.

CHUCK: That's all?

TOMMY: How old is he?

CHUCK: Seventeen.

TOMMY: He's real tired.

CHUCK: I got home from work this morning and he's just lying there. I thought at first he was dead. And then I put my head down to his little body and just listened a while to his breathing, picked him up and took him to bed with me and talked to him. I couldn't sleep so I got up, thought maybe I should put him in this box and take him to the vet. That's when I called you.

TOMMY: You ought to take him in.

CHUCK: Think so?

TOMMY: It's time he was put to sleep.

CHUCK: You think it's that bad?

TOMMY: I think you should take him in. I think you should have a vet take a look at him.

CHUCK: I don't know if I can put him to sleep. I've had this guy for so long. You think he's that bad?

TOMMY: That's my best advice.

CHUCK: I don't know if I can do that. What if they say it's time? I don't know if I can do it. Poor thing. Poor old thing. He's my buddy.

TOMMY: I've never seen a man take to a cat like you take to this one.

CHUCK: Well, I do.

TOMMY: I know you do—

CHUCK: I love this old thing.

TOMMY: Well, you're not doing him any favors.

CHUCK: Do you think he's in pain?

TOMMY: He's not moved since I started looking at him so I think he might be in some kind of pain.

CHUCK: *(To the box.)* Are you in pain, Smiley? Do you hurt, little baby?

TOMMY: He's not going to answer you.

CHUCK: I know that. But the sound of my voice. It makes him feel better.

TOMMY: You're going to have to give that up. The cat's dying and that's all there is to it.

CHUCK: Shut up.

TOMMY: I'm sorry, but he is.

CHUCK: I don't need you to tell me that.

TOMMY: It seems to me—

CHUCK: I said shut up. I know what's happening.

TOMMY: You don't have to get mad at me.

CHUCK: I'm upset. My cat's dying and I'm very upset.

TOMMY: I ought to go home.

CHUCK: You don't have to leave.

TOMMY: Seems to me like—

CHUCK: I'm sorry.

TOMMY: Well—

CHUCK: My cat's sick. That's all.

TOMMY: Well, I'm just trying to help.

CHUCK: I know that and I'm sorry. I didn't mean to snap your head off.

TOMMY: Well—

CHUCK: I should call Jan.

TOMMY: You should call Jan.

CHUCK: Ask her what I should do.

TOMMY: Call her then.

CHUCK: What if she says to put him to sleep?

TOMMY: Then you'll have to do it.

CHUCK: Do you think I should?

TOMMY: I think he's sick.

CHUCK: Should I cover him?

TOMMY: The cat's sick.

CHUCK: I'll cover him with this.

TOMMY: He's probably cold.

CHUCK: *(With towel.)* Here you go, little guy. Little pal. Here you go, you little cutie pie, little thing you.

TOMMY: Your dad's going to take care of you.

CHUCK: That's right. That's right.

TOMMY: If I didn't see it with my own eyes.

CHUCK: What's that?

TOMMY: You. Mooning over a cat.

CHUCK: His name's Smiley.

TOMMY: When I was just a kid—you remember me? I was a bone. A bone of a kid and we had this big cat, a twenty pounder. Rudy was his name. Big thing. Big old thing. Anyway, I woke up in the middle of the night and here's this cat with his paws locked around my throat and his mouth up against my mouth sucking the air out of my lungs. Scared the hell out of me. And so I grabbed hold of him by the throat and I flung him off of me and up against the bedroom wall.

CHUCK: You shouldn't have done that.

TOMMY: He never tried it again and that's for sure—

CHUCK: You're just plain mean, you know it?

TOMMY: He tried to kill me. He was strangling me.

CHUCK: Cats don't choke people.

TOMMY: Well, this one did. A strange, sick cat if you want to know. With a strange, sick hold over my mother. I'd come home from school and there'd be she'd be—sitting at the kitchen table, petting that cat, staring into space like she and Rudy were on some kind of mind trip together. The two of them sitting there smoking cigarettes—

CHUCK: Bullshit.

TOMMY: I'm telling you that fucking cat smoked. My mom would put the cigarette down to his lips and he'd take a drag.

CHUCK: *(Simultaneous to above.)* Bullshit. Bullshit.

TOMMY: He could blow smoke rings, for Christ sake! And he coughed just like my mom. A hacking cough. A terrible, terrible cough that comes from one place and that's smoking. *(Tommy does a loud cat cough.)* And then he'd try to catch his breath like this. *(He gasps and chokes loudly.)*

CHUCK: *(To cat.)* You hear this guy? You hear this bullshitter? *(Suddenly.)* He's looking up.

TOMMY: Let's see.

CHUCK: He's better, I think. You feeling better? Huh? Don't lean in so close.

TOMMY: I'm just looking.

CHUCK: Well, I don't want you to scare him.

TOMMY: I'm not scaring him. I don't think I was scaring him.

CHUCK: He knows when you don't like him. He's not an idiot.

TOMMY: But he's a cat.

CHUCK: They have an instinct!

TOMMY: But he's still a cat. A cat.

CHUCK: I know.

TOMMY: An animal.

CHUCK: I know that.

TOMMY: And this is hurting me.

CHUCK: What?

TOMMY: This. And it's weird.

CHUCK: You scared my sick cat.

TOMMY: I didn't—

CHUCK: I thought you did. I'm sorry.

TOMMY: It's weird. It's strange. It's funny in a weird and strange way.

CHUCK: Sorry. I don't want to hurt your feelings.

TOMMY: Well—

CHUCK: I'm gonna mush his food right now. Is that okay?

TOMMY: Mushing food might make him eat.

CHUCK: I think if I make it soft enough. Maybe I should spoon feed him.

TOMMY: You could try that...so how's Jan doing?

CHUCK: Okay.

TOMMY: Okay?

CHUCK: She's doing okay. I've talked to her twice this morning already. And she sounds okay.

TOMMY: Twice?

CHUCK: Well, she left the place in such a mess. I can't find anything. And I've got these electric and these gas bills and I'm looking at them like what the hell is this! She couldn't take care of this before she left?!

TOMMY: You don't get mad at her, do you?

CHUCK: I don't get mad.

TOMMY: Well, don't...Does she still come by to make you supper?

CHUCK: Yes.

TOMMY: That's a nice thing.

CHUCK: It is nice.

TOMMY: Boy, you know, call me crazy, but I think she still loves you.

CHUCK: She doesn't love me.

TOMMY: Why would she leave you then keep coming back every night to fix your supper?

CHUCK: And she does a load of laundry.

TOMMY: She can't get enough of you.

CHUCK: I don't know. I hadn't thought about it.

TOMMY: She still loves you.

CHUCK: Then why did she leave me?

TOMMY: I don't know...that's what this is, you know? The cat. Your worry about the cat. It's Jan.

CHUCK: I thought you said it was because I was— *(He does the gesture.)*

TOMMY: I was kidding. That girl still loves you. She's just got a crazy streak in her, that's all...Do you remember the day Jan started chasing those boys with an ax?

CHUCK: She was protecting her brother.

TOMMY: What was his name?

CHUCK: Andy. Andrew.

TOMMY: That's it. Andy. Andrew. *(He laughs.)* Don't tell Jan this, but it was my parents who called the police. Jan is a great girl, a smart girl, but I know she broke your heart—and I know she can swing a mean ax. She's got that in her.

CHUCK: She does.

TOMMY: And that's why I'm saying she still loves you. She has an unstable side that makes her walk out on you even when she still cares for you.

CHUCK: You think so?

TOMMY: I know so. I'm sure so.

CHUCK: He's sniffing!! He's licking it!

TOMMY: He's a good boy.

CHUCK: Keep licking, sweetie. Good boy. Good Smiley.

TOMMY: Yea...I'm sorry about...you're not weird.

CHUCK: I know that.

TOMMY: I didn't mean anything.

CHUCK: I didn't think you did.

TOMMY: I'm just worried for you. You're worried, I'm worried, you know?

CHUCK: I know.

TOMMY: Your wife leaves you, you look depressed, you lose weight, you get hypnotized by your cat, a friend has to get worried. He has to.

> *(Beat.)*

CHUCK: She still loves me?

TOMMY: I can't see any other way.

CHUCK: Did you hear that kitty? Mama still loves us. Yea...

As the lights crossfade to a bed in a nursing home, Mae lies in the bed, singing "Jambalayas." Jan sits at her side.

MAE: Why don't you sing with me?

JAN: You don't want me to sing with you.

MAE: Yes, I do.

JAN: You never have before.

MAE: I do now.

JAN: I can't sing.

MAE: Everybody can sing.

JAN: Not me.

MAE: You could if you tried.

JAN: I don't know the words.

MAE: I've been singing that song for a hundred years and you don't know the words?

(Mae and Jan sing a little of the song.)

MAE: That's not bad.

JAN: Yes, it is.

MAE: No, it was pretty. They've asked me to sing for the recreation hour this morning.

JAN: I heard.

MAE: I told them I would have to think about it. I told them I would have to check my voice. "But we love the way you sing. We've heard you sing. Our parents"—get that—"our parents heard you sing. Everyone has heard Mae Pierce sing." Then they start talking about me singing for President Reagan that one time—

JAN: Well, you were a big hit.

MAE: I was a big hit—and Ronny couldn't take his eyes off of me.

JAN: So you say.

MAE: I do say. I do say. And that skinny bitch of his—

JAN: Mom—

MAE: There's not one person in this country doesn't think—

JAN: It isn't—

MAE: It is. It is. It is. She was jealous and everybody knew that, too. Tried to stab me in the back with her comments. I'm prettier than her and everybody knows that. Including Ronny—

JAN: Ronny—

MAE: I call him Ronny. In my head. When he comes dancing in my head late at night.

JAN: Well, you should do it. It'll make you feel better. I noticed you've got your best robe on.

MAE: And this underneath.

JAN: That's a nice combo. And your makeup is pretty.

MAE: Is it too exotic? I don't want to look Oriental.

JAN: You don't.

MAE: I suppose I should do it although I don't feel much like singing, really. And what am I going to sing? And does anybody in this place still have their hearing—

JAN: Mom.

MAE: Well, it's true. I can't mince words, you know that. Is that all you're going to do?

JAN: I have to get this done.

MAE: Give them all A's.

JAN: Mmm.

MAE: Just throw them all away, go into class and tell them "Surprise you all got A's!"

JAN: They would be surprised.

MAE: "A's" from mean, old Mrs. Williamson.

(Beat. Jan looks at Mae.)

MAE: I hear what they say. I know your reputation. *(Beat.)* Is that what you wear when you teach?

JAN: Something like this, yes.

MAE: I think you should try more color.

JAN: I think this is fine.

MAE: I think you should try something brighter. The kids like color, they like brightness. You dress like a tree.

JAN: I beg your pardon.

MAE: *(A little louder.)* I said you dress like a tree—

JAN: I dress fine—

MAE: You would be so much more popular with your students if you wore a little brightness!! You wear some bright reds or yellows or blues and those kids will gather around you like little bees. Like little—*(She waves her hand.)*—bees! Like little—what are those things—they like color-and they buzz around—and they drive me crazy—quick little things—hummingbirds!!

JAN: When have you ever seen a hummingbird?

MAE: I've seen a lot of hummingbirds. They're just naturally attracted to me. All my bright colors. No one would ever mistake me for a tree!

JAN: I dress the way I want to, which I think is just fine.

(Beat.)

MAE: You don't have to jump all over me.

JAN: I wasn't—

MAE: I'm giving you suggestions. That's all I'm doing. I'm a mother and mothers should give suggestions. *(Beat.)* Are you just going to sit there and grade papers?

JAN: Do you want to do something?

MAE: Can't think of what to do. What is that?

JAN: Essays on the poetry of Robert Frost.

MAE: Sounds awful. *(As she sings again.)* I haven't decided to sing, yet.

JAN: They said you were real excited when they asked you.

MAE: I might. I might not. It depends.

JAN: On what?

MAE: If I've got the mood or not. I might not have the mood and if I don't have the mood, I'm not moving from this bed. I don't know why Andy's not here.

JAN: He'll be here.

MAE: I thought he'd call by now. Tell us he was here.

JAN: Do you want to get out of bed?

MAE: No.

JAN: Why don't you get out of bed and come have a cigarette with me?

MAE: I don't want a cigarette.

JAN: You need to get some exercise.

MAE: I don't feel like getting out of bed.

JAN: I feel like a cigarette.

MAE: Go have one then. I won't stop you.

JAN: Why don't you walk out with me?

MAE: Is there a sun?

JAN: It's very sunny.

MAE: I don't like the sun. It hurts my eyes.

JAN: Use my sunglasses. Come on now. Get out of bed.

MAE: I need a wheelchair.

JAN: You can walk.

MAE: Not today. Today, I need a wheelchair.

JAN: You want me to call a nurse?

MAE: They'll never come. It takes forever.

JAN: So what do you want to do?

MAE: I want to lie here and take a nap. Leave me alone.

JAN: All right.

(She begins to grade her papers.)

MAE: Are there any more of those cherry chocolates in the drawer?

JAN: They're sitting right beside you.

MAE: Oh, there they are. Would you get me one?

JAN: You can't reach them?

MAE: You can't get me one?

(Jan gets her a cherry chocolate.)

JAN: Here you go.

MAE: Some of these are missing.

JAN: There are?

MAE: One, two, three, four, five. Last night I had eight.

JAN: You ate more than you thought.

MAE: I had eight when I went to bed. It's that weird woman I told you about. She steals things from me.

JAN: Nobody's stealing things from you.

MAE: She steals my cherry chocolates and my cigarettes.

JAN: Why don't you tell the nurse?

MAE: Why don't you? You're my daughter. You should be protecting me. Somebody should be protecting me.

JAN: I'll say something.

MAE: Don't bother. It wouldn't do any good—

JAN: I'll talk to a nurse.

MAE: A lot of good that will do. The crazy old bag just wanders around this place—in one room and out the other-taking stuff as she pleases. I wake up from a little nap and there she is standing right in front of me with a fistful of my cigarettes and I say to her "Listen, you old bag, keep your hands off my cigarettes and my cherry chocolates or I'll shoot you dead, you crazy bitch."

JAN: Don't use—

MAE: And I then I raise my hand underneath my covers to look like I have a gun—

(Norma, an old woman, comes to door.)

MAE: That's her!

JAN: *(To Norma.)* Hi, can I help you?

(Norma turns abruptly and leaves.)

MAE: Do you see? Do you see?

JAN: She looks harmless.

MAE: She's crazy. What am I doing in a place for crazy people? You put me in a nut house to recuperate from a broken ankle? This is as good as you can do?

JAN: This is a nursing home, not a—and the doctor says—

MAE: Some doctor.

JAN: You should get up and walk everyday.

MAE: Or else he'll cut off my foot.

JAN: He's not going to cut off your foot.

MAE: He'll cut off my foot! That's what he does to people who don't do what he says! He cuts off their feet! *(She begins to cry.)* I don't know what's wrong with me. I have nothing to look forward to. Nothing. You sit there, you grade papers. You won't let me help. I can't do it anymore. I want a cherry chocolate.

JAN: Here you go.

MAE: I'd like a drink.

JAN: You can't have a drink.

MAE: But I'd like one.

JAN: Well, forget it.

MAE: You could sneak one in.

JAN: I'm not doing that.

MAE: How about one vodka martini?

JAN: No.

MAE: Well, thanks for nothing!

JAN: You're welcome.

(Beat.)

MAE: Where is Andy? He said he'd be here today. You bore me, you know that. You just bore me to death.

JAN: Then I'll leave.

MAE: Oh, no. No. I'm sorry.

JAN: You want me to leave?

MAE: No. I'm sorry...*(Picking up the box of chocolates.)* Would you like a cherry chocolate?

 (Beat.)

JAN: All right. Thanks.

MAE: Eat all you want.

JAN: One should do it.

MAE: But you can have all you want.

JAN: One is enough. What are all these labels?

MAE: The nurse brought them to me.

JAN: What are you doing with them?

MAE: They're for you and Andy. I want you to go to my house, pick out the things you want, write your name on the label and then put it on the item.

JAN: Why would I do that?

MAE: So when I die there won't be any argument.

JAN: You're not dying—

MAE: Take the labels.

JAN: You think Andrew and I are going to fight over—

MAE: I want you to do this.

JAN: There's nothing I want.

MAE: Nothing?

JAN: I just said that.

MAE: There is nothing of mine that you want?

JAN: No.

MAE: You are such a bitch to me.

JAN: Don't use that word—

MAE: You are such a bitch—

JAN: I hate that word—

MAE: There is nothing you want?

JAN: Give me some labels.

MAE: *(Handing them to her.)* Put them on everything you think you might want.

(Beat. Mae begins to sing "I Walk the Line.")

JAN: *(Over Mae's singing.)* You know if you exercised more, you'd feel better. The nurses say that you're doing pretty well in physical therapy, but they can't get you to move once they bring you back to the room. If you'd get out of bed and walk, you might get well.

MAE: I have no place to walk. I have no place to go. I don't want to just wander. I don't like that. I look at those people in the halls-and that's all they do. They wander. They wander down the east wing, they wander down the west wing. They keep their heads down and wander like they're following some kind of yellow line that's supposed to lead them out of here. Keep your eye on the yellow line and the next time you look up-the next time you have the strength to raise your head, you'll be free. Can I go home? I want to go home.

JAN: When your ankle is strong.

MAE: And when will that be?

JAN: When you get out of bed. When you start to move around.

MAE: The social worker says I've a low-grade depression. Is that true? Do I have a low-grade depression?

JAN: I think you might.

MAE: I've never been depressed in my life.

JAN: I think you might be now.

MAE: I'm tired.

JAN: You're depressed, too.

MAE: I should be depressed at this stage in my life.

JAN: Mmm, maybe.

MAE: I have good reason to be depressed. I wheel myself down to the lunch room and look out over the tables and there's a sea of depression lapping up at my feet. And the nurses want me to sit in the middle of that, they want me to eat in the middle of all that depression, surrounded by a mess of depressed fish that you keep seeing over and over and over again, their little mouths bobbing at the top, moving their lips like this. *(She does a fish imitation.)* They're like this. *(She does fish imitation again.)*

JAN: They are not—

MAE: Some of them are like this. *(She does imitation again.)* They eat then sink to the bottom. *(Beat.)* Nothing's going right.

JAN: I know.

MAE: I have a whole lot of problems.

JAN: You do.

MAE: I had a major operation. I get put into a nursing home. I have a son who won't visit. *(Beat.)* Help me up here. I want to walk. I want to walk down the halls.

Crossfade to the lobby of the nursing home. Andrew stands there waiting as David enters.

DAVID: She's in 214, Hall B.

ANDREW: Oh.

DAVID: Should we go in?

ANDREW: I'm not ready, yet. Do you mind? If we just sit. For a minute.

DAVID: I don't mind.

ANDREW: Just for a minute. I have to gear up for this. I have to figure out what I'm going to say.

DAVID: Okay.

ANDREW: Thanks. *(Beat.)* You can see my grade school from here.

DAVID: Where is it?

ANDREW: There. Behind the trees. The courthouse is there. That clump of trees hides a statue of Lincoln—on a horse, galloping somewhere or other. A log cabin behind him. That's the roof of Reagan's boyhood home—

DAVID: Where?

ANDREW: Right through there. A bus has probably just pulled up and a group of students is pouring out and into the house, I would imagine. I would imagine...well...

DAVID: You're all right?

ANDREW: It's been a long time.

DAVID: But you're doing okay?

ANDREW: I suppose so. We used to come here and sing for the old folks. Used to sing Christmas carols. Strange...we would line up in the cafeteria and the residents would gather around us like we might be something good to eat. Weird. Strange.

DAVID: I'll bet.

ANDREW: I'm not crazy about what it's doing to me. I don't feel good about this. I feel...small suddenly. Very small. And a little embarrassed.

DAVID: You're with me.

ANDREW: That's why I'm embarrassed. I don't like you to see me like this.

DAVID: It's okay.

124   New Plays from Chicago

ANDREW: I shouldn't have talked to Jan like I did.

DAVID: You were rude.

ANDREW: She never did anything to me. Never. I suppose she's here. I suppose I should apologize.

DAVID: Where's your house from here?

ANDREW: You can't see it. But it's in through there. The trees are in the way...

DAVID: Maybe we'll drive by.

ANDREW: Yea.

DAVID: I'd like to see it.

ANDREW: Maybe.

DAVID: I'll drive really quickly.

ANDREW: I don't know. I'm not real sure—

DAVID: You're so hunched over.

ANDREW: That's what I mean.

DAVID: What?

ANDREW: This place has shrunk me a few inches. I go to the gym everyday just to keep this from happening, but I can see it's done me no good. *(Mimicking.)* I'm melting. I'm melting...what should I say when I see her?

DAVID: Who?

ANDREW: My mother.

DAVID: What do you want to say?

ANDREW: Oh, God, I don't know. I'd thought for a while that my entire childhood was a figment of my imagination and then Jan calls. Things were going fine, weren't they? Weren't they going fine?

DAVID: Yes.

ANDREW: Things were fine.

DAVID: Things were fine.

ANDREW: What do you think I should say?

DAVID: What do you want to say?

ANDREW: Nothing.

DAVID: Really?

ANDREW: I can't think of anything. In fact, I can barely picture the scene in my head. And what I do picture is me standing at the foot of her bed, head down, silent. I'm mostly scared right now.

DAVID: I'll take her down.

ANDREW: Will you?

DAVID: If she gets rough.

ANDREW: That I would like to see.

DAVID: I can handle mothers.

ANDREW: She's pretty fierce.

DAVID: Me, too. One thing to remember. *(Whispering.)* I love you. *(David reaches for him.)*

ANDREW: *(Standing.)* Oh. Good. Good. Okay...I look at a place like this and it blows my whole theory on life. Does anything about life really matter if you finish it here—wandering the halls of a nursing home? Live your life to the fullest so that you can someday end it with a glazed eyed lack of memory.

DAVID: Perhaps there's some peace in that kind of existence.

ANDREW: Really, you think so?

DAVID: I don't know for sure, but I know my grandfather ended up that way. And he was this larger than life Socialist Agitator who picked up the world with his bare hands and literally wrung it dry. Like this. *(He does a movement. And then the voice).* "David," he'd say! "You must fight for the masses!!!" And I'd say, "Yes! Grandpa!! Bring me the blood of a capitalist!" He'd flip out if he had to sit and look at these pictures of Reagan everywhere.

ANDREW: Be careful what you say. He was a hometown boy.

DAVID: He'd pull himself up, *(Standing.)* look the guy straight in the eye and holler out, "You, sir"—sir because grandpa was always a gentleman—"were bad for the Jews!!"

ANDREW: Shhhh.

DAVID: But he was bad for the Jews. Some Jews, anyway. The good Jews.

ANDREW: Sit.

DAVID: No one even looked our way.

ANDREW: The man in the wheelchair hasn't taken his eyes off of us.

DAVID: Trust me, he hasn't noticed us.

ANDREW: God.

DAVID: What?

ANDREW: You'll kill me before you put me in a nursing home, won't you?

DAVID: I'll hire someone.

ANDREW: I'm serious, David. I don't want to be put in a nursing home. Promise me. Promise me right now. If you can't take care of me, you'll off me somehow.

DAVID: I'll off you somehow.

ANDREW: I mean it.

DAVID: I mean it, too. I'll push you out a window.

ANDREW: How bad will I have to be?

DAVID: What do you mean?

ANDREW: Before you kill me?

DAVID: Pretty bad.

ANDREW: How bad?

DAVID: ...Pretty bad.

ANDREW: In a wheelchair like that guy?

DAVID: Yes.

ANDREW: What if I can still feed myself and go to the bathroom?

DAVID: You can't dance or go shopping?

ANDREW: No, I just sit there like that guy.

DAVID: I'd still kill you.

ANDREW: You're not taking any of this seriously.

DAVID: No, I'm not.

ANDREW: But I think we should talk about this.

DAVID: Because we're in a nursing home?

ANDREW: Because we've never talked about it before.

DAVID: It's a little premature, don't you think?

ANDREW: Not if I'm thinking about it.

DAVID: Well, I'm not thinking about it. When we get home, write it all down and put it in a safe deposit box. When you get dementia—which I'm sure you will—I'll open the box and carry out all of your wishes.

ANDREW: *(Seriously.)* Thank you...Will you cremate my body?

DAVID: Jews don't cremate.

ANDREW: But I want to be cremated.

DAVID: Marry a protestant. Ever heard of the holocaust? I don't do cremations. The body goes back the way it was found. That's a Jewish thing.

ANDREW: So you won't go through with my wishes.

DAVID: No.

ANDREW: I'm a helpless dead person and yet you wouldn't go through with my wishes?

DAVID: All right. Let's pretend for a minute that you're dead. *(Pause. He closes his eyes.)* Okay. Now you're dead. And, okay, so I have you cremated.

ANDREW: Thank you...I want a small service by the lake. Invite all our friends. Say something really nice.

DAVID: That will be hard.

ANDREW: It will?

DAVID: I'm kidding you, Andrew.

ANDREW: Oh...what will you say?

DAVID: I don't know.

ANDREW: No idea?

DAVID: I don't have one fucking idea.

ANDREW: Are you kidding?

DAVID: You really think I should have figured out your eulogy?

ANDREW: It just seems like it should pop into your head.

DAVID: Well, it doesn't.

ANDREW: Oh...seems like it should.

DAVID: It doesn't.

ANDREW: Oh...I have a eulogy for you.

DAVID: What?

ANDREW: I know what I'm going to say when you die.

DAVID: You're joking?

ANDREW: I've thought about losing you. I've thought about it. *(Taking out his wallet.)* See what I have here.

DAVID: What is it?

ANDREW: *(Reading from a piece of paper.)* "In case of emergency, call David Sabin at Home: 773-404-1132 or WORK: 312-728-9177." So if something happens, you'll be the first to know.

DAVID: You're so depressing.

ANDREW: Am I?

DAVID: Today, yes, you're depressing.

ANDREW: I think about it. I worry about it. I go to work, I ride the train and I begin to think about what if something happens to me and I don't make it home. What will happen to David? What will he think? Shouldn't he know immediately? And who else do I have, huh? Who else?...I think you should do the same.

DAVID: As soon we get home.

ANDREW: I don't want to be waiting. If you're killed, I want to know. I want someone to call me. That way I can start immediately making funeral arrangements—

DAVID: Oh, God—

ANDREW: And memorizing the eulogy which I have already begun to prepare.

DAVID: Are you kidding me? I cannot believe it. You're nuts, you know it. You're crazy—

ANDREW: *(Overlapping.)* And I'm going to say something about how meeting you saved my life.

DAVID: What?

ANDREW: You heard me.

DAVID: No, I didn't.

ANDREW: Well, I won't say it again.

DAVID: I saved your life. What? Really?

ANDREW: Yes.

DAVID: I didn't know.

ANDREW: You did.

DAVID: *(As he leans into him.)* I truly didn't know—

ANDREW: *(Jerking away.)* Does it smell in here? I think it smells in here? I think it smells like *(Whispering.)* urine? Is that a urine smell?...I think it smells like *(Whispering.)* shit or something. *(Andrew stands up and sniffs.)* It does. It smells like *(Whispering.)* feces. It smells like *(Whispering.)* shit. What kind of a nursing home is this?

DAVID: One that smells like shit. Sit down.

ANDREW: But is that right? Does that seem right to you? Don't they clean in here? Have they never heard of Pine-Sol?

DAVID: I don't know.

ANDREW: Pine-Sol would get rid of the odor. *(Beat.)* Or Lysol. Lysol does it, too.

DAVID: Go buy some Pine-Sol-or Lysol and start scrubbing.

ANDREW: What am I doing here, anyway? I said I'd never come back. You heard me say it.

DAVID: I heard you.

ANDREW: And what nerve, you know? My sister calling me in the middle of the night. Like it's an emergency.

DAVID: So she wanted to—

ANDREW: And leaving messages. How many messages did she leave?

DAVID: About fifteen hundred.

ANDREW: She's the one who decided to stay here. She didn't have to stay. It's not like Mom was any better to her. You should have heard the way Mom talked to her. You should have seen some of the things she had to do because Mom couldn't cope. Couldn't cope. Shit. And now suddenly I should care? I should care about any of this?

DAVID: Would you slow down—

ANDREW: And why is my name and work number not in your billfold.?

(David takes his hand. Andrew jerks away.)

ANDREW: Don't do that. Don't hold my hand here.

DAVID: What?

ANDREW: Don't hold my hand here. This isn't the place.

DAVID: This isn't the place?

ANDREW: No.

DAVID: What place, then?

ANDREW: Not here, that's all.

DAVID: You're a lunatic.

ANDREW: I'm a lunatic, fine. Just don't come back to my hometown expecting to hold my hand. Don't do that to me, David. Don't do that. Not here.

David looks at him. Andrew turns away as the lights crossfade to Tommy and Chuck. There are two more beer bottles in front of Tommy.

TOMMY: Terrible.

CHUCK: I know.

TOMMY: Terrible, terrible.

CHUCK: I know it was.

TOMMY: What a situation. When I was a kid every time we'd drive by their house, my old lady would say "saddest house in town." Every time. "Saddest house in town. This is the saddest house in town." This and that and this and that and saddest house in town.

CHUCK: It was sad.

TOMMY: Jan's little sister dies.

CHUCK: It was terrible.

TOMMY: Then her dad. Think about it.

CHUCK: Terrible stuff, no doubt.

TOMMY: Nice man, too.

CHUCK: He was quiet, I remember.

TOMMY: My parents used to go to Jimmy's to hear the old lady sing.

CHUCK: Mine would never—

TOMMY: They said she was always half-drunk by the time the night was out—

CHUCK: I heard that, too.

TOMMY: (Continuing.)—telling off colored jokes—she was a dirty old thing, that I heard.

CHUCK: But she can sing.

TOMMY: Then marrying Jimmy—

CHUCK: That was something.

TOMMY: Raising a family like two drunks on a pogo stick.

CHUCK: But Jan did all right.

TOMMY: She took care of things. Took care of that nutty family.

CHUCK: She did that.

TOMMY: She did.

CHUCK: And it got to her. It gets to her still.

TOMMY: Exactly.

CHUCK: There's been a few times, she's locked herself in the bathroom. Sometimes for two or three hours and always in the middle of the night.

TOMMY: You're kidding.

CHUCK: So I stand outside saying: Open the door! I'm your husband!

TOMMY: Exactly. You're the husband. With an emphasis on you're and husband.

CHUCK: She wouldn't come out until I'd gone to work—

TOMMY: That's instability. She has a general instability. You should call her, Chuck. You call her. You ask about Smiley. You say he's real sick. You ask her what should you do.

CHUCK: Okay.

TOMMY: Then I would ask "are you coming by tonight to make my supper."

CHUCK: She always does though.

TOMMY: So she'll say yes and you'll say "why do you do that, Jan? Why do you come over every night to make my supper?"

CHUCK: She straightens up a little, too.

TOMMY: She's crazy about you.

CHUCK: Yea.

TOMMY: She is. You know, Chuck, it may be menopausal, that's all. It may be strictly menopausal. My wife is menopausal right now and it's driving me nuts. In fact, I wish she would leave, you know? Cook my supper and then leave.

CHUCK: That bad, huh?

TOMMY: She's hot; she's cold. She's hot; she's cold. It was menopause that turned her into a Jehovah's Witness.

CHUCK: You think so?

TOMMY: I'm sure so. I say, honey, why this—why the Jehovah's Witness and you know what she does?

CHUCK: What?

TOMMY: Just stares at me like I got fire coming out of my head. "Put Satan behind you," she says.

CHUCK: Satan?

TOMMY: That's right.

CHUCK: I didn't know she'd gotten that bad.

TOMMY: I can't get within ten feet of her.

CHUCK: So you think Jan is going through menopause?

TOMMY: I think there's a chance, yes, I do.

CHUCK: I don't know.

TOMMY: What?

CHUCK: Jan's pretty distant with me—

TOMMY: That's menopause.

CHUCK: Like I'm not there. When she told me she was leaving, she barely moved. She didn't blink an eye. Liked she'd practiced or something. Like it'd been years of thinking and planning. Years. Just last year, I built her this brand new kitchen. Look at the place. She says she wants ceramic tiles; I put in tile. Look at this stuff: like a golden sidewalk, for Christ sake! Like a sheik lives here or something. The floor alone cost five thousand dollars—

TOMMY: (Overlapping.) I helped put it in. I know!

CHUCK: I do everything she asks. I say where do you want the stove? She says "put it over there" and so I put it over there. And look at this stove. There are so many gadgets and goofas—

TOMMY: You're a goofas—

CHUCK: —and computer chips chipping away inside the thing that she could practically fly the son of a bitch to the moon! She could run the universe! She could reshape and remake the laws of physics. Solve the problems of the world. Make visits to the Pope. Go to Hollywood and meet some movie star—

TOMMY: (Overlapping.) Loni Anderson!!

CHUCK: And the whole time suckin' the air out of my backside-my aching backside. Now I have Smiley here, dying on me, slipping out the back door like my daughter in college, like my wife in some tiny apartment without any furniture. Years, she planned this. Saved up for it, I know. Years. She even planned to quit her teaching position without telling me. The whole thing mapped out for herself. This is the reason she comes back to cook for me. She misses this kitchen; this space ship; this Sheik's paradise! I'm telling you, Tommy, I want to die! I just want to die. Just die.

TOMMY: You stop talking like that—

(Chuck picks up box with Smiley.)

CHUCK: I ought to take him in, I ought to just take control and say "This is it. Gas him."

TOMMY: I'm telling you now, you stop that talk. Pull yourself up, pick up the phone and call her. I'll stand by you.

CHUCK: Yea?

TOMMY: Go to the phone—

CHUCK: She's at the nursing home.

TOMMY: Call the nursing home—Put the box down.

(*Chuck puts the box on the floor.*)

TOMMY: Now make your call.

Chuck picks up the phone. The lights crossfade to Jan and Mae who are walking up and down the hallway.

JAN: This feels good, doesn't it?

MAE: It's okay. It's rocky going.

JAN: You're doing great. You're doing better than I thought you would.

MAE: Can we go to the patio?

JAN: Yes.

MAE: I want to look out the window. I want to see if Andrew has come. I want to wait for him.

JAN: We can do that.

(*Silence. They walk for a bit.*)

MAE: I can't stand the way some of these people look. Do I look like that? Do I look that poorly?

JAN: No, you don't.

MAE: I will if you keep me here. A month, a week, one more day even and I'll be just like that. (*To another patient.*) What are you looking at, honey? I'm just walking. People walk up and down this hall all day. There's nothing special about it. Just keep your eyes to the floor, keep your eyes on the yellow line—

JAN: Mom.

MAE: There's part of the problem. These people have lost their minds. I've still got a mind. I can still think clearly. This is not a place for me. These people don't remember that they're going to die. But I remember! Did you see her staring at me? Gives me the creeps. Makes me very nervous. I'm not sure I'm even safe here with that kind of woman. Unless they tie her down at night who knows what she might do while I'm sleeping. I could be murdered. I could be strangled. You could choke that bitch to death and she wouldn't know what was happening to her. (*To invisible woman.*) I could choke you to death and it wouldn't even faze you, would it?! But I'd know. I'd know I was going to die. (*Beat.*) How far is the patio, anyway? I thought it was just down the hall.

JAN: Hall D.

MAE: Hall D? I can't go all the way down to hall D. This is only hall B. Hall B! How long, oh Lord, how long must I suffer? *(To another patient.)* What are you staring at? You know, honey, I wish I could be oblivious just like you.

JAN: Stop it, Mom—

MAE: I want to be drifting off somewhere just like you, sweetie. I don't want to recognize anyone.

JAN: Would you stop it!?

MAE: I don't want to know where I am. I don't want to be aware of what's happening to me. I like the idea of crying for no reason. Shouting for no reason. Laughing for no reason. And staring right back at you. *(To patient.)* That's very rude, staring at people like that—

JAN: Shhhh.

MAE: Oh my God, we have so far to go. I can't do it. I just can't do it. How long, oh Lord, how long?

JAN: Oh, stop with the religion stuff—

MAE: I'm religious.

JAN: *(Laughing.)* You are not religious. You're suspicious. You're superstitious, but you are not religious!

MAE: The way you talk to me!

JAN: And the way you talk!

(Mae suddenly freezes in her tracks.)

JAN: What are you doing? *(Beat.)* I said what are you doing?

(Beat. Mae begins to recite The Lord's Prayer.)

JAN: Mom.

(Beat. Mae continues reciting until her next line.)

JAN: Mom? *(Beat.)* This is ridiculous. *(Beat.)* Everybody knows "The Lord's Prayer," Mother. That doesn't mean anything. *(Beat.)* I'm going back to the room. *(Beat.)* You want me to leave you here? *(Beat.)* You're just like them, Mother. Crazy just like them. *(Jan starts to walk away.)* I'm going back to the room. *(Jan walks a bit farther.)* Mom?

MAE: *(Suddenly stopping her recitation.)* Do you have any idea how angry I am? Do you have any idea at all?

Mae starts to walk past Jan who stands there a beat as lights crossfade to David and

Andrew. Andrew turns and looks at David.

DAVID: You're going to sit over there?

ANDREW: Yes.

DAVID: You're going to sit over there?

ANDREW: Yes. Right here. I'm going to sit right here.

DAVID: Jesus.

ANDREW: What? I can't sit over here? I can't sit where I want?

DAVID: I'm coming over.

ANDREW: Don't.

DAVID: I'm coming.

ANDREW: Shut up.

DAVID: Here I come.

ANDREW: *(As David, acting like a very weird old person, moves over to him.)* Stop it. Stop it.

DAVID: *(As old person.)* Take my hand. Hold my hand, sonny, honey. I just want to hold your hand. Let me hold your hand.

ANDREW: *(Overlapping.)* Don't do that. David. Don't.

DAVID: *(As himself.)* You're embarrassed, you're scared, you're repulsed? What? What?

ANDREW: No. This isn't the place—why do I have to explain this to you? Why is that?

DAVID: Because I don't get it. You're nervous and upset—so this is the place—

ANDREW: No, this isn't the time—

DAVID: Seems like the perfect time to me.

ANDREW: It's not.

DAVID: I don't like you here. I want to leave.

ANDREW: Just because I won't—

DAVID: You're embarrassed to be seen with me.

ANDREW: I'm not. I tell you I'm not—

DAVID: You jerked away from me.

ANDREW: I did not jerk. I moved. Like this. Watch me. That's what I did. Like this, see? This is what I did. That is not jerking.

DAVID: It was a jerk. That's either embarrassment or repulsion or fear.

ANDREW: I'm not doing this—

DAVID: And every time I've tried to—

ANDREW: I'm not. And that's it.

DAVID: Okay. What do I know, Andrew, about what happened to you here?

ANDREW: That's right.

DAVID: I'm just a nice Jewish boy from Skokie.

ANDREW: Sometimes, you're nice. Sometimes, you're not so nice—

DAVID: *(Overlapping.)* Okay, okay...And I know my parents indulged me so much that when kids started picking on me, they sent me to a different school—no expense spared.

ANDREW: Lucky you.

DAVID: Lucky me.

ANDREW: Exactly. And so what do you know, huh? What do you know?

DAVID: Nothing.

ANDREW: That's for sure.

DAVID: So tell me.

ANDREW: You don't know anything.

DAVID: Okay. I don't know anything.

ANDREW: That's for sure!!

DAVID: I love you and want to give you a little sense of comfort in a place that makes you feel so bad about yourself, about yourself, but you won't let me do it. And I'm telling you now, I'm telling you now that what I want for myself—easy or not—is to get away from this damaged soul stuff—I want to get away from it—and what I want from a partner, a lover is that same thing. To get away. To get away from it.

ANDREW: Because I won't hold your hand, I'm damaged?

DAVID: Because you won't include me—

ANDREW: Won't include you? I'm damaged?

DAVID: Can I be a little bit more than the person who claims your body when you die?

ANDREW: What does that mean?

DAVID: Can I get close enough, can I be important enough to take your hand here in the lobby of your hometown nursing home without you being too scared to admit your feelings to me—

ANDREW: I do—

DAVID: —or to yourself or to the old man dribbling in his chair or to some hometown ghost—

ANDREW: I do.

DAVID: You don't.

ANDREW: I do!

DAVID: Because I won't stay—

ANDREW: *(Softly.)* I do. I do.

DAVID: I will hold my lover's hand anywhere, Andrew, anywhere in the world—and no one, no one tells me that I don't have the right, that it's bad taste, that it makes someone uncomfortable. And I won't stay with anyone too frightened to do the same. But that is going to be so hard for me because I thought, I'd been thinking that here he is, this is who I want. Andrew Morris. Age: 37. Tall. Fair. In all things. Finally. You. And so it breaks my heart. It breaks my heart. To think about it. It does. It does.

The lights crossfade to Mae and Jan. Mae is standing with her crutches outside of her room. Her back is to the audience. Jan comes up to her.

JAN: Still having your temper tantrum? *(Beat.)* Hello? *(Beat.)* Are you going in? *(Beat.)* You want me to help you? *(Beat.)* You can't stay out here all day. *(Beat.)* The doctor says a week or so and then you can go home. A week, that's all. That's not very long. But you have to get up and move around more. You have to keep moving. *(Beat. Then Jan touches Mae)* Come on. Let's go in.

(Mae withdraws slightly.)

JAN: All right. *(Beat.)* Do I need to get someone? *(Beat.)* If you won't come in, then I'll have to get someone.

MAE: You're moving when?

JAN: At the end of the semester.

MAE: End of the semester?

JAN: Twenty-four school days from now.

MAE: Where?

JAN: To Bloomington.

MAE: You're going to live with Sarah?

JAN: No. Sarah has a boyfriend.

MAE: She lives with him?

JAN: Yes.

MAE: Oh...she must like him.

JAN: I think she does. Is that what this is about?

MAE: No. Have you found a place?

JAN: Not yet, but I'm going down this weekend, and Sarah and I are going to look.

MAE: You could live with me.

JAN: I cannot live with you.

MAE: And why not?

JAN: Because I don't want to.

MAE: I could be at home. That's something to think about. If you were home, I could be, too.

JAN: I'm not taking care of you the rest of your life.

MAE: But if you were home—

JAN: I'm not taking care of you the rest of your life.

MAE: I wouldn't mind moving to Bloomington. I could get used to a bigger town.

JAN: No. Absolutely not.

MAE: Why?

JAN: Because, Mother, this phase of my life is over.

MAE: This phase? This phase?

JAN: Yes.

MAE: What do you mean, this phase?

JAN: This part of my life—

MAE: You know he visits every day.

JAN: Who visits?

MAE: Chuck.

JAN: He visits you?

MAE: Every day. Before I fell. After I fell. Every day since you left.

JAN: He comes here?

MAE: Yes, he comes here.

JAN: I didn't know the two of you were so close.

MAE: We're not so close.

JAN: So what does he want then?

MAE: He just wants to figure out life, that's all.

JAN: *(Chuckling.)* And so he comes to you?

MAE: Yes. *(Chuckling herself.)* That is funny, isn't it?

JAN: And so what has he figured out? What have you helped him figure out?

MAE: A few things.

JAN: Such as?

MAE: None of your business.

JAN: All right.

MAE: I just thought you should know that he comes here and he talks to me and that he has been talking to me for a while. I just thought you should know.

JAN: Well, keep up the good work.

(She starts to exit.)

MAE: Where are you going?

JAN: Back into the room.

MAE: What am I supposed to do?

JAN: Stand out here. Or come back in.

MAE: I want a cigarette.

JAN: Then go to the lounge.

MAE: By myself?

JAN: I think you can do it.

MAE: I don't have my cigarettes.

JAN: I'll put them here in your pocket.

MAE: You should go with me. *(Beat.)* I said you should go with me.

JAN: I'm going to grade papers in the room.

(Jan continues moving.)

MAE: Stupid bitch!! You stupid, mean bitch!

JAN: *(Stopping, in a harsh whisper.)* Don't you call me that.

MAE: You are a bitch, you know that?

JAN: I've told you—

MAE: A fucking bitch. Or should I say non-fucking bitch—

JAN: What?

MAE: And don't use that school teacher stuff with me—

JAN: I've told you never to use that word. That is a vile, ugly word used against women—

MAE: I used it against you.

JAN: I don't know what kind of conversations you're having with Chuck—

MAE: I want you to go with me.

JAN: I'm not going with you. In fact, I'm going into your room, gather up my things and leave.

MAE: *(Throwing her cigarettes to the floor.)* I want a cigarette.

JAN: *(As Jan picks them up and puts them in Mae's pocket.)* Then go have one.

VOICE OVER PA: Good morning, residents. This is Brenda. Today is Monday, April 15. Our resident of the day—tada—is Mae Anne Pierce in room 214. Mae Anne was born December 20, 1932—

(During this, Mae grabs the sleeve of Jan's sweater. Jan wiggles out of sweater and leaves with Mae holding sweater.)

MAE: *(Overlapping.)* She said my age! You old bag! Fat bitch!

BRENDA: *(Overlapping.)* And is a lifelong resident of Dixon. She was married twice—

MAE: *(Overlapping.)* Oh, why does she have to say that? She hates me.

BRENDA: —to the late Benjamin Morris and Jimmy Pierce. She's probably best known as Dixon's answer to Connie Francis—

MAE: *(Overlapping.)* I was better than Connie Francis—

BRENDA: *(Overlapping.)* But according to Mae Anne, her proudest moment was singing to former President Ronald Reagan at the 1984 opening of the Reagan Boyhood Home. According to Mae, she didn't "wash my hips, I mean my lips for a week." *(Brenda chuckles.)* She's funny, isn't she? Just a great gal.

MAE: *(Overlapping.)* Fuck off.

BRENDA: And to help us celebrate this bright, new spring April 15 day, our resident of the day will be singing a selection of songs during the day's morning recreation.

(Jan returns to get sweater during this. We hear one person applauding.)

BRENDA: So warm up those vocal cords. And we'll see you real soon!

(Beat. Mae hands sweater to Jan. As Jan reaches for it, Mae drops it to the floor. Jan picks it up.)

JAN: There you go, Mother.

(Jan leaves.)

MAE: *(After looking around a bit.)* All right, then.

Mae begins to move down the hallway as the lights crossfade to David. Andrew and David look at one another. Then...

ANDREW: Sounds like we're just in time. *(Beat.)* I'm not sure what to say. Probably because I'm damaged.

DAVID: I don't mean for you to take it that way.

ANDREW: Oh, okay, then I'll take it another way.

DAVID: Can we—

ANDREW: And what does it mean? Damaged? What kind of bullshit is that? Damaged. Fucking damaged—

DAVID: Andrew—

ANDREW: You think that's going to make me open up to you—

DAVID: So you admit—

ANDREW: *(Continuing.)* Saying bullshit like that—

DAVID: I told myself—

ANDREW: Who cares? You think I can't do this alone?

DAVID: I know you can.

ANDREW: You think I haven't been doing it by myself for the last thousand years?

DAVID: You're very self-sufficient.

ANDREW: That's right.

DAVID: Very controlled.

ANDREW: Yes...Very...all that. *(Beat.)* I saw a ghost once.

DAVID: Really?

ANDREW: Yes. I did.

(Beat.)

DAVID: Can I ask—

ANDREW: The sister who died? Alice Renee? A couple of weeks after, I was playing in the backyard—I was by myself—don't remember what I was doing exactly, but I do remember that I looked up at the house, and up at the second floor and, at the window of my parent's bedroom, as clear as day, was my sister, Alice. And she was looking down on me—right at me, I swear to God! And I remember that I said "Alice!" and then waved. A little wave. A shy, little wave because she didn't look happy and I wasn't sure if waving was the right thing to do. She did not wave back. And I never saw her again, but every time I was in the backyard, I'd look up to see if she was there. Her ghost—later—came in very handy. When I was in the second grade and kids started to pick on me—my parents did not send me to a special school—I would turn to them and say 'You know, my sister died." And they'd back up. "Her name was Alice and she was ten." They'd back up a little more. "She died of leukemia." Back, back. "And now she looks at me from the upstairs window." Back, back, back. Staring at me, but quiet at last. Did I tell you this?

DAVID: No.

ANDREW: I didn't tell you? Funny. Good story, though, isn't it?

DAVID: *(Startled.)* Yes.

ANDREW: Good story. Full of—oh, you know, all that great damaged soul stuff—

DAVID: Andy—

ANDREW: I had a big garden. Did I tell you that?

DAVID: No.

ANDREW: I did. I had a big garden. And my stepdad used to stand at the same window where I saw Alice and watch me working in my garden. I waved at him once, too, but...again, no response. He hated my flowers. Thought it was a weird thing for a teenage boy to be interested in. Sometimes he'd come outside and stand there watching me. Like he was John Wayne or something. "You quit that gardenin' or I'ma gonna kill ya." It was a beautiful garden, though, and I had the show ribbons to prove it. In fact, I used to wear the ribbons that I won around my neck-all around the place-sashay like this with my ribbons. Up in my bedroom, I'd imagine myself some kind of prince with all my ribbons to prove it. I never took the things off and Jimmy hated it. Hated it. And when I refused to take them off, he chased me out to the front lawn and around a tree—my mom flailing—her hands over her ears—the whole neighborhood watching, I'm sure—ribbons flying and my stepdad screaming "You sissy son of a bitch"—and my mom saying, "Jimmy! Jimmy! Don't kill him! Don't kill him! We'll just have him move out!" And two days later, I was packing my bags and sitting on the front steps waiting for Ted and his mom to pick me up and carry me to a safe spot. I was sixteen the year my head fell. Like this I was all the time. *(He drops his head.)* Shame, shame, shame. This was me—I didn't mean for you to ever see this. Never, never, never were you supposed to see this. My head down so far I could practically carry it in my hands, like some ghostwalking decapitation.

(Beat. David lifts Andrew's head.)

ANDREW: *(As he drops his head.)* Don't.

(David lifts it again.)

ANDREW: *(Dropping his head again.)* I said don't.

(David lifts it again and does some kind of adjustment that "keeps it in place." They look at one another.)

DAVID: I get worried you know. There's always this arms length between us. *(Stretching out his arm.)* About this far.

ANDREW: That far?

DAVID: It feels like it. I lie in bed beside you sometimes and I worry about it. That distance between us and I worry more because I don't think you know it's there and I don't know how to talk to you about it...that distance disappears for a brief few moments when you turn towards me in the morning—and you kiss me—and I think this is our purest time together. No memory of anything, really, except of us. But then the day and the memories somehow work themselves back. And you don't turn to me anymore. I don't know what happens, Andrew. And so the distance—

(Andrew suddenly tucks his head. Mae has limped on with her crutches. She walks past the both of them and looks out a window. Beat. As she looks, Andrew curls his head farther and farther in to his lap. Mae does not notice them. David watches Andrew as he becomes increasingly more invisible. Mae walks past. She looks at them, smiles at David and Andrew who has looked up. Andrew and Mae look at one another. Andrew stands. He suddenly pulls David up beside him. He takes David's hand and puts it up to his chest. A beat. She goes off. Beat.)

DAVID: That was her?...Andy...that was her? Andy...Andy?

ANDREW: Goddamn her. Goddamn her.

He stands there as the lights crossfade to Chuck and to Mae's room where the phone is ringing. Tommy sits there with Chuck, pretending not to listen.

JAN: *(Answering phone in Mae's room.)* Mae Pierce's room.

CHUCK: Jan. Chuck.

JAN: Hi, Chuck. *(Beat.)* What is it, Chuck?

CHUCK: Smiley's sick.

JAN: He is?

CHUCK: I was wondering what I should do?

JAN: Take him to the vet.

CHUCK: I suppose I could do that.

(Beat.)

JAN: What's wrong?

CHUCK: What if they think it's time?

JAN: Time for what?

CHUCK: To put him to sleep.

JAN: Then you'll just have to do it.

CHUCK: Oh.

JAN: He's seventeen.

CHUCK: I know.

JAN: It's a miracle he's lasted that long.

CHUCK: I suppose.

JAN: Do you want me to do it?

CHUCK: Take him in?

JAN: Yes.

CHUCK: No. I'll take him in. I'll see. I'll give him a couple of days. Should I call Sarah?

JAN: If you want. I'm not sure she cares that much anymore, but you might want to let her know all the same.

CHUCK: All right...How's your mom?

JAN: Okay.

CHUCK: Still depressed?

JAN: I suppose so.

CHUCK: Tell her I'll stop in.

JAN: Okay.

CHUCK: Has she told you I've been coming in?

JAN: She told me.

CHUCK: Well, I have been. I figured I should...Tommy's been here all morning—

JAN: You're with Fatboy?

CHUCK: He doesn't like to be called that anymore.

JAN: I can't help myself.

CHUCK: Well, he doesn't like it.

JAN: All right....Is there something else?

CHUCK: I'll see you tonight?

TOMMY: Now's a good time to ask.

JAN: *(Overlapping.)* Yes. You know what you want for supper?

CHUCK: I hadn't thought about it.

JAN: Pork chops, maybe? There's some in the freezer if you can remember to take them out.

CHUCK: I'll take them out. One for you?

JAN: Do I ever stay for supper, Chuck?

CHUCK: No...

TOMMY: Now would be a good time to ask.

JAN: Is there something else?

CHUCK: Well, I've got another question for you.

JAN: And what is that?

CHUCK: Do you love me?

JAN: What?

CHUCK: Do you love me?

JAN: Why are you asking me that?

CHUCK: I want to know.

JAN: Did Fatboy put you up to this?

CHUCK: No, he did not. And stop calling him that!!

TOMMY: What?

JAN: I'm not having this conversation over the phone.

CHUCK: I'm sorry. I didn't mean to yell at you. I'm sorry. I think you should let me know.

JAN: Goodbye, Chuck.

CHUCK: Do you still love me?

JAN: I refuse to do this.

CHUCK: Please. *(Beat.)* Answer the question. Please.

JAN: No, I don't.

CHUCK: What?

JAN: No.

CHUCK: What?

JAN: No, I said no. I don't love you.

    (Beat.)

CHUCK: Did you though? At one time? Did you? *(Beat.)* Did you?

JAN: ...Yes.

CHUCK: Oh. But you stopped, right?

JAN: I stopped.

CHUCK: Okay. That's what I wanted to know. I needed to know that. I needed the information. *(Beat. Then suddenly.)* You know, you told me you were going to clean out the basement!

JAN: And I will—

CHUCK: Goddamn it, you told me you were going to do it a long time ago. None of that stuff is mine! Not one goddamn thing down there is mine!

JAN: Plenty of it—

CHUCK: Not one goddamn thing!

TOMMY: Jesus, Chuck.

JAN: So I'll do it.

CHUCK: Well, I hope so! And there's other things! Other things! Why do I always have to get on you? Why is that, huh? And Fatboy will be here when you get here—he's not going home just because you're coming!

    (Beat. Tommy is horrified.)

CHUCK: *(Suddenly very soft.)* So...I'll see you around six...Around six or so? Jan?...Hello?

    (Jan, quietly, hangs up. Lights fade on Jan.)

TOMMY: What the hell were you doing? Chuck? What the hell was that? Are you crazy?

    (Chuck, hiding his face, begins to cry.)

TOMMY: What happened?

    (Chuck continues to cry.)

TOMMY: Oh boy. Oh boy. Catch your breath now. Catch your breath. Oh, boy. Oh boy, oh boy, oh boy. Hold on. Hold on. *(Rubbing Chuck's back a little)* Things don't work out sometimes, do they?...I buy my wife a special gift for Christmas, a very special ring with a diamond because I think so much of her. I love her. And when I go to hand it to her, she won't take it. The Jehovah's Witness don't believe in Christmas. And so I just stand there with my hand out, with this special gift, this special ring with a small diamond, the smallest diamond in the world, but at least my hand's out. "I can't take that," she says. But I want you to have it, I say. My hand is reaching out like this— and she fixes me with that Jehovah's Witness look and says, "I don't want it." But I want you to have it—"No, no, no I don't want it." My hand's out the whole time. I'm embarrassed, ready to die, not sure how to bring my hand down. But I do. And instead of screaming like you did with Jan, I just go into the bathroom, say a few swear words like Goddamn fucking b-i-t-c-h and just cry and cry and cry. Terrible. I'm shaking, I'm crying so much. But I pull myself together. I pull myself up and you know what I do with that ring? I swallow it. Pulling myself up. Pulling myself together. And I swallow the smallest diamond ring in the world. Down the hatch like a fucking aspirin! Poof! Headache's gone! Poof! The veins relax, the brain opens like a medical miracle. And that's what you've got to do, Chuck. You've got to pull yourself up. Pull up and pull out. But the trick is that you never get mad. You never let them see that part of you. Can you hear me? Are you listening? Up, up now. Up, up, buddy. Up.

The lights crossfade to Jan who dials and then...

JAN: *(On the phone and in a bright voice.)* Sarah, it's your mom. I thought you might be— (She begins to cry and hangs up very quickly. Beat as she pulls herself together. She dials again.) Sarah, it's your mom again. I apologize for hanging up...I thought you and Mike might be in class, but on the off chance you weren't—*(She begins to cry again.)* I have to—*(She hangs up. Beat. She gets herself together and calls.)* Despite what you may think, your poor mother is not losing her mind. Your grandmother and your father are driving me crazy, that's true, but otherwise, I'm all right. I wanted to tell you that I will be down this weekend. I'm looking forward to it. You have a list of places we can look at? I don't need air-conditioning and I don't need a complex with a pool. I was thinking an old house—an apartment on the second floor with a window looking out on the street. I want to look out on the street through a shade tree. An old retired English professor living downstairs. One who has turned from poetry to painting walls and plumbing. Am I being too romantic? Hopeful? And I will do what you suggest: Face forward and into the wind! Bye, sweety. And hello to Mike—and apologies for those ridiculous hang ups...ridiculous, ridiculous.

(Mae has come in. She stands there as Jan hangs up.)

MAE: You're here? Just can't get enough of this old bird, can you? *(Beat.)* I'm sorry. *(Beat.)* I'm sorry. *(Beat.)* I'm sorry.

JAN: I can hear you, Mother.

MAE: Oh. Still no Andrew?

JAN: No. Did you have a cigarette?

MAE: Yes. He's not coming. I don't think he's coming.

JAN: Maybe there was traffic.

MAE: Did he say he was coming?

JAN: He said he was coming.

MAE: I don't think he is.

JAN: He said he was coming.

MAE: I don't think he'll make it. We might just as well forget it. Close the door and forget it. Can you help me into bed?

JAN: Try it by yourself.

MAE: I cannot do it by myself.

JAN: Try it.

MAE: Boy, you never give up, do you? *(Mae struggles into the bed, groaning all the way.)*

JAN: I'd say you're about ready to go home.

MAE: I'm never leaving here. *(Beat.)* You would think after all these years, he'd forget about it, wouldn't you?

JAN: I don't know, I'm not him.

MAE: Was I that bad?

JAN: You're concerned?

MAE: Was I?

JAN: You abandoned him.

MAE: I did not.

JAN: You did.

MAE: I protected him.

(Jan looks at her.)

MAE: Jimmy would have eventually killed him. I'm sure of that. *(Beat.)* He wanted to live with those people. And I thought it was the best thing. *(Loudly.)* I thought it was the *(Jan still looks.)*

MAE: I protected him!!!!

JAN: You let Jimmy harass and threaten him—

MAE: Andrew flaunted himself—

JAN: He was in high school. He was sixteen.

MAE: I stood in between—

JAN: If I had been home—

MAE: You would have what?

JAN: I would have stopped him.

MAE: But you weren't, were you? You weren't home, were you?

JAN: No.

MAE: Were you, Miss Thing? Miss Teacher Thing.

JAN: No.

MAE: Where were you?.....Allrighty.

> *(Beat. Jan looks away.)*

MAE: I think he liked living at Ted's, anyway. He said he did. And it was Jimmy's money that sent him to college. Sent him to Boston U. That was a very expensive school. *(Beat.)* He has no business staying away this long. *(Beat.)* He sends me money.

JAN: Does he?

MAE: Did you know that?

JAN: No.

MAE: He does. He sends me two hundred dollars a month.

JAN: I didn't know that.

MAE: He doesn't visit, but he sends money. And always with the same note. "Thought you might need this. Andrew." That's something, I guess. Isn't it?

JAN: That's something.

MAE: And I write him each time. A very short note, to thank him for the money—and each time I send him some kind of newspaper article or magazine article about something...about gay this or gay that, something I thought he might want to read or know about if he didn't already. "Thought you might want to see this," I say. Each time. "Thought you might want to see this." *(Chuckling.)* It took me forever to come up with that. "Thought you might want to see this." Forever that took. That was something, wasn't it?

JAN: I suppose it was.

MAE: ...You're pretty like my mom, you know it?

JAN: Mmmm.

MAE: You have her hair and profile. I always thought she was the prettiest mother in town. I thought about her when I fell and was lying on the ice and my whole life was passing in front of my eyes. And everything that had ever happened to me was racing around me and I kept thinking "Hurry up. I can't stand seeing all this shit again!" It ended with the face of my mother smiling at me. I think she was welcoming me into the afterlife like a sweet mother angel. I'd thought she'd still be mad at me, but she wasn't. And I thought to myself "just go numb. Let yourself melt into the ice and fly down into your mother's arms"...I was thinking of writing to Ronny.

JAN: Ronny?

MAE: The man couldn't take his eyes off of me—

JAN: Why would you—

MAE: To tell him where I am. To tell him I've been put in a nursing home. To remind him of who I am. I thought I would write.

JAN: Okay.

MAE: He'll remember me. He'll know who I am.

JAN: I don't think so.

MAE: I think he will. And maybe it will help bring him around. Maybe it'll jog a memory or two. Would you help me?

JAN: Yes.

MAE: I'd like to do it today. I'd like to do it now.

JAN: We don't have any stationery.

MAE: Go get some. Just get a pen and paper. You can write and I'll sign.

JAN: I'll bring some tomorrow. I want to finish these papers.

(Mae begins to cry.)

JAN: We can do it tomorrow.

(Mae continues to cry.)

JAN: I'll help you tomorrow. Why are you crying?

MAE: I can't help it. I'm sorry. I'm sorry.

(Beat. Jan continues to grade.)

MAE: I had a dream last night. A terrible dream that woke me up.

JAN: What?

MAE: I dreamt that I was at home and you were a young girl and that I was chasing you around the house and beating you. You were asking me to stop, but I wouldn't. Somebody had to pull me off of you, but I can't remember who—

JAN: Mom—

MAE: *(Continuing.)* Why would I have such a dream? After all, you're the one who took care of things. You did everything you were supposed to do.

JAN: I don't know.

MAE: Took care of me. Cleaned my house once a week! Took care of Alice, sweet thing that she was—

JAN: Don't talk about Alice.

MAE: Sweet thing that she was.

JAN: I said don't talk about her.

MAE: It hurts still, doesn't it? Thirty years later. And all that you did. Carried her from room to room. Her dried up little body, skinny as a bone—

JAN: I don't want you—

MAE: With her crying and screaming. Little bitty Andrew running behind you. Your dad in the basement rearranging the tools. Rearranging the tools. Sweeping the floor. But you were right there. And I thank you, Jan—thank you for what you did. Someone should have thanked you. I should have thanked you. Thank you for all you've done. We should have a thank you day for Jan. We should put up streamers. That's what we should do. How would you like it if we did something like that?

JAN: I wouldn't.

MAE: Come here, sweety.

JAN: I'm grading papers.

MAE: Come over here to me.

JAN: What do you need?

MAE: Just come over here.

JAN: No.

MAE: I'll give you a cherry chocolate.

(Jan comes over.)

MAE: I can't get this pillow, here. Can you reach over—

(Jan does. Mae reaches up and pulls Jan into her.)

JAN: What are you doing?

MAE: Let me give you a hug.

JAN: Don't do that. Let go of me.

MAE: Let me give my good daughter a big hug.

JAN: I don't want a hug. Let go of me. Mom!

(Mae does.)

JAN: How dare you do that!

MAE: Wha—?

JAN: How dare you try to hug me!!

MAE: I wha—?!

JAN: You never hugged me in your life. You've never even held my hand. And you want to hug me? You want to hug me, Mother? How dare you! *(She goes back to her grading.)*

BRENDA: *(Over the PA.)* Good morning, everyone. This is Brenda again. And today is Monday, April 15 and, ohhh, is it ever a wonderful, sunny, spring day. Take a look out your window! In just a few minutes, our resident of the day Mae Anne Pierce will be singing for us in the cafeteria. So get up! Take in the day! And sing-a-long with Mae Anne.

(Mae gets her crutches. She walks over to Jan who does not look up.)

MAE: I saw Andrew in the lobby. He's waiting in the lobby.

JAN: What?

MAE: Looking at me so hard—so angry—you tell him "never mind." Tell him that. Tell him "never mind."

She walks out of the room. Jan stands up and, in great frustration, holds both hands up and gives her the finger. The lights crossfade to lobby where Andrew and David sit. Andrew still holds David's hand, but has his face half-buried in to his chest. We hear the last of Brenda's announcement.

BRENDA: *(Over the PA.)* The cafeteria is filling up so get yourself down here for the big Mae Anne Pierce sing-fest!!! This is going to be the big spring event here at Lee County!!!

DAVID: You okay? Andrew? Andy? I'm so sorry...You breathing? *(Andrew nods.)* You weren't breathing for a while. I thought I was going to have to grab that guy's oxygen. But you're breathing, right? *(Andrew nods.)* Good. You're breaking my hand, by the way...no, no, no, no, no don't let go, just easier, just easier that's all...that's better...I like it. Such a simple thing. Holding someone's hand. A simple touch. The blood underneath your skin. I feel all of that. Can you hear? *(Andrew nods.)* Why don't you come up? Come on up. She's gone. I think you scared the shit out of her. Scared the shit out of me, that's for sure. You were so fucking butch, whooaa, fucking butch, baby. Like a Ronald Reagan cowboy or something. Like Nancy Reagan on a horse.

ANDREW: *(Whispering.)* I gotta get out of here.

DAVID: What?

ANDREW: I gotta get out of here.

DAVID: Okay.

ANDREW: Help me out of here.

DAVID: Sure.

ANDREW: I shouldn't have come—

DAVID: Maybe—

ANDREW: I don't think I should have.

DAVID: I'm sorry.

ANDREW: It's not your fault.

DAVID: It is.

ANDREW: No. It's not. I want to kill her before I leave. What if I kill her before we leave?

DAVID: We'll do it together.

ANDREW: *(Laughing a little.)* Yes. We'll do it together.

DAVID: I'll push her out a window.

ANDREW: *(Looking at David.)* Hmph...I'm going to try, you know, David.

DAVID: I know.

ANDREW: Do you?

DAVID: Yes.

ANDREW: *(He stands.)* Okay, then.

   (David stands. A beat. David takes Andrew's hand.)

DAVID: Would you have anyone deny us this pleasure, Andrew?

   They exit. The lights crossfade to Chuck and Tommy. Chuck wipes his eyes.

TOMMY: You okay?

CHUCK: Okay.

TOMMY: You sure?

CHUCK: I'll be all right. *(He stares out.)* I used to think while I was lying in bed with Jan, I used to think about who was going to die first. I used to lay there and think—with Jan right there next to me—who was going to die first, me or Jan? I couldn't get to sleep thinking about it. I hoped that it would be me because I couldn't imagine what it would be like without her—

TOMMY: *(Quietly.)* Pull up—

CHUCK: It's what I'm thinking—

TOMMY: It bothers me—

CHUCK: I can't help it—

TOMMY: You can pull up-go get it!!

CHUCK: I don't want to be alone. I can't be alone.

TOMMY: You're not alone. I'm here. And you've got Smiley there. He's hanging on. And, shit, I can cook. You got two pork chops in there, I'll cook it up. I'll eat with you.

CHUCK: You will?

TOMMY: I've got a wife who thinks I'm Satan. So I'll cook. I don't mind.

CHUCK: You don't mind?

TOMMY: Why would I?

CHUCK: I don't know.

TOMMY: I'll tell you what. We take Smiley into the vet, get him all checked out, come on back home here and cook up some pork chops. How's it sound?

(Pause.)

CHUCK: *(Quietly.)* We take him in?

TOMMY: Sure.

CHUCK: Okay. *(Chuck picks up the box and looks in. Quietly.)* Smiley, old thing. Old pal. Old thing. I love ya. Love ya...Okay. Let's go.

The lights crossfade to Mae's room. Norma comes in the room. She stops when she sees Jan.

JAN: Oh. Can I help you?

(Norma doesn't move.)

JAN: Can I help you?

(Norma takes out a folded newspaper article and hands it to Jan.)

JAN: What is this? *(Jan unfolds it and begins to read.)* "Nursing Home Resident Dated Hometown President." You dated President Reagan? Is this you? Norma Brown? The newspaper wrote an article about you, huh? That is very nice, very nice.

(Norma just stands there looking at Jan. Jan reads the article.)

JAN: This is you at the high school prom, isn't it? I think that's great. And you are both so handsome there. Tell me now, did he kiss you goodnight?

(Beat. Norma stares at her.)

JAN: I'll bet he did, didn't he? I'll bet.

(Beat. She gives the article back to Norma who stands there.)

JAN: Would you like a cherry chocolate?

(Jan offers her the cherry chocolates. Norma takes one.)

JAN: You can have more. Go ahead. Take all that you want.

(Beat. Norma takes one. Jan keeps the box in front of her. Norma continues to take one and then another and another. Jan starts to laugh as Norma takes them. Norma begins to smile with her. When she has finished, there is a beat.)

JAN: How about some cigarettes? Would you like some cigarettes?

(Jan begins to give Norma all of Mae's cigarettes, stuffing them into Norma's pockets. Norma laughs as she does so.)

JAN: *(Laughing with Norma.)* That's right! You laugh! You laugh! In here. And here. And there.

(Norma looks at Jan. She smiles at her.)

JAN: Anything else I can get you?

(Norma looks at Jan smiling. She suddenly hugs Jan very tightly. Jan tenses at first, but then slowly hugs her back.)

JAN: Now...you need to let go of me, honey...You need to let go...Come on now...Come on...what a big hug...Come on...Such a big, big hug....Well...well...A little hug back...Hmmm...You lost all your memory, but you kept this, didn't you? This you didn't forget...I have a daughter named Sarah. She's twenty-two. And a graduate student. And soon I'll be living very near her...I have a daughter named Sarah. She's twenty-two. And soon I'll be living near her. *(Still hugging Norma.)* I have a daughter named Sarah. Yes. And I'll be living near her very soon. Remember that. Yes. Very soon. Very soon.

The lights crossfade to Mae sitting in a chair-center stage. Mae is in her element. She has a microphone in her hand.

MAE: Hello, everyone—*(Looking out.)*—Oh my God, look at you people, you're all in wheelchairs! I feel like I'm in an old folks home! *(She cackles loudly.)* And what happened to you, honey? Stroke? Did you have a stroke? Yes? I'm so sorry. Is that what's wrong with your hand? But you're hanging in there, aren't you, honey? How about a little applause for this beautiful woman here.

(One person applauds.)

MAE: I take one look at you and say "there but for the grace of God, go I. Go me. Whatever." *(She cackles loudly.)* Is it hot in here? You say you're hot, honey? I'd say you haven't been hot since 1952. *(She cackles loudly.)* Have I told you my "Puss and Boots" story? Oh, I love the puss and the boot story because it's such a dirty, dirty story that's all about a great big, black boot and two sweet pu-oh my God, Seizure!! Over there!! Seizure!!! You are such a fun crowd, you know that? Give yourself a hand.

(One person applauds.)

MAE: So I guess I'm here to sing a couple of songs for you.

(One person applauds.)

MAE: Thank you, sir. Give that guy a better seat! *(She cackles.)* Now I thought I would start with one of my favorites, and I hope it's one of yours, too. It's called "I Walk the Line" and boy, have I ever. Life's hard, you know? You walk the line, you walk life and that's all there is to it. Ronald Reagan walked that line and helped me walk it, too.

(One person applauds.)

MAE: You out there, Ronny? Can you hear me? This is for you, you sweet, sweet, sweet goodlooking thing.

(One person applauds.)

MAE: And a one and a two and a three—

(A piano begins to play "I Walk the Line.")

MAE: Faster, honey. Faster.

(The music begins to play. Mae begins to sing with the recording of the Johnny Cash version of "I Walk the Line" As Mae sings in background, Chuck and Tommy return to kitchen with an empty box. They both sit at table. Jan walks into lobby as Andrew and David are walking out. They look at one another. Beat. Jan, tentatively, waves at Andrew. He returns the wave as the lights crossfade and Mae Ann finishes her singing.)

END OF PLAY

Heat

by Marsha Estell

ALL INQUIRIES CONCERNING RIGHTS, INCLUDING AMATEUR RIGHTS, SHOULD BE ADDRESSED TO:
Russ Tutterow, Artistic Director, Chicago Dramatists, 1105 W. Chicago Avenue, Chicago, IL, 60622
Email: rtutterow@chicagodramatists.org; Phone (312) 633-0630

ORIGINALLY PRODUCED by Chicago Dramatists

For theatre profile and information on Chicago Dramatists, see page 2.

* * *

I directed *Heat* to rave reviews and packed houses at Chicago Dramatists in 2004 when the playwright, Marsha Estell, was still a member of our associate playwright program that we call The Playwrights' Network. The following year, we invited her to Resident Playwright status. Directing *Heat* was one of the most joyous experiences I have ever had in the theatre. This play is so big-hearted and alive, it's like an embrace from the big, safe, loving arms of Mudear, the grandmother. The humor is all character based and absolutely uproarious. Although the playwright has, if you will, a strong Chicago voice, *Heat* is a very Midwestern play. It's about three generations of African American women in a small Midwestern town, which is something unusual, I think, because most plays I've seen about African American families have been set in big cities or the rural South. I feel that Marsha is an important young playwright, with her own distinctive, rich voice, and someone every theatre in the country should know. Every audience that saw our production (and a subsequent production at the Bloomington Playwrights Project in Indiana) was enthralled and uplifted. Each of them had one of the best nights in the theatre in their whole life. Here's how we described the play in our publicity materials:

1 front porch, 3 generations, 105 degrees—A big-hearted play full of storytelling, laughter, and healing about an African American family of women. When the youngest comes home from the big city one summer weekend, she finds a broken air conditioner and a family heat wave to match the temperature. Sharing their laughter, regrets, and fantasies about sweethearts, Sidney Poitier, and sweet potato pie, these women are determined to hold the family together.

Russ Tutterow
Artistic Director, Chicago Dramatists

BIOGRAPHY

Marsha Estell is a new Resident Playwright at Chicago Dramatists, after having been a member of Chicago Dramatists' associate program, The Playwrights' Network for three years. Chicago Dramatists' production of *Heat* earned Ms. Estell a Jeff Award nomination for New Work. *Heat* was subsequently produced at the Bloomington Playwrights Project in Bloomington, Indiana, a finalist in the Dayton Futurefest 2002, 3rd Place winner of the 2001 Theodore Ward Award for African American playwrights, and featured in the 2002 Voices from the Edge Festival at New

Perspectives Theater in New York City. Her plays have received readings at Chicago Dramatists, Goodman Theatre, Chicago Theater Company, ETA Creative Arts Foundation, Dayton Playhouse, New Perspectives Theatre in New York, and Famous Door Theatre. She was awarded a 2001 Illinois Arts Council Fellowship for Playwriting. *Mama Said There'll be Days Like This* was commissioned and produced by Chicago's Black Ensemble Theatre for an extended run in the 2003-2004 season. She is currently working on a musical about the life of Etta James and *Before I Wake*, a post Vietnam War play. Ms. Estell is a member of the Dramatists Guild, Women's Theatre Alliance, Actors' Equity, and AFTRA.

DEVELOPMENTAL HISTORY

In addition to developmental readings at Chicago Dramatists, *Heat* was a finalist in the Dayton Futurefest 2002, 3rd Place winner of the 2001 Theodore Ward Award for African American playwrights, and featured in the 2002 Voices from the Edge Festival at New Perspectives Theater in New York City.

AWARDS AND HONORS

The Chicago Dramatists' production of *Heat* earned Ms. Estell a Joseph Jefferson Award nomination for New Work. *Heat* was subsequently produced at the Bloomington Playwrights Project in Bloomington, Indiana.

ORIGINAL PRODUCTION

Heat premiered at Chicago Dramatists on March 19, 2004.
It was directed by Artistic Director Russ Tutterow with the following cast:

MUDEAR . . . . Saralynne Crittenden
ROSE . . . . Felisha D. McNeal
SHARON . . . . Mimi Ayers
SHELLY . . . . Jillian Pollock-Reeves

and the following production staff:

Set Designer . . . . .Joey Wade
Lighting Designer . . . . .Jeff Pines
Sound Designer . . . . .Joe Plummer
Costume Designer . . . . .Tiffany Trent
Stage Manager & Props Designer . . . . .Barbara Walk

CHARACTERS

MUDEAR: 68, African American, light complexion, battling the early stages of senility.

ROSE : 49, African American, oldest daughter of Mudear. In her heyday, she was considered a "Brick House" 36-24-36. Now her body is constantly at war with gravity…it is losing.

SHARON : 47, African American, youngest daughter of Mudear, Shelly's mother, recently divorced, attractive but shy.

SHELLY : 25, African American, medium complexion, long hair, lives in Chicago, recently underwent major surgery. A little spoiled. (Actress should wear a long wig in Act I. Short hair will be revealed in Act II.)

TIME & PLACE

Early 1990s, mid-summer, a small town about 200 miles south of Chicago, IL.

AUTHOR'S NOTE

I would like to dedicate *Heat* to the following women who have had a major influence on my life: my mother Gloria Lomax, Luda Esteves (the original Mudear), Verdina Carter, Earlene Estell, Lula Heard, Eleanor Wicks and Gloria Bullock.

Felisha D. McNeal (left) as Rose and Jillian Pollock-Reeves as Shelly in Chicago Dramatists' 2004 production of *Heat* by Marsha Estell, directed by Russ Tutterow.   Photo by Jeff Pines

Heat

ACT I

SCENE 1

Mid-morning. Front porch of a framed house in a small town 200 miles outside of Chicago. It is summer, the final days of a heat wave. There is a porch swing, rocking chair, watering can, and a few house plants. A small garden is suggested in the back of the house.

RADIO: *(Voice-over male.)* And it looks like another sweltering day. The heat index has reached a record high. Let's cool off with this mellow tune. *(Music plays.)* Aw, yeah let's get on back to the dusties...

(Lights up on Mudear, resting her eyes, After a couple of moments Rose enters, turns up radio, dances around, then adjusts a dress that's a little too tight.)

ROSE: It's like this—*(Looks down at breasts, cups them.)*—y'all need to do something. *(Beat.)* You used to stand up remember? Without any help. Now you ain't got nothing to say to nobody, all depressed. Getting on my last nerves! *(Beat. Dances.)* Ooooh, used to be the center of attention! A man could never tell the color of my eyes. He looking-looking-looking and his lips smacking like he's 'bout to chomp down on a Sunday dinner. Soul food, of course: greens-macaroni and cheese-fried corn-smothered-chicken-smothered-pork-chops-smothered-fish-smothered everything! Damn, Mama, you put gravy on anything that went across the stove.

(Beat. Mudear ignores Rose.)

ROSE: Every job interview I went on. If it was a man there—got it. I used to wear this suit, see, the blazer would open up like this, and y'all be busting out of a hot pink lace camisole. Night before, take a bath in Jean Nate. Smelling gooooooooood. Smelling good! And I would watch his left eye twitch or was it the right? *(Laughs.)* Shoot, it was both of 'em. And he act like he looking down at my resume and I would bend down too, pointing out my qualifications. On paper! So all this bending and pointing, and twitching, and then I'd sit back down in my seat hard and they would bounce! Then I just count 4, 3, 2, 1 and Old Blinky's throat would clear. "So uh when can you start?" *(Laughs.)* Bingo!

MUDEAR: You did all that to get a cashier job?

ROSE: My point is, back then I didn't have to do anything but breathe. *(She exhales, pushing out her chest.)*

MUDEAR: If you had finished school, you could have been anything you—

ROSE: *(Overlapping from "you could...")* I could have been anything I wanted to be! Starting early this morning huh? Before you had your coffee. *(Beat.)* Anyway, if it was some heifer interviewing me, I'd have to change my tactics...

MUDEAR: You still talking 'bout that mess?

ROSE: Go on inside, if you don't want to hear.

MUDEAR: I will, I'm fixing breakfast. Thought Sharon would have started it.

ROSE: Mudear...Sharon's not here...

MUDEAR: I know that. I don't know where she off to.

(Beat.)

ROSE: Remember...she went to see 'bout Shelly this week.

MUDEAR: She coming back today?

ROSE: Yes.

MUDEAR: Oh, then I need to get to it! Make my grandbaby some rolls and some gravy and—

ROSE: Ma, it's already eighty degrees outside, no baking today.

MUDEAR: This is my house, and if I want to make my baby some rolls then I will. *(Beat.)* I thought she would never come back home. Thought she was going to stay up there and work in the big city.

ROSE: She's not moving back, just needs to take more time off, Sharon says she didn't sound right, when she called her last week ...

MUDEAR: I don't see why she going back. Nasty, dirty, stinking, Chicago.

ROSE: You ain't been there in 50 years.

MUDEAR: Don't need to go back. Didn't like it the first time. When Papa Joe and me went up there I should of known it was a sign.

ROSE: Papa Joe? *(Beat.)* You can't blame Chicago for marrying the wrong man. Anyway, what 'bout the other two?

MUDEAR: What?

ROSE: Marriages.

MUDEAR: Don't you worry 'bout that. Should be worrying 'bout why you don't have nary one ring on your finger.

ROSE: Ooh, you got me, two in a row.

(Rose turns off radio.)

ROSE: It's gonna be another two weeks before her house is ready. I don't know if I can take it, house full of grown women. You and Sharon, be like having two Mudears. Didn't she say it got four bedrooms? *(Beat.)* Told her to buy a condo. Talking 'bout she need grass under her feet. That's why she got big feet, walking around barefoot all the times. *(Beat.)* What you think she gonna do with those extra rooms? *(Beat.)* Shelly ain't moving back if she got good sense...

MUDEAR: You did. And you said, "I ain't never ever coming back to this sorry ass town!"

ROSE: Came back to take care of you

MUDEAR: Oh, that's what you doing? *(Beat.)* Whew, it's gonna be another hot one!

ROSE: *(Jokingly.)* Flashing?

MUDEAR: What?

ROSE: You still getting flashes?

MUDEAR: Nawh. In case you haven't noticed it's hot!

(Beat.)

ROSE: You take your medicine?

(Rose picks up medicine, checks amount.)

MUDEAR: Quit questioning me, I'm not a child. *(Beat.)* Yes, I already did.

ROSE: Uh-hun...well let's take them again.

(Hands Mudear pills and a glass.)

ROSE: I need a touch up, hope Sharon will give me one.

MUDEAR: Why don't you just press it?

ROSE: Too hot to be burning my head.

MUDEAR: Either way you are burning it. I don't know why you are so worried, you got a good grade of bad hair. *(Beat.)* Where is it anyway?

ROSE: What?

MUDEAR: *(Suddenly agitated.)* You know what, Missy! What did you do with my hot comb?

ROSE: Mama, I don't use it. Where did you put it?

MUDEAR: You took it and now you can't find it.

ROSE: You ain't gonna worry me today.

MUDEAR: *(Mumbling.)* Getting on my damn nerves. *(Beat.)* I don't see why she got to have that done way up there in Chicago. What time they coming?

ROSE: *(Looks at watch.)* Should have been here. *(Beat.)* She went to see that specialist.

MUDEAR: She should have gone to see Dr. Frank. He's a good doctor.

ROSE: And he's fine.

MUDEAR: Sex. Is that all you think 'bout?

ROSE: What else is there?

MUDEAR: Women shouldn't talk that way.

ROSE: And it's okay for men?

MUDEAR: That's their way. Doggish. *(Beat.)* That dress is too tight.

ROSE: It's fine.

MUDEAR: Want me to let it out?

ROSE: No, thank you. Anyway it's supposed to accent the behind!

MUDEAR: Your behind don't need no accenting.

> *(Beat.)*

MUDEAR: Too old.

ROSE: So, I'm just supposed to stop living, huh? Stop feeling the heat. Shoot, I'm in my prime. Kills me, folks always acting like there's no use for an older woman. Look at the television or movies, and they act like over thirty-five is a sin. But let it be a man...and it's okay. *(Beat.)* Look at Clint Eastwood, for instance, now he's a good actor, but if a woman looked like that, with all those lines in her face, she could only play the dead grandmother.

MUDEAR: You way past 35.

ROSE: I still look good. Plus I know what I like and ain't afraid to ask for it. That's what scares men. When I was younger, I just figured they knew what they were doing. Believed anything they said. Now they got to do something!

MUDEAR: That's a subject you always making a big deal out of sex-sex-sex. What's the big deal 'bout it?

ROSE: The way you talk, sound like you never had an orgasm.

> *(Long pause.)*

ROSE: Well, have you?

MUDEAR: I'm not answering no nasty question!

ROSE: It's not nasty.

MUDEAR: I did what I had to do to have my children.

ROSE: You mean you only had sex four times?

MUDEAR: Fool, I had five children. Just cause I buried Scottie…he still counts.

(Beat.)

ROSE: I know that. That's not the point.

MUDEAR: What is the point?!

ROSE: I'm asking 'bout your sex life.

(Mudear waves her off, starts toward door.)

ROSE: *(Yells.)* Mudear, don't you turn that oven on!

(Mudear exits.)

MUDEAR: *(Offstage.)* I'm fixing my Sanka! *(Long beat.)* Don't sit in my chair!

ROSE: *(Rose sits in Mudear's chair. Distracted, looks up the road.)* Ma, why don't you just stay inside for a while? Sit under the air.

MUDEAR: *(Offstage,)* Now you know I don't like no air.

ROSE: You ready to eat something?

MUDEAR: *(Offstage.)* Too hot to eat. You won't let me cook my grandbaby something. I know, I know it's too hot.

(Mudear reenters with Popsicle for Rose. She waits for Rose to get out of her chair. After a moment, Rose sits on porch swing.)

MUDEAR: In my day we didn't let no heat stop us…

ROSE: I know Ma back in slavery times. *(Looks down the road.)*

MUDEAR: Slavery? Oh, see you trying to be funny.

(Rose looks at her watch, then down the road and fans herself. Then…)

ROSE: WELL, HELLO THERE ! *(She waves. Beat.)* Hello! I'll meet you half way…

(Rose exits toward road. Very long beat. Mudear closes her eyes for a moment. Mudear gets out of chair, picks up watering can, waters and prunes plants as she speaks.)

MUDEAR: You better hurry up, Joe. Pastor Wayne ain't gonna wait for ya. *(Beat.)* Pastor Wayne big ole hypocrite, always talking 'bout praise God, and while we busy praying, he back there with who knows who. Joe was right 'bout that one. Say he don't trust no man that's always smiling, say he could see it in his eyes—*(Beat.)*—big ole dollar signs. *(Laughs.)* All of them not like that though, the new one at Fellowship, he's very nice, always asking me how I'm doing, do I need anything…that's who Rose should go after, settle down. Humph, but she don't wanna do that. Well, guess the apple don't fall far from the tree.

(Rose returns with mail, hands it to her.)

ROSE: *(To Mudear.)* Who you talking to?

MUDEAR: You must be hearing things, I ain't said a word. *(Beat. Laughs.)* 'Cept ain't nothing like an old fool!

ROSE: You know I'm a sucker for a man in uniform.

MUDEAR: A mailman?

ROSE: Don't matter.

MUDEAR: You know the garbage man coming on Monday.

(They laugh. Sound of a car with an old loud muffler pulling up. Sharon and Shelly enter. Shelly is walking slowly and carries a small bag. Sharon enters behind her struggling with two. She tries to grabs the small bag from her.)

SHELLY: *(Offstage.)* I SAID I GOT IT, MA!

ROSE: Here comes the storm.

MUDEAR: There's my grandbaby, oh my God, she so skinny, need to fatten you up. Why you got your long pretty hair tied up like that, girl. Just a waste.

(Mudear rushes over to Shelly and hugs her. Sharon puts bags down.)

SHELLY: Hey, Grand. Good to see you. Hey, Auntie Ro.

ROSE: Girl, didn't think y'all were going to make it. That car overheat again?

SHELLY: You know it. I told Ma I could catch the train. It was like a ride through hell.

SHARON: You're welcome.

MUDEAR: What you know 'bout hell?

SHELLY: Been there and back. Could go for some ice water.

ROSE: I'll get it. You hungry?

(Rose exits into house.)

SHELLY: Too hot to eat.

SHARON: Bring me a glass too.

MUDEAR: Come closer, daughter, them doctors been good to you?

SHELLY: Yeah, Grand, I'm all right.

MUDEAR: What the test say?

SHELLY: Get the results on Monday, but the doctor says I look good.

SHARON: Well, of course you do. One thing 'bout the Williams women: we live forever.

MUDEAR: 'Cept for sister Alice falling in a well, or Debbie getting shot by that crazy milkman.

SHARON: Mother dear, you take your medicine yet?

(Rose reenters balancing glasses of ice water.)

ROSE: Yeah, she took it.

MUDEAR: She was talking to me, I ain't deaf you know. How's life in the big city?

SHELLY: Okay. This heat is murder.

ROSE: Yeah, lots of folks dying up there.

MUDEAR: City folks ain't use to no heat.

SHARON: It's worse up there, Mudear. All that concrete, people are baking in their own apartments.

SHELLY: Mostly old folks.

(Beat.)

MUDEAR: Why y'all get quiet, I ain't going nowhere.

ROSE: We know you too ornery.

MUDEAR: You just can't wait to get my fur coat.

ROSE: Mama, you been saying that for years. Why would I want that dead possum?

SHARON: *(Imitating Mudear.)* Possum?! I have you know this is genuine beaver!

SHELLY: *(Imitating Mudear.)* Got it from a rich white lady, I used to do laundry for. What was her name?

ROSE: Ms. Reams. *(Sings.)* Meanest woman you ever did know.

ROSE/SHELLY/SHARON: *(Sing.)* Dropped a watermelon on my big toe.

MUDEAR: Oh y'all just so funny, one day I'm...

SHARON: We got it from you, you make fun of everything.

MUDEAR: Got that from my papa, he was the funniest man. *(Beat.)* I never seen a colored man play tricks on white folk and get away wid it.

ROSE: Colored? You mean Black or African-American.

MUDEAR: I mean what I say. I never got used to saying Black. We are not Black. Like the dirt on the ground.

ROSE: 'Cause Mama's color struck!

SHARON: Rose, don't start.

MUDEAR: Or African-American. Now they use ta call us nigger, coon, pickaninny and...Negro. Shot Iris' son in the back, over stolen milk bottles...And you know that cracker didn't do no time. *(Beat.)* Colored was a step above. *(Beat.)* I like it, has a softer sound to it. Now I been saying colored for 65 years and I guess I'm gonna say it to the day I die.

(She exits, the screen door slams behind her.)

ROSE: I thought she made 68 this year.

(Sharon nods.)

SHARON: I'll check on her. You coming in, Shell?

SHELLY: Gonna stay out here with Auntie.

SHARON: No, Shelly, it's too hot out here.

(Beat. Shelly ignores her.)

SHARON: Well, don't stay out too long. Rose, did you pick up her medicine? *(Beat.)* The new one?

ROSE: I knew there was something I forgot to do.

SHARON: I need to lay down for a while. Wake me up in a couple of hours, we'll go.

(She exits.)

SHELLY: Oooh, Mudear mad at you.

ROSE: It's my duty to pick with her, keeps her alive. *(Beat.)* So what's new kiddo?

SHELLY: Nothing.

ROSE: Is that specialist fine?

SHELLY: Please. Not at all.

(A phone rings offstage.)

ROSE: Should have gone to see Dr. Frank

SHARON: *(Offstage.)* Shelly.

SHELLY: Not Dr. Frank again...

(Beat. Sharon stands in doorway with cordless phone.)

SHARON: Shelly.

SHELLY: What?!

SHARON: It's your Daddy...

SHELLY: I'll call him back later.

SHARON: *(Back to phone.)* Yes, here she is.

(Sharon holds out phone to Shelly who stomps upstairs to porch and grabs phone, Sharon exits. Rose watches Shelly.)

SHELLY: *(Bored.)* Hello. Oh, hey. Yeah, it's hot out. Un-huh. Auntie Rose says hey. *(Beat.)* Nothing, just got here. What 'bout you? Un-huh. Mudear's fine. Of course, she can't cook, too hot. *(Pause. To Rose.)* He say, "is that the same air conditioner he installed years ago?"

ROSE: Yep, same one, from the 70s.

SHELLY: *(Beat.)* Yeah, okay. Wal-Mart has a good deal but they're running out. *(Beat.)* Oh really? Under $400. Wow. Okay.

(Mudear enters with comb, brush, and hair oil. Sits in rocker.)

SHELLY: Yeah, well maybe I don't know 'bout fishing. *(Beat.)* No, I'm not scared of the worms, never been scared. *(Fake laugh.)* Okay. Yeah, tell her I said hi. Un-huh. Yeah okay. You too. *(Hangs up phone.)*

MUDEAR: Have a seat by me, baby girl.

ROSE: Yeah, Shell, rest yourself.

SHELLY: I'm okay, I've been resting all day.

(Mudear gestures for Shelly to sit down by her rocker, Shelly does. Mudear unties scarf on Shelly's hair, takes braid or pony tail loose, and gently brushes her hair. A moment passes. Sharon enters.)

SHARON: Mama, I thought you were going to stay in for a while.

ROSE: Yeah, thought you were mad at me.

MUDEAR: You just better find my hot comb.

ROSE: Thought you were gonna take a nap, Sis?

SHARON: I am, gonna make some tuna salad. I see you didn't buy any groceries this week. *(Long beat.)* Oooh, Mudear, Shelly won't let me comb her hair, not even in the hospital.

(Very long beat. Sharon and Rose watch Mudear brush Shelly's hair.)

MUDEAR: What kind of conditioner you using, baby? *(Shelly shrugs.)* Hair is little dry.

(Beat.)

SHARON: Now that was my favorite thing, Shell, sitting under mama. Getting my hair done every morning, or sometimes at night, go to bed smelling like Dippity Do. Your auntie hated it, but that brushing soothed me, put me to sleep.

ROSE: Mama didn't know what a brush was, always the comb first…

MUDEAR: How you expect me to get the kitchen?

SHARON: And if you were bad that day she used the one with the tiny teeth!

ROSE: Ma, remember when you were working two shifts, and Miss Flossy would do our hair, pack it down with grease.

MUDEAR: *(Laughing.)* Took four washings to get it out.

SHELLY: Uncle Petey and Uncle Paulie were lucky being boys, just wash up, brush your teeth and go.

ROSE: *(Laughs.)* Girl, you've seen their grade school pictures, I wouldn't want to walk around with that—that bowl cut.

(They all laugh.) (Beat.)

SHARON: It's Paulie's turn to have the barbeque right?

ROSE: Yeah.

SHARON: I was thinking about taking his turn.

ROSE: We did it last year.

SHARON: I know, but hopefully the house will be ready, it'll be fun, we can sit out on the deck. Let's make a change and go up there for Christmas...

ROSE: I was looking forward to going next month. Not when it's cold, too much snow in Michigan.

SHARON: All right then, how 'bout Thanksgiving?

MUDEAR: You know I always fix Thanksgiving dinner. I want all my children home with me.

ROSE: Fine Sharon, if you wanna do all the cooking, 'cause technically it's his turn, then Petey, Then ours.

MUDEAR: No, we got to hold it here, get to hold my first great grandbaby. Petey sent us a picture last week, Rose go and get it, You should see how fat and healthy that baby is. He's not walking yet, is he? I can't wait to see him.

(Awkward beat. Shelly gets up to exit.)

ROSE: You know Mudear don't like to travel or eat anybody else's food. She barely eats mine. And everybody says my food taste just like Mudear's. Right, Shell?

SHELLY: I guess so.

(She exits. Lights fade on women.)

SCENE 2

Lights up on Rose and Shelly sitting on the porch drinking piña coladas. Bob Marley's "Waiting in Vain" plays on the radio.

SHELLY/ROSE: *(Sing.)* I don't wanna wait in vain for your love, I don't wanna wait in vain for your love, I don't wanna, I don't wanna, I don't wanna. I don't wanna wait in vain.

(Sound of an old loud muffler. Sharon enters with groceries. She waits for someone to help her but no one does. Shelly and Rose continue to sing. Rose dances seductively.)

SHELLY: Eh, Mahn, won't you come join us?

ROSE: Pretty Oman like yourself! Won't you come join us?

SHARON: *(Irritated.)* Won't you come help me?

ROSE: Oh, sorry.

(She grabs bags. Shelly tries to help, but they shoo her away.)

SHARON: Shelly, I know you are not drinking! Aren't you taking antibiotics?

ROSE: It's virgin Sharon.

(Rose exits into house with groceries.)

SHARON: Let me smell it.

SHELLY: Dag ma!

SHARON: Rose, you were supposed to wake me up four hours ago.

ROSE: *(Offstage.)* Take it easy, Mahn.

SHELLY: Yeah, Mahn.

(Beat. Rose enters.)

SHARON: Did you check on Mudear?

ROSE: She probably sleeping under da air, Mahn.

SHELLY: *(Imitates Mudear.)* Now ya know I don't like no air!

(They laugh. Rose pours Sharon a glass.)

SHARON: Is there rum in there?

ROSE: Virgin, Mahn. Virgin.

SHARON: *(Sips.)* Rose, this is too strong.

SHELLY: Dat's 'cause you're a virgin, Mahn. Virgin.

SHARON: How long have you been out here? This heat is murder.

ROSE: Da Natives can take it.

SHARON: *(Laughs.)* Will you stop talking like that?

(She sips again, relaxes. Beat.)

SHARON: Whew, this is just what the doctor ordered. *(Beat.)* On the islands, your Auntie and I drank pitchers of this stuff, and rum punch.

SHELLY: I know, she told me you were doing the limbo with Mandingo!

SHARON: What? No, that was Rose.

ROSE: Uhn-uhn sis, I got the pictures to prove it. She brought three swimsuits and never got in the water.

SHARON: Yeah well, we must have looked ridiculous, two middle-aged women running around an island with hardly anything on. Man, you go on vacation you lose your mind.

SHELLY: And blond hair at that! Who did you think you were, Ma, Farrah Fawcett?

ROSE: Nawh. Marilyn Monroe

SHARON: I had so much rum punch I probably did.

ROSE: *(Pours another.)* Well, I'm not middle aged.

SHARON: What are you?

ROSE: Ripe! Like de watermelons hanging from de tree.

SHELLY: Watermelons grow on a vine, out of the ground, Rose.

ROSE: Oh dat's right, Mahn.

(Long beat.)

SHARON: You guys want to go by the house tomorrow? See how far they got?

(Shelly shrugs.)

SHARON: Shelly, you'll be surprised 'bout the colors I picked. Look like they came straight out of a Pottery Barn catalog.

SHELLY: Really?

ROSE: House gonna look like mud and shit.

SHARON: *(Laughs.)* You don't have to like it.

SHELLY: Earth tones, Rose.

ROSE: OOH, can't tell you nuthin'.

SHELLY: I'm glad you got out of that yellow stage, every room bright yellow.

SHARON: Sunflower. To match my sunny disposition.

SHELLY: *(Laughs.)* Whatever.

SHARON: Let's go Sunday after Church.

SHELLY: Nawh, I don't feel like seeing Sister Fannie's fat arms flapping fans.

ROSE: *(Laughs.)* You know they got air now, don't work half the time but they got it.

SHELLY: You go to church now? Hmm, I wonder who he is.

(Rose winks.)

SHARON: Hey, Rose, wanna go to Home Depot tomorrow? I need to pick out some faucets...

(Rose pours the last of the drink.)

ROSE: Well, I guess we've finished the last of this bad boy.

SHELLY: Yeah, Mahn

(Long beat.)

SHARON: How was Mudear this week?

ROSE: Fine. *(Beat.)* Well, been talking to herself a lot. *(Beat.)* And been talking 'bout Papa Joe.

SHARON: Really? She never talks about Papa Steve, Papa Henry, any of them. *(Beat.)* Have you noticed that, Shell?

SHELLY: I just got here.

ROSE: Especially Papa Joe, caught her out here earlier, just a talking and laughing, like he was sitting right next to her.

SHARON: She was laughing?

ROSE: Like a schoolgirl. *(Beat.)* Two weeks ago she wandered up the road. I asked her what she looking for? She didn't know. Then accused me of stealing whatever it was.

SHARON: She didn't mean it.

ROSE: Mama means everything she says. Even if it's crazy talk she means it.

(Beat.)

SHARON: I guess it is her turn...

SHELLY: For what?

ROSE: *(Nods.)* Runs in the family.

SHELLY: What does?

SHARON: Well, I hope you get it before me, 'cause I don't want you taking care of me.

ROSE: Why not?

(Beat.)

SHARON: You know how you are, Rose.

SHELLY: What runs in the family?

ROSE: Nawh, why don't you tell me?

SHARON: You are liable to forget 'bout me one morning, go off with some man.

ROSE: Oh, I'm just so irresponsible that I would just leave you drooling in your oatmeal.

SHARON: Don't get mad.

SHELLY: *(Yells.)* WHAT RUNS IN THE FAMILY?! *(Panicky.)* Are you talking 'bout heart disease? Sugar? What?!

SHARON: No, honey, talking 'bout senility. I don't know if you remember your great uncle Sal, we would have to go looking for him. He would wander off almost every day. Bless his heart; thought everyday was Sunday, trying to go to church. Your Aunt Sadie too, she would...

(Shelly takes Rose's drink and sips.)

ROSE: I'm tired of it, Sharon, always talking to me like I'm irresponsible. A child!

SHARON: The pharmacy was closed.

ROSE: What?

SHARON: You were supposed to pick it up last week when I went to Chicago, then the day I came back. Well, I'm back and now they are closed. You can get mad all you want but...

ROSE: So I forgot okay? You act like you're perfect.

SHELLY: Here we go.

SHARON: Not perfect. Responsible.

ROSE: We're out here having some fun and you got to rain on it. You always got to ruin a good time, Sharon.

SHARON: There is more to life than a good time. You never learned that lesson.

ROSE: And sometimes there ain't! Sometimes a good time is all you have left. I'm sorry okay. I forgot. You just need to fuss 'bout something. I'll get up first thing in the morning.

SHARON: I already took care of it.

ROSE: What?

SHARON: Drove over to Dr. Frank's brother-in-law, he filled it.

ROSE: Then what the hell are you fussing 'bout? It's too hot for all this carrying on.

(Mudear enters from house unnoticed, she leaves the door open, she has flour on her hands, face, and dress. She is sweating profusely, she wrings her hands.)

SHELLY: Amen, Mahn.

(Shelly drinks.)

SHARON: Then go sit under the air.

ROSE: You go! *(Beat.)* I'm sitting in the island sun minding my business.

MUDEAR: I'm sorry, Joe. Real sorry, ain't no more sweet potatoes out back!

SHARON: Mama? What's the matter?!

MUDEAR: Gotta find them!

SHELLY: What's that smell?

(Shelly exits into house.)

SHARON: Bring me a wet towel.

ROSE: Mama, come sit down.

(Mudear pulls away from Rose.)

MUDEAR: No! I know what I'm looking for, gotta hurry up, Joe, late for church. Pastor Wayne ain't gonna wait for us. *(She begins to cry.)*

SHELLY: *(Offstage. Yells.)* Oven is on, up to 500!

MUDEAR: It don't matter, Joe. I don't care what my poppa says. Dat don't matter to me.

(Shelly enters with towel and glass of water. Sharon tends to Mudear.)

SHARON: Responsible right? Damn it, you are the oldest! Supposed to check on her! Shshsh, Mama, it's okay. How long you been out here, Rose?

MUDEAR: Rose, can't find it. Got to find it!

ROSE: Not long!

SHARON: And you didn't bother to check on her? Shelly, quit standing there, go call Dr. Frank!

(Beat. Shelly is in shock, doesn't move.)

ROSE: I'll do it.

(Rose exits into house.)

MUDEAR: *(Weeping.)* Got to find them, you seen them? Huh? 10:00 already late. Gotta sneak down the back so Papa don't see. Wearing big clothes so nobody can tell.

Shshsh.

SHARON: Ssshhh, Mama. It's all right. Just sit with me…

MUDEAR: No—*(Weepy.)*—we gotta hurry before it's too late…

SHARON: Mama, what's my song, huh? You used to sing.

MUDEAR: I don't know nothing 'bout no song.

SHARON: Sure you do, you used to sing it to me when I was a baby.

MUDEAR: Baby? Pastor Wayne ain't gonna wait. Hurry.

(Sharon hums while tending to Mudear, who mutters to herself anxiously. Lights fade to black.)

SCENE 3

Several hours later. Lights up on Shelly sitting on porch. The radio plays. Sound cue: car. Shelly stands as Sharon enters.

SHARON: She's okay, Shelly. *(Beat.)* They just want to keep her overnight, let the house cool down. You call your daddy?

SHELLY: Left a message. Where's Auntie?

SHARON: I don't know. She left after we talked to Dr. Frank.

(Beat.)

SHELLY: It was an accident, Ma.

SHARON: You put the air conditioner on full blast?

(Shelly nods.)

SHARON: I suggest we make a palette on the floor tonight. I'll pick her up first thing in the morning. I don't know how we going to keep that woman in the house.

SHELLY: She was just trying to cheer me up, have some fun. It was my fault too.

SHARON: I'm too tired, Shelly. I'm going to take a shower.

(Sharon starts to exit.)

SHELLY: This is something else I get to look forward to. *(Beat.)* With my luck I'll probably get it in 5 years.

SHARON: Don't talk like that; you won't get it.

SHELLY: How do you know, Ma? Nobody knows anything.

(Shelly brushes past Sharon, enters the house, leaves the door open, music plays louder.)

SHARON: *(Yells.)* Shut the door. *(Beat.)* Letting the good air out.

(Sharon closes door. Beat. She sits in Mudear's rocker. Rose enters, stops when she sees Sharon. Beat. Rose sits on steps with her back to Sharon.)

ROSE: You only been here a few months, but I been staying with Mama! Taking care of her, watching her. You come in here ordering like you always do. She blames me for everything, things she forgot, or can't find. Gotta hear her putting me down, and I take it. But I am not going to take you doing it too.

(Sharon exits into house.)

ROSE: Try switching places with me for a change; try being Rose, the incompetent one for one day and I bet you can't handle it. *(Beat.)* Nawh. You'll move in your new house, teach school, and forget. But I'll be here…still taking Mama's shit—*(Beat.)*—cleaning it up.

(Rose turns around. Lights fade on Rose watching door. Blackout.)

SCENE 4

Midnight. Soundcue: Crickets. Low lights up on Rose sitting on the porch step, she lights a joint, takes a drag, closes her eyes, relaxes. After a beat, Shelly creeps toward the house. Turns on flashlight. Beat.

SHELLY: *(Whispers.)* Boo!

(Rose jumps up. Almost falls, trying to put it out.)

ROSE: You scared the hell out of me! *(Laughs.)* What are you doing out here?

SHELLY: Don't even try to put the focus on me. *(Sniffs air.)* I know that's not ma-ra-ja-wana?!

ROSE: Mind your own business...

SHELLY: Give me some!

ROSE: No.

SHELLY: I'll tell.

ROSE: Girl, I'm 49 years old, you think I'm scared? And when did you start smoking?

SHELLY: TT Rose?

ROSE: What did you call me? *(Laughs.)* You haven't called me that since you were two. *(Beat.)* Couldn't say Auntie. Just TT Rose, can I have, TT, can I go too? Following me all over the place. Getting on my last...

SHELLY: I wanted to hang out with the cool Auntie. Remember those lime green hot pants you had?

ROSE: With Black Power printed on my behind!

SHELLY: I wanted some just like that and Grandmama got mad at you 'cause you wrote it on the back of my diaper. Ooh, those pants were the talk of the town.

ROSE: I can't believe you remember that, you were just a baby. *(Beat.)* Your mama's real mad at me.

SHELLY: Don't worry, Mama don't stay mad. She'll wake up tomorrow act like nothing happened. *(Beat.)* Actually, the doctor recommended it.

ROSE: What?

SHELLY: To counter the side effects of the chemo.

ROSE: You must really think I'm a fool. You had radiation not chemo. Here.

(Hands it to her, looks back at porch door.)

SHELLY: Why are you smoking anyway? *(Takes a drag.)* You depressed?

ROSE: Just trying to take the edge off—*(Beat.)*—turning 50.

SHELLY: Oh, tomorrow's your birthday?!

ROSE: *(Looks at watch.)* Well officially, it is now here.

SHELLY: I'm sorry, I forgot. You want to go to a movie tomorrow? *(Beat.)* I mean today.

ROSE: Ain't nothing else to do in this town. I don't think that air conditioner going to last much longer, the way we been using it. Maybe we should turn it off, give it a break. *(Beat.)* Ooh! I know what I wanna do tomorrow, go to the video store and rent some...

SHELLY: No, Auntie Rose...no.

ROSE: It's my birthday.

(Beat.)

SHELLY: All right. How many?

ROSE: Six of 'em. We'll have us a Sidney Poitier marathon, start with "Blackboard Jungle," "Lilies of the Field," "A Patch of Blue," then skip ahead to "Buck and the Preacher" then jump back to "A Raisin in the Sun" then. What time the video store open?

SHELLY: 10:00. Rose, you seen those movies a hundred times.

ROSE: Add them to my fantasies and that's 1,000 times x-rated.

SHELLY: That old man? *(Passes joint.)*

ROSE: Watch it. He wasn't always old. Yeah, Sidney and me had some good times. Add "In the Heat of the Night," "They Call Me MISTER Tibbs!" Mmmm, mmmm, chocolate Sidney. You know I always did like dark skinned men.

SHELLY: Me too, I wondered where I got that from. *(Laughs.)* Mama too.

ROSE: We all do except Mudear. Say she don't even like chocolate cake. Though, tell you the truth I think she does. *(Beat.)* It's just that Papa Joe, he was real dark skinned and —*(Beat.)*—hurt her. Had that smooth black skin, didn't look like he was from here, you know?

SHELLY: I've seen a picture of him.

ROSE: Nawh, couldn't have, Mudear got rid of those pictures years ago. *(Beat.)* I remember when you were born. The first thing she did was check your ear lobes.

SHELLY: For what?

ROSE: To see if you were going to turn darker. Then she fell on her knees and prayed to the heavens, "God, please let her hair stay good."

SHELLY: *(Laughs.)* No, she didn't.

ROSE: Okay. Maybe she didn't pray, but I know she wished it. *(Beat.)* What ever happened to that boy you brought down here?

SHELLY: What boy?

ROSE: The one from college—*(Takes a drag.)*—only one you ever brought to the house. Mudear kept going on and 'bout his hair until I told her, it was a curl. He was cute though. We were so surprised when you asked Mudear if he could stay the weekend.

SHELLY: I know. Y'all thought I was gay.

ROSE: No, we didn't. *(Beat.)* So what happen to him?

SHELLY: We broke up shortly after I brought him here. *(Beat.)* Maybe I'm following the Williams women tradition.

ROSE: What's that?

SHELLY: Can't keep no man.

ROSE: Speak for yourself, I ain't dead yet.

(Long beat.)

SHELLY: Why did you come back?

ROSE: I don't know but at the time I needed something familiar…calm me down. That was the year Mama broke her hip, came down to take care of her. Stayed.

SHELLY: Why?

ROSE: I don't know, Shell, don't know why I do half the things I do.

SHELLY: Must have been a man.

(Beat.)

ROSE: *(Laughs.)* Yeah, must've been…matter of fact, you seen his picture on the wall at the high school. Made All-State Track, captain of the basketball team, even played baseball.

(Beat.)

SHELLY: Oh, you mean the Black and White photos?

ROSE: Smarty. Yeah, he come by one day, heard I was back. He still looks good. *(Beat.)* Back in high school every girl wanted him. I just daydreamed 'bout him til…thirty years later we uh. *(Laughs.)* Guess some fantasies should stay in your head.

SHELLY: You didn't date him in high school? You were one of the popular girls.

ROSE: Yep, me and your mother and Doris Witherspoon.

SHELLY: Ma?

ROSE: 'Course Doris looks real bad now. But that's what drugs will do to you. *(Relights joint, inhales.)* I've told you that, how boys were always sniffing around this house…seemed a whole lot bigger back then. I couldn't wait to get away, never thought I'd be sitting on this porch…

SHELLY: Smoking a J…

ROSE: Shoot, your mother had a cute figure, although she would never show it, too busy with her eyes in a book. The boys knew it though, seem like they had x-ray vision. Hooked your father, the minute he saw her, James' nose was wide open. Used to sit right up here and do their homework till dark, till Mudear chase him away. But he would be back the next day and the next…

SHELLY: Yeah, Daddy told me. How you tried to steal him away from her.

ROSE: What? See, people don't understand me, I wasn't flirting, that's just my way, that's the way I communicate. I'm very—*(Beat.)*—expressive. Your father needs to quit telling that lie. *(Beat.)* Why didn't you wanna talk to him?

SHELLY: I don't know, he don't talk 'bout nuthin'.

ROSE: Anything.

SHELLY: With your country bumpkin butt, I know you're not correcting me.

ROSE: I have an excuse, you don't, you went to college. He's worried 'bout you, Shell, your mother too.

SHELLY: I told them I'm all right!

ROSE: Okay. Okay. Don't blow my high. *(Passes joint.)* Change the subject.

SHELLY: Okay. *(Inhales.)* Well, I have a movie fantasy dream.

ROSE: Let's hear it.

SHELLY: Been dreaming the same dream since I was 11. I think it was after seeing "Duel in the Sun." You remember that movie with Gregory Peck and uhm Jennifer Jones . . .?

(Rose shakes her head no.)

SHELLY: You seen it. He's the bad boy who falls in love with this woman who is a half-breed. And she loves him too except she doesn't want to, 'cause she is also in love with his brother who is the good guy. Well, in my version, it's post slavery times. Out west and...

ROSE: Is that the movie where they kill each other on the mountain?

(Shelly nods.)

ROSE: Dying is your fantasy?

SHELLY: We don't die in my version, anyway I'm like her, I'm a woman no man can tame, cause I'm half-Indian.

ROSE: Every Negro wants to be half something, anything but completely Black.

SHELLY: Are you going to let me finish my story?

ROSE: I bet you were Cherokee, everybody claims that, like there is no other tribe.

SHELLY: TT Rooooossssse?

ROSE: Okay, quit whining.

SHELLY: So I'm wild see and nobody wants me 'cause I raise hell, and won't do anything a man says. So one day...

ROSE: But ya got good hair.

SHELLY: What?

ROSE: If you are half Cherokee, you more than likely got good hair, and probably are a little lighter than the rest. So a lot of them will want you, back then. *(Beat.)* Hell, even now. *(Beat.)* Finish.

SHELLY: Forget it.

ROSE: Come on now, finish your story.

SHELLY: I can't remember the rest.

ROSE: Well, all right. *(Beat.)* I'm hungry, I'm gonna get some chips, cookies, you want a sandwich?

(Shelly doesn't answer Rose starts to exit.)

ROSE: Is he fine?

SHELLY: Than Michael Jordan and Sidney Poitier...

ROSE: Oooooh. The chips can wait!

SHELLY: When he sees me, he's got to have me but I won't have anything to do with him 'cause he's bad news. Even though he has that smooth Black skin and white teeth. When he smiles, his whole face lights up, makes me want to go back to the motherland. I watch him sometimes chopping wood or when he's in the field, the sweat seems to grab hold then dance around his muscles, and he has those deep set eyes, eyes that know what I'm feeling, like he knows. *(Beat.)* All the women want him, but I'm going 'bout my business, living off the land, protecting my heart.

(Sharon stands in doorway, unnoticed.)

SHELLY: He's a gambler and bets that he can tame me, so he picks me up, throws me over his back and I beat on it like all the White women do, in all those movies. And he takes me to his house but—*(Beat.)*—we don't do anything and every time I run away he finds me and brings me back. Till one day he gets tired of chasing 'cause I'm tired of running and he just—*(Beat.)*—looks at me. *(Beat.)* And I know, I feel, I want it to happen. *(She turns away from Rose.)* And then, two months later I'm late. *(Beat.)* I'm supposed to be! *(Beat.)* He walks in, tired and sweaty from a hard day's work, but I don't mind, I like his scent, and he lays his hat down, and I'm smiling at him and he says to me—*(Beat.)*—what you smiling at baby, what? And I say I got to tell you something. I say you...we're gonna have—*(Beat.)* But I can't have that dream no more, can I? Huh? Nawh, 'cause I'm fixed now right? *(Holds her stomach.)* Can't have that dream, it don't end right.

SHARON: Shelly, honey.

SHELLY: God, Ma. Eavesdropping?

(Shelly storms in the house.)

SHARON: *(Yells.)* You out here doing drugs, Rose! You got my daughter out here smoking!

(Rose puts joint out.)

ROSE: Ain't nobody smoking.

SHARON: So I'm wrong? I didn't see you smoking with my baby? You don't have any respect for anything! Not even your own mother's house.

ROSE: Shelly's grown! You can't see that! You know what I see?

SHARON: I don't care what you do with your life! 50 years old going on 10.

ROSE: I am still 49. I was born 6: 43 in the p.m.!

SHARON: You will not ruin Shell's life too. She has an education, she's gonna make something out of her life...

ROSE: You just mad. Mad cause Shelly talks to me! Oh yeah, we been out here 'bout 2 hours just a talking and a laughing...

SHARON: Mama is not coming with me!

ROSE: What?!

SHARON: Calling me! Asking me why didn't I get ranch style. What did I need an upstairs for?

ROSE: I don't care 'bout that!

SHARON: Talking 'bout she can't make it up the stairs, looking for an excuse to move her in with me.

ROSE: Don't nobody care 'bout your stanky house. Anyway, it's your turn. I been taking care of her, the house...

SHARON: Rent free! No responsibilities. Shoot. You got it made. I see what you trying to do. Just like when we were kids, you might as well quit worrying 'bout how much room I'm going to have.

ROSE: You the one always worried 'bout the world! What everybody else is doing! Just like that time we went swimming at Dutchman's pier! Too scared to go in.

SHARON: What are you talking 'bout?

ROSE: Scared to test the water! Standing on the sidelines, watching. *(Teasing.)* Come on, Sharon, put your big toe in. Sharon on the sidelines mad! Mad cause you too scared. Mudear, all of us in the water having fun. *(Beat.)* Papa Henry told me to go get you.

SHARON: That was Papa Steve.

ROSE: Wouldn't even put your big toe in!

(Beat.)

SHARON: I couldn't swim.

ROSE: Wasn't even deep, could have put your big...

SHARON: He didn't teach me yet. Papa Steve taught me how to float...summer before... I was watching Petey and Paulie!

ROSE: Could have learned. Could have. Sitting on the sidelines too scared. Papa Henry taught all of us the dog paddle, breaststroke then...

SHARON: THAT WAS PAPA STEVE...MY DADDY! You pushed me! *(Sharon starts toward Rose.)* Then ran away. Pushed me in the back, thought I didn't see. Couldn't catch my breath just water, couldn't reach the pier, just laughter and babies crying and nobody sees Sharon—*(Beat.)*—nobody hears me and, I'M DROWNING! I'm waving my arms and I can't get over the water the laughter—*(Softly.)*—Mommy, can't you see me? And I hear my daddy whispering, say relax and breathe...Nobody ever talk 'bout him...nobody see him. Papa Steve saved me, I see him I do.

(Beat.)

ROSE: *(Gently.)* Sharon…What are you talking 'bout? *(Beat.)* I don't remember pushing… If I did, I'm sorry. We were just kids…Papa Henry was with us. Papa Steve…your daddy, died summer before.

(Beat.)

SHARON: *(Calmly.)* I ought to know when my…Maybe you're right. Nobody ever talked 'bout it. She don't. Summer before…summer after, don't matter. By Spring had us a new Papa.

(Lights fade on Rose and Sharon.)

END OF ACT I

ACT II

SCENE 1

Next morning, early, lights up on Mudear seated on porch, sipping coffee.

SHARON: *(Offstage.)* Mama?

MUDEAR: Hmmm?

(Sharon enters.)

SHARON: Oh, you're out here. 11:30 and it's already 90 degrees. Mama, that air conditioner making a lot of funny noises, I think we need to look around for another one. Guess I'll look today. *(Beat.)* Don't stay out too long, we just got you home. Heard you gave those nurses hell. *(Beat.)* Birthday girl still asleep?

MUDEAR: Mmm hmm.

SHARON: I was thinking of surprising Rose, since it's too hot for you to bake, maybe some home made ice cream. Is the maker still up there in the attic?

(Mudear nods.)

SHARON: Throw some fish on the grill, salad, something light. I noticed how big Rose's behind is getting. I know I got my nerve, just seem like you wake up one day every part of your body headed for a vacation-down south. *(Beat.)* Men don't have it as bad as we do. My weight went up, down, fat left, came back, left again only to return stronger than ever. James still looks the same after 20 years, except for a little stomach. *(Beat.)* Come asking me what ever happened to that little dress you used to wear, I say what dress? He was talking 'bout the one I wore to the library, the day he met me! How come I never wear it? *(Laughs. Beat.)* It's funny, I look at those old pictures. And I don't know who that young girl is. *(Beat.)* Who is that hiding behind that big ole man? *(Beat.)* I know him though…His half smile…like a smirk, like he knows the joke and can't wait to tell it. Those fearless laughing eyes. *(Beat.)* Arm round me protecting. But I don't know who she is. Shy-girlie in the picture, the one at the beach. Look like I was trying to say something or catch my breath. *(Beat.)* James walks in a room and takes all the air out. Never thought I would get tired of that.

(Mudear looks at her.)

SHARON: What? Mama, I don't want him back! I don't. I like room to breathe. *(Beat.)* Yeah, something light, some salad.

MUDEAR: Ham me munna mose maedas ba ber.

SHARON: What?!

MUDEAR: Mose maedas. *(Beat.)* Mose maedas!

SHARON: Mama, what's the matter? You can't talk? *(Exits quickly.)* Rose! Rose! Mama's sick!

(The following happens very quickly: Sharon runs in house to get cordless phone. Reenters. Dials. Rose enters, runs over to Mudear.)

ROSE: Mama, look at me! Look at me!

MUDEAR: Met mo of me.

SHARON: Hello, I need an ambulance at 241- Yes, hello, Cheryl Lynn, it's Mama, she's sick. *(To herself.)* Oh my God, I hope she didn't have a stroke.

(Sharon hangs up phone, runs over to Mudear.)

MUDEAR: Met...mo...of...me!

ROSE: Mama. *(Beat.)* Put your teeth in. Sharon cancel the ambulance!

(Sharon hits redial on the phone.)

SHARON: Hello, Cheryl Lynn, false alarm. *(Beat.)* Huh? No, she's fine. Procedure? *(Beat.)* You still got to send it? But she's fine. It was a mistake. Okay? *(Beat.)* Thank you. Yes, I'll see you on Sunday.

(Sharon hangs up phone. Mudear reaches in her pocket to put teeth in.)

ROSE: *(Laughs.)* Lord have mercy, you gonna kill us both, Mudear. Give us a heart attack.

SHARON: Why didn't you tell me you didn't have your teeth in?

MUDEAR: You wouldn't let me! Running around like a chicken with his head cut off.

SHARON: What were you trying to say?

MUDEAR: I said hand me one of those tomatoes back there! You were talking 'bout making a salad.

SHARON: Well, I had my laugh today. Guess I'll go to the store.

ROSE: Don't forget ice for the ice cream. See if they got some decent peaches at the store, Sis?

SHARON: You heard? It was supposed to be a surprise. Shelly up?

ROSE: She's gone. You didn't hear her as loud as that muffler is? Left out early.

SHARON: She didn't ask me if she could take it.

(Beat.)

MUDEAR: How is she doing?

(Beat.)

ROSE: She's fine, right, Sharon? Doctors said they got it all, radiation treatments were just a precaution.

(Long beat.)

SHARON: I had to make her go. She missed her last appointment, and was going to skip this one, if I hadn't escorted her. I can't talk to her, everything I say don't soothe her, just make her mad. I haven't seen her cry, she won't. It's like she blames me.

ROSE: She's lashing out, Sis.

MUDEAR: Sharon, it's not your fault.

SHARON: No? I could have taught her something. I don't know, to take better care of herself. Taught her everything else, stupid…shit that wasn't important, I preplan everything, making sure her clothes matched, knew what college she was going to before she was even born. Trunk full of toys, receiving blankets for my future grand-babies, names already picked out.

(Beat.)

MUDEAR: It's all right, Sharon…

SHARON: Put her on the same floor as the maternity ward, nurse told me she was supposed to be on the fifth floor, with post-op. But this surgeon wanted his patients on the floor closest to his office. *(Beat.)* When they wheeled her in the room, the nurses snatched the pink and blue pictures of Winnie the Pooh down. *(Beat.)* Shelly would visit those babies every day; just stare at them through glass. *(Beat.)* Every day…like she needed them to breathe.

(Beat.)

MUDEAR: Well…I was happy when they took mine, not happy, but I tried not to dwell on it. I had my children. It was a relief. Doctor didn't sew me up right though, told him I had the keloid, but the scar gone down some. *(Beat.)* You young people got a lot more to face in life. It could be worse.

ROSE: I can't believe you calling me young.

MUDEAR: You need to act your age.

ROSE: Why? Acting my age never got me anywhere…

SHARON: It is worse, Mama. It's cancer! *(Beat.)* Something you can only whisper 'bout. It's worse than fibroids. And I tried to be like you…strong…but my way, I talked 'bout it, faced it with her, tried to educate, bought every book on the subject.

(Beat. Rose crosses to comfort Sharon on swing.)

SHARON: I went over the anatomy chart, pointing out every organ and, and it's so small, you know? I couldn't believe it. *(Breaking down.)* The uterus. Cervix. How could removing cause so much pain? *(Beat.)* And I learned all I could 'bout those little, tiny, horrible cells, you think of it as some big monster, but they're just weak, mal-formed…insignificant… pathetic…

MUDEAR: Stop it, Sharon. We will do whatever it takes, if we all got to go with her next time then that's what we'll do. *(Beat.)* I'm really sorry it happen to her so young. Hopefully, she will adopt. *(Beat.)* It looks like we all had it done.

(Long beat.)

ROSE: *(Trying to cheer her up.)* Sharon, remember when I had mine? After surgery they won't release you until you're able to go to the bathroom.

(Low ambulance siren.)

MUDEAR: What so funny 'bout that?

ROSE: You remember, Sharon, when you were helping me wash up, and the two little Filipino nurses kept asking me "Did I go?" "Did I, did I go yet?"

SHARON: Yeah, over and over again. *(Laughs.)* Then you broke wind!

(Everyone laughs.)

ROSE: And they started clapping and cheering, and we laughed so hard, I thought my stitches were going to burst. *(Beat.)* I never wanted to have any children. Nope. I want to be the only baby.

MUDEAR: That's 'cause you're spoiled rotten and selfish.

ROSE: I love you too, Mudear. You're the one that spoiled me.

(Siren is louder.)

SHARON: That damn Cheryl Lynn, I told her to cancel it. They better not charge us.

ROSE: I bet Leon's driving, I'll go talk to him.

MUDEAR: *(Yells.)* He's married, Rose!

ROSE: *(Yells.)* What?

SHARON: *(Yells.)* Got married last week.

ROSE: Shit. I mean shoot. *(Looks down the road.)* Ooh, they sent a fire truck too.

(Rose exits. Ambulance/fire truck lights flicker. After a few beats, an old loud muffler. Shelly rushes in, with bag of videos.)

SHELLY: What's the matter?

MUDEAR: Nothing had a false alarm. Where you been?

SHARON: And who told you to take my car? You put gas in it?

SHELLY: I was over at Miss Dee's place.

SHARON: What you doing over there?

SHELLY: You know, they changed the name of the shop. Her daughter Verlena took over since Miss Dee has carpal tunnel real bad.

MUDEAR: What?

SHARON: It's like arthritis in the hands.

MUDEAR: Well, they should call it that. I know how that feels. What they change it to "Verlena's"?

SHELLY: Nawh. "Happy to be Nappy."

SHARON: Really?

MUDEAR: That child was never right in the head. I always knew that, didn't want you running with her, but you was always up under her crowd.

SHELLY: Verlena's okay. I knew enough not to do everything she did, but girl could hook up some hair.

SHARON: Yeah, her whole family has that gift. So now it's a natural hair shop. I guess you got to change with the times.

SHELLY: I'm glad you agree, Ma.

MUDEAR: Change with the times? Natural hair ain't nothing new, wore our hair like that till Madam CJ Walker came out with the pressing comb...

SHARON: I know you jumped for joy when that happened, Mudear.

SHELLY: With your hair natural, you don't ever have to worry 'bout it going back.

MUDEAR: You know she was the first female millionaire in this country. 'Course, I think she went too far with the bleaching cream.

(Rose enters swinging a small piece of paper in her hand.)

ROSE: *(Sings.)* "I shot the sheriff, but I didn't shoot the deputy." Guess what I got here?

MUDEAR: Leon's phone number, after we told you he was married.

ROSE: No, Mother dear. Give me more credit than that. Anthony Sans was driving with him, you know him Sharon, guy that was always so shy in high school, I told him it was my birthday, and so he's taking me out tonight. Leon had the nerve to look jealous, staring at me. Hell, he better go home and stare at his wife. *(Beat.)* Where should I tell him I wanna go?

SHARON: I thought we were going to grill, and have some home-made ice cream.

ROSE: Oh.

SHELLY: Have a Sidney Poitier marathon. I got all the ones you wanted plus "To Sir with Love."

(Beat.)

ROSE: We can do that tomorrow, right? I mean, you know me, I celebrate all weekend. I need to get inside and see what I can fit.

SHARON: Sure, Rose. *(Beat.)* We'll do it tomorrow. I'm still going to the store. Shell, come with me.

SHELLY: I don't feel like sitting in that hot old car again.

ROSE: You wanna paint my toes?

SHELLY: Uh. Can't, gotta go with Ma.

(Rose exits into house.)

MUDEAR: Nobody asked me if I wanted to go.

ROSE: *(Offstage.)* Why is it so hot in here? Somebody turn the air off? *(Beat.)* Oh no.

(Rose enters.)

ROSE: Y'all ready for a funeral?

SHARON: Dead?

ROSE: Yep. *(To Shelly.)* Didn't James say Wal-Mart got them under $400, but they're going fast?

SHARON: C'mon, Shell.

MUDEAR: Maybe you should call first.

SHARON: Good thinking, Ma.

(She exits into house. Shelly pulls her bandana off. Her hair is cut off to a short hair style, Afro or cornrows or dreadlocks, depending on texture of hair. She stands proudly, waiting.)

ROSE: Oh my God. What did you do?

MUDEAR: *(Squints.)* She done lost her mind too. Sharon! Come look at what your daughter did.

(Sharon rushes in with phone in hand. Beat.)

SHELLY: Well, come on with it. The comments, throw the heat I can take it. I know you got something to say. Ma? Mudear?

MUDEAR: *(Eyes closed, rocks.)* Lord have mercy, lord have mercy.

SHELLY: Rose? I know you do. *(Beat.)* Nothing? Say it now or forever hold your peace. Nobody wants to say anything. Huh? Well, I do. I'm grown, so I can do with it what I want. Hear? It's my head, and I wanted a change and it's not like I did it spur of the moment. Been thinking 'bout it a long time. Wanted a change to match me. 'Cause I'm different. *(Beat.)* I was going to have it done in Chicago, had the appointment and everything. But I had to come down here, right, Ma? Had to be here, even though I didn't want to go. Wanted to stay in my place. Alone. In my apartment.

SHARON: Apartment, you hadn't cleaned in weeks, sleeping in your day clothes!

SHELLY: It was mine. It was my choice not to clean it. *(Beat. Brightly.)* So anyway I got up early this morning and had this feeling like I had to get out, just felt trapped, couldn't breathe, had to feel free? You felt like that before right, Rose?

ROSE: Don't be putting me in it.

MUDEAR: All that hair—*(Beat.)*—that beautiful hair.

SHELLY: Yep, Grandma, all that hair don't mean nuthin'. It's just something that grows out of your head. Just like a weed out the ground. Don't worry I kept it. Didn't want the Dee's putting a curse on it. I got it right here. *(Takes pony tail out of bag, gestures to Sharon.)* You want to hold on to it, Ma?

SHARON: Get out of my face, Shelly.

SHELLY: Guess not.

SHARON: What is wrong with you? You did this to get back at me? To hurt me?

SHELLY: This has nothing to do with you. It's 'bout me, Ma! Me! *(Beat.)* So anyway I went for a drive, sorry I took the car without asking. I rode all over town, back to high school. Sat in the driver's education range and went in circles fast as I could go. Drove over to the Dairy Queen, it was closed. And then I went over to the bad side of town, where you told me to stay away from. I drove past "Happy to be Nappy," and Verlena was sitting outside on the stoop braiding hair. Air conditioner broke down too. Guess whose hair it was? *(Beat.)* Guess.

SHARON: Just tell us, Shelly!

SHELLY: Okay, Mother Dear. Poochie Walker. *(Beat.)* You know Poochie. Ev'rybody know Poochie. Girl must have had six babies, and nine abortions. Sitting on the stoop. And Poochie's holding her newest contribution, a little boy. Must be 'bout 6 weeks old. She asks me if I want to hold him, I shake my head no. I ain't never been much on babies that young. She say he might be a little stinky 'cause she forgot the diapers again, but could I please hold him for a few minutes, 'cause her arm was falling asleep and so I—*(Beat.)*—did. *(Beat.)* Fed him too. He smiled at me and seemed to…Poochie say, I'll be damn, I been trying to get that Negro to smile at me, first times he see you, you got him smiling. Should have known he'd go for somebody pretty with good hair. *(Beat.)* I told Verlena cut it off.

ROSE: And that wasn't spur of the moment?

SHELLY: Nawh, it wasn't, Rose. Oh, wait, that's not right, it was after. *(Beat.)* After Poochie said sorry to hear. Does that mean you can't have any? What 'bout the sex, can you still enjoy that? Here some heifer opens her legs for at least six babies, three of 'em taken away from her and she asking me! Asking how come I can't have one. *(Beat.)* And all I'm thinking is: How people know before I can get used to knowing myself.

(Beat. Phone rings. Nobody answers.)

SHELLY: How my business get in the street? Huh, Ma? How it get there?

(Lights fade on Shelly staring at Sharon as phone continues to ring. Blackout.)

SCENE 2

Lights up, several minutes later. Shelly is sitting on porch drinking a glass of lemonade. Sharon talks on the cordless phone.

SHARON: Well, try to hold it for me. I'll be there in 15 minutes. Can't you hide it in the back? All right, I'll take my chances, be there in…I'm leaving right now. *(Clicks over.)* Oh, hey, James. Can't talk long, gotta pick up the air conditioner—*(Beat.)*—they got one more left. *(Beat.)* Yeah, I'm still the same, I always wait to the last minute. Here's Shelly.

(Shelly shakes her head no. Beat.)

SHARON: She'll call you back, she's going with me to pick it up.

(Shelly shakes her head no.)

SHARON: Well, okay. Gotta go. *(Hangs up.)*

SHELLY: Ma, I don't feel well, can't Rose go with you?

SHARON: *(Stares at Shelly. Yells.)* Rose!

ROSE: *(Offstage. Yells.)* Huh?

SHARON: *(Yells.)* Go with me to pick up the air conditioner!

ROSE: *(Offstage. Yells.)* Can't, my nails are wet.

SHARON: Well, call your dad back, he wants to take you fishing tomorrow. *(Beat.)* Do you hear me, Shelly?

SHELLY: Yes.

SHARON: You mad at him too, huh? What did he do?

SHELLY: Nuthin'.

SHARON: Act like an adult and tell me what did the man do to you?

SHELLY: He doesn't do anything, he wasn't even there at the hospital when…

SHARON: What are you talking 'bout? He was there. He drove us to the hospital.

SHELLY: Yeah, but then he left, run an errand or something. Now he wants to hang out.

SHARON: You think you know everything, Shell. But you don't.

SHELLY: I know what I saw.

SHARON: He went to the chapel.

SHELLY: Yeah, right.

SHARON: He just couldn't watch his baby being wheeled in there helpless. But he was in the waiting room the whole time. *(Beat.)* Do you know what it did to him? Huh? Knowing that there was nothing he could do to make it better. That you had to suffer, and…I know that man, lived with him 20 years, and he was scared, and praying for his little girl to make it.

SHELLY: He don't say nothing, just how ya doing kiddo, talking 'bout the Bulls, fishing, Mama, I don't care 'bout!

SHARON: He's still trying, trying to connect to you. *(Shelly turns away.)* Look at me. I can't see you like you are now, grown up-all I see is that my little girl is hurting and scared. *(Beat.)* But it stops now, you hear me? The attitude, the disrespect stops. You want to be a child and yell and scream in your room then that's fine, but you will not disrespect me. Do you hear me?

SHELLY: Yes.

(Beat.)

SHARON: Yes, what?

SHELLY: Yes, ma'am.

(Sharon exits.)

SHELLY: Ma, I…

(Long beat. Shelly picks up the phone, dials, and then hangs up. She starts to cry but stops herself. Rose enters with dresses, holds them up.)

ROSE: This is wearing me out. How come we can't do this in my room?

(Beat.)

SHELLY: It's hotter in the house than out here. *(Looks at dress.)* Too slutty. You want to look like an innocent slut, like it's not really in your nature.

ROSE: You're right. Don't want to give the wrong impression. What 'bout this one?

SHELLY: It's okay.

(Beat.)

SHELLY: Rose. *(Beat.)* You think I'll ever get married?

ROSE: Sure. Well.

SHELLY: What?

ROSE: Maybe after you grow some hair back.

SHELLY: *(Laughs.)* Shut up.

ROSE: Bald head, bald head. *(Laughs.)* You know I was gonna get you. *(Beat.)* I guess you can be mad at me. *(Beat.)* When I heard 'bout...you know the cancer, I was so worried I called my girlfriend Teresa who's a nurse at the hospital...

SHELLY: And a member of our church.

ROSE: I guess she told. Sorry, Shelly.

SHELLY: Okay. *(Beat.)* How come you never got married, Rose?

ROSE: I don't know. Guess 'cause—nobody asked.

(Shelly tries to speak.)

ROSE: I was popular 'cause of these—*(Points to breasts.)*—like that's all there is. *(Beat.)* Like there's nothing inside me.

SHELLY: Somebody must have asked...

ROSE: I said nobody. You think I had so many I can't remember? Don't answer that. *(Beat.)* With me, most of it's just talk. Talk-noise to fill up the quiet. *(Beat.)* Quiet always make me think too much. Nobody asked, and tell you the truth back then, I didn't want it. When I came up, women, we were just getting our freedom. The pill, legalized abortion, didn't have to worry 'bout walking round with the big belly, while he go on his merry way. Bring shame to the house, hell, the whole neighborhood or worse have to marry someone you don't love.

SHELLY: Like my mama.

ROSE: No, that's not true. James and Sharon loved each other back then. I do know that. They were very much in love, but they were young too. *(Beat.)* Sometimes people just fall out of love. Sometimes that happens. But at least they had that, had them some good years together. Plus they're still friends. *(Beat.)* Anyway, I came up when feeling free was the only way to be.

SHELLY: Sounds like a song.

ROSE: I'm sure it is.

(Beat.)

SHELLY: Somebody asked.

ROSE: You going to call me a liar, you know you ain't too old to whip...

SHELLY: Shelton Lee. *(Beat.)* Didn't he?

ROSE: *(Softly.)* Yes.

SHELLY: I was 'bout twelve, and waiting for you to come home from your date, I think y'all went to the fair over by Dutchman's pier. And he promised to win me one of them stuffed animals, can't remember which one I wanted.

ROSE: A zebra.

SHELLY: Yeah, I was collecting them. I was supposed be in bed, but I hid over there. *(Points.)* He asked you and you said no. Plain as day, didn't blink an eye…just no. And he cried, I never seen a man cry before, he didn't say nothing, just closed that little ring box, I could see his tears in the moonlight and…

ROSE: Shut up, Shell.

SHELLY: No, wait. And I thought to myself that's love. Somebody cry over me, somebody want me so bad that he…

(Rose starts in the house, turns around suddenly.)

ROSE: You don't care do you, Shell, who you hurt? Or you just don't think. Finish the story, Shelly. What happened to him?

(Beat.)

SHELLY: I don't remember.

ROSE: Drowned. The next day, so it don't count, see!

(She exits, slams door. Long beat. Mudear enters from garden with a tomato.)

MUDEAR: Who dat slamming doors?

SHELLY: Rose.

MUDEAR: Your mama get back with the air conditioner?

SHELLY: No.

MUDEAR: You should have gone with her. *(Long beat.)* Think it's gonna rain?

(Shelly shrugs.)

MUDEAR: I do. Can feel it in my bones. *(Beat.)* You know I would never do anything to hurt you, right?

SHELLY: What? You told somebody too?

MUDEAR: When we got the news 'bout the second opinion being the same as the first, Charlene was standing there, I told her mom to send her over for some tomatoes out in the garden. She was in the kitchen rinsing them off, when we got the call.

SHELLY: Guess it don't matter, Grand.

MUDEAR: Turn around, let me look at that head.

(Shelly turns around.)

MUDEAR: I ain't gonna lie to you, I don't like it.

SHELLY: I know.

MUDEAR: But I understand it.

(Beat.)

SHELLY: *(Softly.)* You do?

MUDEAR: Sometimes, we hurt so bad, we have to do something, change the outside, make us feel better. You ain't the only one. You remember when your mom dyed her hair blond? *(Shelly nods.)* That was right after the divorce. Dye or cut our hair— *(Beat.)*—and shopping, women are good for that. Watch Rose, every time she talks 'bout losing weight, she ends up with a new hair do or outfit. It's quicker. After the baby died, I...

(Beat.)

SHELLY: What did you do?

MUDEAR: Well, I didn't have that luxury, shopping or doing something to my hair. Couldn't afford it. After the baby died I just stopped taking care of myself and I was a good looking woman back then, had them big legs. *(Laughs.)* I didn't have no energy, couldn't get out of bed. For a while couldn't budge, then all of a sudden, I had to do something! Move. So I started cooking, making sweet potato pies, 'cause that was his favorite. I made one every day like if he smelled it, might make him come back. *(Beat.)* I must have looked like a crazy woman, baking all those pies in the summertime, sitting them outside the window.

(Beat.)

SHELLY: I've never been in love. Did you love him?

(Beat.)

MUDEAR: He was my first. Loved to watch him work, that man was one hard worker. Had them big strong arms, made you feel safe, when he held you. And his skin was smooth, and Black, like he was from Africa, or the islands.

SHELLY: Ooh, Grandma, listen to you talk, all fast, sound like Auntie Rose.

MUDEAR: Where do you think she got it from?

SHELLY: I'm surprised to hear you talk like that. Rose says you don't even like chocolate cake!

(Long beat.)

MUDEAR: *(Softly.)* That ain't me talking, that's my daddy. Cursed the day I married Joe. Said he was bad luck! Black was. I know I say those things, but that ain't me, that's the way I was raised, but when I met Joe, I stopped listening to my daddy's words—I listened to those arms wrapped around me. *(Beat.)* But—*(Beat.)*—when little Scottie died in my arms, it was like my daddy's words come back in my head. *(Beat.)* I blamed Joe, he wasn't working and…it was like poison in me. I told him he killed him.

(Rose enters quietly.)

SHELLY: You didn't mean it.

MUDEAR: Nawh, I didn't was out of my head with fever. But it didn't matter I said it, even after my fever broke, couldn't stop the words…wouldn't let him near me. Wanted him to hurt like I hurt inside. I wouldn't let him touch him, not once. Not even to say good-bye to his son. Held that baby, even when he stiffened up, held on. He was cold, tried to warm him up. Tried to. My milk came down. Still. Like my body didn't know that I was no use to him. Couldn't be a mother to my other baby. Rose crawling on the floor hungry. Ms. Flossy come by took her. Took care of her until my mind came back. *(Beat.)* Worse than me saying it, was the look in his eyes, told me he believed it. Believed all those terrible words Black folks say to each other. He was always so proud, but when he heard me, the little gal who always looked up to him, say—*(Beat. She has a hard time saying it.)*—Git!

ROSE: *(Whispers.)* Git yo Black ass way from here, Git

(Mudear looks at Rose.)

MUDEAR: *(To herself.)* Keep your dirty Black hands off my baby. *(Beat.)* He left, and I baked sweet potato pies trying to bring him back home to me. *(Beat.)* And my business was in the street, folks talked 'bout me thought I had lost my mind.

(Beat.)

ROSE: He came back once. He tipped his hat. Didn't come in the gate, just waited—*(Beat.)* He looked good, had on some kind of uniform.

MUDEAR: *(To Rose.)* Yes, he's a porter now. *(Beat.)* By that time I was with Papa Steve, had my babies to feed. You have to understand, had to feed my babies. *(Beat.)* Joe saw—*(Beat.)*—he knew. Tipped his hat. *(Beat.)* He understood—*(Beat.)*—sometimes you have to have a baby—*Beat.)*—in order to feed the ones you got. *(Long beat.)* Didn't have no birth control then. No. *(Beat.)* Rose running around, I'm holding Sharon. And your Uncle Pete was due in a few months. Can't move my feet, want to run to 'em, but I was holding Sharon, and seem like Rose, you knew, grabbed me around my waist held on tight. *(Beat.)* He tipped his hat. Then—*(Smiles.)*—he went on his way.

SHELLY: You ever see him again?

(Beat.)

MUDEAR: Sometimes I find myself, looking up the road, thinking I'm gonna see him.

SHELLY: This is the most you ever talked 'bout him.

MUDEAR: I know. Seem like your sadness bring up mine. We're connected like that, daughter. *(Beat.)* Now cutting off your hair. You feel better, Shell?

SHELLY: Yes, I do.

(Beat.)

MUDEAR: Come closer.

(Beat.)

SHELLY: Why, Grandma?

MUDEAR: I got to tell you something.

(Shelly walks over to Mudear. Mudear stands behind her.)

MUDEAR: It's okay, Shelly, now do as I say, okay?

(Mudear gently massages Shelly's back as if she is trying to coax the anger, pain, sadness out.)

MUDEAR: Breathe, Shelly. Breathe. Let it out

SHELLY: *(Anxiously.)* I'm all right.

MUDEAR: Breathe, Shelly. Breathe. Let it out. You don't have to be brave right now 'cause you with me. You with Grandmama. Remember when you used to come here every summer when you were little? Seem like you were always falling and skinning your knee. Grandmama would have to beat up the stairs, or the wall for hurting my baby. Don't worry 'bout being strong, you are already that. *(Beat.)* Now I want you to say whatever you got to say. Be mad at whoever, can you do that for me?

(Shelly shakes her head no.)

MUDEAR: Sure, you can. I want you to do that, cry whatever you need to do. Get it out cause it's like poison, baby, it's eating away at you. You want me to start? I will, Grandma will say it! That damn cancer hurt my baby!

(Rose walks over to Shelly.)

ROSE: You mad, Shell? Let it out. I'm not going to let it hurt no more, hear? You want to scream, Shell? Go ahead, come on, scream.

(Shelly screams.)

ROSE: Louder, Shell! Let it know!

(Rose and Mudear continue to hold Shelly. Shelly tries to run, but they catch her and continue to hold her. Sound cue: car pulls up.)

MUDEAR: Does it hurt, Shell?

SHELLY: This hurts me, God help me, this hurts me...please, I can't breathe.

ROSE: Yes, you can, let it out baby.

(Rose and Mudear continue holding Shelly. Sharon enters.)

SHARON: Let her go!

ROSE: Let it go, Shelly, come on, let it go!

SHARON: Let her go!

SHELLY: *(Screams.)* Mommy, help me, please!

(Shelly runs to Sharon, collapses in her arms. Her final release affects all of the women. Lights fade to blackout.)

SCENE 3

> *Radio plays soothing R&B music. Lights up on Mudear, Shelly, and Sharon, 3 hours later. Shelly's head is resting in Sharon's lap.*

RADIO: *(Voice-over male.)* Awh, yeah, finally a break, a little coolness, light air, it may not be over but for now, this moment, let's appreciate the breeze.

(Long beat as mellow instrumental music plays softly under. Rose, dressed to kill, enters with ice cream. Dishes it out.)

ROSE: So he says since I didn't tell him where I wanted to go I have to leave it up to him. So I'm nervous, I can't believe I'm nervous, and so I'm talking, just babbling 'bout how we planned to have a Sidney Poitier marathon. And he starts imitating him in "Raisin in the Sun." I mean had it down pat "Williiiieeeee Wiiiillieeee, that money was my father's blood." I'm laughing so hard and I'm starting to get over the fact that he's short.

SHELLY: How short?

SHARON: He's short, not Rose's usual type.

ROSE: But then I noticed he ain't driving toward downtown, and I'm thinking I know he ain't taken me to the Chicken Shack. But I try to play it off like I don't notice and he steady talking like Sidney!

MUDEAR: Gotta good deal at the Chicken Shack.

ROSE: Anyway, he drives up along Dutchman's pier, and I'm thinking this cheap MF. The Fisherman's cove been closed down for months, if he thinks he's gonna pretend like he...and then I'm mad. I'm 'bout to tell him to take me home.

SHARON: Awwh, that's too bad, Rose. He was always nice in high school.

SHELLY: Did you have his nose open too, like Daddy's?

SHARON: What? *(Laughs.)*

ROSE: Hold on, let me finish. So he parks the car and says to me. I always wanted to do this—*(Beat.)*—have a picnic with you. *(Beat.)* Then he pulls out this blanket and champagne, caviar, and cheese, and fruit. Hands me a rose, and says happy birthday, 'bout time for me to be treated like the beautiful flower I am. And I know it's corny but I just let loose, I started crying right there and at first he thinks I don't like it and he starts apologizing, and you know what I noticed?

MUDEAR/SHARON/SHELLY: What?!

ROSE: He was looking directly in my eyes the whole time. *(Beat.)* The whole time. And then after we ate, we didn't say anything, he's still shy and quiet, we just sat there and looked at the stars. Listened to the crickets.

(Beat.)

SHARON: You going to see him again, Rose?

ROSE: Saturday, he wants to know if y'all want to go to the dunes.

SHELLY: Yeah!

MUDEAR: Me too?

ROSE: Of course, Mommy!

(Beat.)

MUDEAR: Hey, Shelly. Next time let's make chocolate ice cream!

SHARON: Mom?

MUDEAR: And some hot fudge. We got any in the icebox?

ROSE: I want to see this.

(Shelly hands Mudear Hershey's syrup.)

MUDEAR: This ain't the real thing. I want the real thing!

SHELLY: I know that's right, Grandma!

ROSE: Let's start my marathon today.

SHARON: House should be nice and cool by now.

ROSE: Let's get started.

(They start to exit. Mudear picks up her Bible, and pulls out a picture of Joe.)

MUDEAR: Shoot, Sidney Poitier ain't got nothing on Joe.

SHARON: *(Looks at picture.)* I don't think I ever seen this one.

ROSE: Mama, I looked everywhere for that picture. Thought you threw it out.

MUDEAR: If you read the Bible sometimes, you might have found it.

ROSE: He sure was handsome.

MUDEAR: Joe is fine.

SHARON: What 'bout my daddy? *(Beat.)* My daddy was handsome.

MUDEAR: No…he wasn't. He was a good man, though. You should be glad you look like me, daughter.

ROSE: She got his feet, though.

(Sharon and Rose begin to clear dishes.)

SHARON: SHUT UP! *(Laughs.)*

(Sharon and Rose exit into house with dishes.)

MUDEAR: You going fishing with your daddy?

SHELLY: Yep. Talking 'bout I'm scared of the worms. *(Laughs.)* Ain't never been scared. Don't like pulling the hook out the fish, though.

MUDEAR: Catch me a big ole catfish, and I'll fry it up for you.

SHELLY: Yuck, Grandma.

MUDEAR: Since when you don't like catfish?

SHELLY: Not out of that water!

MUDEAR: *(Laughs.)* I guess nowadays, fishing is good for passing the time, enjoying each other, and the quiet. *(Long beat.)* Now I'm gonna have good days and bad. But I hope I have more of the good. I hope I do.

SHELLY: Me too.

(Rose and Sharon enter.)

SHARON: No, Rose. Come on in y'all.

ROSE: Oh, come on, Sis, it's not hot in the house anymore.

SHARON: I'm not your personal hairdresser. Better make an appointment with Happy to—well somebody else.

SHELLY: What she want, a touch up? *(Laughs.)* Hey Rose, you should cut it all off like me, be free, Mahn.

(They all start into house.)

MUDEAR: You don't want to do that, daughter.

ROSE: I thought 'bout doing that before, but I don't have the right shaped head.

SHARON: What are you talking about?

MUDEAR: She gotta hook back there.

ROSE: See. Mama knows.

MUDEAR: When you was a baby, colored doctor say he ain't never seen anything like it.

ROSE: Got it from you.

(Lights fade on all exiting into house laughing.)

END OF PLAY

Taking Care
by Mia McCullough

For Ida and Israel

ORIGINALLY PRODUCED by Steppenwolf Theatre Company

Founded in 1976
758 W. North Ave., 4th floor, Chicago, IL 60610
www.steppenwolf.org

Martha Lavey, Artistic Director
David Hawkanson, Executive Director

Committed to the principle of ensemble performance through the collaboration of a company of actors, directors and playwrights, Steppenwolf Theatre Company's mission is to advance the vitality and diversity of American theatre by nurturing artists, encouraging repeatable creative relationships and contributing new works to the national canon. Long known for its productions of seminal contemporary American plays like *True West, Balm in Gilead* and *Of Mice and Men*, in 1995 Steppenwolf instituted the New Plays Initiative, a new play development program that today allows Steppenwolf to commission and develop new works by local and nationally-recognized writers. The NPI has developed many plays that have been given their world premieres by Steppenwolf, including the Pulitzer Prize finalist *Man from Nebraska* by Tracy Letts and works by Stephen Jeffreys, Joel Drake Johnson, Bruce Norris, Pulitzer finalist Alexandra Gersten-Vassilaros, Austin Pendleton, Charles Mee and many more. In 1985, Steppenwolf Theatre Company was awarded the Tony Award for Outstanding Regional Theatre, and received the 1998 National Medal of Arts from President Clinton.

*   *   *

I first became aware of Mia's work over ten years ago, when a small storefront theatre I headed produced an early play of hers as a late-night. Over the years, we stayed in contact, and I continued to read her work. *Taking Care* seemed an ideal match for our Garage space, a venue devoted to the cultivation of new voices, and for Steppenwolf's aesthetic. Mia's work is consistently notable for the complexity and intense inner life with which she imbues her characters. In *Taking Care*, she offers a subtle and heartbreakingly empathetic view into the shifting mother/son relationship between Ma and Benny as each is called to care for the other. In the painstaking, and at times painful, rendering of the daily minutiae of their lives, Mia explores the essence of familial devotion in the face of the inexorable passing of time.

Edward Sobel,
Director of New Play Development, Steppenwolf Theatre Company

BIOGRAPHY

Mia McCullough's recent productions include  *Since Africa* at Chicago Dramatists, *Echoes of Another Man* at Actors Express (Atlanta), *Cyber Serenade* and *Suicide* at Stage Left Theatre (Chicago), and *Chagrin Falls* at Cincinnati Shakespeare Festival and Stage Left Theatre. *Chagrin Falls* was published in the Smith & Kraus anthology "New Playwrights: Best Plays of 2001." *Chagrin Falls* has garnered many awards including the American Theatre Critics Association's (ATCA) 2002 M. Elizabeth Osborn Award for up-and-coming playwright, the Joseph Jefferson Citation for Best New Work, the After Dark Award for Best New Work, and first prize in the 2001 Julie Harris Playwriting Competition. Ms. McCullough has received commissions from Steppenwolf Theatre Company and Cincinnati Shakespeare Festival. Her plays have received staged readings at many theatres in Chicago as well as at development organizations in New York City, Los Angeles, and Ashland, OR. She is also the author of several screenplays, short stories, and half a novel. Ms. McCullough is a member of The Playwrights Collective, Stage Left Theatre Ensemble, and The Dramatists Guild. She lives outside Chicago with her husband and son.

DEVELOPMENTAL HISTORY

Taking Care was originally developed through the Women's Theatre Alliance (Chicago) and The Playwrights Collective. It received staged readings in the Women's Theatre Alliance New Plays Festival and at Chicago Dramatists in 2002.

ORIGINAL PRODUCTION

Taking Care premiered at Steppenwolf Theatre Company's Garage Theatre, Chicago, March 6, 2003.
It was directed by Tim Hopper with the following cast:

BENNY . . . . Guy Van Swearingen
MA . . . . Roslyn Alexander

and the following production staff:

Set Designer . . . . .Russell Poole
Lighting Designer. . . . . .Adam Friedland
Sound Designer. . . . . .Joshua Horvath
Costume Designer . . . . .Jennifer Roberts
Stage Manager . . . . .Malcolm Ewen
Dramaturg . . . . .Edward Sobel

CHARACTERS
BENNY: A man in his 40s
MA: Benny's mother, 76 at start of play
Various voices heard on the television or radio. All prerecorded.

TIME & PLACE
1996 to 2003. A small apartment that has not altered in appearance in many years.

AUTHOR'S NOTES

Benny is an unmedicated schizophrenic. I no longer refer to his specific illness in the play because audiences have gotten very caught up in their own misconceptions of what schizophrenia is, and I have no interest in turning my play into a psychology lesson. For the audience members, I don't think the diagnosis is relevant as long as Benny's behavior is clearly that of someone who is not well. For the actor playing Benny, the diagnosis is important. Benny has been ill since his teenage years. He has never been medicated and he no longer exhibits many positive symptoms (positive symptoms include hallucinations, lashing out in a violent manner, speaking nonsensically). For the most part, he exhibits negative symptoms of which the most obvious is withdrawing from human contact and communication. Schizophrenics are prone to compulsive and repetitive behaviors, and those behaviors tend to become more exaggerated when they are agitated. Often, as schizophrenics pass into their forties and fifties, the disease releases some of its hold on them.

Taking Care is inspired by actual events.

Guy Van Swearingen as Benny and Roslyn Alexander as Ma in the world premiere of *Taking Care* by Mia McCullough, directed by Steppenwolf ensemble member Tim Hopper.　　　　　　　Photo by Michael Brosilow 773-235-4696

Taking Care

SCENE 1

A small and slightly dingy apartment. The furniture is tacky. Ornately carved wood, stained white with faded upholstery that was once loud and garish. Shawls and throws cover everything. Downstage are two armchairs and a small coffee table. Far downstage left is a TV that faces upstage right. Stage left is a daybed. Upstage is the kitchen area. A refrigerator and a sink are along the back wall. A table, about twice the length of a card table divides the kitchen area from the living room. There are three chairs around this table, and a small portable TV is set on top of it. Upstage left is a hallway that leads to the bedroom and bathroom. The door to the apartment is stage left. On the wall is a portrait of a woman in her 30s, a portrait of a man in his 30s, and between them their wedding photo. The wedding photo hangs askew on its hook. Benny, a man in his 40s, sits at the kitchen table watching TV. He has long hair, but it's matted and gnarled into a mass. Ma, a woman in her 70s, enters from the hallway carrying two full grocery bags. She is addressing someone in the hall.

MA: Yes, Mrs. Heinemann. Yes. Yes, I'll have a talk with him...Of course...I understand. I'll see you later. *(Ma closes the door with her behind.)* Uh! You're going to have to cut your hair. You're scaring the neighbors. *(She sets the groceries on the table. She takes out a prescription bottle and squints at the label.)*: Here. These are yours.

(She sets the bottle down in front of Benny. She begins pulling her own prescription medication out and filling up a large pill planner. Benny takes his bottle and tosses it in the trash.)

MA: Don't do that! Don't throw them out. Those pills cost a lot of money. Don't take them if you don't want to, but don't insult me by throwing them out! *(She pulls the pills out of the trash and sets them on the counter.)* I don't know what the hell is wrong with you. Two pills a day. Believe me, two pills is not such a chore. How many pills do I take a day? Eight, sometimes twelve. You don't see me complain.

BENNY: You complain.

MA: Shut up. The point is, I do it. I take the pills because I'm supposed to. I don't waste them.

BENNY: I told you not to buy them.

MA: That would be...that would be...What do they call it? Aiding and abetting. That's not right. Co-dependent. No. What's the word I'm thinking of?

(Benny ignores her, watching TV. She puts groceries away.)

MA: You could be well. You could be just as normal as anyone. As me, if you'd take two pills a day.

BENNY: I never felt normal.

MA: You didn't give it a chance.

BENNY: You don't know.

(While she talks, she makes two identical sandwiches. As she works, she takes a dish rag from a hook by the sink and flings it over her shoulder.)

MA: I never should have been so easy on you...You were always so difficult and I let it slide. Your sisters are right about that. I treated you better. Obviously, a huge mistake. But I will not give in to your unwillingness to help yourself. I won't do it. Fine if you won't take your pills. You can let them sit on a shelf and stare back at you. Remind you that it's no one's fault but your own that you're like this. You know some things they don't have a cure for. Some things they can't fix at all. You at least, you they have medication for, and what do you do? Waste it. Here's your sandwich.

(She sets a sandwich in front of him. He picks it up and begins to eat without acknowledging her. Ma takes her own sandwich and sits down in her armchair. Benny gets up, grabs the dish rag off her shoulder and carefully puts it back on the hook, then returns to his sandwich. Ma shakes her head. Pause. She looks at her sandwich.)

MA: Ethelyn Goodman died last night. Stroke. Only 73. You remember her? The one with the bubble voice?

(No response, though he does glance over at her.)

MA: She's one of my only friends who wasn't afraid of you.

(Lights fade to black as they eat in silence. The TVs flicker in the darkness and white noise swells. Different voices of TV personalities overlap one another.)

WEATHERMAN: It's a blustery one out there today. Looks like autumn is really here. Tonight's temperature will be in the low...

NEWS WOMAN'S VOICE: ...reporting on last night's Academy Awards ceremony...

SCENE 2

Ma sits in her armchair on the phone. The cradle is on the wall behind her, and the cord is long enough to reach anywhere in the playing area.

MA: Oh, you know. Nothing changes. I'm surviving. How's Kayla doing?...She must be getting big. I wish you'd visit more often...How is that husband of yours?...I know he has a name...I wasn't insulting him. Believe me, if I wanted to insult him, I'd do it right...Oh, you know. He's the same. No, he's out right now. Smoking, loitering, I don't know. Oh, wait, his coat is here. He can't be out. He must be sitting in the bathroom...How should I know what he does? He has that chair in there. Sits for hours...So then I tell him to get out, and he gets out...Yeah. You know, he cut his hair...No he didn't let someone, he cut his own hair. Well, how do you think it looks? The boy's never been to beauty school...It's a sight. I can't say it looks better. Nearly gave me a heart attack to see it all lying there in the garbage can when I got up in the morning. It looked like his whole head was in there... *(She laughs.)* You talk to your sister? She called last week. Sounds like she's doing well at that job...Yeah...Busy. Everybody's busy. Everybody but me.

(Benny enters from the back hall. His hair is shorter, but not neater.)

MA: Oh, here's your brother. Coming out of his lair.

(Benny makes his way over to the kitchen table, ducking under the telephone cord that is stretched across his path.)

MA: (Into phone.) I don't know why you always do this. *(To Benny.)* Benny. Benny, you want to talk to your sister?

BENNY: No.

MA: You hear that? Benny, talk to your sister. She wants to talk to you. He's coming. It's Sharon.

(Benny walks over to Ma and takes the receiver.)

BENNY: Hi. *(Pause.)* Okay.

(Pause. While Benny talks, Ma gets up and straightens the wedding photo on the wall. Benny straightens the throw that hangs on the back of Ma's chair.)

BENNY: Yeah. *(Pause.)* Yeah. Okay.

(He hands the phone back to Ma, tilts the wedding photo back to the way it was, and then sits at the table in the kitchen and turns on the TV.)

MA: I don't know why you bother. It's like talking to a potato. I may as well live by myself for all the company he is. Of course he's not taking the medicine...You want to come over and shove the pills down his throat, be my guest.

(Benny turns up the volume.)

MA: Not so loud!

(He turns it down, but gives her a resentful glare that she doesn't see.)

MA: You and Shayna had better decide what it is you're doing with him when I die. The neighbors won't stand for him here and he can't take care of himself. I do everything for him. I cook, I clean. "You know, you know." Stop saying you know. You'll know when I die and he has to move into your house...So, what? He's going to live with Shayna?...Well, have you even discussed it?...You're right, I'll be dead and it'll be none of my business. Did you ever think it might give me some peace to know what will happen to him?...How can you say that, Sharon? If I didn't care he'd be out on the street...No, he's not listening, he's watching TV. He never pays attention to a word I say, he never did. None of you ever did...Why do I start? Does it ever occur to you that maybe you start?...Oh, that's right, I forgot. I am the horrible woman and you are the innocent children...Yes, that's fine. Goodbye. *(She gets up to hang up the phone.)* What did I do to deserve such miserable children? The whole lot of you. Your sisters say it's my fault they never visit. They make up these wild stories. These horrible things I've done to them. If I'd done such things, don't you think I'd remember? I swear, they're crazy. How could I have driven them away? What could I have done? I didn't drive you away. You're still here.

(He gives her a quizzical look.)

MA: You, who I would like a break from now and again. You have never left the nest.

BENNY: I left.

MA: You came back.

(Ma goes over and inspects the back of his head. Benny waves her hand away as if swatting at flies.)

MA: I could even it up a bit.

BENNY: No!

MA: Fine.

(Ma pours two glasses of juice and puts five crackers each on two plates, during this she puts the dish rag on her shoulder again. She sets one glass and one plate in front of Benny, then takes her own snack over to her chair. She pulls out a little portable table for her food and sets it on top. Benny pulls dish rag off her shoulder and puts it back on its hook. Ma turns on her own TV and looks for something to watch. Benny sits back down and takes a bite of a cracker.)

MA: I'll bet they put you in a home.

(Benny looks at her. He stops chewing.)

MA: Maybe they'll put us both in a home.

(Lights fade. The TVs flicker in the darkness. In the half light, Ma clears away her dishes and Benny's. Benny gets up puts his coat on and exits. Ma settles down into her chair and falls asleep.)

SCENE 3

Ma is asleep in her armchair. The door to the hall opens and Benny enters. He sees Ma asleep in the chair, and he purposefully closes the door loudly enough to wake her up. Ma stirs and turns around to see him hanging up his jacket. He is obsessive about how the jacket hangs from the hook. He futzes with it until it's just right.

MA: How can you wear that coat in this heat? I've never understood that about you.

(Benny crosses the room and sits on the daybed. He stares at her, waiting.)

MA: I suppose you want me to go to bed.

(They look at one another.)

MA: You'd think I'd be past waiting up for you by now. I'm always afraid you won't come back...I've never gotten over you running off to California like that. My baby, my boy, picking up and leaving. Driving to the other side of the world with a bunch of who-knows-what and you didn't even say goodbye. I know it wasn't always the happiest home, I know, but I think I deserved a goodbye, at least. I don't think I can ever forgive you. For making me afraid like that. Like this.

(Benny shrugs and looks away.)

MA: Well goodnight, then.

(Ma gets up with effort. She's stiff. The dish rag is draped over her shoulder. She waddles off towards the back of the apartment. As she passes Benny, he grabs at the dish rag but she beats him to it, yanking it off her shoulder and then throwing it at him. He hangs it in its spot as she exits. Benny straightens the throw on her chair. He reaches under the daybed and takes out a pillow and some blankets. He arranges them on the daybed. He grabs the remote and turns on the TV with the volume very low. He curls up on the daybed, with the covers over him. The lights fade. The TVs flicker in the darkness. In the half-light, Benny gets up and puts away his bedding. Ma enters and pulls out a menorah from a cabinet, which she sets on the table. Benny moves the menorah to a slightly different position and sits at the table.)

SCENE 4

(Benny is watching his TV. Ma sets a box of Hanukkah candles on the table.)

MA: You want to pick out the candles?

(Benny turns off the TV. He pulls out two candles, putting one in the Shamas spot and one in the right-most spot. He pulls out another candle and switches it with the Shamas. Ma is rifling through the kitchen drawers.)

MA: I know I have matches around here somewhere.

(Benny takes out a lighter and flicks it on, holding it out for her to see.)

MA: You can't use that. You don't celebrate ancient miracles with Bic lighters...Here we go. Would you like to light the Shamas or should I?

(Benny takes the matches and lights the Shamas. Ma then lights the first candle with the Shamas and sets it back in the menorah.)

MA: Well. Happy Hanukkah. Here's your Hanukkah gelt.

(She holds out a dollar. Benny shakes his head, amused.)

MA: You don't want it?

(Benny takes the money before she can put it back in her purse.)

MA: That's what I thought. Your sisters yell at me for treating you like a child, but lord knows you don't discourage it. *(She puts her coat on.)* Somedays I wonder, when I die, will you turn into a man? Will you function? Or will you need someone else to be your mother?

(They look at one another a moment.)

MA: Well, I'm off to the party, then. Your supper's on a plate in the ice-box...You sure you don't want to come?

(Benny shakes his head.)

MA: Your Aunt Beena said it would be all right if you just sat in the den and watched TV. She wants the whole family to be together.

(He shakes his head again.)

BENNY: Ma, could you turn the light down?

(Ma dims the light.)

MA: All right. Don't go for your walk until the candles are all out.

(Ma exits. Benny watches the flames as the lights fade. The TVs flicker in the darkness. Benny slowly blows out each of the candles. He very carefully brings the menorah and the candles into the kitchen area and puts them away out of sight.)

SCENE 5

Benny is watching the big TV. He is pacing back and forth, agitated, smacking himself in the head.

BENNY: No! Stupid, stupid, STUPID! What is electromagnetic! Magnetic!...Duke of Wellington, what is the Duke of Wellington...I don't know. No...Oh! Oh! The Magna Carta! WHAT IS THE MAGNA CARTA! God, you people are idiots!...No, don't risk that much. You're going to lose it. You don't know anything about opera.

(He hears a key in the lock. He rushes up to the TV and turns it off, then retreats to the kitchen. Ma is talking to a neighbor in the hallway.)

MA: Yeah, it was a beautiful service. Very nice...Yes...Not a good day to be standing outside wearing black, but what can you do?

(Ma enters the apartment. She closes the door on whoever it is.)

MA: Yeah, okay. See you later.

(She shuts the door and lets out a weary sigh. She is in a black dress and a black hat.

She goes to her chair and sits without looking at Benny who is watching her. Pause.)

BENNY: Who died?

(Ma turns around and gives him a hard stare, though she is not the least bit startled to find him there.)

MA: Who died? *(Pause. She turns back and faces out.)* Your father's cousin Ruth. You remember Cousin Ruth?

BENNY: Yeah.

MA: Well, she's dead.

BENNY: *(Unemotional.)* You didn't tell me.

MA: I told you. I told you. You just weren't listening to me. As usual.

BENNY: *(Matter-of-fact)* You didn't tell me.

MA: You must have heard me talking about it on the phone.

BENNY: I don't listen to you on the phone.

MA: Ha.

BENNY: You didn't tell me.

MA: What? You were going to go to the funeral?

BENNY: No.

MA: So what does it matter if I didn't tell you? *(Pause.)* But I did. I remember telling you. *(A long pause. She takes off her shoes and her hat. She is exhausted from the day's events.)* Everyone asked after you. "How's Benny?" "How's Benny doing?" "Oh, you know, he's fine. The same. Nothing changes." *(Beat.)* What am I supposed to say? "Oh, Benny? He's good. He met a nice girl and they got married in a small, private ceremony, and now he's got a successful textile business in Philadelphia and a baby on the way." *(Pause.)* Sometimes I make up a whole life for you. I name your kids...I even kind of like your wife. But I never tell people about it when they ask. About your make-believe life. I'm probably the only one who would think it was funny. Get me a glass of juice, will ya? There's always too much standing around at these things.

(Benny gets up and pours a glass of juice and brings it over, then goes back to his kitchen seat.)

MA: Your cousin Alyssa said she saw you the other day. She was driving down the street and she saw you walking. She said she slowed down and called out to you, but you looked at her and kept going. Didn't you know it was her?

(Pause. Benny stares at the little TV.)

BENNY: I knew.

MA: So, it would have killed you to stop and say hello?

BENNY: I don't like her.

MA: You used to play with her all the time when you were kids.

BENNY: She used to play with me.

MA: She's a very nice woman now.

BENNY: She's stupid.

MA: She's not stupid. She's a doctor. Who are you to call other people stupid?

(No response. Ma gets up and carries her shoes and hat into the back. Benny watches TV.)

BENNY: *(Quietly.)* What is osmosis.

MA: *(Offstage.)* Did you say something?

BENNY: No.

(Ma returns without her jacket and with house slippers on her feet. She goes back to the chair. Big sigh.)

MA: So that's the last of your father's family. Well, you know, your cousins, but no one left to carry on the family name. You were the last one. The line dies with you.

BENNY: What do you care?

MA: I care...I care. Your father was so happy when he had a son. For a while.

(Long pause.)

BENNY: So, what's my wife's name?

MA: Rachael.

(Lights out. The TVs flicker in the darkness. Ma gets up and puts her glass in the sink. She puts the dish rag on her shoulder and opens the fridge.)

SCENE 6

Benny sits at his table. Ma carries a piece of cake with a candle on it to him, cupping the flame with her hand, singing. She sets the cake in front of him.

MA: Happy Birthday Dear Benny, Happy Birthday to You. That's the kind you like, right?

(Benny nods. He leans forward to blow out the candle. Ma stops him with a fairly fierce yank of the shoulder.)

MA: Make a wish first!

(Benny stares at her long and hard. He grabs the dish rag off her shoulder and puts it back on the hook, then returns to his seat and blows out the candle. Ma hands him a long rectangular package.)

MA: Here.

(He unceremoniously unwraps the gift. It is a carton of cigarettes.)

BENNY: Thanks.

MA: Use them in good health.

(She laughs at her own joke and sits down.)

MA: At least you're easy to shop for, Benny.

(She turns on the TV. They both watch. After a moment.)

BENNY: Did Sharon or Shayna call?

MA: Not yet. They might have forgot. We're not a high priority with those two, you know. Not top of the list. Uh! So dusty. Where does it come from? The windows are closed, we don't drag dirt all the way up three flights of stairs. It's never made any sense to me.

(Ma grabs a rag and begins to wipe down surfaces and tchotckes.)

BENNY: They always call.

MA: Yeah, well, some year they won't. Maybe this year. You can't count on people, Benny, not even your sisters. If there's one thing I've learned in life, it's that you can't count on anyone. *(Pause. She continues to dust. She wipes across the radio and accidentally turns it on. She tunes it and finds a station with Lawrence Welk-ish music.)* I wonder if we just sat here in our chairs perfectly still for months and months, if we died and your sisters never came looking for us—which is not so out of the realm of possibility— would the dust pile up like snow? And how much? Would it ever stop?

BENNY: They call almost every day.

MA: And you never want to talk to them. Why do you care if they remember your birthday? I remembered. Isn't that enough?

(Ma moves on to the photos on the wall. She straightens the wedding photo. She dusts her own photo first, then she takes the photo of the man off the wall and dusts it ever so gently. After a moment she begins to sway a little, then dance and twirl with the photo held up like a partner. Benny looks on with irritation.)

MA: Your father was so handsome. It's too bad he hated dancing. I would've liked to have gone dancing a time or two. I guess we never had any money, anyway. *(She twirls around.)* Well, you're dancing now, aren't you, Saul? *(She stops, out of breath. She wipes the glass tenderly with her rag.)*

BENNY: He left you. He moved out and then he died.

(Ma's spell is broken.)

MA: How would you know what happened? You weren't here. You were in California getting high and wandering the streets with no shoes on.

BENNY: Sharon and Shayna told me.

MA: Well, your sisters don't know everything. Your father and I had a good marriage. Thirty-four years.

BENNY: He didn't even like you.

(Pause.)

MA: Get out! Get out of my sight if you're going to say such horrible things to me!

(Benny and Ma stare each other down for a long moment.)

MA: Get out!

(Benny turns off the TV, gets up, grabs his coat, puts it on carefully, buttoning every other button.)

MA: He didn't like you either!

(Benny slams the door closed as he leaves. Ma hangs the photo back on the wall. She goes over to the window, perhaps looking for Benny. Outside is the faint sound of an ice cream truck passing, children playing and shouting. As the lights fade, a strong wind swells and buffets against the windows replacing the sounds of children. Dry leaves swirl in the wind. Ma backs away from the windows and slowly retreats to her bedroom as a snow plow goes by outside. A voice from a megaphone outside.)

MEGAPHONE: If you are parked on the north side of the street, please move your vehicle immediately so we can plow. If you're parked on the north side...

(The voice fades.)

SCENE 7

Ma is at the wall by the phone wearing a bathrobe. She is frantically speaking into the receiver.

MA: Hello! Hello! Yes, my son is missing. Yes...I need someone to go out and look for him...He lives with me. No, no, he always comes home. He goes out for his 10 o'clock walk and then he comes home, watches television and goes to bed...He's 45. No, you don't understand. I can't wait 48 hours. He's not like a regular person. He's ill. No, not like he has the flu. He's mentally ill...You don't understand, he does the same exact thing every day. Watches the same programs, eats the same things. Goes for walks...Well, I don't know where he walks, exactly. I don't follow him. The point is, he should be home by now. He should've been home last night and it's minus ten outside. He might be frozen to death on a park bench...No, I haven't looked for him. I'm 80 years old. You want me to go outside, walk on the ice and break my neck? Is that what you want? Maybe if the city cleared the sidewalks, maybe then I could go out and look for my son...You're telling me you can't look until 10 o'clock tomorrow night?...But he's not an adult. He's not well...No, he's not retarded, he's crazy...No, not dangerous. He's a gentle boy. Wouldn't hurt a fly. His name is Benjamin Painter. Yes, with a "P." I...Thank you. You've been so helpful. *(She hangs up and immediately begins to make another call.)* ...The machine...Sharon? Sharon? Are you there?...This is your mother...Sharon, your brother didn't come home last night, will you pick up the phone?...I knew you were there. Your brother never came home last night...No, we didn't have a fight. We don't even speak, how could we have a fight?...I already called the police. They say they can't look for him until he's been gone 48 hours...Yes, I explained all that, they don't care...I should call the hospitals? Why can't you call the hospitals?...It's my fault you live long distance? I didn't tell you to move half way across the country. I want to keep this line open in case Benny calls...I don't know if he knows the number. I don't know...

(The front door opens and Benny steps inside. He does not close the door or take his coat off. He is shaking. Ma drops the phone as she runs to him.)

MA: Benny! Oh, my God. Did you stay out in this all night? Don't you have any sense? You've had me worried sick! On the phone with the police! With your sisters!

(Benny tries to take off his coat, but his fingers are too stiff. He falls against the wall.)

BENNY: There's something wrong with my feet.

MA: Your feet? What's wrong with your feet?

BENNY: I can't feel them.

(Lights fade to black. TVs flicker in the darkness. Benny exits out the front door. Ma goes into the back.)

Ambulance sirens can be heard in the distance as the wind swells again. The siren grows closer and closer, then fades. Benny enters from the back rooms with a walker and his feet bandaged. He walks gingerly. He grabs one of the chairs from the kitchen table and pushes it downstage with his walker. He sits in it and lights a cigarette.

SCENE 8

Benny sits in one of the kitchen chairs. It is far downright. He is smoking. He leans down a little to blow the smoke out an unseen window in the fourth wall. His feet are wrapped in bandages. Behind him, next to his chair is a walker. Ma enters from the back rooms.

MA: Jesus! It's freezing in here! Will you shut that window?

BENNY: I'm smoking.

MA: Well, stop it. Stop all of it. It's minus ten degrees out there! If it weren't for your smoking, you wouldn't have been outside in this and you wouldn't have lost three of your toes. *(Ma looks at the clock.)* I'd better change your bandages while I'm thinking of it. Put that out and close the window.

(Ma exits to the back rooms. Benny sucks on the cigarette, getting the last puffs out of it. Then he puts it out in a tea cup. Ma returns with gauze, sterile tape and a tube of ointment. Benny shuts the window as Ma drags a tray table up and sets up her first-aid materials.)

MA: I guess the upside of this is you have to wash your feet every day. Maybe I can get the doctor to tell you to wash the rest of you every day. Or every other day. Even that would be a vast improvement. You know your nieces won't even come to visit because it smells so bad in here. That's why they don't come to see me. Because you stink. I don't even notice anymore. *(Ma pulls a chair up opposite of him and sits.)* Okay, which foot do you want to start with?

(Benny stares at her meanly. He does not respond or move.)

MA: You know, I could have let you be institutionalized. That doctor asked me, "Does Benny take his medication?" I say, "No, of course he doesn't. He never takes his medication." And then the doctor said, "Well, this incident seems indicative that Benny is a danger to himself. It's enough to have him committed to the psychiatric unit. And if he was committed they'd make sure he took his medicine." And I said, "Oh, no. Benny and I are fine. This was a one time thing. I don't know why he didn't come home that night, but I'm sure he's learned his lesson and it will never happen again, Doctor." That's what I said to him. That's what I did for you. Because if they put you in one of those places, you'll have people telling you what to do every moment of the day, and they'll put you on that Thorazine stuff, and then you'll find a real appreciation for your horrible mother. Your sisters thought maybe we should, but I said no. Because they don't understand what a nice arrangement we've got here. So you've got to cooperate. Start behaving yourself. You can't be doing these crazy things ever again, Benny, or else we are both going to get put in a home. Do you understand?

(Ma gives Benny a moment to let this sink in.)

MA: So what's it going to be? Which one of those decapitated little piggies do you want to start with?

(Benny lifts one leg up, and after a second, lets it rest gently on her knee.)

MA: All right, then.

(She begins to unwrap the bandage as the lights fade. The TVs flicker in the darkness. In the half-light Ma pulls off both bandages and takes them and her first-aid stuff into the back. Benny folds up his walker and puts it in the closet. Ma brings out his shoes and he puts them on, methodically tying the laces. Outside, perhaps the sound of birds in spring.)

SCENE 9

Lights up on the apartment. There is a banging on the front door, a jiggling of the door knob, the sound of keys. Benny's coat is on its peg, but he's nowhere in sight.

MA: *(Offstage.)* Benny! Benny! Are you in there? Will you let me in? Benny! ...No, Mrs. Heinemann, I'm fine. Something happened to the lock. My key isn't—oh, there it goes. No, I'm fine, thank you. Bye. *(Ma enters the apartment with her purse and a couple of grocery bags.)* Benny? Are you here? Of course, you're here. *(She gives his jacket a swat, knocking it from its hook. Yelling.)* What's wrong with you that you can't come to the door? *(She begins to put groceries away. The phone rings.)* Hello? Shayna? Why are you calling me now, it's the middle of the afternoon. What?...I'm fine. He called you?...I'm fine. I lost track of what floor I was on and tried to get into his apartment. It's not a crime, I was just distracted...I was thinking and I didn't notice which floor I was on. I do think, you know...Let me ask you something: Does everyone in this building have your number? Do they? What about that idiot across the hall?...Look, I've got to put the lox in the fridge. I know it can reach, but I don't want to talk to you anymore, so goodbye. *(Ma hangs up the phone.)* Nosy good for nothin'. *(She stomps her floor on the floor, sending a message to her downstairs neighbor. She resumes putting the groceries away.)* That stupid goy who lives downstairs called your sister on me. It was an innocent mistake, and everyone's got to act like I'm losing my mind. All the floors look the same. Bastard got me so flustered I couldn't open my own door, followed me halfway up the stairs, everybody peeking out their doors at me. Who could open anything with such an audience of nosy-bodies? *(Ma shuffles over to the TV, hits the power, and collapses into her chair.)* What's the matter with the TV? *(She gets up, turns it on and off a few times.)* What the...? *(She checks to see if it's plugged in.)* Is the power out? *(She turns a lamp on and it works.)* Benny, what did you do to my TV?! Benny, get out here...I said, get out here!

(Benny comes out from the bathroom with a mixture of trepidation and defiance.)

MA: What did you do to my TV?

BENNY: Nothing.

MA: Don't lie to me, Benny. I know you watch it when I'm out. I hear you scurrying around in here when I'm outside the door. I'm not stupid, you know, now what did you do to it?

BENNY: Nothing. It's not working.

(Benny sees his coat on the floor, and goes over to hang it up and fix it.)

MA: I can see that it's not working. Did you hit it? Did you get excited watching your game show?

BENNY: It's not on until three.

MA: Was the television talking to you? Is that why you broke it?

BENNY: No. I didn't break it. It stopped working.

MA: So you were watching it.

BENNY: I didn't break it.

(Benny sits at his table.)

MA: Well, what am I supposed to do? What am I supposed to do for company, now?

(Benny does not respond. Reflexively he looks at his TV, maybe even reaches to turn it on, but then realizes he'd rather not call attention to his TV. Ma glowers at him. Lights fade. Benny turns on his TV. In the half-light, Ma searches in some drawers and pulls out a deck of cards. She sits down next to Benny and starts dealing for a game of solitaire. Benny scoots his chair a little farther away from her.)

SCENE 10

Benny sits at the kitchen table watching the mini TV. Ma sits next to him playing solitaire. Benny watches her play out of the corner of his eye. When he can take it no longer, he reaches over and moves her cards, then returns his attention to the TV.

MA: I'm playing.

BENNY: You suck.

MA: It doesn't matter. I don't want your help.

BENNY: You never win.

MA: *(Not talking about the cards.)* No. I never do. Not in my whole life. (*Pause.*) You watch stupid programs.

(She continues to play. Benny watches the cards out of the corner of his eye.)

BENNY: You're cheating.

MA: Shut up.

(Ma throws down the cards in frustration. Blackout.)

Lights come up again briefly on Ma watching Benny's TV, which she has pulled over to her side of the kitchen table. She is laughing at the show along with the laugh track. Benny sits watching, not amused. Lights fade. In the half-light, Benny picks up each card, and squares up the deck as evenly a possible, checking it from every angle before he slides it into its box. He puts it back in the drawer in the kitchen.

SCENE 11

The lights come up on Ma in her chair, wrapped in blankets and an afghan. Benny's TV is back in its spot and a new TV sits on an ottoman. It's bigger than Benny's but smaller than the original. The phone rings. Ma gets up to answer it.

MA: Hello?...Lois! Where are you? Are you home? *(She crosses to downstage, peering out the "window" in the fourth wall and across the street. She waves energetically.)* Hi!...Happy Thanksgiving to you, too. Can you believe this? Two feet and it's only November...I know. We may not get out for a walk until April. *(She looks across the street at her friend and nods sadly. Then she makes her way to the stove and turns the heat on under a kettle, puts the schmata on her shoulder.)* I know. It makes you see why everyone moves to Florida...Yes, you're right. Prisoners of Mother Nature...I know. *(She shuffles back to her chair and sits.)* Oh, you know, it was good...Yes, the girls are fine...No, I didn't cook. I haven't cooked a big meal in I don't even remember. No, Sharon and Shayna cook? If they do, they keep it secret from me. All they ever want is to go out. Always in a restaurant where it's distracting and loud and you can't have a conversation...Oh, no, even for Thanksgiving dinner we went out...*(She laughs.)* Shayna calls me up and says, "Ma, we're going to a topless place for Thanksgiving dinner." I say, "A what place?" She says, "A topless place." So I think maybe this is a new name for some trendy kind of restaurant, but I don't say anything, because you know everything I say is wrong with those girls, and besides, I think maybe it'll be interesting. A good story to tell. "Yes, I'm eighty-two years old and my daughters took me to a topless bar for Thanksgiving dinner." As if Phyllis could top that! *(She laughs again.)* Hang on, I'm telling you...So we get there, and right away I'm disappointed because everyone's got their clothes on. And on the menu it says "Tapas." T-A-P-A-S. I still don't know what it means. It's Mexican or something...Yeah, it was okay. Salty, but good. Oh! and I had shrimp! Well, I only had one...I was about to bite into the second one when my stupid daughter yells out, "Ma! What are you doing!? You can't eat that, it's not Kosher!" As if she's Kosher. As if she's been Kosher since the day she left this house. Who made her the Parve police?

(The whistle on the kettle starts to blow.)

MA: That's my tea. How was your Thanksgiving?

(Ma gets up and walks toward the stove. Benny enters from the back, ducks under the phone cord, but then is trapped by it as Ma walks past him with the phone. He waits for her to realize what she's done, but she doesn't appear to notice him.)

MA: Uh huh...Oh, that was nice...Uh huh...Really?

(Ma puts some tea bags in a tea pot and then fills it with hot water. Then she waddles back to her chair, releasing Benny from the coils of the phone cord without acknowledging him. Benny continues into the kitchen and sits. He does not turn on the TV. He merely stares at Ma.)

MA: Oh, no. They got out Saturday morning before it got bad...They never stay a whole weekend. Sharon says she needs Sunday to recover from the trip before she goes back to work. Recover from what, is what I want to know. She sleeps in a hotel, she eats at restaurants, she sits in my apartment and doesn't say anything. What's to recover from? And you know Shayna, she won't visit when Sharon's not here... *(She gets up again to pour her tea. She reaches into the cupboard with a little groan.)* Oh no, Benny didn't go to the topless place...I don't know what he did. Probably sat in the bathroom all evening, in his chair, staring at the wall. You know... *(She takes down one cup, fills it with tea and sets it in front of Benny.)* Yeah. I'm going to worry all winter now, with him going out for his walks. You remember last year with his toes. It's amazing he walks at all now, but, you know, nothing keeps him from his routine... *(She gets another tea cup pours some tea, spilling some. She looks for the dish rag on the hook.)* Dammit. Where's the? Where's the schmata? Benny? Where's the—never mind, you're useless. It's nothing. I just spilled some tea.

(She shuffles off to the back. Benny is amused and triumphant.)

MA: I know...I know...

(Suddenly there's a loud thud, and the phone cord falls to the floor. Benny is startled but does not move.)

MA: *(Offstage.)* Oh! Oh! Benny! Help me. My hip! Oh, I felt it pop! Benny! Will you do something! Ohhhhh.

(After a moment Benny jumps up. He goes into the back and backs out holding the phone.)

BENNY: Hello...Yeah...She fell.

MA: *(Offstage.)* Benny, will you help me up!

BENNY: No, I can call...Bye.

(Benny hangs up and dials 911.)

MA: *(Offstage.)* Ohhhh. How can you just leave me here?

BENNY: Yeah, hi. My mother fell on the floor. She wants me to help her up, but I don't think I should.

(Ma groans in pain as the lights fade. The TVs flicker in the darkness. Benny paces, nervously, and then puts on his coat for comfort. He continues to pace. Then grabs the remote for Ma's TV and sits in her chair.)

SCENE 12

Benny sits in Ma's chair watching TV. The volume is turned up loud. After a few moments, the phone rings. Benny turns down the volume and looks at the phone. It rings a second time, then stops. He gets up and stands by the phone. After a moment the phone rings again. Benny picks up.

BENNY: Hi...Yeah, hi...I'm okay...Yeah, it was good, thanks...Oh. She is?...Where am I going to sleep?...Oh. Okay...No, I can do it...Yeah.

(Benny hangs up the phone. He takes a long look at the arm chairs and the daybed and then begins to rearrange the furniture. He puts the daybed where Ma's chair was. He lays in the daybed, and finds that he cannot comfortably see the TV from there. He shifts the daybed. He arranges the armchairs in a suitable fashion, with one of them in the corner that the daybed occupied. He picks up his bedding from the floor and begins to lay it out on the daybed. He plumps the pillow and sets it carefully down. Then he moves it slightly. He stares at it all a moment. Then he picks up the pillow and sniffs it. He grabs the rest of the bedding and walks to the back rooms. Lights fade. The TVs flicker in the darkness. In the half-light, a Paramedic helps Ma back into the apartment and gets her into the daybed. Benny comes in, not acknowledging anyone and pulls the walker out of the closet. He sets it up near Ma. The Paramedic exits.)

SCENE 13

Lights up on Ma in the daybed, swaddled in blankets. A walker is to the left of the daybed. Benny sits in an arm chair, opposite her. They both look over at the front door, which is being pulled closed by an anonymous hand.

MA: *(Weary.)* We'll be fine. Thank you.

(The door closes. Benny and Ma lock eyes—Benny tense and uncertain, Ma tired and scared.)

MA: Did they bring my pills?

BENNY: They're on the table. Do you want one?

MA: No, I...there's a schedule...I don't know when—

BENNY: It's on this paper.

MA: Okay.

(He tries to hand her the paper.)

MA: No, you keep it. You'll have to tell me when.

(Long pause.)

MA: You were okay while I was gone?

BENNY: I was okay.

MA: You ate.

BENNY: I ate.

MA: Shayna said she stayed with you.

BENNY: Yeah. Some of the time.

MA: That was okay?

(Benny shrugs. After a moment, the phone rings. They both look at it, up on the wall. It rings a second time and then stops. Benny gets up and stands next to the phone. He and Ma continue to stare at one another.)

MA: What are you doing?

(The phone rings again. Benny picks it up and holds the receiver to his ear, but says nothing for a moment.)

BENNY: ...I'm here...Yeah...I got it...Yeah...Thanks. I got it...Yeah, she's here. She's okay. I thought you would come today. *(To Ma.)* You want to talk to Sharon?

(Ma wearily shakes her head "no.")

BENNY: She doesn't want to talk to you...I got it...I know...I know! I KNOW!

(He hangs up the phone. Ma and Benny stare at one another for a long while. Suddenly Benny breaks their stare and goes to the kitchen. He pours some water in a glass and brings it to Ma.)

MA: Your sisters are not relaxing people. I'm glad they went back home. Every day in the hospital for two weeks. Sitting there. Fretting. I think they were hoping I'd die. Some days I was hoping I'd die, but something just makes you go on. Like it or not. I could hear them talking when they thought I was asleep. I heard Shayna say, "You know, these broken hips, they're usually the beginning of the end." And Sharon said, "I know." She didn't sound too unhappy, though.

(Benny sits in the arm chair and looks at his mother.)

MA: The beginning of the end. The beginning of the end has long since come and gone.

(Again they stare at one another.)

MA: Did you miss me?

(Benny stares at her unresponsively.)

MA: I have to go to the bathroom.

(Benny looks terrified at the prospect. He does not move.)

MA: Could you pull the blankets? I can't move my legs.

(Benny carefully pulls the blankets out from around Ma's legs. He then helps her set her feet on the floor. Ma grimaces in pain.)

MA: Okay, okay. *(Ma lets out a long sigh.)* You remember how the guy showed us?

BENNY: *(Hopefully.)* You want the walker?

MA: I'm not strong enough for the walker, yet.

(Benny steels himself, then bends down and puts his arm under Ma's arm. He holds out his other hand for her to brace herself. She rocks herself in preparation as she counts.)

MA: Okay. One, two, threeeowahhh! Ow. Okay.

BENNY: You're okay?

MA: Yeah.

BENNY: It hurts.

MA: Yes...Okay. I can walk now.

(Very slowly he walks her offstage.)

MA: It's a good thing you're here, Benny. Otherwise I'd put Sharon and Shayna in the poor house. They wouldn't let me stay with them. They'd put me in a convalescent home. Or take me out back and shoot me like a horse, if they could get away with it.

(Lights fade as they disappear into the back. The TVs flicker in the darkness. In the half-light, Benny guides Ma back to the daybed. He puts on his coat and leaves.)

SCENE 14

Lights up as Benny enters from the hallway. Ma is on the daybed watching TV.

MA: You're back. That was fast.

(Benny takes off his coat and hangs it up carefully.)

MA: Didn't you buy anything?

BENNY: He wouldn't let me.

MA: Who wouldn't let you?

BENNY: Mr. Schuller. He asked me to leave.

MA: Didn't you tell him I was sick?

(Benny paces frantically.)

BENNY: No.

MA: I'm sure he's heard what's happened to me.

BENNY: He asked me to leave. In front of everybody.

MA: Oh, Benny. I'll call him. You've known Mr. Schuller since you were five years old. He probably didn't recognize you.

BENNY: He knows who I am.

MA: Hand me the phone. I'll explain.

BENNY: No.

MA: I'll explain and you can go back.

BENNY: No...I can't do it.

MA: You can't do what? Go into the store?

BENNY: I can't...buy things.

MA: Of course you can. You buy cigarettes all the time.

BENNY: It's different. They know me. I don't have to ask. I go in. I put my money on the counter. And they know. Camels. No filter. They give me my change and I leave. They don't look at me. They don't talk to me...Everyone was staring at me...He said I was too dirty. That he'd have to throw out the tomatoes I touched.

MA: Benny...

(Benny starts rocking slightly.)

BENNY: I can't...I can't.. . It...It...Hurts...To have them all looking at me.

MA: *(Quiet, but firm.)* Well, how are we going to eat? I can't go to the store.

(He stares at his hands.)

MA: I'll have to call your sisters. They'll figure something out. Will you hand me the phone?

(Benny retrieves the phone for her.)

MA: I want to know where this cordless phone is that Shayna said she sent. Have you seen a box downstairs?

(Beat.)

BENNY: There's a box.

MA: Is it for us?

BENNY: I don't know.

MA: Well, will you check, please? It's probably the phone.

(Benny puts on his jacket, slowly buttoning every other button.)

MA: How long has it been there?

BENNY: I don't know. A few days.

MA: And you didn't think to see if it was for us? Someone could have stolen it.

(Benny leaves as she talks. Ma dials a number.)

MA: Busy.

(She looks around a moment, then drops the receiver on the floor. Benny comes back a few moments later with a smallish box. He hands it to her, then takes off his jacket and hangs it up carefully, meticulously.)

MA: I can't open it, will you get me a knife?

(He hangs up the phone and gets her a steak knife from the kitchen. She pokes at the box with it, but her hand is a little shaky.)

MA: Maybe you should open it.

(Ma hands him the box and the knife. He slices it open, pulls the lid up, hands it to her, and brings the knife back to the kitchen.)

MA: Oh, look. There's a card. *(She pulls out the phone.)* Will you figure out how this works?

(Benny takes the phone over to the kitchen table. As Ma talks he looks over the directions.)

MA: "For our dearest mother on her birthday." My birthday was weeks ago. "How does it feel to be 83?" Eighty-three! I'm not 83.

BENNY: Yeah, you are.

MA: No, I'm not, I'm only 80. Eighty-one at the most.

BENNY: You're 83.

MA: No...Really?...This is a conspiracy. My children are trying to make me crazy. You're in cahoots with them. Eighty-three.

BENNY: I don't like this phone.

MA: I don't remember turning 82...I don't...Did we do anything special when I turned 82? Did anyone visit me?...I can't remember it at all. *(Pause.)* Did I hit my head when I fell?...Benny?

BENNY: I don't know.

MA: Didn't you see?

BENNY: You were in the bathroom.

MA: Ever since I fell I've been...

(She looks at Benny. He is messing with the phone.)

MA: Do you think I was a good mother?

(He looks at her a long moment, then goes back to poking at the phone.)

MA: How's the phone? Can you figure it out?

BENNY: It smells funny.

(Pause. She looks at the card again.)

MA: Eighty-three. I should be dead by now.

(The lights fade. The TVs flicker in the darkness. In the half-light, Benny sets up the phone, and puts the old one away. Ma pulls her self up with the walker and goes over to the wastebasket to throw the card away. She goes back to the daybed and sits. Benny pulls some things out of the refrigerator.)

The faint sound of arguing can be heard, perhaps from downstairs, perhaps the TV, or perhaps from the depths of the past.

MOTHER: You are not wearing that. You are not leaving this house.

DAUGHTER: I hate you!

MOTHER: Yeah, well, I hate you, too. Go change your clothes.

SCENE 15

Lights up on Ma sitting in her daybed, watching TV, flipping through channels. Benny has just finished making sandwiches and is bringing one to Ma as she talks on the phone.

MA: Who's your fourth now?...Oh? How is she? You know, you're all welcome to come here to play. I can't move, but I could play cards. Thank you, Benny. Did you see that? He just brought me lunch. He's waiting on me hand and foot...Shayna's got some sort of Internet service bringing us groceries. Otherwise I don't know what we'd do. Did you hear what happened with Benny over at Schuller's? It would be one thing if he'd never met Benny, but he's known him his whole life....How can you say that, Lois? He's never attacked anyone. He's a lamb. He doesn't even talk to people...Look, I've gotta eat my sandwich. Say hello to everyone for me...You're not comfortable with it. Fine. Fine. Maybe someday I'll be well enough to come over to your place again...Yes. Goodbye. *(Pause. She stares at the receiver.)* Benny, could you hang this up? I don't know which button. But leave it here. With me.

(Benny gets up, takes the phone, pushes a button, moves to return it to the wall, remembers, and with great effort sets it down next to Ma. Meanwhile, Ma takes a bite of her sandwich.)

MA: Euh! This tastes so funny. *(She peels up the bread.)* What is this? Is this tongue? It doesn't taste like tongue.

BENNY: It's ham.

MA: Ham!? These Internet people gave us ham?! Why didn't you tell me?

(Benny is eating his sandwich at the table.)

BENNY: It's all they brought.

MA: You're going to eat it?

BENNY: It's all they brought. It's good.

(She looks at her sandwich, then at Benny. She takes a small bite and begins to giggle with her mouth full. Benny joins in.)

MA: A nice couple of Jews we are.

(They laugh for a moment, Ma heartily, Benny more subdued. After the laughter subsides, Ma sighs.)

MA: No one will come see me.

(Ma sighs. Benny looks on as the lights fade. The TVs flicker in the darkness. Ma pulls herself up with the walker and goes in back. Benny begins to rearrange the furniture to its original set up.)

SPORTSCASTER: Stay tuned as March Madness continues...

WEATHERMAN: Folks, it's the longest day of the year, so enjoy, because they all get shorter from here on out.

COMMERCIAL: ...We've got costumes, candy, tricks and treats for all ages...

SCENE 16

Benny sits at the kitchen table reading the newspaper. Ma comes out from the back using her walker. She's in some kind of hurry. She wears a pretty dress that is not zipped in the back.

MA: Benny, would you zip me please?

(Benny stares at his mother, confused.)

MA: What're you looking at me for? I need to be zipped. I can't reach.

(Benny gets up and gingerly zips up her dress.)

BENNY: Where are you going?

MA: Where am I going? Your sister's wedding. You've gotta help me find my purse.

The green one. The one that goes with this dress.

(Ma maneuvers around Benny and heads towards the pegs next to the door where Benny's coat rests among other jackets.)

MA: See if it's over there. On one of those hooks. Behind the coats.

(Benny places himself between Ma and the door.)

BENNY: Whose wedding?

MA: Shayna. Your sister. Don't you pay attention?

BENNY: I thought Shayna was married.

MA: You're not looking for my bag.

(Pause. He searches her face.)

BENNY: Who's she getting married to?

MA: She's getting married to Jonathan. Remember him? She brought him here and he brought us that nice pastry. She got divorced from that other loser. Kevin. *(Pause.)* What?

BENNY: Shayna didn't invite you to her wedding.

MA: Of course she...She didn't?

BENNY: Shayna married Jonathan in 1982 and she didn't invite you.

(Ma is taken aback. She's trying to remember, to get her bearings.)

MA: What year is it now?

BENNY: Two thousand.

MA: Two thousand?

(Ma is completely baffled by this. She looks around the room. At herself. Her walker.)

MA: And she didn't invite me?

BENNY: No.

MA: Did she invite you?

BENNY: She didn't invite any of us.

(Ma begins to walk back to her room, sniffling as the lights fade. The TVs flicker in the darkness. All the while a Christmas carol is being sung on TV.)

TV: It's the most wonderful time of the year...

(And then.)

TV: If olde acquaintance be forgot and never brought to mind...

SCENE 17

Ma is sitting upright in her chair. She is waving her finger at someone who is not there.

MA: You never do anything around here! I cook, I clean, I wash your clothes. Stop crying! You're so selfish.

(Benny comes in the front door. He watches Ma, neither surprised nor concerned at first. But maybe a little curious and irritated.)

MA: Why do you waste your time with these things? No one cares if you can paint a picture. You don't get a husband by painting pictures. Men want a woman who can keep a good house. Give me those! I said give them to me!

(Ma reaches out toward the invisible person she's talking to.)

BENNY: Don't hit her!

(Ma spins around. Benny closes the door.)

MA: Benny.

(She is disoriented for a moment. Benny hangs up his coat in his usual meticulous way.)

MA: You're back from your walk.

(Benny goes to the kitchen and starts making sandwiches.)

MA: I was having the strangest...the strangest...Your sister. She was little. She was on the back steps. Not here. No. Where we used to live. When you were a baby. She was painting. She had made a...what do you call it? That painters lean their pictures on.

BENNY: An easel.

MA: Yes. An easel. I asked her to do the dishes, but she said, "No, I'm painting. Don't interrupt me." *(Pause.)* And I grabbed the paint sticks. The...the...the...

BENNY: Brushes.

MA: And I smeared them across the paper, mixing all the colors. I said, "That's what I think of your picture! Go wash the dishes!" And she was crying. Screaming...

BENNY: And you hit her.

(Shocked, she looks at Benny.)

MA: How do you know? How do you know about my dream?

BENNY: I was there. I remember it.

MA: In my dream?

(He looks at her for some glimmer of understanding, but does not find it. Lights fade. The TVs flicker in the darkness.)

SCENE 18

Ma sits in her chair talking on the cordless phone.

MA: I'm so glad to hear that. How's Kayla? What grade is she in now? She's doing well in school?...That's good. Is she there?...Oh, that's too bad. I haven't spoken to her in such a long time...Oh, he's all right. I want you to talk to him though. He's been yelling at me....I don't know. Because I can't remember things...He doesn't like me asking him questions. He gets mad and he yells. I don't like to have people yell at me...Is he? I don't remember. What time is it? Benny?! Benny!?...Are you here?! *(Pause.)* Sharon wants to speak to you. *(To Sharon.)* I don't know if he's here...Oh, you're right...Yes, I see his coat.

(Benny has come out of the back silently and is standing right beside Ma.)

MA: Benny! Oh! Benny! Don't sneak up on me like that! Here.

(Benny holds the phone up to his ear.)

BENNY: ...Yeah....Yeah?

(He glares at Ma and turns away from her.)

BENNY: ...uh huh...I understand...I'll try...I know...Yeah, okay, bye.

(He hangs the phone up and puts it in its cradle on the other side of the room.)

MA: I wasn't done talking.

BENNY: You were done.

MA: I didn't even get to ask about Kayla.

BENNY: You asked her eight times about Kayla. You ask everything eight times. A hundred times!

MA: You're yelling at me!

(Benny paces, trying to regain composure.)

MA: Don't pace like that. You make me nervous.

BENNY: Do you want me to tell them about how you tried to go to synagogue at three in the morning? Do you want me to tell them those things? *(Muttering.)* God you make me crazy!

MA: I don't remember that.

BENNY: You don't remember anything!

MA: Don't yell at me, Benny. Please don't yell at me.

(Benny stalks off to the back. The bathroom door slams shut. Ma is very upset, crying.)

MA: Oh. Oohhhh. Benny! I think I had an accident...Benny?

(Benny comes out, still mad but much calmer. He comes up and stands by her.)

BENNY: I'm sorry.

(Ma wipes her nose and eyes. Benny holds out his hand, tenderly—for him.)

BENNY: Come on.

(She looks at him. He waits patiently. She places her hand in his. The lights fade. The TVs flicker in the darkness. In the half-light, Benny sets up his daybed for sleeping and lays down. Ma goes back to her room.)

SCENE 19

Benny is asleep on the daybed. Ma comes in with her walker. She goes over to the daybed and sits in the chair near his head. She turns the lamp on, awakening Benny.

MA: Do you ever hear voices? *(No answer.)* Sharon said that you told her once, a long time ago, that you heard voices. That a voice told you to go to the desert and that's why you went to California. *(Pause.)* Do you still hear it? The voice?

(Benny does not respond. Ma turns back to the front.)

MA: Sometimes I think I hear voices...I think I'm going crazy.

BENNY: You're just old.

(Ma stands up and leans over him.)

MA: Turn over.

(Benny does not move.)

MA: Turn over.

(They look at one another for a long time. Then Benny turns, and Ma pulls up his shirt, searching at his back for something. Suddenly she freezes, then rubs a spot on his back, ever so gently. Benny stares out, expressionless.)

MA: You have a scar. *(She continues to feel it.)* It's so...

(She pulls her hand away from him and then takes her walker over to the arm chair and sits. She looks at him. He sits up. Pause.)

MA: I was lying in bed and I just...This vision of something flying across the room, hitting you in the back. I don't even remember what it was.

BENNY: It was a piece of an ash tray.

MA: How can you remember that? You were so little.

BENNY: You were throwing it at Shayna. You missed.

MA: ...No. No, I wasn't throwing it at...

BENNY: Because she burned the latkes.

(Pause. Ma seems to remember.)

MA: Are there other scars?

(Pause.)

BENNY: Probably. You'll have to ask them.

MA: Do you think that's why?...Do you think that's why you're sick?

(Pause.)

BENNY: No.

(She holds her hand to her mouth, teary and afraid of her own thoughts.)

MA: I don't want to hear the voices, Benny. I don't want to remember.

(Lights fade. The TVs flicker. Ma returns to the back. Benny puts his bedding away, takes his coat and exits. Ma goes to her chair.)

SCENE 20

Benny sits at the kitchen table, his hands clamped over his ears, the TV on fairly loud. Ma is in back, out of sight, yelling and throwing things.

MA: *(Offstage.)* God damn you and your books! All you ever do is read. You come home, you read at the dinner table. Then you sit in your chair and read, then you come to bed and read! As if I'm not even here! As if none of us were here!

(Benny turns up the volume on the TV and continues to clamp his ears. The phone starts ringing. Benny looks at it. Desperate.)

MA: *(Offstage.)* And you! I know what you're scribbling in that diary of yours. How much you hate your mother. What an awful beast I am. I've seen it. You can't hide things from me. This is my house. I can look at anything I damn well please!

(Benny turns down the TV and answers the phone.)

BENNY: Hello?...Hi...No, she's sleeping.

MA: *(Offstage.)*...Someday you'll come home and you won't find your little diary...

BENNY: That's the TV. Oh. Did they? They must have heard the TV. She turns it up loud now...Yeah, I'll turn it down.

MA: *(Offstage.)* And you. You'll come home and all your books will be gone. I'll give them away! Burn them!

BENNY: No, everything's fine...We're fine...She's fine.

(There's a sound of something toppling over.)

BENNY: I gotta go. I'll have her call you when she wakes up.

(He hangs up and heads into the back. Lights fade. The TVs flicker in the darkness. In the half-light, Benny watches Ma walk over to her chair and sit. She cannot work the remote. He turns the TV on for her and goes over to his chair.)

SCENE 21

Ma sits in her armchair. Benny is at the table.

MA: Who was that woman who was here this morning?

BENNY: Marta.

MA: Who is she? Why is she coming here?

BENNY: To help.

MA: To help who?

(Pause.)

BENNY: You.

MA: Me?

BENNY: Yes.

MA: How does she know about us?

BENNY: Sharon pays her to come.

MA: Sharon?...She pays her to help me?...Do, I know Sharon?

(Pause.)

MA: She was nice. This woman. What did you say her name was?

BENNY: Marta.

MA: Is she Jewish?

BENNY: I don't know.

MA: We should ask her.

BENNY: No, Ma.

MA: Why not? I want to know.

BENNY: It doesn't matter.

MA: Of course it matters...I think she must be Jewish. She's very nice. *(Pause.)* I'm having a good day today, don't you think? Could you take me for a walk later? Just around the block? It looks nice outside.

BENNY: We went for a walk.

MA: Today?

BENNY: Yes. You don't remember.

MA: I know I don't remember. I know...Sometimes I think you lie to me. You tell me we went for a walk because you know I don't remember, but we never had a walk...Tell me about it, Benny. Were there flowers? Is it the time of year for flowers?

(Lights fade. The TVs flicker in the darkness. In the half-light, Benny gets up and puts his coat on and exits. Then Ma gets up, she straightens her wedding photo, and takes the photo of her husband off the wall and carries it back over to her chair. She wipes the dust from the photo and then embraces it. Lights fade to black.)

SCENE 22

Lights up on Ma in her chair, her eyes closed. She holds the photo of her husband. Benny comes in the front door and sees her asleep. He closes the door, not trying to be quiet. Ma does not stir. He hangs up his coat in his usual meticulous fashion. He goes to the kitchen and puts her pills in a paper cup. He pours her a glass of juice and brings everything over on a tray. He sets the tray down in front of her.

BENNY: Ma.

(Still, she does not stir. He pulls the photo from her grasp and her hands tumble lifelessly into her lap.)

BENNY: Ma.

(No response. Benny shakes her shoulder. She tilts to the side.)

BENNY: Ma?

(He realizes she is dead. He sits in the opposite arm chair and stares at her, holding the photo of his father much the way she had been holding it. Lights fade to black.)

SCENE 23

Lights up on the apartment. It looks the same, except no one is in it. The phone rings twice and stops. It begins to ring again. After many rings, Benny comes in from the back room. He wears a suit that fits him well and is carrying a yarmulke. He is struggling with his tie, which is hanging at odd lengths. He answers the phone.

BENNY: Hello?...Yeah...No, I'm coming...I'm ready...I know...I did...I did...I know!...I DID!

(Pause.)

BENNY: I don't have to say anything, do I?...Do I have to wear a tie? I can't tie it. I don't remember how...Okay...Sharon?...Will I stay here?...By myself?...Who will pay the rent?...Really?...No, I want to....No. I'll wait outside.

(He hangs up the phone. He is about to try again with the tie, but he gives up and leaves it like it is. He is about to put the yarmulke on, but then shoves it in his pocket instead. He goes over and takes his shabby jacket off the peg. He starts to button it over his suit, but then he realizes how that would look. He takes it off and carefully hangs it back on the peg. He stares at it a moment, then puts it back on, but does not button it. He returns his parents' wedding photo to his preferred skewed angle, then he goes out into the hall. He looks over the empty apartment for a moment, then pulls the door closed behind him. Lights fade.)

END OF PLAY

The Liquid Moon

by John Green

Dedicated to Rebecca and Ed

ORIGINALLY PRODUCED by Chicago Dramatists

For theatre profile and information on Chicago Dramatists, see page 2.

* * *

John Green has been a Resident Playwright with Chicago Dramatists for about fifteen years. His plays are always audience favorites, not just because he frequently writes comedies, but because he writes from the heart about the things that worry him, which just happen to be the things that worry audiences. In most all of his plays, and notably in *The Liquid Moon*, he does what I think is the hardest thing in the world to do: he writes funny. But *The Liquid Moon* is much more than a sex comedy, a frustration comedy, a guilt comedy, and a middle-age crisis comedy. It is also a very thoughtful and contemporary contemplation of personal morality. And, yes, it has a nude scene (which resulted in parking lot protests and sold out houses when it was produced at the venerable Barter Theatre in Virginia). When the rave reviews came out for our world premiere production at Chicago Dramatists, we suddenly had packed houses. Interestingly, I've seen other plays get rave reviews, but the audiences never turned out. With *The Liquid Moon*, they read the reviews and decided it was something they really wanted to see. And they loved it. It even earned John a well-deserved Joseph Jefferson Award for New Work. Here's how we described the play in our publicity materials for our Chicago Dramatists' world premiere:

Fearing the three "M"s (Middle-age, Mortgage and Mother-in-law), Ryan beginsa platonic "experiment" with a wounded, young poet. Torn between what feels good and what is good, Ryan dares to explore what's in between.

Russ Tutterow
Artistic Director, Chicago Dramatists

BIOGRAPHY

John Green's geopolitical farce, *The (W)Hole Thing*, was first produced as part of Stage Left Theatre's new play festival, Leapfest, and then chosen by them for full production. John's musical, *Let It Play*, was first produced at Chicago's Body Politic Theatre and then moved to the 78th Street Playhouse in Manhattan. *I Have Found Home* (musical) was staged at New York's South Street Seaport. His comedy, *Hamburger Twins*, was produced by Michael Leavitt at the Body Politic and Briar Street Theatres. It has since been done at the Creede Repertory Theatre in Colorado and in Paris at Theater de La Main D'or. John's comedy, *Mr.*

Happy, was developed through a series of readings and workshops at Manhattan Punchline Theatre and Chicago Dramatists, where it was first produced, as was his play *The Duchess*. *Mr. Happy* was also produced at Shadow Box Cabaret in Columbus, Ohio, as was his comedy, *Choke Chain*. *My Song*, a full length play with music premiered at the Circle Theatre in Forest Park, Illinois. The one act version of his play, *Twilight Serenade*, was published by the Dramatic Publishing Company. The full length version received its world premiere at Chicago's Red Hen Productions, as did his autobiographical musical, *Going Up*. John's play, *Hiding*, was a finalist in the national Tennessee Williams/New Orleans Literary Festival One Act Play Contest. He is a Resident Playwright at Chicago Dramatists. As an actor, John won the Joseph Jefferson Award (*Of Mice and Men*) and was nominated two other times. He has appeared in film, television, and on stages across the United States and Europe. He teaches acting at Act One Studios.

DEVELOPMENTAL HISTORY

The Liquid Moon was developed through a series of table readings at Chicago Dramatists and the Goodman Theatre, as well as a staged reading at Chicago Dramatists.

AWARDS AND HONORS

The Liquid Moon won a Joseph Jefferson Award for New Work and an After Dark Award for Outstanding Play. It then had a sold out run at the Barter Theater in Virginia in the fall of 2003.

ORIGINAL PRODUCTION

The Liquid Moon premiered at Chicago Dramatists on October 5, 2001.
It was directed by Producing Director Ann Filmer with the following cast:

RYAN . . . . .Norm Boucher
PAUL . . . . .Stephen Spencer
KELLY. . . . . .Carrie Layne
BARBARA. . . . . .Judy Blue

and the following production staff:

Set Designer. . . . . .Joey Wade
Lighting Designer. . . . . .Jeff Pines
Sound Designer . . . . .Edward Reardon
Costume Designer . . . . .Michelle Lynette Bush
Special Make Up Designer. . . . . .Sandy Morris
Stage Manager . . . . .Barbara Walk

CHARACTERS

RYAN: 40-55. A writer, husband, seeker and unfulfilled romantic—a Democrat. Kelly is both inspiration and temptation at a time when his wife is emotionally unavailable. He is driven by a deep spiritual longing to experience and name the ineffable.

PAUL: 40-55. A husband, father, businessman, unfulfilled poet—a moderate Republican/ Independent. He needs to hear Ryan's story as much as Ryan needs to tell it.

KELLY: 20s. A wounded poet in search of her own voice. She sees in Ryan the "mythical lion" that can undo the spell put on her by her father. She is passionate and hungry for healing.

BARBARA: 40-55. Teacher, paleontologist, wife, reluctant caregiver trying to deal with her aging mother without losing her sense of self. More than anything, she needs her husband to be on hold in this time of crisis.

The actress playing Barbara also plays the OLD WOMAN at the top of the play, using a walker, disguising herself in a robe, slippers, and head scarf.

TIME & PLACE

The present. Chicago. Various locations.

AUTHOR'S NOTES

The dialogue and debate between Paul and Ryan must be understood as immediate and passionate and not merely "intellectual" in order for the play to work. It is essential to understand that Paul is friend, audience, and Ryan's conscience as he shadows him throughout the play.

The setting is both simple and symbolic, hinting at a drama that is both natural and abstract. The stage is framed by a pair of sculpted male/female figures entwined like the twisting trunks of trees, one stage right and the other stage left. Their arms extend above their heads, becoming branches reaching toward one another, arching across the top of the stage, meeting in the middle. Subtle images of dense foliage and primitive growth appear on a scrim upstage, evoking The Garden of Eden. Ryan's home and Kelly's apartment are represented by a simple couch, a small end table to its left and a small desk and chair down right that is also used for the bookstore scenes. All bars, restaurants, and the coffee shop scenes are played at a round table with two chairs downstage left. Behind the scrim upstage are two trees, one barren and the other with healthy leaves, representing youth and aging, as well as the "tree of life," and that of "good and evil" referred to in The Garden of Eden. During the pre-show setup, the two trees are subtly lit, then disappear until the end of act one. They remain continually lit as the play opens up both spiritually and psychologically in act two. No one appears behind the scrim until the end of act two, making it a mysterious and important space for the end of the play. The setting for the original production at Chicago Dramatists (a smaller proscenium stage) was simple and symbolic. The main playing area was a slightly raked platform made of light blonde, refinished wood that ran on a small angle from center right to down left. This odd angle hinted that the play was both natural and poetic. The down left edge of the platform was warped, curling into the air, representing "the edge" at which the drama unfolds. Ryan's home and Kelly's apartment were represented by a simple futon couch with a small end table stage right. All bars, restaurants and the coffee house were played at a round table stage left with two wooden chairs that matched the color of the platform.

The costumes remain the same throughout to match the fluidity of blocking and storytelling (even though time shifts back and forth). The only costume change is for Kelly. During her last scene in the coffee house she adds a conservative cardigan sweater to signify a shift in her relationship with Ryan.

Graceful solo piano music is used sparingly to emphasize the sense of delicate humor, poetry, and the theme of "touch" inherent in the script.

CENTRAL IMAGES AND DEFINITIONS

Liquid 1. Flowing freely like water 2. Neither solid nor gaseous: characterized by free movement... 3. Shining clear 4. ...readily takes the shape of its container 5. ...is opposed to fixed; opposed to rigid or stiff and may stress susceptibility to change of form or pattern

Moon 1. The earth's only known natural satellite shining by the sun's reflected light... 2. To spend in idle reverie: Dream; to behave abstractedly

Eternal 1. Having infinite duration: Everlasting. Characterized by abiding fellowship with God 2. Continued without intermission

Cherubim (Cherub) 1. A biblical figure often represented as a being with large wings, a human head, and an animal body and regarded as a guardian of a sacred place.

Author's Image: The inconstant moon reflects the light of an eternal sun.

Carrie Layne (background) as Kelly, Judy Blue (left) as Barbara, and Norm Boucher as Ryan in Chicago Dramatists' 2001 production of *The Liquid Moon* by John Green, directed by Ann Filmer.   Photo by Jeff Pines

The Liquid Moon

Act I

In dim light, we see Ryan and Paul seated at a table down left, silently sipping wine. The two trees appear upstage behind the scrim. An Old Woman, bent over her walker, enters up left. She is in silhouette. We cannot make out the features of her face. She moves across the stage, stops to gather strength, and then exits right. Lights fade on the two trees. The images of dense foliage and growth return to the scrim, remaining there throughout the play. Lights come up on Ryan and Paul. Ryan seems giddy, delighting in a secret. Paul watches him, bemused.

RYAN: Thanks for meeting. I know how busy you are.

PAUL: Of course.

RYAN: Thanks.

PAUL: What's going on?

RYAN: It's hard to explain.

PAUL: Right.

RYAN: Are you good? Things okay with Lisa? The kids?

PAUL: Yes. Things are fine.

RYAN: Good.

PAUL: You seem...

RYAN: I know. I think I'm on the verge of a nervous breakthrough.

PAUL: *(Chuckles.)* Sounds like it. *(Beat.)* What is it?

RYAN: Nothing. Yet.

PAUL: Okay.

RYAN: Listen, before we start...it's weird but—you're the only one I trust. With this.

PAUL: Thanks. I guess.

RYAN: No, it's good. But, well...Look, I'm concerned about telling you because, well...

PAUL: You can tell me stuff.

RYAN: I know. God, you're the only guy I talk to. I mean, about real stuff.

PAUL: You too.

RYAN: It's just—we had that fight, you know, about the suburbs and having children and...

PAUL: Republicans?

RYAN: Yes.

PAUL: It's okay, Ryan. We should be able to fight. You know, best friends argue.

RYAN: I know. It's just that the last thing you said before getting in the car—it bothered me.

PAUL: The last thing?

RYAN: About you weren't "voting for the man." The Supreme Court nominations?

PAUL: Oh, right. *(Beat.)* Right.

RYAN: We're so different.

PAUL: Which is good.

RYAN: Which is good, yes. But, well, now that you have kids and your own business—and you go to church.

PAUL: I see.

RYAN: You do.

PAUL: You're afraid I'll judge you.

RYAN: Kind of.

PAUL: I won't. *(Beat.)* I'll try not to.

RYAN: "Thou shalt not judge."

PAUL: Exactly.

RYAN: Hey, even some people in the Christian Coalition are speaking out against the death penalty, right?

PAUL: The Christian Coali—?!

RYAN: I'm not implying—

PAUL: Jesus, Ryan, it's not that way.

RYAN: I didn't mean—

PAUL: I'm not born again or fundamentalist or—

RYAN: Good. I mean...

PAUL/RYAN: "Not that there's anything wrong with that."

(They share a much needed laugh.)

RYAN: On the way here, I was standing on the El platform, waiting for the Red Line.

PAUL: Uh-huh.

RYAN: My eyes were drawn to the top of this trash can. I saw a series of amazing snowflakes or frost or—whatever. One was a perfectly formed clover leaf. Another, a six-pointed star. I'd never seen anything like it. I mean, if I tell you I saw an amazing snowflake, you'd think, "sure, I've seen snowflakes." But I am telling you—*(He looks around, then leans in. Intensely.)*—I have never in my life seen any like these.

PAUL: *(After a beat.)* Really.

RYAN: I had to show someone. Before they melted. I looked around the platform. There was this big Hispanic guy-he'd probably beat the shit out of me. This old woman seemed too preoccupied. Finally, I spotted a young man. He looked like a college student-sweet faced, open. It was my only chance before the train got there. "Excuse me," I said. "Can I show you something?"

PAUL: *(Cringing.)* Oooh.

RYAN: It was awkward as hell. But he came over. He stood there. And he saw it. He whispered, "awesome."

PAUL: "In awe." You literally stood "in awe."

RYAN: It was like a prayer, like...

PAUL: *(Teasing.)* Worshipping?

RYAN: Exactly. *(Beat.)* The train arrived. The moment collapsed. We didn't say a word. He went to a separate car. And I'm glad he did. It too would've felt uncomfortable as hell. But the moment, the moment itself was pure.

PAUL: That's you.

RYAN: What?

PAUL: Looking for snowflakes.

RYAN: *(Defensive.)* I suppose.

PAUL: You're always looking at things. Even when we were kids.

RYAN: Was I?

PAUL: You remember this football game? We were playing down at Gilson Park, without gear? It must've been seventh grade. In the middle of the huddle you look around at the team, all of your friends standing in a circle, and you go *(In awe.)* "this is so cool."

RYAN: *(Embarrassed.)* Did I really?

PAUL: The other guys thought you were nuts.

RYAN: *(Deep appreciation.)* But not you.

PAUL: *(Deep affection.)* Not me. *(Pause.)* So, is that it, the snowflakes?

RYAN: Not exactly. But looking at things.

PAUL: Really seeing them.

RYAN: The whole picture.

PAUL: Right. *(Beat.)* So, tell me. From the beginning. *(Beat.)* What's going on?

RYAN: Okay. God, this sounds corny but—"there's this girl."

PAUL: Oh, boy.

RYAN: Hey.

PAUL: Sorry. Go ahead. Seriously.

RYAN: Yeah.

(Lights crossfade as Ryan picks up a box from behind the table and crosses to the desk down right. It is covered with copies of his novel, "The Liquid Moon.")

RYAN: Well, she comes up to me one evening...

(Kelly enters from stage right, approaching him.)

RYAN: ...after a book signing...

(He sits, placing a book inside of the box as Kelly approaches.)

KELLY: Excuse me.

RYAN: Hm? *(Looks up.)* Oh. Oh, hi.

KELLY: Hello again.

RYAN: You were at...

KELLY: Borders and Barnes & Noble.

RYAN: Both signings. I remember.

KELLY: Don't worry, I'm not stalking you.

RYAN: Too bad. *(They laugh. He stands.)* Wait, wait don't tell me. Kelly, right?

KELLY: That's right.

RYAN: *(Sings Woody's tuneless song from the TV show "Cheers.")* "Kelly Kelly Kelly Kelly..." *(No response.)* I'll bet you never heard that before, huh?

KELLY: Only about a thousand times since it was on "Cheers."

RYAN: Sorry.

KELLY: You're blushing.

RYAN: Am I? Great.

KELLY: No. I like that.

RYAN: You do?

KELLY: Yes. It's human.

RYAN: Ah, human. Yes, well, listen-don't tell anyone but it's all an act.

KELLY: Is it?

RYAN: Can you keep a secret?

KELLY: I'll try.

RYAN: I'm actually an alien.

KELLY: I knew there was something different about you.

RYAN: It doesn't scare you?

KELLY: Not after the boys I've been dating.

RYAN: *(Laughs.)* That's good. That's very very good.

KELLY: Thanks. *(Beat.)* Anyway, I wanted to tell you I loved your selections tonight. *(She takes out a notebook and pen.)* And the talk on writing, how you write.

RYAN: That's very nice of you.

KELLY: I mean it.

RYAN: Thank you. *(Beat.)* So...

KELLY: So...

RYAN: Well, I'd better get "organ-i-zized." You know, like in "Taxi Driver?" You know the Scorsese film.

KELLY: *(She opens the notebook and begins to write.)* "Taxi."

RYAN: "Driver." With De Niro. Not the TV series, "Taxi." That was Andy Kaufman.

KELLY: Oh, yes. "Man on the Moon." I loved that.

RYAN: Jim Carrey.

KELLY: Oh, yes.

(Their eyes lock.)

KELLY: I love him.

RYAN: *(Entranced.)* Incredible. He is an incredible minor—*(Quickly correcting.)*— mimer-mimic!

KELLY: Very convincing.

RYAN: Totally. Anyway, I'm glad you enjoyed the lecture.

KELLY: Can I... *(Raises her hand.)* I had a question.

RYAN: Yes, you, in the first row.

(They chuckle.)

KELLY: I'm sorry.

RYAN: No. No, it's sweet.

KELLY: Oh, great. Well, anyway, do you have a second?

RYAN: Um, sure. I just have to gather some of the-too many unsigned copies no one purchased. *(Picks up box.)*

KELLY: Oh, I loved your book.

RYAN: *(Puts the box down.)* This can wait. What's the question?

KELLY: It's about the subconscious. What you said, about stimulating or engaging the imagination or...

RYAN: Preparing the soil.

KELLY: Preparing the soil. Yes. Yes, does that apply—"preparing the soil"—to poetry as well as prose?

RYAN: Poetry.

KELLY: Do you? Write poetry?

RYAN: Not for a long time.

KELLY: Oh.

RYAN: Do you?

KELLY: I guess I do...I do. Yes.

RYAN: Tell me about it.

KELLY: It's a bit...

RYAN: Personal?

KELLY: Yes. And...

RYAN: What?

KELLY: Dark.

RYAN: Okay.

KELLY: How about you?

RYAN: My...

KELLY: Poetry.

RYAN: Is it dark?

KELLY: Can I buy it?

RYAN: I've never published...I mean poetry, it's...

KELLY: Private.

RYAN: To me.

KELLY: But it's all personal. You said that today. "All fiction, every character is ultimately personal. If you find the connections to your self."

RYAN: You really listen, don't you.

KELLY: I want to learn. It means everything to me.

RYAN: Writing?

KELLY: Everything.

(She rushes to Ryan's chair, sits, opening her notebook, pen in hand, anxiously awaiting his lecture.)

RYAN: Well. Poetry. I think-see, poetry. When I used to write...It seems to me that it is direct. More in the moment. No plotting. No outlining. Just...

KELLY: Rhythms of the heart.

RYAN: That's lovely. *(Beat.)* You're lovely.

KELLY: My turn to blush.

PAUL: *(Interrupts, mocking.)* "Rhythms of the heart?"

(Lights crossfade. She sits at the table in dim light, studying her notebook. Ryan walks toward Paul.)

RYAN: Come on.

PAUL: Sorry.

RYAN: *(Studying Kelly.)* She's beautiful, Paul.

PAUL: *(Pondering.)* Rhythms of the heart.

RYAN: Yes.

PAUL: I love poetry.

RYAN: I used to.

PAUL: Remember in college, reading William Blake?

RYAN: You used to do sketches. Of his poems.

PAUL: I did, didn't I?

RYAN: Some bird. A large bird.

PAUL: A raven?

RYAN: That was Poe.

PAUL: No. Blake. Something about flight.

RYAN: Oh, yes.

PAUL: *(Quotes Blake.)* "So he took his wings and fled:

Then the morn blush'd rosy red:

I dried my tears & arm'd my fears

With ten thousand shields and spears.

Soon my Angel..."

RYAN: An Angel.

PAUL: But I drew a bird. Half bird—

(Ryan crosses to Paul.)

RYAN: Half man. A dark Angel. This wild flying creature.

PAUL: *(Excited.)* A Cherub.

(Ryan looks slightly puzzled.)

PAUL: In Genesis, The Garden of Eden-Adam and Eve are kicked out for disobeying. These Cherubim are placed at the gate. To guard and protect. To keep them out.

RYAN: *(Sits.)* They're angels, right?

PAUL: Kind of. Everybody thinks they're these cute little creatures. But they're not. Half of them is animal. Half beast, half angel.

RYAN: It's a riddle.

PAUL: What?

RYAN: The parable ends with these, um—

PAUL: Cherubim—

RYAN: Cherubim guarding the gate. It ends with a kind of question. We all want to get back. We all want to get back to paradise, right?

PAUL: Right.

RYAN: So, the riddle is: How do you get back? How do you get past the Cherubim?

PAUL: *(Deadpan.)* Stop watching cable.

(It takes Ryan a second before he gets the joke. He chuckles. They drink silently.)

PAUL: *(Finishes quote.)* "Soon my Angel came again;

I was arm'd, he came in vain:

For the time of youth was fled

And grey hairs were on my head."

RYAN: You sure you're a Republican?

PAUL: I'm an Independent and you know it. Don't get me started, Ryan.

RYAN: I'm just teasing, Paul.

PAUL: Just don't get me started.

(Pause.)

RYAN: "Grey hairs were on my head."

PAUL: *(Touches his head.)* Prophetic, eh?

RYAN: *(Wistful.)* What the hell did we know then?

PAUL: I miss it. The poetry. The time.

(Ryan stands, looking at Kelly.)

RYAN: She's there.

PAUL: Where?

RYAN: Rhythms of the heart. Poetry. She's alive with it.

PAUL: She's young, right?

RYAN: I suppose.

PAUL: What, eighteen, nineteen?

RYAN: Twenty-something.

PAUL: Well...

RYAN: I know. I know but still—*(Ryan crosses toward Kelly.)*—there it is. In her eyes. In her voice-poetry. It's alive in her.

PAUL: You're smitten.

RYAN: No. Yes. Look, I know the syndrome-older man looking for his lost youth in a younger woman. But still...

PAUL: She's a doorway.

RYAN: To?

PAUL: Your soul.

RYAN: Are you putting me on?

PAUL: *(Nods "yes" but says:)* No.

RYAN: No? *(Paul nods "no.")* Yes, you are.

PAUL: I'm serious. It may be clichéd. But in your experience it's real. It's real between you and...

RYAN: Kelly.

PAUL: "Ryan and Kelly." Sounds nice.

RYAN: It does. It is. Real. How come you understand all of this?

PAUL: *(Stands.)* You'd be surprised.

RYAN: You? Have you—

PAUL: That's another story. This is about you.

RYAN: You son of a bitch.

(Paul crosses up and sits on the edge of the couch.)

PAUL: Your story. So, she likes poetry, she's—

RYAN: A "doorway to my soul."

PAUL: Continue.

RYAN: All right. All right...

(Lights change.)

RYAN: So, she brought some of her poems to my next signing.

(Ryan crosses to Kelly. She hands him a few pages of her poetry. He studies them.)

RYAN: And they were good, Paul. *(To Kelly.)* Really good.

KELLY: Oh, my God.

RYAN: I mean it.

KELLY: You can't imagine what this means. From you.

RYAN: Listen, you haven't read my mine yet.

KELLY: No. But you're a professional and I love your work.

RYAN: Thank you.

KELLY: "The Liquid Moon" is incandescent.

RYAN: But not commercial.

KELLY: I disagree. It's personal and universal at the same time.

RYAN: Man, I wish you'd written a review. A number of critics found it "turgid."

KELLY: I beg to differ.

RYAN: Please do.

KELLY: I found it lyrical. Highly metaphorical. Not to be taken literally.

RYAN: That's right. *(Beat.)* Still, we'll see if it goes anywhere.

KELLY: It already has.

RYAN: Huh?

KELLY: I'll tell you exactly where it's gone. *(She touches her heart.)* Right here.

> *(Beat.)*

RYAN: Can I buy you a drink?

PAUL: *(Stands.)* Look out.

RYAN: *(To Paul.)* I know, I know. What can I say?

> *(Paul crosses right. Kelly crosses down left and sits at the table, placing her notebook on it.)*

PAUL: "Rhythms of the heart." You're hooked.

RYAN: Tell me about it.

PAUL: *(Sits at the desk down right.)* So?

RYAN: So—we went to The Cavern. *(Ryan sits at the table across from Kelly.)* This intimate little bar with soft lighting and major ambience.

PAUL: *(Teasing.)* "A doorway to the soul." *(He watches them.)*

RYAN: I was surprised. Pleasantly surprised. There's a depth to your work. A perspective. An older point of view.

KELLY: I've been through a lot.

RYAN: That resonates.

KELLY: Would you—forget it.

RYAN: Please.

KELLY: There's one I didn't show you.

RYAN: Too personal?

KELLY: Painful.

RYAN: Then don't. There's no need to.

KELLY: I want to. May I?

RYAN: Of course.

(She opens her notebook, starting to read, then stops, closing it.)

KELLY: In "The Liquid Moon," the boy grows up too quickly. Was that personal?

RYAN: Not the exact circumstances but the core. The emotional core of—

KELLY: Abandonment?

RYAN: The core, yes.

KELLY: Good. I mean…

RYAN: My mother died when I was twelve. My father disappeared, became a ghost.

KELLY: Like in the book.

RYAN: "The man in the moon is a liquid balloon."

KELLY: "Nothing is solid."

RYAN: "Things seem solid. They hold form for a while, and then, poof—they disappear."

KELLY: "Like clouds."

RYAN: *(Amazed she knows his book so well.)* Like clouds.

KELLY: Okay, this is—my father was…he used to…

RYAN: He was cruel.

KELLY: Terribly.

RYAN: I'm sorry.

KELLY: I'll just begin.

(She opens her notebook and reads, fighting back emotion.)

KELLY: "Like lightning

His fists splintered my soul

Black and blue

Deep wine colored blood

Swirling in delicate pools on the wooden floor

Following the fragmented pieces of my self

I-both child and woman before my time-

Move forever in nervous circles

No beginning

No end

Chasing after my broken heart"

(She closes the book quickly. She is unable to look at him.)

RYAN: I am so sorry. *(Beat.)* Did he...

KELLY: Not sexual. Fists and words and once...The words cut deepest. They haunt the soul.

RYAN: The power of words.

(She looks deeply into his soul.)

KELLY: You have beautiful eyes.

RYAN: Blush time.

KELLY: They're kind. Like a mythical lion. There's this light. A kind of softness.

RYAN: I would never hurt you, Kelly. *(He touches her hand.)*

KELLY: I know. *(Takes his hand.)* I know that that is true.

(Lights crossfade, She exits right.)

PAUL: *(Standing.)* She hooked you.

RYAN: Totally. But she wasn't manipulating.

PAUL: Not consciously.

RYAN: That's not fair.

PAUL: I don't mean it in a bad way. I mean—look, we all need healing.

RYAN: Yes, we do.

(Paul crosses toward Ryan.)

PAUL: I read somewhere—not Christian by the way.

RYAN: Okay.

PAUL: I read this idea that relationships are all about healing each other. Healthy relationships.

RYAN: That sounds right.

PAUL: What about you?

RYAN: Me.

PAUL: *(Sitting at table.)* What are you healing?

RYAN: You sure you've never done therapy?

PAUL: I read a lot.

RYAN: Well, I guess, I guess I have a lot of fear-and need-to touch. This hunger for—to immerse myself in flesh, in...

PAUL: Sensation?

RYAN: Heat.

PAUL: Love?

RYAN: No. No, I have love.

PAUL: Barbara.

RYAN: *(Deeply felt.)* Yes, Barbara.

PAUL: Are things okay? With you two?

RYAN: Yes. But not magic. It's not...I don't think this girl has anything to do with some problem in the marriage. The marriage is...

(Paul is pressing hard here.)

PAUL: Solid.

RYAN: No question.

PAUL: I believe it.

RYAN: I think the marriage-a good, long-term marriage is what it is. It can't be...

PAUL: New.

RYAN: I don't buy that you're suddenly infatuated with someone else because something's missing in the marriage. A marriage can't—

PAUL: You can't have it all.

RYAN: Are you being sarcastic?

PAUL: Not at all. I think this is a big myth. "You can have it all." It makes people crazy.

RYAN: And you can't get it all in one person. One person cannot fulfill all the aspects of your self.

PAUL: Right.

RYAN: We play all of these...

PAUL: Roles?

RYAN: The husband, the writer—

PAUL: The lover—

RYAN: The romantic.

(Pause.)

PAUL: (Pressing hard.) How are things? With you and Barbara?

RYAN: Good. I mean, it's been stressful. Buying the house. Dealing with her mother.

PAUL: How long have you been there?

RYAN: (Sighs.) Three months. It's something she's wanted her whole life.

(Lights crossfade. Barbara enters, a newspaper in hand.)

RYAN: A house. The yard. But I was afraid. I kept saying, "The next book will put us over." I didn't want to go into debt. I saw that when mother died, the medical bills and all that.

PAUL: I remember.

RYAN: Yeah. So—(Ryan crosses right.)—after Barbara's uncle left us enough for a down payment—(He sits on the couch.)—she was determined.

(Barbara joins Ryan on the couch.)

BARBARA: (Reading.) Here's one. "Two bedroom ranch. Near the bus. One car garage. Ravenswood area."

RYAN: I'd rather be near the El. That way I can avoid parking downtown. I really don't want to have to take a bus and then the El.

BARBARA: I know, but this is in our price range and the bedrooms would all be on the first floor.

RYAN: Right. But didn't we want her bedroom on the first floor, only hers? Don't we want some—?

BARBARA: Distance.

RYAN: I don't mean it as an insult. I really don't object to living with your mother.

BARBARA: I do. Why shouldn't you?

RYAN: Well...

BARBARA: You're going to be with her more than I am. She'll make you crazy, Ryan.

RYAN: I'm already crazy. (Beat.) No, it's the right thing to do. I welcome the challenge.

BARBARA: (She studies him, bemused.) Okay. (Back to paper.) Why is it so hard to find a first floor bedroom?

RYAN: Maybe a ranch would work. Maybe there's one with a bedroom at one end separated by a kitchen and dining room.

BARBARA: A long long dining room.

RYAN: With soundproof walls—

BARBARA: And a small football stadium in between.

(They laugh.)

RYAN: It'll be all right.

BARBARA: I feel terrible. She's my mother, for God's sake. I should be glad to have her live with us.

RYAN: "Should should should."

BARBARA: You're right. *(Beat.)* But I should. My God, she's got arthritis, her memory's going...I mean, God.

RYAN: This is why people ship them off to nursing homes.

BARBARA: I could never do that.

RYAN: I know. That's why I love you.

(She tears up.)

RYAN: I really do. Come here. *(He holds her.)* I could take the bus. Really.

BARBARA: No. We'll find something. *(Sigh.)* Why is everything so complicated? Why can't you just picture it and, voila—it manifests.

RYAN: I don't know. *(Beat.)* When do you have to be in Montana?

BARBARA: April twelfth. We meet at the university in the morning and then drive to the site. The dig begins the next day.

RYAN: That should give us time.

BARBARA: I can't miss this one. It could put me on the map.

RYAN: Indiana Jones look out.

BARBARA: I need this, Ryan.

RYAN: I know. I know you do. We've got four months. We can do it. *(Looks at paper.)* Hey, here's a place. In Rogers Park.

BARBARA: By the Red Line.

RYAN: "Two story. One car garage. Enclosed porch on first floor." We could, maybe we could—

BARBARA: Convert the porch—

RYAN: Into a bedroom.

BARBARA: How much?

RYAN: A little high. *(He shows her the paper.)*

BARBARA: That's above our range.

RYAN: True. But if we paid down points...

BARBARA: And we will have mother's social security.

RYAN: I wish...if "Liquid Moon" would just take off.

BARBARA: We'll be okay. *(She sits forward, slightly worried.)* We will.

    (She studies the paper. He studies her.)

RYAN: I felt close.

    (Paul rises, crossing to Ryan.)

PAUL: Like partners.

RYAN: Best friends.

PAUL: Lovers?

RYAN: No.

PAUL: Close but—

RYAN: You never hear a poem about:

"The lawyers sat on either side

Discussing points and taxes

    (To her, mock romantic.)

Speak to me of interest rates

Of candlelight and faxes"

PAUL: Or arthritis.

RYAN: Hardly. *(Ryan rises, walking toward Paul.)* No. God, her mother. She's sweet, you know. I mean, she handles it with grace and dignity.

PAUL: But there it is.

RYAN: Every day. And Barbara—

    (She rises. He watches her.)

RYAN: It's eating at her.

    (She exits.)

RYAN: They never got along. Before. They don't fight. But it's all formal. Very stiff.

PAUL: And now it's in your house.

RYAN: Every day. Every damn day. And I'm the one who feeds her, watches TV—

PAUL: That's good of you.

RYAN: I know how I want to feel about her. I want to be the Dali Lama. You know, I want to be Jesus washing her feet. *(Beat.)* But I can barely make it through "Wheel Of Fortune" without wanting to strangle her!

PAUL: It's hard.

RYAN: Numbing.

(Kelly enters, walking to the left side of the couch.)

PAUL: But this girl...

RYAN: *(Watching her.)* Kelly.

PAUL: She's young.

RYAN: *(Gazes at her.)* Untouched.

PAUL: Hardly.

RYAN: Touché.

PAUL: She's damaged, Ryan.

RYAN: Wounded.

(Ryan walks to her. Paul crosses downstage and watches with the audience.)

PAUL: You have to be careful.

(Lights crossfade. Ryan stands next to Kelly, looking around her apartment. Kelly is clearly in charge during this scene.)

KELLY: *(Crossing to front of couch.)* It's kind of small.

RYAN: Are you kidding? When I was in college I never had my own place. I lived in this burnt out rat trap with two roommates from the land of the bizarre. We had a refrigerator and a hot plate. We had to do the dishes in the bathtub.

KELLY: *(She sits.)* No.

RYAN: I swear. We called it the "pismire."

KELLY: What's a pismire?

RYAN: Exactly. One of the bizarro twins was this older guy—well, thirty, which was old at the time.

KELLY: I understand.

RYAN: Anyway, he smoked a pipe like Sherlock Holmes. James Whalen. He was from North Dakota but he spoke with this phony British accent. "My dear sir, I must tell you."

KELLY: That's funny. You are extremely funny.

RYAN: No..

KELLY: Yes.

RYAN: Not...really?

KELLY: Your accent is so good.

RYAN: *(Theatrical.)* I've trod the boards with the bard a bit in my day.

KELLY: Huh?

RYAN: Acted. In college, I did some Shakespeare. You know, "the bard?" In my day.

KELLY: *(She jumps up, kneeling on the couch.)* You are multitalented.

RYAN: I don't know.

(She leans in toward him.)

KELLY: *(Passionate.)* You are.

RYAN: *(Moving a few steps away from her.)* Yes, well-anyway, the accent—his accent— drove me nuts. So I'd really lay on the Midwestern twang. You know, *(Flat "a.")* "How's your aunt, James?" And he'd get all huffy. *(Proper "ah.")* "My auuuunt is perfectly fine." And I'd go, *(Nasal, flat "a.")* "Right. So, is your aunt visiting again?" He'd turn bright red, totally unhinged and go, "My dear sir, she is not an ant, she is not a PISMIRE. She is my aaaaaaaaaunt!"

KELLY: That is precious. *(Applauds.)* That is perfect. *(She lifts a bottle of wine and two glasses from behind the end table.)* More?

RYAN: Please.

(She pours them each a glass.)

KELLY: I love hearing stories. *(She holds out a glass to him.)* I love hearing what people have been through.

RYAN: Older people?

KELLY: I suppose. Yes.

(He takes the glass and then steps back a safe distance. She makes just enough room for him to sit close to her.)

RYAN: I always did. *(He starts to sit next to her, and then decides the arm of the couch is proper.)* When I was young. I couldn't get enough of my dad or my uncles—Grandma Hannah. They'd tell these stories, about their childhood. You'd feel connected to the past. To these quieter times before television or cars. You felt like you were sitting with them on a front porch—on one of those swinging chairs, you know? *(He mimes the back and forth motion.)* You'd listen to their stories about their youth. About general stores and old men playing checkers and how their parents met at church socials. And how their parent's parents met and on and on, stretching back in time.

(He is mesmerized by his own story. She grows distant.)

RYAN: Until I felt that if I just reached my hand out far enough I could touch the pioneers. Actually touch them.

(She is silent.)

RYAN: Are you okay?

KELLY: Hm? Oh, yes, fine.

RYAN: *(Sits next to her.)* What?

KELLY: Nothing. *(Pause.)* I guess...I never had that. Stories. We were kind of cut off, isolated. My father didn't talk much. Screamed but rarely talked. After we, well, escaped-mom was focused on surviving. I kind of ran the house. She took any job she could. There weren't any—no frills. I envy you.

RYAN: I was lucky.

(She impulsively takes his unfinished glass of wine away from him, placing both hers and his on the end table.)

KELLY: Tell me a story.

RYAN: A real one?

KELLY: It doesn't matter. *(She lays her head on his lap.)* Please.

RYAN: *(Stunned, not knowing what to do with his hands.)* Oh. Well, okay then. Let's see.

(Kelly freezes. Ryan stares at Paul. Paul crosses quickly in toward them.)

PAUL: She put her head on your lap?!

RYAN: I swear.

PAUL: Man.

RYAN: I didn't know what to think. I mean, it felt intimate.

PAUL: I'd say. And a little—you know.

RYAN: Unclear. Like, women are weird that way. It could be affectionate and sexual.

PAUL: At the same time.

RYAN/PAUL: Amazing.

(Paul crosses toward the down left table.)

RYAN: It was odd. Because obviously I'm the father here. Telling a story to a little girl.

PAUL: *(Wry.)* The father thing is clear.

RYAN: But still, her head was on my lap. And her hair is so beautiful. I just wanted; I wanted so badly to stroke her hair. To run my fingers through it. *(Fighting the urge to touch her face.)* To touch the side of her—

PAUL: *(Obsessed.)* Her head in your lap. Right in your lap.

RYAN: You're not listening to me.

PAUL: Come on, Ryan.

RYAN: It was tender. I felt more tender.

PAUL: But still...

RYAN: I'm telling you.

(Paul sits. Kelly lifts her head.)

KELLY: It doesn't have to be real. Make it "poetic."

RYAN: Clever. Very very clever.

KELLY: I like to think so. *(She snuggles back on his lap.)* Go ahead.

PAUL: Go ahead.

RYAN: Okay. *(Beat.)* Okay, here goes. Once upon a time there was a man, a very tired man, wandering through an enchanted forest at night. He came to the edge of a dense thicket of gnarled trees and damp hanging vines that seemed to—*(Tasting the words.)* —twist and hiss like vicious snakes. *(Enjoying his own creativity.)* He was soaked to the bone, deeply chilled. He felt numbed and exhausted, bereft of all hope.

KELLY: "Bereft." I love that word.

RYAN: *(Making love to her with the word.)* He was bereft.

KELLY: Mmmm. Go on. Go on.

RYAN: Yes. So, finally he came upon a cabin, a thatched hut at the edge of the forest. In the window was a lamp...no, a lantern, its soft light spilling across the wet forest floor. He carefully approached the window and peered inside. He saw a glowing fire in the brick chimney with a large pot of steaming stew hanging from a chain. He entered. He was alone.

KELLY: *(Brushing her hand across his cheek.)* Poor man.

RYAN: Yes.

KELLY: *(Adjusting herself on his lap.)* So? What happens next?

RYAN: He fixes himself a bowl of the hot stew and warms himself before the inviting fire...or the inviting heat from the warm fire. Or—

KELLY: *(Sensual.)* "Inviting fire." Definitely. *(Beat.)* And then...

RYAN: And then, the door opened.

KELLY: And a young woman entered.

RYAN: A beautiful young woman.

KELLY: With long flowing hair.

RYAN: And eyes the color of the purest summer sky.

(The two poets joyously indulge in the heat of their own storytelling.)

KELLY: *(Sitting up.)* She saw that he was still a boy inside, but time and life had worn him down, slowing his gait, causing him to mistrust himself and the world.

RYAN: *(Intense.)* "Please," he said. "The world has become a senseless whirlwind from which there is no escape. I have buried the angels but don't remember where. All color has been sucked out of my world."

KELLY: Vanquished.

RYAN: Vanquished. "Help me," he says. "I am holding my breath until I am offered an ironclad guarantee that life will not bring me pain or loss again. EVER!"

(She kneels on the couch, facing him.)

KELLY: She looked at him with pity. A tear fell from her eye. "Here," she told him. "Take this tear and place it upon the center of your forehead. It will slowly heal you." *(She places it on his forehead.)*

RYAN: It will revive you.

KELLY: "It will protect you. From the cold rain. The cruel rain. The horrible rain that poisons the soul."

RYAN: *(Breaking the trance.)* That's beautiful, Kelly. You have a gift.

KELLY: So do you.

(She kisses him passionately. He tries to not react.)

KELLY: So do you.

(Lights crossfade. Ryan watches Kelly exit.)

PAUL: Unbelievable.

RYAN: Intense.

PAUL: Like a movie. God, I kind of envy you.

RYAN: Really?

PAUL: The energy.

RYAN: Lots of energy.

PAUL: The problem is...

RYAN/PAUL: Barbara.

(Ryan crosses toward Paul.)

RYAN: No matter what I tell myself. You know, "It's a fantasy" or "It has nothing to do with Barbara." Still, it happened. It is real.

PAUL: It's the withholding.

RYAN: Is it...do you think it's, I don't know, immoral?

PAUL: How would I know?

RYAN: You're a Republican. *(Beat.)* And you go to church. *(They laugh.)* Aren't you the only ones who care about this stuff anymore?

PAUL: Very funny. Very funny. *(He stands, crossing to Ryan.)* Look, the thing about church, for me...I told you it's not literal, Jesus, for me is...When Jay turned eight I wanted a place, a place I could take him where people acknowledged another dimension. I found this church where people gather to-you sit there, once a week, with people and there's this shared sense of the eternal. That there is something beyond the physical. And that, yes, it matters what we do. Our actions matter. I wanted Jay to know that. To sit with people who believe that that's true. So that he'd have a choice. A starting point. It's a good church. The minister is bright. He doesn't lay on the guilt or make you feel separate. It's very "inclusive." It's not about Jesus. Although, of course, that's the story. That's the map—Christianity.

RYAN: That's nice.

PAUL: Are you being sarcastic now?

RYAN: No. It is. It's nice. For you. I feel...Barbara and I don't have that. We still kind of "do our own thing." We don't have kids. I'm still "in the arts." There's a kind of—

PAUL: Passion.

RYAN: Yeah. A certain freedom. But lately...it can be floaty. Ungrounded.

PAUL: This girl...

RYAN: Kelly.

PAUL: Kelly. It's like having a child. It reminds me of telling stories. Bethany's four, still in the magical thinking stages. It reminds me of reading to Bethany.

RYAN: Yuck. Isn't that kind of creepy?

PAUL: I didn't mean—

RYAN: I mean, your daughter never kissed you like that.

PAUL: No, but still, there is an attraction.

RYAN: Really?

PAUL: Not, you know, sexual exactly, but what-there is this sense of male/female energy.

RYAN: But still.

PAUL: All I'm saying is, the same needs come up. Like being a parent.

RYAN: True. Barbara teaches. She takes care of a lot of young people.

PAUL: Parents them.

RYAN: I don't have any of that. The writing is isolated. Cold. But this girl...such warmth. *(Pause.)* Is it, do you think it's wrong?

PAUL: What you've told me so far seems loving really. It's just...

RYAN: Barbara.

PAUL: Not telling her. Having a secret.

RYAN: *(To Paul.)* I kissed the girl.

(Barbara enters. She stands in darkness, next to the couch. Ryan rises.)

RYAN: All I had done was kiss her. Once. That's all.

(Paul crosses down left and watches with the audience.)

PAUL: One kiss.

RYAN: That's all.

(He crosses to Barbara. Lights fade on Paul and up on her. We now see that she is holding a bouquet of flowers. She smells them.)

BARBARA: They're beautiful.

RYAN: *(Beyond sincere.)* So are you, Barbara.

BARBARA: Were they on sale?

RYAN: Does it matter?

BARBARA: I'm just teasing. Lighten up.

RYAN: I thought you'd like them.

BARBARA: I do. I'm sorry, hon, it's been so long. I love them, I really do.

RYAN: I just...it's been difficult, with your mom downstairs. And you've been so good with her.

BARBARA: So have you.

RYAN: I try.

BARBARA: You're doing fine.

(She kisses him lightly, then crosses up to put flowers away.)

RYAN: I feel distant. *(She stops.)* Even when we make love. *(He takes her hands.)* It's like—I don't feel you. In your hands, in your touch.

BARBARA: I know.

RYAN: Is it me? Is it—

BARBARA: I try to put it out of my mind. I try to pretend things are the same. But I feel her watching. It's like I'm back in that tiny apartment growing up. There was no privacy. She was constantly staring at me. And she was—me, trying to become me. Living through me. *(Hands him back the flowers, determined to not let her mother win.)* Start again.

RYAN: I don't know.

BARBARA: I mean it. *(She sits on the couch.)* Start all over.

RYAN: Okay. *(Beat.)* Okay. *(He steps away, attempting to get into character.)* Oh, honey, I'm home.

BARBARA: *(Southern accent.)* Well, I declare, is that you? Rhett? Oh, Rhett, honey, are y'all back from the war?

RYAN: Scarlet, my dear, I realized I do give a damn. These are for you. *(Holds out flowers.)*

BARBARA: Oh, now, y'all shouldn't have bothered. Not all this fuss over little ol' me.

RYAN: Well, Scarlet, I had my fresh values card from Dominick's and they were on sale, so, I thought, "she's worth every half off penny of it!"

(He hands her the flowers. She gives him her hand.)

BARBARA: Oh, Rhett, Rhett, I'm all agog. *(Leans her head back.)* Kiss me quick you fool.

(He kisses her hand, her arm, and then dives over the back of the couch and kisses her neck. They laugh joyously.)

RYAN: This is good. It's good to laugh. With you. It's been so grim.

BARBARA: I know I've been distracted. I'm always listening for her. I'm so afraid she'll—

RYAN: Fall.

BARBARA: Or call out. And I won't hear her.

RYAN: It's like having a child.

BARBARA: I'll say.

(Ryan takes the flowers and places them on the table.)

RYAN: We have got to have our life. To preserve it.

BARBARA: I know that.

RYAN: We need to—

BARBARA: I know. Don't you think I know?

RYAN: I miss you, Barbara.

BARBARA: Me too.

(He kisses her tenderly.)

BARBARA: I miss you too.

(They begin to make love. They kiss. He gently draws her down on the couch, beginning to lie on top of her. She struggles to relax. They begin to kiss again when she "thinks" she hears a noise downstairs.)

BARBARA: *(Stopping him.)* What was that?

RYAN: What?

BARBARA: Did you hear a noise?

RYAN: No. No, it's okay. *(He reaches for her.)* Don't worry about it.

BARBARA: I'm sorry. *(She forces herself back into his arms.)*

RYAN: It's okay.

(He kisses her. She tries to respond.)

BARBARA: *(Distracted again.)* Wait a minute.

RYAN: Don't worry about it.

BARBARA: Wait!

RYAN: Goddamnit!

(He sits up. She reaches for him.)

BARBARA: I'm sorry, I thought I...

RYAN: It's okay. *(He moves away.)* It's not your fault.

BARBARA: *(Looking away.)* I'm so sorry.

RYAN: We'll figure it out. We will.

(Lights fade on Barbara. During the following, she exits and Kelly enters, standing right of the couch, establishing her apartment again. Ryan begins pacing.)

PAUL: *(Crosses up left.)* Trouble in paradise.

RYAN: *(To Paul. Pacing, upset.)* That was it. I couldn't take anymore. I bolted from the land of arthritis and Ben Gay. Her mother haunted that house like some decaying icon of death. The sound of her walker scraping across the floor. The vacant look in her sad eyes. The stories of her past repeated over and over and over again. Loss. Loss of memory. Loss of dignity. Loss of everyone you love. If this was aging. If this was the booby prize before you disappear forever-then to hell with it! God didn't care. Why should I?! *(He crosses to Kelly.)* I had to see you again.

KELLY: You do. You did?

RYAN: I do.

PAUL: Did she know you were married?

RYAN: She knew. *(To her.)* You know I'm married, don't you?

KELLY: I thought so.

RYAN: *(Holds up his hand.)* The ring?

KELLY: Not just that.

RYAN: What?

KELLY: You've been trained.

RYAN: Huh?

KELLY: You're tender. You listen. In a certain way. Like a woman's trained you.

RYAN: Trained?

PAUL: *(Steps in.)* Housebroken.

RYAN: Shut up.

KELLY: I don't want to hurt anyone.

RYAN: You won't. *(He crosses away from her.)* I could.

KELLY: I guess it makes me feel safe, that you're married. It sort of defines things. But I don't want to hurt her.

RYAN: That's between me and her.

KELLY: What's her name?

RYAN: Does it matter?

KELLY: I suppose not. *(Beat.)* What is it?

RYAN: If I tell you her name—then it will be real.

KELLY: Isn't it?

(They look at each other, heat rising.)

RYAN: *(Sensual.)* Is it?

KELLY: *(Sensual.)* I see what you mean.

(She moves closer. They are about to embrace.)

RYAN: *(Breaking, quick save.)* Have you ever heard of courtly love?

KELLY: Kind of, I—

RYAN: *(Sits on couch.)* In Medieval times, the knights would woo married ladies, through music and gifts—

KELLY: And poetry.

RYAN: Especially poetry. But they chose to remain platonic.

KELLY: I've heard the word, of course, but—

RYAN: It means...well, it's come to mean not physical, and you know "just friends." But originally it's from Plato. The Greek Philosopher?

KELLY: Duh.

RYAN: You never know these days. Anyway, in the original meaning, according to Plato, it meant that the feelings between you-the individuals-are used to transcend your subjective selves toward the ideals they represent. In other words, you project your feelings and desires onto the other person but instead of believing it's all about them—or limited to them—you use these emotions to remind you or reflect or return one to the divine.

(Paul crosses in to left of the couch.)

PAUL: No sex.

RYAN: Platonic.

KELLY: *(Sits on couch.)* Wow.

RYAN: Yeah, wow.

PAUL: Is that possible?

KELLY: Do you think it's possible?

(Paul and Kelly wait for his answer.)

RYAN: It's worth a shot.

KELLY: What do we do?

PAUL: What did you do?

RYAN: *(To her.)* I'm not sure. *(To him.)* It's hard to explain.

KELLY: Have you ever, you know, tried this out with anyone else before?

RYAN: No.

PAUL: No?

RYAN: Never.

KELLY: Good. I mean, that makes it kind of special.

RYAN: You are.

KELLY: No.

RYAN: Yes. *(Realizing.)* Ooh, ooh I think that's it.

KELLY: What?

RYAN: See, I tell you how I feel—about you—what qualities I like, what they inspire—

KELLY: In you.

RYAN: But instead of—

KELLY: Sexualizing them...

RYAN: Have you done therapy?

KELLY: Have you?

RYAN: Once.

KELLY: Twice.

RYAN: Six months.

KELLY/RYAN: A year.

KELLY: Cool! So, then...

RYAN: So, then, instead of "acting out," we investigate.

PAUL: Oh, brother.

RYAN: Give me a break.

(Paul crosses and sits at the table down left.)

PAUL: Good luck.

(Kelly takes his hands, facing him.)

KELLY: I'm ready. Tell me. Project all over me.

RYAN: *(To Paul.)* Don't even start. *(To her.)* Alright. Let's see, I look at you: Your skin, your hair, your eyes—are perfect.

KELLY: "Perfection."

RYAN: Absolute.

KELLY: It's an ideal. Perfection is an ideal.

RYAN: You're right. Okay, okay, you are perfection.

KELLY: But I'm not. I'm filled with doubts and fear. I judge, I whine—

RYAN: "Perfection."

KELLY: The ideal of perfection. Not me but—

RYAN: Yes. So when I when I hear you speak, look into your eyes—I see your essence. Your—

KELLY: You do?

RYAN: Absolutely.

KELLY: Oh my.

RYAN: Perfection.

KELLY: Perfection.

RYAN: *(Looks at her face.)* Your skin. The tone, the texture, it—what—comforts me. It's soothing.

KELLY: Weird.

RYAN: And your hands. *(Takes her hands, studying them.)* Your hands are beautiful. Delicate but strong. They're—

KELLY: Like a baby's?

RYAN: Like a mother's.

PAUL: *(Does the Twilight Zone theme.)*

RYAN: *(To Paul.)* They were beautiful. *(To Kelly.)* They were beautiful.

KELLY: Your mother's hands.

RYAN: She used to play the piano. I remember her hands flying across the keys. Her strong hands, filled with love.

KELLY: *(Touching his face.)* She sounds wonderful.

RYAN: She was. *(Takes her hands.)* I look at you, Kelly, and I see warmth, kindness-female beauty—

KELLY: "Beauty—"

RYAN: "Absolute." And I want to touch you and be touched by you.

KELLY: *(Turned on.)* Me too.

RYAN: *(On fire.)* This heat, this longing rising up...

PAUL: Rising straight up.

RYAN: You look perfect. But maybe what I'm really hungry for is—

PAUL: Sex!

KELLY: Passion!

RYAN: Connection. I'm hungry to connect!

KELLY: Yes!

(They grab each other's shoulders, dying to make love. Their lips quiver. They move in, about to touch, then quickly break apart an instant before they actually kiss.)

RYAN: Whoa, shit!

KELLY: This is hard!

PAUL: So is Ryan.

KELLY: The more we delay.

RYAN: The stronger it feels.

KELLY: Like a dam building.

PAUL: It can't work.

RYAN: Yes, it can.

PAUL: It can't.

RYAN: It can work.

KELLY: My turn.

RYAN: Good idea.

(They quickly face each other, holding hands.)

RYAN: Go ahead.

KELLY: When I look at you I long for wisdom.

RYAN: Good luck.

KELLY: Your skin is ruddy. Your hands are strong, a bit coarse—

(Ryan breaks contact, staring at his hands.)

RYAN: They are, aren't they?

KELLY: I like that.

RYAN: This is... *("Hard." Looks at Paul, choosing a different word.)* ...difficult. I'm not used to being the...

KELLY: Object?

RYAN: It's odd.

KELLY: How do you think women feel?

RYAN: Self-conscious.

KELLY: And worse. *(Takes his hands again.)* But it's my turn. Wisdom. I see wisdom. That's my ideal.

RYAN: Projected on me.

KELLY: It's there. I see it. There is wisdom.

RYAN: I suppose.

KELLY: There is kindness.

RYAN: I try.

KELLY: I look at your face and I see someone older.

RYAN: You see lines and wrinkles.

KELLY: No wrinkles. But it wouldn't matter. *(Touches his face.)* It would add to it. To a face that's been lived in, that's seen sorrow and loss and rejection. But still you're alive, you haven't surrendered. There is light in your eyes. A softness. Kindness. *(Moved.)* Wisdom is kindness. This longing to touch.

(She reaches for him. He takes her hands.)

RYAN: To connect.

KELLY: *(Painful longing.)* To be held.

(They stare into one another's eyes. Ryan breaks the trance, turning to Paul as if to ask, "What do you think?")

PAUL: That's remarkable.

RYAN: *(Crossing to Paul.)* But is it cheating?

PAUL: I'm not sure.

(Lights crossfade. Kelly crosses and sits at the desk down right, picks up her notebook and studies it. Barbara enters in the dark with her laptop computer. She sits on the

couch studying it.)

RYAN: Every culture seems to have these odd definitions. Like in Argentina if you're a man screwing another man you're not considered gay. But if you're the one taking it up the pooper then you are.

PAUL: It's about power.

RYAN: Who's screwing who.

PAUL: You're a man if you're doing the screwing.

RYAN: It's like prison. *(Flirting.)* Would you be my bitch?

PAUL: *(Looks him over.)* A little work on the abs wouldn't hurt.

RYAN: Hey!

(They laugh. Paul rises, stretching.)

RYAN: It's all about eggs.

PAUL: Eggs.

RYAN: The woman has the eggs. The male wants to plant his seed and run. "Sorry, babe, I hate to fertilize and run." It's built in.

PAUL: Evolution.

RYAN: Don't tell me you have a problem with evolution.

PAUL: Well...

RYAN: Jesus, Paul, don't be an idiot.

(Paul turns sharply, attacking.)

PAUL: Screw you! You keep jumping to conclusions, these clichés about—

RYAN: *(In Paul's face.)* Right-winged Neo Nazi suburbanites!

PAUL: Pedophile do-your-own thing left wing liberals?!

RYAN: CLICHÉ!

PAUL: TOUCHÉ!

RYAN: OKAY! *(Pause.)* Man, this hits all the hot buttons, doesn't it?

PAUL: Yes. But I think—I'm actually more of an Independent than you realize.

RYAN: You swing both ways.

PAUL: I'm bi-votal.

(Ryan chuckles.)

RYAN: What were you saying? About evolution?

PAUL: Well, I was just saying...Of course, we're part of evolution. I see that. It's just as an explanation; I don't think it covers everything. Not as neatly as science would like. That's all.

(Lights slowly, subtly rise on the two trees upstage of the scrim during the following dialogue.)

PAUL: I don't think it covers everything. Not in the terms in which we experience ourselves.

RYAN: Maybe not.

PAUL: Like "planting the seed." I mean, God, yes, I have those feelings. But we don't simply act on them. It's more complicated.

RYAN: We see the future.

PAUL: We imagine it.

RYAN: Consequences.

PAUL: The burden of knowledge.

RYAN: The "poison apple." *(Ryan rises.)* There are two trees, right?

PAUL: Two trees?

RYAN: In The Garden of Eden. The tree of knowledge is what, death?

PAUL: Good and evil, I think.

RYAN: What's the other one?

PAUL: The tree of life.

(Ryan crosses center, now framed by the two trees.)

RYAN: *(Obsessed.)* What is the point? Knowledge keeps you out of Paradise? That makes no sense.

PAUL: No. No, I think the tree of life is eternity. Paradise is eternity. So, maybe you have to understand good and evil before you can enter the eternal.

RYAN: *(Frustrated.)* They were already eternal! They got kicked out! For eating knowledge?!

(Beat.)

PAUL: Here's something that's always intrigued me. At the end, God says, "Behold Adam, he is one of us, knowing good and evil."

RYAN: It says that?

PAUL: Yes. First of all, who is "us?" Who is God talking to?

RYAN: The other gods?

PAUL: Exactly. You never think of "the gods" in the Old Testament, but there it is. And secondly, this knowledge makes you God-like. You become...

RYAN: Conscious.

PAUL: Yes. And that requires discipline. Now you have to define: what is right, what is wrong.

RYAN: Which means...?

PAUL: You're responsible for your actions. *(Beat.)* Which means...?

(Pause. Lights sneak up on Barbara and Kelly.)

RYAN: You have to choose.

(Paul sits, takes a drink, enjoying a moment of triumph.)

PAUL: I'm afraid so.

(Ryan looks, first, at Kelly, then Barbara. As the lights begin to fade, he slowly turns back to Paul, giving him a withering look. Blackout.)

END OF ACT I

Act II

Lights up on Ryan and Barbara. He is seated on the couch looking at a photo album. She is standing behind, to the side, studying him. Her coat is draped across her suitcase, which sits on the floor downstage. The two trees are lit behind the scrim throughout the act.

BARBARA: I still think it's strange.

RYAN: What's wrong with looking at photos?

BARBARA: Nothing. For me. Or mother.

RYAN: A man can't enjoy, can't be nostalgic.

BARBARA: Of course, a man can. But not you.

RYAN: I love your albums. I love the care you take. I love all the little captions. *(Reads.)* "The dreamer dreams. The novel awakens." I love that. I remember that. I am touched by that.

BARBARA: Has some strange spirit taken over my husband's body?

RYAN: Come on, Barb. Jesus, I just...You take such care with things. Little details. Like the house. The plants, the antiques. *(Carried away.)* I love the way you fold laundry, the way you write poetry.

BARBARA: I don't write poetry.

RYAN: *(Caught off guard.)* You could.

(Paul steps in from off stage right. Barbara freezes.)

PAUL: That was close. Real close.

RYAN: I know.

PAUL: Did you tell her?

RYAN: About—

PAUL: The girl.

RYAN: No. Not directly. I didn't see the point. I mean—

PAUL: "Eatin' ain't cheatin'?"

RYAN: And we hadn't even done that. No. I thought "keep the platonic courting deal alive with Kelly and bring all of that energy home to Barbara."

PAUL: *(Crossing left.)* Slippery slope.

RYAN: You're telling me. *(To Barbara.)* You could write poetry. *(Picks up the album.)* "The dreamer dreams." That's poetic.

BARBARA: *(Trying to follow.)* Thank you.

RYAN: *(Walks to her.)* We could take a night school course. Together.

BARBARA: I suppose.

RYAN: Go line dancing. *(Makes up a dance move.)* Something fun. Together, you know?

BARBARA: I know. I know, it's difficult-with mother, the house, all of this...

RYAN: Reality.

BARBARA: Too much reality.

RYAN: I hate reality.

BARBARA: You always have, honey. That's why you write fiction. *(Beat.)* You sure you can handle being alone?

RYAN: I'm sure.

(She grabs her coat from off of the suitcase and puts it on.)

BARBARA: It's only ten days.

RYAN: We'll be fine.

BARBARA: You're not just...

RYAN: I want you to go.

(She gets her purse from the end table.)

BARBARA: Okay. *(She removes a slip of paper from her purse.)* Here's the phone number. You can leave a message with Schneider's secretary. We'll be in the field. But someone can always reach us if there's an emergency.

RYAN: Got it.

(She picks up her suitcase.)

BARBARA: The freezer's full. Plenty of frozen dinners. You'll have to buy fresh milk and fruit. You know where the vitamins—

RYAN: What about the, um... *(Gestures.)*

BARBARA: Suppositories? In the fridge. But only if she starts bleeding again. And remind her they're just hemorrhoids. She gets frightened.

RYAN: I can't wait. I've always wanted to shove something up your mother's ass.

(He laughs. She slams down her suitcase.)

BARBARA: Thank you. Thank you very much.

RYAN: I'm kidding.

BARBARA: I'm not going.

RYAN: Don't be ridiculous.

BARBARA: This is extremely important to me, Ryan.

RYAN: I know that.

BARBARA: It is the biggest dig since they found those T-Rex bones in Wyoming.

RYAN: It was a joke.

BARBARA: Well, it's not funny! If you resent me leaving you alone with her, then tell me!

RYAN: Oh. Oh, we've gone beyond Paleontology. You're a therapist now!

BARBARA: Shhh, you'll wake her.

RYAN: *(Whispers.)* It was a joke.

BARBARA: I need to trust you.

RYAN: *(Stunned.)* Huh?

BARBARA: Can I trust you?

RYAN: *(Sudden guilt.)* I have done nothing. Nothing wrong. I've been good. Really really good.

> *(Pause.)*

BARBARA: Are you having an affair?

> *(Paul crosses in.)*

PAUL: Holy shit! What? What did you say?

RYAN: *(To her.)* No.

> *(Paul stands behind him.)*

PAUL: No?

RYAN: I wasn't.

PAUL: Not technically.

RYAN: I was walking around with a pair of blue balls the size of Tahiti! Not touching this girl! In order to be able to look my wife straight in the eye and say *(To Barbara.)* I-am-NOT-having an affair!

PAUL: *(Clinton.)* "I did not have sexual relations with that woman."

RYAN: *(To Paul.)* I didn't. *(To Barbara.)* I didn't. Am not. Having an affair. I'm—

> *(Sound of car horn.)*

RYAN: —not.

BARBARA: The taxi's here.

RYAN: I'll take care of her. I will.

BARBARA: You sure?

RYAN: It was a dumb joke. I'll—*(Gestures.)*—you know. I'll just do it.

BARBARA: The latex gloves are in the hall closet. *(Car horn.)* Well...

RYAN: We'll be fine.

BARBARA: Okay.

> *(She picks up suitcase, starts off.)*

RYAN: I love you.

BARBARA: *(Stops.)* Me too.

> *(She exits. Paul crosses and sits on the couch, looking at photo album.)*

RYAN: *(To Paul, extremely frustrated.)* It's not an affair!

PAUL: Of the body. What about your heart?

RYAN: Good question. *(Sighs.)* It's hard for me, someone like me, to get excited about fixing up the house or gardening.

PAUL: Mowing the lawn.

RYAN: And her mother. I find myself consumed with doctor appointments and "should we build a wheelchair ramp? Is it more cost-effective to install an electric lift?" I mean, these are not the questions that stir the soul and spark the imagination.

PAUL: She is not a muse.

RYAN: We are not amused. *(Beat.)* You're right, Paul. It's hard to find inspiration.

> *(Kelly enters.)*

RYAN: The only place lately—is with her.

> *(Ryan and Kelly sit at the table, sipping wine. They are tipsy, giggling at his story.)*

KELLY: County sewer?

RYAN: County sewer. I was trying to sound suave.

KELLY: How old were you?

RYAN: Seventeen. She was really old.

KELLY: How?

RYAN: A college girl. Eighteen.

KELLY: That old?

(They clink glasses.)

KELLY: And you took her to a French restaurant.

RYAN: I saved up for months. Summer jobs. Mowing lawns and such. So I told the maitre d' in this really bad accent, "Yes, masseuse, I am a wine county sewer." Connoisseur. I had heard it on some public TV show but I couldn't remember the right word so I said—

KELLY/RYAN: "County sewer."

(He picks up his glass and starts to drink.)

KELLY: Do you like pornography?

(He spits out his wine.)

KELLY: Oh, dear. Here.

(She takes a napkin and begins to wipe off his shirt.)

RYAN: I'm sorry, Kelly. It's just...you know.

KELLY: *(Wiping off his lips.)* I didn't mean to shock you.

RYAN: No no no. You didn't. *(He gently moves her hand away.)* Shock me. I was simply-surprised. You surprised me.

KELLY: You're blushing again.

RYAN: Am I? *(Beat.)* I am.

KELLY: Two thirds of all money made on the Internet is from pornography. I read that.

RYAN: Where?

KELLY: Some magazine. Glamour or Cosmo. Some rag featuring a stick figure model with a new boob job on the cover.

RYAN: Boobies.

KELLY: Hooters.

RYAN: Headlights.

KELLY: Headlights?

RYAN: They used to call 'em headlights. Back in the nineteen sevent—*(Quick recovery.)* Go on.

KELLY: *(Obsessed. More to herself.)* All these men pay hundreds of dollars to see women.

RYAN: *(Feigning disgust.)* Pathetic.

KELLY: Odd at least. A part of me thinks "it's humiliating. Who are these women?"

RYAN: *(To himself.)* Who are these women?

PAUL: How do you meet them?

(During the following, Kelly is looking out front, lost in thought. The more powerful she feels, the more uncomfortable and rigid Ryan's body becomes.)

KELLY: But another part, a wicked little part thinks, "What a trip. What incredible power." Like, the power to seduce, to affect. To see that response. Like watching some dignified, powerful man—

PAUL: Like a "writer?"

KELLY: To see him transformed from this coat-and-tie civilized pretense into an animal—all sweaty and needy and vulnerable. It would be—I don't know—affirming, somehow.

RYAN: *(Unnerved.)* The power.

KELLY: The control. *(She looks at him.)* A part of me...

RYAN: Yes?

KELLY: This wicked but...

RYAN: Powerful...

KELLY: Part of me.

RYAN: Yes.

KELLY: Wants to...

RYAN: Wants to...

KELLY: Wants to... *(Gathering courage.)* Wants to undress in front of you.

RYAN: Un...

KELLY: Yes...

RYAN: Dress.

KELLY: In front of you.

PAUL: For real?

RYAN: *(To her.)* For real?

KELLY: For real.

(She freezes. Paul rushes to above them.)

PAUL: Oh my God. Tell me she didn't say that.

RYAN: She did. I swear. It's like—

PAUL: A dream.

RYAN: A dream come true.

PAUL: It's like one of those centerfolds you've dreamed about.

RYAN: Worshipped.

PAUL: *(Crossing down right.)* Beat off to.

RYAN/PAUL: Since Boy Scouts!

PAUL: As if one of the most beautiful playboy bunnies...

RYAN: Miss April.

PAUL: ...floated off the page and came to life. Right there in your bedroom.

RYAN: I know. I know I know I know.

PAUL: How does that fit with courtly love?

RYAN: My question exactly. *(To her.)* How does that fit with courtly love?

KELLY: *(Teasing.)* They weren't online back then, eh?

RYAN: I don't think so.

KELLY: Was there pornography?

RYAN: Paintings I suppose.

KELLY: Well, they had those feelings.

RYAN: I'm sure. But the idea is to transcend them.

KELLY: We would.

RYAN: We would?

KELLY: We'd bring it all to the surface.

RYAN: Wouldn't I be using you?

KELLY: Yes.

RYAN: Isn't that wrong?

KELLY: Not if I choose it. What does Vonnegut say? Something about being used properly by life? To be used the way we choose is the goal.

RYAN: But Kelly...

KELLY: What?

RYAN: You were mistreated. Your father, he hit you.

KELLY: I know that. I told you that.

RYAN: I don't want to hurt you.

KELLY: *(Firm.)* I know what I'm doing. I am not a child.

(She exits. Paul crosses quickly to him.)

PAUL: What happened?

RYAN: Nothing.

PAUL: Nothing?!

RYAN: Not yet.

PAUL: You mean...

RYAN: Tonight. I'm seeing her tonight.

PAUL: That's it? End of story? Tune in next week?

(Paul sits at the table with Ryan.)

RYAN: That's why I needed to see you.

PAUL: Oh, man, I'm on the edge of my seat. I'm waiting for the—

RYAN: Climax?

PAUL: Damn.

RYAN: Sorry.

PAUL: It's terrible. You come to me for advice, moral advice—and I'm waiting for the cum shot. *(Beat.)* To be honest, I'm all caught up in your story. I was hoping you had gone through with it—the posing, the sex, wild animal sex—then afterwards you gave me the—

RYAN: "Blow by blow?"

PAUL: Exactly. Then I'd give the moral proclamations.

RYAN: You're no help.

PAUL: It's so strong. The drive.

RYAN: The fantasy.

PAUL: It's like that dream of going back in time and making love to all the girls in college, the ones you could have but didn't want to offend.

RYAN: You didn't want to hurt them.

PAUL: Or you thought they were just doing you a favor.

RYAN: Because back then you thought women didn't really like sex.

PAUL: *(Cocky.)* Until you got into bed.

RYAN: *(Cocky.)* And they'd go nuts.

(Beat.)

PAUL: Sometimes.

RYAN: Yeah, sometimes. And also, the fantasy of going back is to get it right.

PAUL: To go back, knowing all you've learned about foreplay and tenderness.

RYAN: And sensuality. Not being afraid of your own emotions. *(Pause.)* Would you?

PAUL: It's so tempting. But I don't think I'd ever be in your situation.

RYAN: You wouldn't put yourself there.

PAUL: No.

RYAN: Too pure?

PAUL: I'm not as open. There's too much at stake.

RYAN: Your children?

PAUL: And Lisa. To create the situation. But if it was there, staring me in the face... I don't know.

RYAN: Is it wrong?

(Pause.)

PAUL: You should call it off. Now.

(Paul exits. Ryan picks up a glass behind the end table and sips nervously. Kelly enters, drink in hand.)

KELLY: *(Excited.)* It was really quite interesting. She's a graduate student. *(In awe.)* In psychology.

RYAN: Really.

KELLY: Really. So she says everything, everything comes from dirt. *(She waits for his reaction.)*

RYAN: *(Forced.)* Wow.

KELLY: I know. Everything. Like cars? They're made of steel which is made from iron and carbon that comes from the earth. And tires from rubber that grows on trees that are planted in... *(Waits for his answer.)*

RYAN: Dirt.

KELLY: See how it works? She's really amazing. And we talked about the "big bang." We all come from—

RYAN: Dirt.

KELLY: No. Before that even. The big bang. "In the beginning..." Out of nothing. (Beat.) The ultimate mystery.

RYAN: *(Forced.)* Wow.

(Uncomfortable pause.)

KELLY: Would you care for more?

RYAN: Please.

(Kelly nervously pours a small amount and hands it to him, then crosses upstage.)

RYAN: It's like new physics. The more they discover, the more it all begins to sound like science fiction.

(Kelly takes off her shoes and socks.)

KELLY: It does. It really does.

(He catches a glimpse of her undressing. Both pretend it's not happening.)

RYAN: Order and chaos...particles and such.

(She slips off her skirt. He continues to steal glances.)

RYAN: Like "Jurassic Park." Jeff Goldblum. *(Holds up his hand.)* "It's random...guess."

(Awkward pause.)

KELLY: I have to tell you something. May I?

RYAN: Of course.

KELLY: This is difficult.

RYAN: We don't have to do all this.

KELLY: I want to.

RYAN: You sure?

KELLY: I am. It's just...Look, he—he made me ugly.

RYAN: Who?

KELLY: My father.

RYAN: Oh.

KELLY: I want you to see. If you want.

(He stands quickly.)

RYAN: I do. *(Beat.)* If it's okay.

KELLY: Could I...

RYAN: Say it.

KELLY: See...

RYAN: Go ahead.

KELLY: You. Would you... *(She gestures "undress.")*

RYAN: Oh.

KELLY: Sorry.

RYAN: No. No, it's fair. Of course it's...wow.

(He crosses to stage left, facing her. He starts to undo his trousers, stops, turns away shyly, and then reluctantly undresses down to his underpants and a t-shirt.)

RYAN: Love handles. *(Embarrassed.)* I used to be...I mean I could eat anything when I was younger.

KELLY: You look nice.

RYAN: A little saggy, I'm afraid. My friend Paul says I'm growing breasts.

KELLY: You look nice.

(She takes off her blouse.)

RYAN: Underwear. Who invented it?

KELLY: Yeah.

(While she takes off her panties, he takes off is t-shirt.)

KELLY: He cut me.

RYAN: Show me.

(She starts to undo her bra, and then stops. She steps downstage, facing away from him.)

RYAN: Please.

KELLY: *(Looking out.)* He called it his tattoo. He caught me making out with this boy. On the couch. We were sixteen. My bra was undone. That was all, I swear. We were just making out. And he grabbed the boy, my father did, and he screamed at him and he threw him out on the front lawn. I was frozen. On the couch. I couldn't move. And then he came back. He came back with his hunting knife. And he...my father picked me up and threw me on the floor and he cut me. *(Fighting tears.)* He cut me. He cut me and called me...My father. MY FATHER called me a WHORE! *(Quiet.)* He called me a whore.

(Ryan takes off his underpants and slowly, gently steps toward her.)

RYAN: Show me, Kelly. Show me what he did.

(She turns cautiously, studies his naked body, then turns away, undoing her bra. There is a long, hideous scar running across both breasts. She turns back and stands facing him. They are both framed by the two trees behind the upstage scrim.)

RYAN: That son of a bitch.

KELLY: *(Covering herself.)* It's ugly.

RYAN: No. No, it's not. It is not ugly. You are not ugly.

KELLY: I am.

RYAN: No. Listen. Please. He was sick. It was evil. But not you, Kelly. You're beautiful. You are. And you're good. *(To a fragile child.)* You are a good girl.

KELLY: I'm not.

RYAN: You are. My God, look at you. Your eyes. Your hair. Your poetic soul. You are irresistible. There is something so good, so kind and pure about you. And these scars, these tiny little marks on your chest—

KELLY: Kiss me.

RYAN: I can't.

KELLY: Don't you want me?

RYAN: More than I can say.

KELLY: Then do it. Kiss me. *(Pleading.)* Why won't you kiss me?!

(He steps forward. He takes her hands firmly in his. He begins to kiss her on the lips. Stops. He goes to kiss her on the cheek. Stops. Awkward pause. He decides. He places his hands gently on her arms, leans forward and kisses the scars on her breasts. She cries softly. He kneels, resting his head against her chest. She struggles to trust him, her arms fighting to embrace his head.)

RYAN: We just stood there—ten minutes, half an hour. I don't know. I could feel the warmth of her skin, the sound of her heart beating. And I—we imploded. From head to toe. She returned me to myself. It was—*(To her.)*—beautiful. I feel beautiful.

KELLY: You are.

(Paul speaks, as he enters.)

PAUL: For real? That's all you did.

RYAN: We just stood there. Every pore of my body drank in her spirit. The flesh of her. The heat. Her loveliness.

KELLY: You are beautiful.

RYAN: So are you.

PAUL: You are on the edge.

RYAN: Gloriously.

(Ryan stands. Kelly gathers her clothes and exits.)

RYAN: It was—

PAUL: *(Sitting on the couch.)* I get the picture.

RYAN: Divine.—

(Ryan dresses during the following.)

PAUL: Right.

RYAN: I felt, I don't know...the opposite of dying. You know?

PAUL: How could you not...

RYAN: What?

PAUL: Do it. For God's sake. How could you not make love?

RYAN: We did. We made love. We created love.

PAUL: Too weird for me.

RYAN: It was enough. It was more than enough. It was healing. If we had done more it would've felt like less. If we had—

PAUL: Released.

RYAN: Yes. If we had climaxed it would've ended up feeling, I don't know—separate and lonely. But this felt complete. Implosion. You see?

PAUL: *(Agitated.)* I don't know what to do with all of this.

RYAN: You don't have to do anything.

(Pause. Paul rises from the couch.)

PAUL: *(Difficult.)* I don't like it. I just...You come to me and ask my advice. You know where I stand. And then you go ahead and do what you want anyway.

RYAN: It was beautiful, Paul. It was innocent.

PAUL: You're fooling yourself.

RYAN: Bullshit.

PAUL: No. No, we always try to find agreement, to support each other no matter what. But you come to me, knowing how I'd feel. You used me.

RYAN: What are you talking about?

PAUL: To justify your actions. But I don't. I do not agree. You got naked. With another woman. A younger woman. An abused child. It's real, Ryan. What you did is real.

RYAN: I know it's real. It was more than real. It was transcendent.

PAUL: You have a wife. You took vows. How do you think she'd feel?

RYAN: It was beautiful, Paul.

PAUL: So what. So fucking what. You can't do things because they're beautiful. It—our whole generation: "if it feels good do it." There's no center. It's all about you. What about Barbara? What about your wife? How would you feel if she was hugging some naked twenty-five year old hard body with a washboard stomach? How would that "feel?"

RYAN: We didn't do anything.

PAUL: You are lying to yourself.

RYAN: Look, look, I feel—I'm sorry but I believe in feelings...and I feel renewed. I feel alive again. I feel like I can walk back into that house and look into my mother-in-law's frightened eyes with love. And I feel like I can take Barbara in my arms and have something to give her. It's not about sex. It's energy and—

PAUL: *(Mocking.)* Groovy, man.

RYAN: No. No, Goddamnit, listen. Listen to me, Paul. It is. Everything is energy. It—

PAUL: It's dangerous, Ryan. This is a very slippery slope. People can justify all sorts of things and before you know it we don't know what's real. "Anything goes." "Do your own thing."

(Pause.)

RYAN: *(Discovery.)* You want punishment.

PAUL: What?

RYAN: It's time to pay for my sins. It's time for "Scarlet Letters" and boiling bunnies and—

(The following lines overlap.)

PAUL: There are—

RYAN: Good old fashioned—

PAUL: Consequences—

RYAN: Old Testament—

PAUL: For our—

(Simultaneously.)

PAUL: Actions!

RYAN: Punishment!

PAUL: *(Pained.)* I almost lost Lisa!! Jay was only three. I'd lost my job. I was "downsized." The country was in a terrible recession. I had a house, a child. Lisa had to go back to work. I was home alone with Jay. I felt humiliated. Anyway, this woman, a single mom-she was beautiful. Red hair. Warmest smile you can imagine. We'd be playing with our kids in the park. She was lonely. I guess I was too. She'd ask advice and I'd get all philosophical—you know how I get. She loved it, this woman, and I loved the look in her eyes. It made me feel, well, like a man. I convinced myself that it was good. That being with her would "revive" me. That it would be good for Lisa and Jay. It all "felt" right. *(Beat.)* Anyway. Anyway, Lisa came home from work one day. Early. She came home sick. And she caught us—in bed. In our wedding bed. *(Tearing up.)* It broke her heart, Ryan. I slept on the couch for six months. Jay was so confused and upset. And the pain, the look in Lisa's eyes when she found us. It broke her heart, Ryan. *(Sits at table.)* I broke her heart.

(Pause. Ryan crosses to him.)

RYAN: I'm sorry. For you, for Lisa, and especially Jay. But—there is another way of seeing it. An impossible possibility.

PAUL: What are you talking about?

RYAN: Lisa walks in and finds you.

PAUL: Yes.

RYAN: She's shocked, horrified.

PAUL: She was.

RYAN: I know. It's so immediate, that response. It's reflexive, instinctual—

PAUL: It's real.

RYAN: Perhaps. Here's another possibility. *(He crosses to Paul.)* A woman walks in and sees her husband making love to another woman. He's not stabbing this woman, he is not humiliating her. He is making love.

PAUL: He's fucking a stranger!

RYAN: Do you see? Do you see how quickly—?

PAUL: It was wrong.

RYAN: I'm just asking you to look—

(Stands, moving away from him.)

PAUL: It's impossible.

RYAN: I'm asking you to consider—

PAUL: I committed adultery!

RYAN: Don't you see how quickly you have to label it!

PAUL: I don't understand!

RYAN: You and this woman made love. Reached out to one another. Lisa comes in and sees it. It crushes her. But not because you took vows or it's ordained by God or—she can't handle it. She can't look at you and go, "how wonderful. The man I love is connecting with someone. Kissing, caressing, sharing love in our bed."

(Paul crosses and sits on the couch.)

PAUL: *(Incredulous.)* You're out of your mind.

(Ryan crosses above him.)

RYAN: No. You are. We all are. The problem is not the intimacy. The problem is us. How little we touch. How guilty we feel.

PAUL: And you could handle this?

RYAN: I don't think so. We need rules. We need definition. But not because sex and intimacy are meant to be shared with one person, sanctioned by God. But because we can't handle it. The next time you go to church and you're sitting there with Jay sensing eternity, remember those nights when you sneak into the study and masturbate, dreaming about that beautiful woman in the pew across the aisle. And realize how many people in that church long to be with one another but end up alone late at night touching themselves. Because it's too threatening to reach across that aisle. *(Beat.)* Wouldn't it be great if the minister could say, "I know that most of you fantasize and masturbate. Some of you are carrying on affairs. Hell, I was whacking off in the shower this morning thinking about Ms. Demby, our organist. *(Beat.)* Isn't that ironic? *(Sincere.)* Don't be ashamed. Celebrate this longing. Forgive yourselves. Forgive me. Forgive God for creating us this way."

PAUL: *(Stands.)* I get that. But still, doesn't it feel wrong?

(Ryan crosses down toward him.)

RYAN: Of course, it does. I've been conditioned. By the culture, by the church—

(Paul moves away. Ryan pursues him about the stage.)

PAUL: *(Mocking.)* "Free love, man."

RYAN: You have to label it.

PAUL: It's wrong.

RYAN: Okay, do that with it.

PAUL: Human relationships are too complex.

RYAN: Do that, do this, do something with it. Because it's too confronting.

(Paul stops, facing him.)

PAUL: Tell me what you want.

RYAN: The truth.

PAUL: Free love?

RYAN: No.

PAUL: Open marriage?

RYAN: No way.

PAUL: What then?

RYAN: The truth.

PAUL: Your truth, my truth?

RYAN: Exactly.

PAUL: *(In his face.)* WHAT THE FUCK ARE YOU TALKING ABOUT?!

RYAN: "The truth shall set ye free." It's not about choosing. It's about stepping up to the moment and allowing the truth to reveal itself. "Right/wrong, good/evil, animal/spirit?" Beyond that. Standing at the edge. Listening. Waiting. Holding paradox. *(Beat.)* "The truth shall set you free."

(They stand face to face, dangerously still, intensely focused, speaking quietly.)

PAUL: This is weird.

RYAN: I know.

PAUL: I feel like punching you.

RYAN: Go ahead.

PAUL: Or making a joke.

RYAN: We're outside of the box. *(Pause. Ryan tries to name his truth.)* There are moments. Like the snowflake. Like with Kelly. They reveal themselves, if you pay attention. As you approach these moments, and as you leave them, the mind has to analyze and categorize, put them into a box.

PAUL: We need rules. We need structure.

RYAN: I agree.

PAUL: So what are you saying?

RYAN: People believe in rules. You either obey them or you don't. I'm saying there is a third way. At the edge, the edge of obeying or disobeying.

PAUL: What is that?

RYAN: *(Hypnotic passion.)* Oh my God. Oh my God, I've got it. I have got it.

PAUL: What?

RYAN: The riddle: How do you re-enter The Garden of Eden? How do you get past the Cherubim guarding the gate?

PAUL: How?

RYAN: You don't. *(Beat.)* You become them.

PAUL: You...

RYAN: The answer is: you become a Cherub. Half angel, half beast. Good and evil. You hold those tensions. You live in the balance of those dichotomies until they resolve themselves. In your heart. In your mind. And then the gate opens and you are...

(Paul crosses toward the couch.)

PAUL: *(Stunned.)* In the garden.

RYAN: In that moment, with Kelly. It was lust, it was love. It was at the edge of good and evil. But in that moment, the moment I kissed her scars we became...

PAUL: Human.

RYAN: Yes.

PAUL: The Cherubim are human.

RYAN: A beast with wings.

PAUL: I see that.

RYAN: Do you?

PAUL: I would never go there.

RYAN: You don't have to.

PAUL: But I see it.

RYAN: That's all I ask.

(Ryan crosses and attempts to hug him. Paul reluctantly returns it with a stiff pat on the back. They both sit on the couch. Pause.)

PAUL: That was intense.

RYAN: I'll say.

PAUL: I'm getting a headache.

RYAN: *(Playful.)* I think I need a cigarette. *(He mimes dragging on a cigarette.)*

(Pause.)

PAUL: Wait a minute. Just... *(He gestures "hold on.")* Okay. Okay, so you found your way back—to Paradise. You've experienced a kind of...

RYAN: Transcendence?

PAUL: Right. Right, then here's a riddle for you.

RYAN: Oh boy.

PAUL: You're back in The Garden. You've found the key. *(Pointed.)* What are you going to do with it?

RYAN: Well...

PAUL: Yes?

RYAN: Use it...?

PAUL: *(Leading the witness.)* For...?

RYAN: *(Playful reluctance.)* For "good."

PAUL: *(Playful triumph.)* That sounds "right."

RYAN: *(Playful.)* And "wrong."

(They laugh. Paul playfully gestures "follow me," crossing down left, away from the "heavy philosophical" area. Ryan follows.)

PAUL: Am I allowed to make a practical suggestion here?

RYAN: Please.

PAUL: Lisa had an idea. She suggested we stay at your place, with Barbara's mom. We'd come look after her over Memorial Day. Give you guys some time alone.

RYAN: You told Lisa?

PAUL: About Barbara's mom. The strain on your relationship. Not about the affair.

RYAN: Hey.

PAUL: Sorry. The "naked energy exchange."

(They laugh.)

PAUL: So, if you want, we could look after her mom.

RYAN: That's too much.

PAUL: We want to. I want to. But only if you use it to get it together with Barbara. She's a good woman, Ryan. What you have is—irreplaceable.

(Ryan crosses upstage, deep in thought.)

RYAN: Do you think I should tell her?

PAUL: Do you love this girl?

RYAN: Yes. But I'm not in love. It's not like that.

PAUL: How about Barbara?

RYAN: Am I in love with her?

PAUL: Yes.

RYAN: Always. It's never stopped.

(Paul crosses up to him.)

PAUL: *(Wry.)* Well, then I guess you'd better "explore the edge."

(The two friends look deeply into one another's eyes. Lights change. Paul exits. Piano music plays. Time has passed. Kelly enters and sits at the table. She is wearing a conservative cardigan sweater. Ryan sits, taking two coffee cups from behind the table and placing them on top. Awkward pause.)

RYAN: I like this place.

KELLY: Better than Starbucks.

RYAN: I hate Starbucks.

KELLY: They're so corporate.

RYAN: Money.

KELLY: It's all about money.

RYAN: It is. *(Pause.)* I thought coffee might be a good idea.

KELLY: Definitely.

(Pause.)

RYAN: How are you?

KELLY: I'm okay.

RYAN: That's good.

KELLY: I cried a lot. After we were together.

RYAN: Oh, Jesus. Really?

KELLY: You want everything to be pretty, don't you?

RYAN: I guess I do.

KELLY: I was sad because I'm not used to kindness. I haven't had a great deal of it.

RYAN: Oh.

KELLY: I cried because what we shared was bright. Like shining a light in a dark cave. The light startled me. When you're used to darkness...

RYAN: The light is blinding.

KELLY: It presses against the wounds. It can open wounds.

RYAN: That sounds dangerous.

KELLY: It was healing.

RYAN: And painful.

KELLY: Yes.

RYAN: What about...

KELLY: Us?

RYAN: You weren't expecting...

KELLY: You're too old.

RYAN: Ah, well—

KELLY: Oh my God. Oh my God I didn't mean—

RYAN: No. No, it's true. It could never be real.

KELLY: Not that kind of real.

RYAN: So what do we do?

KELLY: Take it with us. Hold it in our hearts. Say it was good.

RYAN: Wasn't it?

KELLY: I say it was. *(Pause.)* I have a new poem.

RYAN: *(Playful.)* God help me.

KELLY: I want to read it to you.

RYAN: Now?

KELLY: Yes. But first, I want you to tell me a story.

RYAN: Fiction?

KELLY: No.

RYAN: Poetry?

KELLY: No.

RYAN: Ah. A real one.

KELLY: Yes. Make it real.

(Pause.)

RYAN: Okay. Okay, here goes.

(Soft romantic piano music underneath.)

RYAN: Once upon a time there was a boy who met a girl.

(Barbara enters, strolling in the area above the scrim, studying the trees.)

RYAN: A beautiful girl with impossibly warm shining eyes. Her name-is Barbara.

KELLY: Barbara.

RYAN: They met in college. He had been chasing girls, seducing them with poetry.

KELLY: He was a poet.

RYAN: *(Reclaiming it.)* He is.

KELLY: He is.

(Barbara enters left, crossing down past the table.)

RYAN: He was familiar with romance and passion.

KELLY: As play.

RYAN: He loved to play. *(Watching Barbara.)* But with her it was different.

(He and Barbara take hands. He stands, walking and talking with his wife.)

RYAN: When we were first together, I could barely hold your hand.

(They stop. So does the music.)

BARBARA: Tell me about it. I kept thinking, what's with this guy? Everyone else is trying to rip my clothes off but he won't touch me. Let's see, he's artistic, he's sensitive. Oh-my-God, is he?

RYAN: Did you think that, really?

BARBARA: A little.

RYAN: I just couldn't be sexual. Every time I was around you I felt this enormous sense of peace. Like I was home.

KELLY: *(Deep longing.)* Home.

RYAN: You were my home.

BARBARA: And you mine.

KELLY: Home.

(Lights fade on Kelly. She exits. Pause. They sit on the edge of the stage, looking out.)

BARBARA: I love this place.

RYAN: It's a great view.

BARBARA: It was so nice of Lisa and Paul.

RYAN: It was.

(Awkward pause.)

BARBARA/RYAN: Listen I have to, want to, tell you something.

BARBARA: What is—?

RYAN: No, you—

BARBARA: It's nothing really.

RYAN: Please. I mean it.

(Pause.)

BARBARA: It's about mother and...

RYAN: Yes?

BARBARA: I keep blaming everything on her but...

RYAN: What...

(She tears up.)

RYAN: Oh, honey.

BARBARA: My period. I didn't have my period. Again.

RYAN: You're not... *(She looks at him helplessly.)* Oh.

BARBARA: I feel so old. My body is changing. I can't believe it's here. *(Beat.)* It's not all mother. Not making love. It's that too.

RYAN: I understand.

BARBARA: I needed you to know that. *(Beat.)* What did you want to tell me?

(Soft delicate piano underneath.)

RYAN: I...

BARBARA: What?

RYAN: Well...

BARBARA: Tell me.

RYAN: While you were away...

BARBARA: Yes?

(Pause. He steps up to the edge, reaching deep inside.)

RYAN: This is what I want to tell you. One day while you were in Montana, I was standing in the living room.

(Lights shift, a subtle sense of shadows.)

RYAN: It was late afternoon. Your mom was asleep. The house was empty. I was alone. The clock was ticking. Otherwise, silence. I looked at the front door. And I wanted it to open. I wanted to see you. To see you walk through that door. And I realized how I depend on that. Live for that. How a part of me relaxes when you come home. And I have no words. Can you believe it? *(Tearing up.)* Me? Without words? I can't explain it, Barbara. But if you didn't come through that door...

BARBARA: I know. Oh, God I know.

RYAN: Your mother lies on that bed all day. She has no one to scratch her back.

BARBARA: No one to hold her on a cold winter's night.

(They are sitting face to face now, as if renewing their vows.)

RYAN: It's these little things.

BARBARA: They sustain us.

RYAN: You bring me a cup of coffee.

BARBARA: I tell you my day.

RYAN: You lay your feet on my lap watching TV.

BARBARA: You rub them.

RYAN: And you smile. I need to see you smile. I rely on that smile to get me through the day.

(She pulls away. Music stops.)

BARBARA: It's hard to smile. I don't trust things. Nothing is solid.

(He pulls away.)

RYAN: "The Liquid Moon."

BARBARA: "The man in the moon is a liquid balloon."

(A large cold moon appears against the upstage wall. They sit side by side, gently collapsing into one another. Their heads meet, as they gaze at the moon—two life-partners facing their mortality together.)

RYAN: "His face expands into a huge grinning clown with enormous white teeth. Then he suddenly deflates into a hideous demon with wrinkled balloon-skin and hollow eyes."

BARBARA: My body is changing.

RYAN: So is mine.

BARBARA: When you touch me I feel pleasure, then immediate ice.

(He turns to her.)

RYAN: I feel you withdrawing.

(She faces him.)

BARBARA: It's so hard to trust.

(Kelly enters above the scrim. She reads the new poem from her notebook. Piano music builds in urgency.)

KELLY: "Touch."

BARBARA: I try to be present.

KELLY: "Our hands are made to touch."

BARBARA: But there it is.

KELLY: "Touch."

BARBARA: I freeze up inside.

RYAN: I disappear.

KELLY: "Lips can curse and mock you."

RYAN: I love you.

KELLY: "Or bless you with sweet nectar."

RYAN: I love you so much.

(He touches her face.)

KELLY: "Touch."

BARBARA: I'm afraid.

KELLY: "The hand cradles the cold steel gun, trembling with the power to destroy."

(He strokes her hair.)

RYAN: I need to see you smile.

KELLY: "The same hand can lift a flower and caress its velvet skin."

BARBARA: I want to let you in.

(They embrace.)

KELLY: "He placed his hands upon her shoulders. Her body flinched, preparing for familiar punishment."

RYAN: Warmth.

KELLY: "He startled her with kindness."

(They break the embrace, looking into one another's eyes.)

BARBARA: To sustain us.

KELLY: "Warmth."

RYAN: To protect us.

BARBARA: Warmth.

KELLY: "To soothe our mammal hearts."

RYAN/BARBARA/KELLY: Warmth.

(They kiss passionately.)

KELLY: "To sustain us. To protect us. To convince us that it is safe to continue. To continue. To continue to continue to continue."

(Lights fade on Kelly. Barbara and Ryan separate, looking at one another. We hear Kelly's voice in the dark:)

KELLY: Touch.

(Lights fade, except for the moon. The piano plays a final, sustained meditative chord that resonates as the moon disappears. Blackout.)

END OF PLAY

The Face of Emmett Till

by Mamie Till Mobley and David Barr III

ALL INQUIRIES CONCERNING RIGHTS, INCLUDING AMATEUR RIGHTS, SHOULD BE ADDRESSED TO:
Dramatic Publishing Company, 311 Washington Street, Woodstock, IL 60098; Phone: (800) 448-7469 or (815) 338-7170

ORIGINALLY PRODUCED by Pegasus Players

Founded in 1978
1145 W. Wilson, Chicago, IL 60640
www.pegasusplayers.org

Alex Levy, Artistic Director
Arlene Crewdson, Executive Director

In the theatre's 26 year history, Pegasus Players' mission has always been two-fold: to produce the highest quality artistic work and to provide exemplary theatre, entertainment, and arts education at no charge to groups who have little or no access to the arts. Pegasus was founded on the belief that art builds community, enlightening and inspiring people to see through the eyes of the other. The "acting out" of theatre is rooted in the word, and Pegasus is strongly committed to providing a theatre for voices that are frequently unheard and reaching new audiences who have not traditionally been theatre patrons. Pegasus is committed to providing a quality arts experience for those who would normally be denied it, such as inner-city school students and low-income senior citizens. The theatre won the annual James Brown IV Award of Excellence for Outstanding Community Service from the Chicago Community Trust, the Chicago Commission on Human Relations Year 2000 Human Relations Award, the first-ever Joseph Jefferson Citation to an outreach program, and a special cash award from the Chicago Department of Cultural Affairs, which recognized the Young Playwrights Festival. Pegasus has received 73 Joseph Jefferson Citations for theatre excellence, more than any other theatre in this category in the history of the awards.

* * *

The Face of Emmett Till by David Barr III and Mamie Till Mobley, the mother of Emmett Till, was first produced by Pegasus in its 1999-2000 season. Mrs. Mobley's trust in David Barr both as a playwright and as a man made the creation of this work possible. Mrs. Mobley was determined to capture clearly and truly all the circumstances surrounding the death of her only child. The play tells the searing, compelling history of August, 1955, when the body of Emmett Till was discovered floating in the Tallahatchie River. Producing this play, Pegasus was privileged to help stage an event that marked a turning point in United States history. The play gives voice to Emmett Till's mother and her determination that her son's death not go unnoticed. Due to her courage and persistence, Emmett Till's death became a national issue and the springboard for the Civil Rights Movement. *The Face of Emmett Till* is Mamie Till Mobley's lasting, moving, and inspiring memorial to the life of her son and the price he paid to remind America that "all men are created equal." In 2003, Pegasus revived the show to kick off its 25th anniversary season, a season that highlighted Pegasus' proudest and most honored productions.

Alex Levy
Artistic Director, Pegasus Players

BIOGRAPHIES

MAMIE TILL MOBLEY

Mamie Till Mobley was an active member of the Evangelistic Crusaders C.O.G.I.C (Church Of GOD In Christ). She was one of seven members who founded this particular Chicagoland chapter of C.O.G.I.C. in May 1973 under the pastorate of Elder George Liggins. Following the death of her only child, Emmett Louis Till, on August 28, 1955, Mrs. Mobley entered Chicago Teachers College in September 1956. She graduated Cum Lade in three years and finished fifth in her class. Assigned to Carter Elementary School in 1960, she saw the need to continue her education, earning a Masters Degree in Administration and Supervision at Loyola University. She served as an elementary school teacher from 1960-1983. Throughout most of her life, Mother Mobley spoke across the country, recalling the struggle for civil rights and urging her listeners to "be the best they can be." She is the Founder and Director of The Emmett Till Players, a rotating group of her elementary students who delivered public recitations from the speeches and sermons of Martin Luther King, Jr. The Emmett Till Players often accompanied her during her extensive travels. Mother Mobley passed on January 6, 2003.

DAVID BARR III

David has been a proud Resident Playwright with Chicago Dramatists since 1993. During that time, he has been fortunate enough to have many of his works developed there. Several of those plays have been produced in Chicago and across the country including *The Face of Emmett Till, The Journal Of Ordinary Thought, Death Of The Black Jesus, Ev'ry Time I Feel The Spirit,* and *My Soul Is A Witness,* which just completed a 60-city, national tour with the JENA Theatre Company of New York City. His most recent Chicagoland productions include *The House That Rocked!* produced in May 2004 at the Black Ensemble Theatre and *The Upper Room* which premiered at Pegasus Players in

February 2005. David has received a myriad of playwriting honors including two National Play Awards from the Unicorn Theatre in Kansas City, Missouri, winner of the 1993 Mixed Blood Theatre National Playwriting Contest sponsored by Mixed Blood Theatre in Minneapolis 1998 "Best Play Award" from the Mystery Writers of America, winner of the 1998 Theodore Ward National Playwright's Contest, three Illinois Arts Council Fellowships, and the Goodman Theatre's first David Ofner Prize, which he shared with Carson Grace Becker. Lastly, his most recent work, *The Upper Room,* received a 2004-2005 Joseph Jefferson Citation Nomination for "New Work."

DEVELOPMENTAL HISTORY

The Face of Emmett Till was developed with Mrs. Mamie Till Mobley from 1997 through 2003. It is based on the life and tragic death of her son Emmett Till. *The Face of Emmett Till* debuted at Pegasus Players in September 1999, had its West Coast premiere in August 2000 at the Unity Players in Los Angeles, California, and had its East Coast premiere at the Paul Robeson Theatre Company in Buffalo, New York, in February 2001. Both theatre companies restaged the play during the summer and fall of 2001. It made its Southern premiere at Dillard University in New Orleans, and will be produced at the University of Louisville in 2005, prior to a tour of Mississippi.

ORIGINAL PRODUCTION

The Face of Emmett Till premiered at Pegasus Players, Chicago, Artistic Director Arlene Crewdson, on September 9, 1999.
It was directed by Douglas Alan-Mann with the following cast:

MAMIE TILL MOBLEY	Michelle Wilson
EMMETT TILL	Bryan Parker/ Kamal J. Williams
MORRIS DEES/GERALD CHATHAM	Chris Jackson
ALMA SPEARMAN	Sandra Watson
HENRY SPEARMAN	Amos Ellis
ROY BRYANT/JOHN WHITTEN/POLICE CHIEF	Paul Hofmann
CAROLYN BRYANT	Cyndi Rhoads
ROY WILKINS/BISHOP FORD	Jason Lee
MOSES WRIGHT	Willie B. Goodson
WILLIE REED/A.A. RAYNER	Ronnel D. Taylor
MAURICE	P. Francois Battiste

and the following production staff:

Scenic Designer	Jack Magaw
Lighting Designer	Dave Gipson
Sound Designer	Joe Plummer
Costume Designer	Karen Wells
Stage Manager	Katie Klemme

CHARACTERS

MAMIE TILL MOBLEY: African-American woman, referred to as Mamie Till Bradley through the bulk of the play, appears at age 67 and age 33.

EMMETT TILL: African-American teenager, 14-years old, as he was before his death in 1955.

MORRIS DEES: White man, head of Southern Poverty Law Center, Mid to late 40s. (Doubles as J.W. Milam and Gerald Chatham.)

ALMA SPEARMAN: African-American woman, mother of Mamie, early 50s. (Doubles as Sister Margaret Avery.)

HENRY SPEARMAN: African-American man, stepfather of Mamie, late 50s to early 60s.

ROY BRYANT: White man, small-time supply store owner in Money, Mississippi, mid to late 20s. (Doubles as John Whitten.)

CAROLYN BRYANT: White woman, wife of Roy Bryant, early 20s. (Doubles as Mrs. Burke and Reporter.)

J.W. MILAM: White man, stepbrother of Roy Bryant, early 40s.

ROY WILKINS: African-American man, Executive Secretary of the NAACP during its heyday, mid 40s. (Doubles as Bishop Ford and Maurice.)

MOSES WRIGHT: African-American man, great uncle of Mamie and Emmett, mid 60s.

A.A. RAYNER: African-American man, south-side Chicago funeral director, early 50s.

MAURICE: African-American teenager, country cousin of Emmett, 18-years-old.

WILLIE REED: African-American man; Money, Mississippi, resident key witness; early 20s. (Doubles as Whisperer #1 and A.A. Rayner.)

GERALD CHATHAM: White man, District Attorney of Tallahatchie County, lead prosecutor in the Till murder trial, early 50s.

JOHN WHITTEN: White man, defense attorney for Milam and Bryant, early 40s.

SENATOR JAMES O. EASTLAND: White man, Mississippi Senator, early 50s. (Doubles as Strider and Swango.)

SHERIFF H.C. STRIDER: White man, Tallahatchie County Sheriff, early 50s.

JUDGE SWANGO: White man, presiding judge in the trial of Milam and Bryant, early 60s.

BISHOP LOUIS HENRY FORD: African-American man, pastor who eulogized Emmett, late 40s.

WHISPERER #1: African-American man, late teens.

WHISPERERS: Total cast.

SISTER MARGARET AVERY: African-American woman, late 40s.

MRS. BURKE: Southern white woman, early 20s.

REPORTER: Southern white woman, early 30s.

(It is suggested that the following parts be double-cast as follows:)
ALMA SPEARMAN/SISTER MARGARET AVERY
MORRIS DEES/GERALD CHATHAM/J.W. MILAM
JOHN WHITTEN/ROY BRYANT
WILLIE REED/A.A. RAYNER/WHISPERER #1
JAMES EASTLAND/SHERIFF H.C. STRIDER/JUDGE SWANGO
CAROLYN BRYANT/MRS. BURKE/REPORTER
ROY WILKINS/MAURICE/BISHOP LOUIS HENRY FORD

November 1989 and August/September 1955. Civil Rights Memorial, Montgomery, Alabama; various locales throughout the south-side of Chicago; and Tallahatchie County, including Money and Sumner, Mississippi.

AUTHOR'S NOTES

This stage play chronicles the life and tragic death of Emmett Louis Till, a 14-year old Black boy from Chicago who in 1955 was brutally murdered while vacationing in Money, Mississippi. Emmett was accused of whistling at a local White woman. This single incident has been credited for sparking the modern day Civil Rights Movement. The play calls for the singing of various Civil Rights Movement hymns and songs. These songs may be sung by any members of the cast who are able. If members of the cast can't be found to do this, then every effort should be made to hire outside singers to specifically perform these roles. The singing should be framed in as much of a theatrical manner as possible and should reflect the devotion and the intensity of the growing Movement sweeping the nation at the time of Emmett's death. The play should seamlessly blend a series of styles. The "courtroom" exchanges are to be portrayed somewhat realistically. At times, one "testimony" will begin before another ends as one version of this incident will bleed into another. Transitions should be as fluid and effortless as possible. This will give an intended cinematic feeling to much of the play. There are no blackouts anywhere within the play. All scene changes should take place in "twilight" or partially lit scenarios on stage. The cast movement and manipulation of the set from scene to scene should be visible. The set should obviously have one constant feature: The Civil Rights Movement Memorial in Montgomery, Alabama, situated prominently upstage.

(From left to right) Sandra Watson, Barbara Myers, Ronnel D. Taylor and Denzel Henderson in Pegasus Players' 2003 production of *The Face of Emmett Till* by Mamie Till Mobley and David Barr III, directed by Douglas Alan-Mann.

Photo by Jennifer Girard

The Face of Emmett Till

ACT I

SCENE 1

The set is dimly lit. Lights reveal several cast members in shadow singing "We'll Never Turn Back."

CAST: *"We've been buked and we've been torn*

"We've been taught that sure as you're born

"But we'll never...turn back

"No we'll never...turn back

"Until we all...live free

"And we'll have equality."

WHISPERERS: *Shame! Shame! Shame in Mississippi! Shame! Shame! Shame in Mississippi!!!!!! Shame!*

(Lights up on Whisperer #1.)

WHISPERER #1: When I was a little boy living in Canton, Mississippi...I worked for the meanest White woman in town. A few weeks after Emmett Till was murdered...she called me to her family room.

CAROLYN: *(As Mrs. Burke.)* You hear about that little colored boy who was killed up 'round Money?

WHISPERER #1: *(Cautiously.)* No mam.

CAROLYN: *(As Mrs. Burke.)* Do you know how he got hisself killed?

WHISPERER #1: No mam.

CAROLYN: *(As Mrs. Burke.)* He got killed because he forgot his place with a White woman. A nigra boy from Mississippi woulda known better. But this boy was from Chicago. *(Pause.)* Tell me again, how old are you?

WHISPERER #1: *(Nervously.)* Fourteen, mam.

CAROLYN: *(As Mrs. Burke.)* Well I do declare. That Chicago boy was fourteen, too. It's a shame he had to die so young.

ALL WHISPERERS: *Shame! Shame! Shame...in Mississippi!!!*

(Lights fade on Carolyn.)

WHISPERER #1: I went home that night, shaking like a leaf on a tree. She had made me feel like rotten garbage. That entire summer, she had tried to instill in me the kind of fear that kept Blacks in the South docile for centuries. She had tried...and she had failed. But this time...when she talked about this boy named Emmett Till...there was something in her voice that sent chills down my spine. I was never the same. Nothing...was ever the same.

ALLWHISPERERS: *Shame! Shame! Shame...in Mississippi!!!*

(Lights fade on scene. End scene.)

SCENE 2

As the lights slowly fade on the previous scene, the soothing sound of running water is heard in the distance. Lights up on an upstage center platform with a replica of the Civil Rights Memorial in Montgomery, Alabama. The structure itself is a large, circular black granite table that has the names of famous Civil Rights icons carved into the top of an upside down cone-like structure. A brief history of the 50s and 60s Civil Rights Movement is also carved in lines that radiate in the top of the structure like the hands of a fine clock. Toward the center of the wall, Dr. Martin Luther King's well known paraphrase of Amos 5:24..."We will not be satisfied...until justice rolls down like waters and righteousness like a mighty stream"...is engraved in the side of the structure. Lights slowly reveal Mamie Till Mobley staring up at the memorial. It is November 5, 1989, the day the monument was officially dedicated. Morris Dees enters. He sees that Mamie is transfixed by the beauty of the monument. Mamie is holding several promotional pamphlets in her hands. Outside, muffled murmurs and restless voices are heard escalating throughout the following scene.

DEES: You nervous?

MAMIE: No. *(Slight pause.)* Well...maybe a little.

DEES: You'll do fine.

MAMIE: It's strange. I've been waiting for this moment for over thirty years. Now that it's here...I can't seem to steady myself.

DEES: Well don't you worry. You're surrounded by friends.

(Pause. The angry murmurs are growing.)

DEES: I think Rosa Parks is almost finished with her speech. You're on next. *(Pause.)* Can I get you something while you wait?

MAMIE: I'm fine, Mr. Dees.

DEES: Morris.

MAMIE: Morris.

(Beat. Mamie slightly nervous. Angry noises swell louder. Dees senses Mamie's discomfort.)

DEES: Oh…don't worry about them. Security is pretty tight around here.

MAMIE: (Gesturing with the pamphlets in her hands.) I've been reading up on you. (Reading from one of the pamphlets) "In 1971, Morris Dees co-founded the Southern Poverty Law Center." It says here, that Corretta Scott King calls you "…by any measure, one of the most dedicated and effective civil rights lawyers in the history of the United States."

(Half-beat. Dees smiles. Mamie smiles back.)

MAMIE: That's high praise.

DEES: *(Chagrinned)* A lot of that stuff is exaggeration…and *over* exaggeration, I'm afraid.

(Angrier, outside voices swell. They seem to be getting louder…and closer.)

WHISPERERS: *Zeig Heil! Zeig Heil! White Power! White Power!!!!!!!!!!!!*

MAMIE: *(Nerves overcoming her.)* GOD, it never stops. *(Pause. Steadying herself.)* I'm sorry.

DEES: It's all right. Most of those idiots are loud-mouthed fools afraid of their own shadows when the liquor wears off.

MAMIE: *(Beat. Uneasy.)* This is the first time I've traveled South since… *(Beat.)* I guess some things never change.

DEES: Some things don't. *(Half-beat.)* But some things do.

MAMIE: *(Her discomfort growing. Dees smiles reassuringly at her.)* How do you do it, Morris? You build a beautiful Civil Rights Monument to our loved ones. And you organize this affair for the families of the victims of the Movement. You're risking your own life for what some people might say…isn't really your fight. *(Beat.)* You don't need this.

DEES: No mam, I suppose I don't.

MAMIE: Then why do it? *(Dees hesitates. Mamie pointed.)* I'd really like to know.

DEES: *(Uneasy pause.)* Well…*(Beat.)* In 1955, I was twenty…and I was still living on my daddy's farm. One morning, I read about the death of your son. I can't explain it really …but reading about the lynching of a 14-year-old boy just…Well…I felt like something inside of me was born on that day. It made me seriously examine the South. Our way of life. How this child was killed. And *why* he was killed. *(Pause.)* In some ways…I guess he reminded me of the Black fellas I played with on the farm. Whatever it was…he was dead…for no reason…and his mama was crying for all the world to see. *(Pause.)* At the time, I had never sent a letter to a newspaper in my life.

But the death of this innocent little Black boy struck a real chord in me. And I wrote that..."We in the South practice segregation. But we also are supposed to believe in *justice*. If this young boy did something illegal, then he ought to be tried and convicted before he is punished. Not lynched." *(Pause.)* When my uncle read what I had written...he called me a *nigger lover. (Half-beat.)* But...that newspaper published my letter. Even 35 years ago...I suppose there were bastions of moderation on "...the race issue." Even in the South. *(Half-beat.)* One way or the other...the death of Emmett Till changed everything for me. *(Outside angry noises escalate.)* Maybe you better wait backstage until it's time for your speech.

MAMIE: No. I think I'll stand here a little longer. I want to see Emmett's name under these lights. *(Half-beat.)* There's not a day that goes by when I don't think about him. I finally got to the point where I can actually look at his picture without crying. *(Half-beat.)* Even after all of these years. *(Beat.)* But lately...I've found myself thinking of him constantly. No matter how much time passes, losing a child...it's like...a knife, through your heart. It's a pain that never goes away.

DEES: *(Pause.)* I think I understand. *(Pause. Purposely changing the subject.)* Mrs. Mobley...can I ask you a question?

MAMIE: *(Somewhat cautiously.)* Certainly.

DEES: *(With some difficulty. Somewhat chagrinned.)* I realize this might seem a bit out of place, but...

MAMIE: *(Curiosity.)* No, it's fine. Go on.

DEES: Well...have you ever thought...that this struggle...and your struggle...might have been to save someone else's child?

MAMIE: *(Pause.)* Yes. But the way things are in the world today, I'm not sure his death means as much as it once did.

DEES: *(Beat.)* I disagree. Standing here...in Montgomery...just a few steps from Dr. King's church on Dexter Avenue...it's a symbol of just what your son's passing meant to so many people. Even for people like me who never knew him. But knew the sacrifice he made. *(Shifting gears. Trying to change the somber mood.)* It's not a coincidence that less than four months after your son's death...Rosa Parks stood her ground against Jim Crow. *(Looking offstage as if he has been signaled.)*

MAMIE: *(Long pause. Then a knowing half-smile from Mamie. Beat.)* Perhaps, but I still miss him, Morris. So much.

DEES: *(Light applause heard in the darkness.)* I think...they're ready for you.

(Mamie stands stoically. Lost in a memory.)

DEES: Mrs. Mobley? *(Beat.)* Mrs. Mobley?

(Lights fade on Dees as his last sentence echoes throughout the theater. Lights soften on scene. End scene.)

SCENE 3

Previous scene fades to black. Emmett's voice is heard in the background, under with the darkness.

EMMETT: *(Voice-over.)* Mama? *(Beat.)* Mama?

(Mamie crosses downstage to the suggested living room area. Emmett enters wearing a period baseball hat from the Kansas City Monarchs and a Sox jersey. He is wearing a baseball glove and holding a baseball, which he occasionally throws up in the air and catches. Emmett is struggling, trying to deliver a recitation of the Gettysburg Address. He stammers through half of it and forgets the rest. He's distracted. It's game time.)

EMMETT: "FFFFFourr score and sssseven years ago...our ffffatherssss brought forth on this continent, a nnnewww nation conceived in...conceived in..."

MAMIE: *Liberty* Bo...*Liberty.* I know you can do this.

EMMETT: "lllll...*liberty...*"

MAMIE: Good. What do you do when you get stuck on a word?

EMMETT: *(Emmett takes a deep breath and whistles to steady himself.)* M...M... MMMama? CCCCCan't I learn sssomething thattttt's easier to ssssay? Whenever I stutterrrr like thatttt...all the kids laugh at me. And I don't lllllike it.

MAMIE: Don't worry about them. You just worry about this speech, boy.

EMMETT: It's tttoooo hard to rememmmber, Mammma. And I ssssound funny. I know I do.

MAMIE: This is the *Gettysburg Address.* It's Abraham Lincoln's most famous speech. Besides...you sound fine. All you need is practice.

EMMETT: Can't I jjjust lllearn this after the ggggame?

MAMIE: At this rate, you might not make it to another baseball game until football season.

EMMETT: BBBBBBut, MMMMama, they're gonna let m...m....me ppppitch today.

MAMIE: Bo, the last time you pitched your team lost 99 to 1.

EMMETT: The ummmmmpire didn't know how to call the sssssstrike zone.

MAMIE: *(Pause.)* Bo...I was the umpire.

EMMETT: I know.

MAMIE: *(Mamie laughing at Emmett's nerve. They both giggle as Mamie tickles him.)* Boy!

(Door bell rings. Henry Spearman enters.)

MAMIE: Morning, daddy.

SPEARMAN: *(Spearman enters, kisses Mamie and hugs Emmett.)* Hey there, Mamie Lizzie. How you doin' there, young fella?

EMMETT: FFFFFFine granddaddy.

SPEARMAN: That's good. Real good. Mamie I'm looking forward to seeing Bo pitch. I hear he's better than Satchel Paige and Bob Feller.

MAMIE: Well...I'm not so sure we are going to play baseball today, daddy. Emmett's behavior doesn't warrant a baseball game or any other extra-curricular activity.

EMMETT: I'lll bbbbbee goodddd. I pppromise!

MAMIE: He hasn't finished his studies...

EMMETT: I can do that spppeech, MMMMama...just wwwatch mmmme.

MAMIE: In fact, unless I see marked improvement, he may not be playing baseball for a very long time.

EMMETT: "FFFFFour score and ssseven years ago our fathers bbbrought forth on this continent, a new nation, conceived in Liberty, and dedicated to the proposition that all men are cccreated equal."

SPEARMAN: That sounds good, Emmett. Real good. *(Half-beat.)* So how you been, daughter?

MAMIE: Holdin' on, I suppose.

EMMETT: "...that from these honored dead we ttttake increased devotion to that cause ffffor which they gave the last full measure of devotion...that we here resolve that these dead shall not have died in vain."

SPEARMAN: Your Uncle Mose and his boy Maurice will be getting to Chicago late tomorrow night.

MAMIE: *(To Spearman. Trying to hide her enthusiasm.)* Everybody looks forward to Poppa Mose's visits. That's a GOD fearin' man.

SPEARMAN: Yes Lord. *(Beat.)* I suppose you read about what happened to Lamar Smith?

MAMIE: *(Half-listening.)* Who?

SPEARMAN: Lamar Smith. Civil Rights worker down in Brookhaven, Mississippi. He was a colored fella that... *(Beat.)* Lord Mamie Lizzie! The story is all over the front page of the *Defender*. The man was shot down in broad daylight on the front lawn of the courthouse.

MAMIE: Father, father.

SPEARMAN: The *Defender* says he was trying to register Black folks to vote. Same thing happened to Reverend George Lee down in Belzoni three months ago. They shot him to pieces for speakin' out against Jim Crow. *(Half-beat.)* I can't believe you didn't hear about this. I hear the NAACP is planning to send a hundred folks down there to…

MAMIE: The *NAACP* is never going to change anything in Mississippi. Even if the government makes Whites desegregate some things, a lot of the Negroes in the South are too scared to ever take advantage of their rights. Do you know what I hear most folks down there call this *NAACP*? *(Half-beat.)* " *Niggers Ain't All Colored People.*" *(Beat.)* Daddy…the *NAACP* doesn't mean one thing to those White folks in Mississippi. And you know it.

EMMETT: *(Speaking louder, trying to get Mamie's attention.)* "—*and that a government of the people, by the people, for the people, shall not perish from the earth.*"

SPEARMAN: Mamie…change is comin'. I can't tell ya where or when. But when it get here…it ain't gonna be so easy to turn a blind eye.

MAMIE: *(Now loud enough for Emmett to hear her.)* Right now...the only thing I'm interested in changing is my son's behavior.

EMMETT: I'm done with the sssspeech. Can I go to the game, *now*? PPPPlease? PPPlease?!!!!!

MAMIE: What do you think, daddy?

SPEARMAN: Speech sounded fine to me.

EMMETT: MMMMe….ttttooo.

MAMIE: Daddy you didn't even listen to him. And what about this boy's behavior? Honestly…the things that come out of his mouth, sometimes.

SPEARMAN: Young man…are you sorry for the things your mama said you said?

EMMETT: *(Slyly.)* MMMMMost of it.

MAMIE: *Most of it?*

SPEARMAN: Well that's good enough for me. *Play ball!!!*

EMMETT: *Yeah….pppppplay…bbbball!!!!*

(All laugh. Mamie hugs Emmett and Spearman. Lights fade on scene. End scene.)

SCENE 4

A church organ is heard in the distance. Lights up on Mose Wright. He is speaking in the pulpit of a packed Southside Chicago church.

WRIGHT: *(Beat.)* It is right and natural…for us…to ask ourselves in troubled times like these… "How can we sing the Lord's song in a strange land?" How can our spirits sing about GOD's glory when our bodies lie shackled under fetters of iron chains? How can we be happy in bondage? How can we sing—the Lord's song—in a strange land? *(Beat.)* You know, when folks ask me…why I choose to stay in a state like Mississippi…my *home state*…the place of my birth… with all that prejudice down there against colored folks…I tells 'em that GOD ordained it. *(Beat.) Why do I still live in Mississippi?* Because the White man down there lives his life…day and night…like a *free* man. And so should *I*. Freedom is what I want for myself…and for *my* children. *Freedom, in Mississippi. (Beat.) Why do I still live in Mississippi?* Because Mississippi is my home. I love the land. Even though it produced prejudice White folks…like Senator James Eastland and the Silver Knights of Ku Klux Klan. Even though it has exterminated many GOD fearin' Negroes like Reverend George Lee and Lamar Smith…it is *still…my home.* Mississippi is *still* a part of the United States. Seem to me, the rules of this country up North…ought to apply to White folks down South. Whether the White folks down there like it or not…I don't intend on living in my own home as a parasite. *(Beat.) Why do I still live in Mississippi? Because…I can.* Because the constitution of these United States says that I can. Because *GOD* almighty…says that I can. And His law…is the *ONLY LAW*…I've got to obey. *(Half-beat.)*

(The amen corner erupts in gospel shouts. Lights fade on scene and segue to the Spearman family room. Emmett and Mamie are in mid conversation. Alma Spearman is in the room, totally involved in the conversation, wearing an apron and fussing around the kitchen table. Wright is seated at the kitchen table finishing dinner.)

MAMIE: *Mississippi?* But Emmett, you know that we are planning a vacation in Detroit. We've had our hearts set on it. *(Slight hesitation.)* And I thought you wanted to go.

EMMETT: BBBBBut that was before I knew cousin Wheeler and Curtis was ggggoing with PPPPoppa Mose to Mississippi. Wheeler says they have a lot of fun down there every summer.

MAMIE: *(Nervous, confused, and upset.)* I…I don't know about all of this. Mama, what do you think?

ALMA: *(Concerned but staying out of this one.)* Child don't ask me. He's my baby…but he's your son.

EMMETT: PPPPPoppa Mose and Aunt Lizze are gonna bbbbbe there the whole time.

WRIGHT: *That's right.*

MAMIE: Bo, I'm sorry. I've already made plans. Besides, I'm not too sure about you going down there. Daddy just told me about this colored man in Brookhaven who was shot just for...

WRIGHT: *(Defensive and somewhat indignant.) Mamie...girl. Listen at yourself.* Y'all talkin' like things in Mississippi ain't changed since *slavery days.* What happened to Lamar Smith and Reverend Lee coulda happened anywhere in America. *(Beat.)* Mississippi is different than it was when you was growing up 'round them parts. Colored folks down South doin' all kinda fanciful things now. Important things. Shoot, they just about run all of Mound Bayou and everything in it. Them crazy, prejudice folks better not come 'round there actin' a fool.

EMMETT: See, Mama. Even PPPPPoppa Mose says it's all right.

MAMIE: Poppa Mose is not your mother.

EMMETT: *(Beat.)* Y'all don't trust mmmmme?

ALMA: *(Long pause)* It's not *you* she's concerned about, Bo. *(Hugging Emmett. Taking his face in her hands.)* We love you. And we just wanna make sure nothin' bad will happen to you. Thass all.

WRIGHT: Emmett, let me speak with your mama and grandma in private.

(Emmett exits. Wright shoots Alma and Mamie the look.)

MAMIE: I know that you think I'm paranoid. But I have to protect that boy. Maybe I should have let him visit Mississippi more often when he was younger...so he could be exposed to that life...but I knew he wouldn't understand.

WRIGHT: *(Beat.)* Why y'all need that boy to be so dependent on ya?

MAMIE: I had to sacrifice everything...to be a good mother.

WRIGHT: Now you're sacrificing the boy's right to lead his own life. *(Beat.)* It's not right that Emmett don't ever see his kin folks down South. That boy's got a GOD given right to know his family. His *whole* family. Chicago ain't the only place he got kin.

ALMA: Mose, we've been down this road before.

WRIGHT: An' we gonna go down it again. *(Beat.)* Y'all actin' like you 'shamed of where you come from.

ALMA: That's not fair.

WRIGHT: Well that's what folks down South are sayin'. They sayin' y'all done come up North and got all "dicty." That y'all don't want no parts of rememberin' the family y'all left behind in Mississippi. This sound like an example of them bein' right, iffen ya ask me. Y'all got family in Money that ain't seen that boy since he was a baby. No matter how far y'all runs, Mississippi gonna always follow ya.

ALMA: Have you forgotten why we left Mississippi? I moved Mamie Lizzie up here when she was young 'cause I wanted her to have a better life than *we* had. Is that so wrong?

I didn't want her to walk them dusty, country streets with her head always bowed...too scared to lift her face up to the light of day.

WRIGHT: She ain't standin' no taller by runnin' from who and what she is. And neither is Emmett.

ALMA: I didn't want that boy growing up in a world where he'd be constantly reminded that he's just a "nigger." Surrounded and living in a state full of "niggers."

WRIGHT: *(Long pause.)* Is that what you think of *me*? That me...and all your kin folks down South ain't nothin' but a bunch of *niggers*?

ALMA: That's not what I meant.

WRIGHT: Mamie Lizzie...I thought you wanted the best for that boy.

MAMIE: *I do.* But I don't want my son to ever hear this kind of talk. I don't want him to know what you and my parents had to live through in that hateful state.

WRIGHT: I'm sorry to say this...but I got to ask ya...who you really tryin' to protect?

MAMIE: *(Pause. Backtracking.)* If you're saying that this is about my guilt over Louis...

WRIGHT: I'm sayin' that it ain't your fault Emmett's father was the way he was. Ain't no need for you to keep doin' penance over that thing.

MAMIE: Fourteen years ago I chose to have a child with a man I knew would leave me crying one day. My decision cost me years in a bad marriage and it nearly destroyed me and my child in the process. *(Beat.)* He's my whole life, Poppa Mose.

WRIGHT: Then give him a fightin' chance to live his. Don't send that boy out in this world deaf, dumb and blind. Give him the tools and the education to make sure he'll never have to live ignorant. Let the boy learn the right way. Please.

MAMIE: I...I still don't know. *(Long pause.)* Mama?

WRIGHT: *(Pause.)* Now Mamie Lizzie, *you* that boy's mama. Sooner or later you gonna have to untie him from your apron strings. It's a big world out there. Iffen his kin lived on the moon...we *still* blood.

ALMA: *(Long pause.)* Mose...I want you to listen to me very carefully...if we let him go down there...you cannot let this boy out of your sight. If he wants to go into town...you drive him. You understand me?

WRIGHT: I'm gonna take personal care of Emmett. Like I do all them boys in my charge. It won't take him no time to get used to life down there.

ALMA: You've got to promise *me* that you'll protect those children.

WRIGHT: *(Pause. Growing very serious.)* I won't let 'em out of my sight. Don't you worry about a thing.

(Lights fade on scene. End scene.)

SCENE 5

"Come On, Boys, Let's Go To The Ball" by Sid Hemphill and Lucius Smith swells in the distance. Lights up on Senator James Eastland speaking on the floor of Congress.

EASTLAND: "Mr. President. Honorable members of the Senate. We are not going to permit this *NAACP*…or any other Communist organization to control our state. And I'll tell you something else about Southern people. *(Beat.)* The southern institution of racial segregation or racial separation was a correct, and self evident truth which arose from the chaos and confusion of the Reconstruction. Separation promotes racial harmony. It permits each race to follow its own pursuits and its own civilization. Segregation is not discrimination. Segregation is not a badge of racial inferiority and it is not recognized as such by *both* races in the Southern States. In fact, segregation is *desired* and *supported* by the vast majority of the members of *both* races in the South, who dwell side by side in otherwise harmonious conditions. *(Beat.)* Let me make this clear, Mr. President…There is no racial hatred in the South. *(Beat.)* And the Negro race…especially in my native Mississippi… is *not* an oppressed race."

(Beat. Lights fade on scene and cross fade to a flashback to Emmett and his country cousin Maurice. Emmett is standing on a roof. Maurice nervously keeps looking over his shoulder. Soft live jazz music is heard in the far distance.)

EMMETT: *(Emmett doing a very bad James Cagney impression.)* "Top of the world MMMMMa!!! Look at me!!! I'm on the top of the world!!!!"

MAURICE: *"Top of the world…huh?!!!* " We gonna see how bad you is when your mama find us out here. She warned us once.

EMMETT: *(Attempting a Marlon Brando imitation.)* "And suddenly you're the qqqqqueen of the NNNNile. SSSS…Sittin' on your throne. SSSS…Swillin' down my liquor. Well you know what I gggggotta say to that?!!!! (Beat.) Huh?!!!! (Half-beat.) Hah!!!! Hah!!! HAH!!!!!"

MAURICE: Man, Emmett. You been watchin' way too many movies.

EMMETT: *(Having fun now watching Maurice squirm.)* "SSSSSTELLA!!!!! SSSTEL-LA!!!!"

MAURICE: You keep yellin' like that and there ain't gonna be no question somebody is gonna find us. They gonna *hear* us…even iffen they don't *see us.*

EMMETT: *(Imitating a very bad New York accent.)* "HEY MARTY?!!! (Beat.) What you wanna do? I dddddunno no…what you wanna dddddo?!" (Pause. Looking back at Maurice with exasperation.) Stop bbbbbein' such a chicken. I'm the one sssssstandin' on this roof…nnnnot you.

MAURICE: And what's so great about that roof? I mean…what do you see up there that's so great?

EMMETT: *(Slowly)* The *ffffuture*. It's bbbright. And…And I ssssee *colors*…and flashes of

light all over Grand Boulevard. *It's bbbbeautiful. (Pause)* When I'm up here...
I think...I could dddddoo almost anything...I think...I can live forever...if I could just
sssstand right up here...fffforever. *(Long pause.)* Maurice? I think...I think I could
bbbbe...a mmmmmovie star. Like Gary Cooper. Or BBBB...Bogie.

MAURICE: *A movie star?! (Laughing.)* Yeah...you better come down from there, man.
The air from that stanky garage musta seeped out and started messin' wit your brain.

EMMETT: I'm fffffine.

MAURICE: Well you won't be...*fffine*...if *somebody* shows up with a *belt* in her hand.

EMMETT: *(Bravely. Trying to be evasive.)* SSSSSomebody...like who?

MAMIE: *(Offstage voice.) Emmett?!!!!! Emmett Louis Till, where are you?! You're going
to miss your train!!! I sure hope for your sake that you're not standing on top of that
shaky, broken down old piece of a garage I warned you about. And...if you are on that
roof...you are not wearing that new leather belt I just bought. 'Cause I'm gonna wear
that out on somebody...if I find...either one of you over there!!!!*

MAURICE: *(Running. Waving goodbye.)* It's gettin' late. Train's comin'. See ya, Emmett!
(Maurice exits.)

EMMETT: *Maurice?!* Wait fffffor mmmm...me!!! I'm comin'! I'm comin'!

(Lights fade on scene. End scene.)

Scene 6

*Lights crossfade to the 63rd and Englewood train station. Emmett, Alma, Spearman,
and Mamie quickly enter. Emmett is carrying a small suitcase. Mamie is following
closely behind him obnoxiously doting on and over every stitch of clothing he's wearing; ie, feverishly brushing at his collar, combing through his hair, straightening his
hat, etc.*

EMMETT: It's lllleavin'! I gggotta go!!!!

ALMA: Wait a minute, young man. I want you to understand a few things before you go.

EMMETT: You done already told mme all a that stuff, gggrandmama.

ALMA: I know. I know. But you've got to understand, child. When you are colored and
living in *Mississippi*...you are not in *Chicago*. When you are walking on *their* sidewalks and you see a White person walking toward you, just step aside...and give them
the *entire sidewalk*. Do you hear me?

EMMETT: Grandmama. It can't be that bbbbbad down there.

MAMIE: *(Nervous tension.) You better listen to mama!! We are very serious!!! (Long
pause. Calming.)* Emmett, honey, these are *different* people, with a *different* way of

acting…and *reacting* to things they don't understand. If you're in the same room with a White man, you just drop your head. Don't even look them in the eye. I don't care if it makes sense or not. Just drop your head. You are going to *Mississippi*…they *hang niggers* in Mississippi.

WRIGHT: *Mamie!!!*

ALMA: I'm sorry Poppa Mose, but Mamie's right. The boy has got to know.

MAMIE: *(Pushing, but more gently. Calmly, still pointed, however.)* I need to know that you will do everything we say… just the way we are telling you to do it. Promise me, young man?

EMMETT: I promise. BBBBut you all don't have to worry about mmmme. I'll be all right. *(Train whistle blows. Emmett turns to run toward the train station and suddenly stops. Slightly embarrassed, he turns back to Mamie.)* Here…*(Emmett takes his watch off and hands it to Mamie.)* You take this. I won't need this.

MAMIE: Okay…I'll wear it until you get back. *(Beat.)* But… what about your father's ring?

EMMETT: *(Looks at it longingly then back to Mamie.)* I think I'll keep this with mmmme. Show it off to the ffffellas. *(Train whistle blows again. Only this time, it feels more urgent.)*

OFFSTAGE VOICE: *All Aboard!!!!!*

EMMETT: *I gggotta gggo mammma!!! Bye!!!! (He kisses her again and quickly exits.)*

MAMIE: You better call me as soon as you get…*(He is gone. To herself.)*…to Mississippi.

(The train whistle blows for the final time. Mamie stands for several seconds, staring at the spot where Emmett has vacated. Finally, she puts Emmett's watch on and turns to walk away. Alma approaches Mamie and slings an arm around her.)

MAMIE: *(Still grinning and staring toward the last area she saw Emmett exit as the sound of the train is heard pulling away from the station.)* Look at him. He's getting so tall and handsome. *(Half-beat.)* Well…I guess he's gone.

SPEARMAN: Yeah…he's gone. He'll be back before you know it. Ready to go?

(Mamie looks at Spearman smiling, missing her son already.)

ALMA: Let's go home, baby.

(Lights fade on scene and crossfade to Maurice and Emmett. In darkness…we hear Judge Swango in an offstage voice-over.)

SWANGO: *(Voice-over.)* "What do you think happened in the Bryant's store that day?"

MAURICE: "We were all at the church that night. Daddy was preachin'…and we got bored. He tends to go on and on when the Holy Ghost gets a hold of him. Anyway…I had the keys to his car…so we decided to drive to town until he finished testifyin'. The way he was carryin' on that night…I figured we had at least two, three hours to spend in Money before he even got to the offerin'. But somehow, the time just got away from us. It was me, Wheeler, my brother Simeon, my sister Thelma, and Emmett. I was drivin'. We stopped in front of Bryant's store right before we headed back."

(Lights crossfade to Emmett and Maurice standing in front of Bryant's store. Maurice is obviously very nervous.)

MAURICE: *Damn!* We got to go. I gotta get this car back 'fore daddy knows it's gone.

EMMETT: You think he'd get mmmmad?

MAURICE: What *you* think? Ya daggone right he gone be mad. But he ain't gonna know nuthin' ifffen we can get back to the church 'fore he finish that sermon.

(Emmett pulls his wallet out. Maurice glares at him as takes out a few bills. Maurice grabs the wallet from Emmett. A few pictures fall out onto the ground.)

EMMETT: I'mmmm gonna get me sommmm…bbbubble gum. Want some? *(Bending down to pick up the pictures he's dropped.)*

MAURICE: Wait a minute. What kinda pictures you carryin' 'round in that fancy wallet, boy?

EMMETT: Just pictures of some girls I go ttttto school with.

(He nonchalantly hands Maurice a few of the pictures. Maurice looks at the photos and flashes an immediate expression of horror across his face.)

MAURICE: Boy you better get them things away from me!

EMMETT: WWWhat's the…mmmmmatter?

MAURICE: Them pictures of *White* girls.

EMMETT: So?

MAURICE: *(In disbelief.)* You mean to tell me…they let colored go to school with White folks up North?

EMMETT: Yeah MMMMaurice.

MAURICE: *(Pause. Laughing.)* You almost had me goin'. You ain't never gone to school wit' *White* girls.

EMMETT: *(Teasing.)* Yeah I do. Some of 'em are friends of mmmmine.

MAURICE: *(Long pause. Then laughing.)* *White girlfriends, too?* Is that what you sayin' now?

EMMETT: Well we friends…and they just happen to be *girls*. So I guess you can say they my *girlfriends*.

MAURICE: *(In genuine disbelief.)* Naw?!!! *(Pause. Finally laughing.)* Boy, you must think I'm just a simple country fool. Fresh out the back of a turnip truck. Fresh as dew off a collard plant. *(Pause.)* You ain't never been to no school wit' no White folks...and you sho' ain't never 'had' you no *White girlfriends.*

(Lights up on Bryant's store. Carolyn is seen sitting at the counter looking through a copy of Look Magazine. Maurice looks to the store.)

MAURICE: You talkin' 'bout all them white girlfriends you got up in Chicago...but I bet you won't say *boo* to the White lady in that store over there.

EMMETT: *(Blindly taking the dare.)* I bbbbetcha I will. I ain't 'fffraid a White folks.

MAURICE: *(Teasing. Daring.)* Well go on...*fool.* Go on an talk to her like ya talk to all yo' *White girlfriends.*

(Emmett reluctantly crosses to the Bryant's store area of the stage. Lights soften on Maurice. He can still be seen and heard giggling throughout the following sequence. Emmett periodically looks toward Maurice. Carolyn Bryant is unaware of Emmett's presence at first. When she sees him...she stops what she is doing and shadows his movements. Finally, Emmett timidly approaches Carolyn.)

EMMETT: I...I... *(Hearing Maurice's giggles as he nervously addresses Carolyn.)*

CAROLYN: *(Looking at Maurice then back at Emmett.)* He a friend of yours?

EMMETT: N...N...Naw. I mean...*yeah.* Heeee...Heee...mmmmy ccccousin.

CAROLYN: Yeah? Well you better tell 'em to get away from my front door...goofin' around and actin' all stupid like that. *(Cruel sarcasm.)* Lessen *heeeeee*...wants me to call the sheriff. *(Maurice temporarily snaps to attention.)*

CAROLYN: Well...what y'all want?

EMMETT: T...T...T...Two ccccents worth of b...b...bubble gum, please.

(Carolyn turns around slowly and takes the bubble gum jar off of a high shelf that's directly behind the counter. When she turns away from Emmett, Maurice immediately starts laughing again.)

MAURICE: *(To himself. Laughing aloud. Shouting toward Emmett in the store.)* See there! I knew you couldn't do it! You just a old chicken butt!!!

EMMETT: *(Looking at Maurice, Emmett hangs his head and begins to back away from Carolyn and the counter.)* I'mmmmm sorry ma...mammm. Nnever mm...mind.

(Emmett turns to walk out of the store. As he begins to walk out of the store, Maurice laughs louder...and begins making chicken clucking sounds. Rather than slink away and back down in the face of Maurice's obnoxious laughter, Emmett reluctantly turns around and looks at Carolyn.)

CAROLYN: (Almost in a playful, self-absorbed flirt.) Well...what y'all staring at...*boy?*

(Please Note: The following scene is to be played stylistically. Maurice is still standing outside of the store laughing. Emmett stands blind with rage and terror. As he tries to steady himself by whistling, a half-hearted attempt at a wolf whistle is heard. After the wolf whistle all time stops. The intensity can be cut with a knife as Carolyn stares at Emmett with astonishment. Maurice immediately understands the significance of this act.)

MAURICE: *(Sudden panic.)* Awwww. You done it now. I'm gettin'outta here. You crazy!! Just plain crazy!!

(Maurice exits quickly. Emmett stands alone in an isolated spot. Lights fade on scene. End scene.)

SCENE 7

"Chevrolet" by Lonnie Young, Jr. swells. Lights slowly fade on scene and crossfade to the living room where Mamie is still sleeping. The sound of a ringing telephone is heard. Mamie wakes and picks up the receiver.

MAMIE: Yes? *(Long pause.)* Aunt Lizzie...what? *(Beat.)* Slow down...I can't understand a word you're saying. *(Beat.)* No I...I... Aunt Lizzie...*You are talking too fast.* I... *(Beat.)* Bo? What about Bo? *(Long pause.)* Some *men* took him? Took him where? I...I don't understand Aunt Lizzie. My GOD...how long has he been gone? *(Beat. She is starting to melt when she gets the answer.)* How long? *(Half-beat. Trying to maintain her composure, but she cracks.)* Oh my GOD. GOD. I...I don't understand that Aunt Lizzie. I...I... *(Snapping. Very pointed.)* Aunt Lizzie, stop talking. I want you to calm down and think hard. What do you mean Emmett didn't come back to the house this mornin'? *(Getting upset trying to maintain her composure.)* Hang up and we'll call you back. I've got to call mama right now. *(In panic, exasperated finally.)* I...I...*Hang up Aunt Lizzie! I have to call mama!*

(Lights fade on scene. End scene.)

SCENE 8

Lights crossfade to the office of Roy Wilkins, Executive Director of the NAACP. Mamie and Spearman sit opposite him. Wilkins casually flips through a manila file folder.

MAMIE: I don't know why I'm here, really. All I want to do is catch the first train down there and find my son.

SPEARMAN: We talked about this. You can't just run down to Mississippi like a chicken with your head cut off. You ain't goin' to do Emmett no good iffen you don't have the press and some good law on your side.

WILKINS: I'm afraid he's right, mam. Emotion not withstanding, things like this have to be handled delicately and with careful planning. *(Half-beat. Resigned and content with his "inner knowledge." Speaking as if he is reading from a note card.)* Your son has not suffered in vain. His life will continue...to serve as a symbol to the people of this city... and this *nation*. We pray to GOD that a tragedy of this kind will never happen again.

MAMIE: *(Indignant with Wilkins' attitude.)* You're talking like my son is dead. My son is *missing*. And... *(Wilkins sits stoically silent, staring at the folder.)* Mr. Wilkins? Mr. Wilkins?

WILKINS: *(Coldly.)* Do you have a recent picture of the boy?

(Mamie removes a picture of Emmett from her purse. She begins to hand it to Wilkins, but she momentarily hesitates, clutching it to her chest a bit too long. Mamie looks at it longingly and fights back emotion. Spearman tries to comfort her. Wilkins looks on helplessly and is somewhat uncomfortable. Eventually, she lets the photo go and hands to Spearman.)

SPEARMAN: I'm right here, baby. Right here.

(Handing the photo to Wilkins. He stares at it for a time. Then suddenly...)

WILKINS: I'm very sorry. But I can't help you.

MAMIE: I...I don't understand.

WILKINS: *(Long pause. Looking deeply at Mamie.)* Things are a little...*touchy* in Mississippi right now.

SPEARMAN: What do you mean *touchy*?

WLIKINS: Most of the Whites in Mississippi look at *us*...the NAACP that is...as *invaders*. They haven't been very *cooperative* with anything we've proposed.

MAMIE: I can't believe this is happening.

WILKINS: *(Half-beat.)* I'm sorry.

SPEARMAN: You know...the *New York Times* was down in Mississippi when Emmett was kidnapped.

WILKINS: Yes. They were doing a story on Medgar Evers.

SPEARMAN: *(Pause.)* So...you do realize the eyes of the nation are watching every move you all make? *(Beat.)* Or *don't* make.

WILKINS: *(Slow burn, laying down the gauntlet to Spearman and Mamie.)* Yes. I'm well aware of that.

SPEARMAN: *(Beat.)* Well...I suppose the risk, reward ratio is too unattractive for you.

WILKINS: I beg your pardon.

SPEARMAN: I said...maybe the life of this one little *Black boy* is not e
you to risk the reputation of your precious organization.

WILKINS: That was uncalled for. *(Fuming. Glaring at Spearman with contempt...but
remaining calm.)* *Your* responsibility is merely toward your own child. *My* responsibility is for *all* Negroes who suffer unspeakable atrocities in the South and all over
this country. *Now* and in the *future*. My parents were born and raised in Mississippi.
I was born in Mississippi. So I certainly understand your frustrations. *(Calming.
Regaining composure.)* Of course...we at the NAACP anguish for the suffering of
your boy. And...we all applaud your efforts to seek justice on his behalf. But...

SPEARMAN: We are not asking for your *anguish* or your *applause*. We are only asking...for a little courage on the part of the organization that claims to represent ALL
of *my people*.

WILKINS: *(Trying to ignore Spearman.)* I'm sorry, Mrs. Bradley but I...

SPEARMAN: *Man!* How many times are you gonna keep sayin' *I'm sorry*?!!!!

MAMIE: *(Trying to calm her father.)* Daddy please. *(Beat.)* Mr. Wilkins...I realize that
things are very difficult for your people in Mississippi, right now. I can tell you...it's
certainly not fun for my family, for *me*...and for *Emmett*. But this is no idle press
notice in *The Defender*. Not to us. This is my boy. My son. *(Beat.)* I'm sure that you
are doing your best. I have to believe that. It's my only hope. You see...when this first
happened...all I wanted to do was run down there as fast as I could to find my boy.
But everyone tells me that I don't understand what I am getting into. That it could do
more harm than good. And I'll be honest with you...I'm scared. More scared than I've
ever been in my life. But you see Mr. Wilkins...you and the NAACP..have all of the
political machinery in Mississippi on your side. You are the ones with the connections
down there. I'm just a single mother...living in Chicago...trying to raise my *only* child
the best I can. *(Pause.)* My son has been kidnapped, Mr. Wilkins. Can't you understand that? *(Beat.)* Maybe he's been shot...or tortured. Maybe he's been beaten so
badly that these men are just...just keeping him hidden away...until he's well enough
to be released. I don't know. And I don't care. *(Pause. Fighting back emotion.)* All I
want you to do is to... somehow...get in touch with those people down there...and tell
them that I will take Emmett back no matter what they've done. *(Pause. Mamie has
broken down to Wilkins.)* If it's money they want, I'll pay them. If they want me to
make some kind of...of...political statement...I will say or sign whatever they tell me
to. I'll absolve *everybody* of *everything* if that's what it'll take to get my Emmett back.
I'll even stop going to the newspapers. I'll stop giving interviews and speeches. I...I
just want my boy to come home, Mr. Wilkins. *Please. (Long pause.)* He's my only
child. He's...my mother's only *grandchild*. *(Long pause.)* Mr. Wilkins?

WILKINS: Yes.

MAMIE: Did you hear what I said?

WILKINS: *(Beat.)* Yes, Mrs. Bradley.

(Wilkins starts clearing his desk and gathering up his files. Mamie is crestfallen, finally sensing Wilkins' apathy. Spearman stands.)

SPEARMAN: *(Trying to comfort her.)* Let's go, Mamie.

WILKINS: Please understand. The NAACP has hundreds of cases. They are all very important.

MAMIE: With all due respect Mr. Wilkins, this is the only *case...* I care about.

SPEARMAN: *(Trying to usher Mamie out of the door. To Wilkins, bitterly.)* Thanks...for nothin'...*brother.*

WILKINS: *(Abruptly.)* We will work on your son's case.

MAMIE: *(Pause. Relieved, but still firm in her resolve.)* Thank you.

WILKINS: I'm sorry for the *interrogation.* I've worked with a lot of people over the past two or three years and with every important case...they've...well let's just say that they've *changed on me*...when they started getting their names in the newspapers. You understand?

MAMIE: I think so.

WILKINS: I'll provide you with all of the necessary legal assistance and security guards you will need during this time.

MAMIE: Thank you.

WILKINS: *(Half-beat.)* Oh...Mrs. Bradley? I hope they find your boy. I really do.

(Lights fade on scene. End scene.)

SCENE 9

Lights cross fade to the Spearman living room. A telephone rings. Mamie enters and answers it.

MAMIE: Yes? *(Long pause.)* This is the Spearman residence...what? *(Beat.)* This is Mamie Till Bradley. I...who is this?*(Half-beat. Growing suspicious.)* No you can't speak to my mother. She's sleeping *(Beat.)* What about Bo? Did you find him? *(Long pause.)* I just told you, sir, you cannot speak to my mother. Besides, there's nobody in this house more qualified to take a message about my son than I am. *(Getting upset. Trying to maintain her composure.)* Oh, is this really necessary?

SPEARMAN: Who is that, Mamie Lizzie?

MAMIE: Could you hold the phone, please? *(Placing her hand over the receiver.)* It's...some man from the *Associated Press.* He has information about Bo but he won't give me the message. He says if he can't speak to mama he wants to talk to a family friend.

SPEARMAN: *Say what?* Give me that telephone.

MAMIE: No Daddy. *I* have to do this. *(Beat. Trying to remain calm.)* Yes...Yes I'm still here. *(Beat. Holding back tears and frustration.)* All right. You can call Miss Ollie Williams in Argo, Illinois. *(Beat.)* No... she's my best girlfriend. Her telephone number is ATLANTIC-6368. But I... *(In disbelief.)* He hung up on me. *(Beat.)* That man actually *hung up* on me.

SPEARMAN: *(On the edge.)* What in the world is going on here tonight? Well that man might be *crazy*, but I'm not. I'm gonna call the *Chicago Sun*, the *Times*, the *Daily News*, and *The Defender* all night long if I have to. I'm going to get to the bottom of this mess.

MAMIE: Maybe...it was just another one of those crank calls.

SPEARMAN: *(Angry.)* I'm tired of this! I'm tired. The obscene phone calls, the death threats, them nasty...insulting letters we get in the mail *every* single day since this happened. I'm...I'm just tired of it. Why do *we* need...a police car to sit outside this house to protect us?! Think about...how ridiculous that is! *(Half-beat.)* They all afraid that this fuss over Emmett is gonna cause Negroes to march down to Mississippi. Well we ought to march down there and root out every one of them rednecks. It's *time* for a change. *(Beat.)* We ain't done nothin' wrong. We are the *victims*. And it's time somebody started treating us like it.

MAMIE: But what else can we do?

SPEARMAN: *(Frustrated pause.)* I…I don't know. But it's got to be better than pacing these floors every night…praying for the telephone to...

(The telephone rings again. Alma slowly enters and looks at the people in the room as if she is in a dream. She instinctively knows it's bad news.)

ALMA: Is anybody going to answer that? *(Long pause.)* Mamie Lizzie? *(Beat.)* Henry? *(Sensing that something is not right.)* What's wrong with you two? What's happened? Answer the telephone!

(Alma quickly moves toward the ringing telephone. Mamie picks up the receiver before she reaches it.)

MAMIE: Hello? Yes Ollie. I'm fine. *(Pause.)* No...you can't speak to my mama. If there's a message you're going to have to give it to me. See...I know what the message is. But don't give it to me fast. I want to write everything down. I don't want to miss anything. *(Beat.)* No...no…go ahead...I'm ready. *(Beat. Mamie begins writing down the message. At one point, early in the relaying of the message, she gasps and stifles an exasperated cry. She regains her composure and continues writing. The message ends and Mamie places the pen and pencil down.)* Is that all? *(Beat.)* Thank you Ollie. *(Pause.)* No, I'm all right. *(Beat.)* Really…I'll be fine. I'm…I'm going to go now. *(Beat.)* No. That's not necessary. *(Beat.)* Yes. I will. I promise. *(Mamie hangs up. Brief pause.)* Emmett's dead. They found him...floating in a river. *(Beat.)* They say...they say... a young White boy was fishing...and he saw...he saw... *(Beginning to crack.)* Emmett's *foot*... sticking out of the water. *(Beat.)* His body was so damaged... that the only way Poppa Mose could tell that it was my son was because he was still wearing his father's *ring. (Cracking.)*

ALMA: Lord have mercy...no!!!!!! Emmett?!!!! Emmett!!!!!!!

SPEARMAN: Oh GOD! GOD!!!! I can't believe it. I can't believe anybody would do something like that to...

ALMA: *Emmett?!!! Emmett?!!!! Why?!!!!!!!*

(Lights slowly fade on Spearman and Alma, leaving Mamie standing alone in an isolated spot.)

MAMIE: *Mama? (Mamie...about to lose it.)* Help me, Mama. What should I do now? Please...tell me...what to do now. I mean... somebody...somebody has got to tell me what to do!!!

(Lights fade on Mamie and crossfade to Roy Wilkins, delivering the following speech.)

WILKINS: "There is no place with a civil rights record of abuses that even approaches the state of Mississippi...in inhumanity, in murder, in brutality, and racial hatred. It is absolutely at the bottom of the list. But the Emmett Till case has shaken the very foundations of this country. Because this single act is proof...that in the state of Mississippi...even a *child*...is not safe. For the *White* Mississippian...this act represented a chance to prove their manhood. They had to prove it. They just had to prove...that they were superior by taking away the life of a 14-year-old boy. And it was because he was a Black *boy* that they went there...in the dead of night. It's in the *virus.* It's in the blood of the Mississippian. He simply can't help it. Only *GOD* knows how many Negroes have come up *missing* in that state. Or how many more will end up like Emmett Till...unless our federal government is willing to act. *(Pause.)* You know...President Eisenhower was a fine general. But if he had fought World War II the way he fights for civil rights...we would all be speaking *German.*"

(Lights fade on scene. End scene.)

Scene 10

Lights slowly crossfade to Alma sitting on her couch. She is nearly in a catatonic state. The whispers are in her head. Offstage voices: "Shame. Shame. Shame in Mississippi. Shame." The telephone is ringing but she barely hears it. She finally picks up the receiver after several rings. Mamie enters toward the top of the conversation.

ALMA: Yes? *(Beat.)* Yes. This is the Spearman residence. *(Beat.)* What? *(Long pause. Alma bursts into tears of joy. She is almost debilitated with jubilation.) What?!! You what?!!!! Praise Him!!!! Praise GOD!!!!!*

MAMIE: *(Confused and suspicious.)* Mama?

ALMA: *(Ignoring Mamie. Barely able to hold the telephone.)* Bless you, sir!!! GOD bless you!!!!

MAMIE: *(More pointed.)* Who *is* that, Mama?

ALMA: *(Lost in her own euphoria.)* When can I...I mean...when can *we* see him?!!!

MAMIE: Mama, I don't think you should...

ALMA: No...no you're right. That won't be necessary. We'll just wait to hear from you!!!! *Bless you, sir!!! Bless you!!!* You've made us all...*so happy!!!!*

MAMIE: *(Alma hangs up.)* Mama, what is it?

ALMA: *(Grabbing Mamie. Falling to her knees with joy. Almost in a state of delirium.)* They found him Mamie!!!! They've found Emmett!!!! And he's alive!!! Emmett...is alive!!!!

MAMIE: *(Confused. Getting upset.) What?* What are you talking about? Who was that?

ALMA: I don't know. Some...man. He said that he was a police officer. And that he had been working with the FBI on Emmett's case. But it doesn't matter who he is!!! Nothing else matters right now. They've found Emmett!!!! *And he's alive!!!! He's comin' back to us!!!*

MAMIE: *(Slowing down. Suspiciously.)* What else did this man say?

ALMA: *(Panting. Out of breath with happiness.)* He said...that *everything*...this whole incident...was just a terrible mix up and that Emmett has been alive all this time! He said...he said that there wasn't any more need for you to keep talkin' to the newspapers. There ain't no need for any kind of police investigation...or even for you to go to Mississippi. *Because he's coming home! (Half-beat.)* The man also said...that you don't have to fly around the country anymore makin' all those speeches for the NAACP.

MAMIE: *(Pause. Fighting back emotion.)* Momma, please...*don't do this.*

ALMA: *(About to lose it. Delirium.)* I've got to call Henry!!!!

MAMIE: Just stop for a minute...and listen to what you're saying.

ALMA: I've got to let him know that...

MAMIE: Mama...please...stop! *(Beat.)* Did this man tell you why he's waited all of this time to call us? Or why he's kept silent even after the sheriff in Money arrested the two white men who took Emmett from the house? Did he give you a reason why he let the district attorney set a trial date before calling us? *(Tears welling in her eyes.)* Did this man even let you speak with my Emmett?

ALMA: *(Long pause. Reality sets in. Realizing that phone call was nothing but a cruel hoax. She breaks down.)* No. No! Emmett *is* alive. He's coming back to us. Why can't you just accept that?

MAMIE: No. Emmett's gone. He's gone, Mama.

ALMA: *But*...that man on the telephone said...

MAMIE: No.

ALMA: *(Beat. Slow implosion.)* Oh GOD!!!! *(Half-beat.)* GOD.

(Beat. Mamie embraces her crestfallen.)

ALMA: Why?

MAMIE: I'm here, Mama. I'm here. We've just got to hold on...until we find the answers.

(Lights slowly fade on scene. End scene.)

SCENE 11

Lights up on Sheriff H. C. Strider, Wright, and Maurice. The two Black men are holding shovels digging a grave as Strider stands over them supervising the operation.

STRIDER: Now remember Preacher...I want that body buried before sundown.

WRIGHT: Yassah...Sheriff Strider, sir.

STRIDER: *(Half-beat. Grinning at Mose. Spitting on the ground near where the body is supposedly laying.)* Why'd he do it, Mose?

WRIGHT: I...I don't rightly know, sir.

STRIDER: Goddamned fool, iffen ya ask me. *(Half-beat.)* All right y'all, mind what I said.

WRIGHT/MAURICE: Yassah...Sheriff Strider, sir.

(Strider exits.)

MAURICE: We ain't gonna bury Emmett without tellin' Mamie Lizzie, is we?

WRIGHT: Ya heard what the sheriff said. We cross 'em...we liable to end up just like him.

(Maurice defiantly throws his shovel down and exits. Beat. Wright stands motionless and stares at the ground. Wright places his shovel down after a time. Lights fade on scene and shift to Mamie on the telephone.)

MAMIE: But that's what I want. Why is there a problem?

SPEARMAN: Who are you talking to?

MAMIE: It's Maurice. The sheriff's trying to bury Emmett's body down in Mississippi.

SPEARMAN: *What?*

MAMIE: They've actually dug the grave and everything.

SPEARMAN: Well...tell them to stop.

MAMIE: I'm trying daddy, but he says the local sheriff *ordered them* to bury his body by sundown.

SPEARMAN: What do you mean he *ordered them*. He can't do that. And *we* can't let 'em do that.

MAMIE: You're right. *(Beat.)* If they bury Emmett in Mississippi...that will be the end of any chance we have of finding out what really happened. *(Pause. Speaking back into the phone.)* Maurice...I want you to go back to that cemetery and tell whoever you see to stop what they are doing. Tell them my son's body has got to get back to Chicago. Anyway you can. Just bring Emmett home!!!

(Lights fade on scene. End scene.)

SCENE 12

A verse of "Leaning on the Ever Lasting Arms" is sung by the cast. Lights slowly cross fade to Rayner, Mamie, and Spearman at the A.A. Rayner Funeral Home. Spearman guides Mamie through the crowd.

MAMIE: *(Seeing the casket/box being taken from the train.)* Oh...Lord have mercy!!! Take my soul!!!

SPEARMAN: It's all right Mamie Lizzie. We don't have to do this if you don't want to.

MAMIE: No. I'm all right.

RAYNER: *(Fighting back the crowd.)* Everybody get back!!!! Please!!! Get back and give Mrs. Bradley some room!!! We have to go inside and view the body!!!

(Crowd moans in grief upon hearing Rayner's words. Slowly, the crowd noises fade.)

MAMIE: Thank you, Mr. Rayner.

RAYNER: You're welcome. Now...there's a seal on this box that says it is *definitely* not to be opened. The body is to be buried *as is*. *(Rayner produces a pen and slip of paper...trying to hand it to Mamie.)* Now... just sign here and I'll make all of the arrangements.

MAMIE: I don't understand.

RAYNER: Well...the only way the officials down there would allow the body to be released was if your uncle signed an affidavit swearing that none of his family would disturb the remains.

MAMIE: So...you're not going to open that box?

RAYNER: *(Beat. Very apologetically.)* I'm sorry. This ain't none of my doin'. They might hold me liable for the damages...or somethin'.

MAMIE: *(Beat.)* Do you have a hammer?

RAYNER: I beg your pardon?

MAMIE: *A hammer.* Do you have one? Because I didn't sign anything. And I'm going to open that box...with my bare hands if I have to. *(Beat.)* I'm not asking you...I am *telling you.*

RAYNER: You're...you're just upset. Maybe...you should lay down for a spell.

MAMIE: Mr. Rayner...if that is my son in that box... I have a right to see him. And I could care less what the entire state of Mississippi thinks about it.

RAYNER: *(Staring at Mamie. Reluctantly.)* All right, Mrs. Bradley. All right, whatever you say.

(The men begin to tear off the seal of the box and chop the lock that secures it. It is a very hard task. Mamie struggles to remain standing upright.)

RAYNER: *(The men succeed in opening the initial box. They all pause.)* What in the world?

SPEARMAN: There's another box inside *this* box. Somebody wanted to make sure that whatever's inside wasn't gonna be seen.

RAYNER: Oh yeah? Well let's get this other one open. *(Beat. Looking toward Mamie.)* I mean...if that's all right with you, Mrs. Bradley?

(Mamie slowly nods her head and the men resume opening the last portion of the casket/box. Beat. The men step aside as Mamie slowly walks toward the box and opens the lid. As she pulls the lid upward...the stench of the box's contents literally immobilize everyone in the room. The smell is extremely nauseating. Everyone in the room places either a piece of cloth or their hands over their noses. Mamie slowly leans forward to examine the contents of the box. As she reaches inside and brushes away the lime, they see Emmett's mangled face. They all recoil in horror.)

MAMIE: *My GOD!!!!!!!!*

SPEARMAN: What did they do to him?!!!

RAYNER: In all my years...I ain't ever seen anything like this. *(The smell starts to overcome everyone in the room.)* I've got to open up a few windows...before we all get sick. *(Rayner exits.)*

SPEARMAN: They say he was in the water for three days. *(Straining to look inside the box.)* But...it has to be more than just the river water that did that to him. *(Pause. Seeing Mamie creeping up to look inside the box. Rayner enters.)* No, Mamie. Please don't look at him any more.

RAYNER: He's right, Mrs. Bradley. I'll take it from here.

MAMIE: *No.* Daddy...Mr. Rayner, I'm all right. *(Beat.)* I still have a job to do. *(Beat.)*

RAYNER: What kind of *job*?

MAMIE: I have got to check whatever this is that they sent me. Because if this isn't my son...I'm not going to bury...*this*.

SPEARMAN: Mamie Lizzie. You need a *doctor* for that. Somebody that's been trained to...

MAMIE: If this is *not* Emmett...then I want Mr. Rayner to give this poor soul a proper Christian burial. *(Beat.)* But if this *is* Emmett...I'm going to have an open casket at his funeral.

RAYNER: *(In absolute horror.)* An open casket!!! Mrs. Bradley...you can't be *serious*!!!

SPEARMAN: Mamie Lizzie...you should really think about what you're saying. You're...you're just upset.

MAMIE: If I tried for a million years, I could never describe *this*. If that really is my son, I want the whole world to see what's happening in Mississippi. I want them to see what they did to my Emmett.

(Lights fade on the men in the funeral home and intensify on Mamie.)

MAMIE: *(To herself. And the body in the box.)* Emmett...what have they done to you?

(Lights soften on Mamie and scene. She remains in a semi-freeze through the next scene. Church organ swells in the distance. Lights up on Bishop Louis Henry Ford. It is the funeral of Emmett Till. Sister Margaret Avery enters and sings "Been in the Storm So Long.")

AVERY: *"I been in the storm so long...*

I been in the storm so long...children

I been in the storm so long...

Oh...give me a little time to pray."

(Repeat.)

FORD: Today...we will be reading from Matthew...18th chapter.

(Beat. The entire cast reads this passage in unison.)

CAST: *"At the same time came the disciples unto Jesus saying: Who is the greatest...in the kingdom of Heaven? And Jesus called a little child unto him, and said...Who so shall receive one such little child in my name receiveth me. But who so shall offend one of these little ones which believe in me, it were better for him that a millstone were hanged about his neck and that he were drowned in the depth of the sea."*

FORD: This...is a very sad day for anyone who can feel pain...or loss. My heart is very heavy today. My soul...has been rocked to its very foundation. Indeed...this one event has shaken people all over the world. It would seem...that the 'M' in *Mississippi* stands for *murder*. *Mississippi*...the state of jungle fury. It is clear to me...that the *State of Mississippi* has decided to maintain its un Christian-like credo of White supremacy at all costs; even if those costs involve the lynching...of a *child*. *(Long pause. Ford surveys the room and congregation.)* And...if you have any doubts about what I'll say this morning...then simply look inside of this casket and let your heart be your guide.

(As the pastor finishes his last sentence, the famous photo of Emmett's mangled face that was published in the Chicago Defender September 1955 is flashed on an upstage wall or scrim. It remains on screen until the end of the act. Lights fade on church and crossfade to Mamie still leaning over her dead son's body. Suddenly, Mamie, in sheer agony, pulls the ring from the box, holds it up...and clutches it close to her chest. Finally, pitifully, hysterically...Mamie breaks down under the strain.)

MAMIE: OH GOD. *GOD!!!* I don't want to be here. I don't want *this*. Not *this*. Emmett? *Emmett?! Emmett?!!!!!!!*

(Lights fade on scene. Fade to black.)

END OF ACT I

ACT II

SCENE 1

In darkness, the cast is heard singing several verses of "In the Mississippi River."

WHISPERERS: *"In the Mississippi River*

In the Mississippi River

In The Mississippi River

Well you can count them one by one [It could be your son]

Count them two by two [It could be me or you]

Count them three by three [Do you want to see]

Count them four by four...

Well, into the river they go...

Into the river they go...

Into the river they go...

Into the river they go..."

(When the song is finished, lights rise on Wilkins' office. Mamie enters.)

MAMIE: I've been trying to contact you for several days.

WILKINS: We've been very busy.

MAMIE: Yes. But my speaking engagement in San Francisco is next week. My father and I haven't received the financial arrangements from your office.

WILKINS: *(Arrogantly.)* That's because we've cancelled your trip, Mrs. Bradley.

MAMIE: I don't understand.

WILKINS: The NAACP will not fund a free junket to California for you and your *entourage.* Especially if it isn't an NAACP sponsored function.

MAMIE: *(Pause.)* The money they are offering me to speak at their rally will help with my son's trial. And that helps the NAACP.

WILKINS: It's been settled. I'm sorry.

MAMIE: *(Trying to restrain herself.)* I thought it was clear that any money from my speeches will go directly to the NAACP lawyer you promised me. That's what you said. *(Beat.)* The trial is in two weeks. You promised that the NACCP would be with me every step of the way.

WILKINS: That's not true, Mrs. Bradley. I said no such thing.

MAMIE: *(Beat. Bewildered by this switch.)* You most certainly did. (Half-beat.) I am not independently wealthy. I've had to take a leave of absence from my job until this business is completed. My father had to leave his job to travel with me. So I've had to put him on a salary. All of his expenses are up to me. When we go to Mississippi...

WILKINS: You don't need anybody to travel with you to Mississippi. There will be someone from our Jackson office to meet you.

MAMIE: But what if I am recognized? I can't travel alone anymore. I can't go *any-where...alone* anymore. I need my father to protect me from the crowds wherever I go. Since this happened, I can't even think straight. People will ask me where I am going and half of the time I'll tell them where I am. I get so many cards and letters from all over...I've had to hire a secretary to manage my affairs.

WILKINS: *(Bemused.) A secretary?*

MAMIE: How else am I supposed to answer all of that mail? I am not making any money at all...but I still have a life to maintain. What else do you expect me to do?

WILKINS: Mrs. Bradley...we are not going to fight your case. *Mississippi* will fight *your* case. *(Pause.)* Let me be frank about something. The NAACP feels that your case has far reaching implications...well beyond this trial. That's why we feel it is much more important to use the money you raise on our behalf to fight the kind of racism that killed your son *through the federal courts.* It is our best chance to finally kill Jim Crow where he lives. I don't know if you're aware, but America is trying to position itself as the great, moral center of the universe. But this is *our* chance to show the world what's really happening in this country. Especially to Negroes. Putting the White killers of a little colored boy on trial in the bowels of rural Mississippi will accomplish more for Negro rights than when we won the right to desegregate public schools. *(Half-beat.)* Can't you see how important this case is to *all Negroes* and not just *your* son?

MAMIE: *(Beat. Anger and frustration swelling.)* Do you know what kind of Hell I'm going through? My son is dead, sir. My *son* is dead...and the men who killed him are walking the streets of Money, Mississippi...like nothing ever happened. Still laughing and grinning over their little *lynching party.* Looking for the next *nigger boy* they'll toss into the Tallahatchie. *(Half-beat.)* Now, when I try to get justice for my boy's murder...no one is willing to lift a finger. *(Slow burn, bubbling to the surface.)* When Emmett's body was found, the news reached the local television stations in Chicago. They interrupted *I Love Lucy* to speak of his murder. *(Half-beat.) I* received *hundreds* of angry letters for that. *(Beat.)* My son's life was sacrificed in the name of *our* struggle, *sir.* And you have the nerve...to speak to me like that? I wasn't raising money for the NAACP so they could assume the right to martyr my Emmett. All I've ever wanted for my son was *justice*; not a dedicated statue in his likeness. *(Beat.)* You specifically led me to believe that the NAACP was going to provide me with legal counsel to take to the trial in Mississippi. That is the *only* reason I agreed to speak publicly on the NAACP's behalf.

WILKINS: The *NAACP* doesn't provide personal lawyers for private citizens. *Mississippi* will give you a lawyer.

MAMIE: So in the entire NAACP there's no one who is willing to go down there with me?

WILKINS: Like I said, we've been very busy lately. There's simply no one available for such a trip. *(Half-beat.)* I'm sorry you believe the world shouldn't go on until your son's murder trial is over. *(Pause.)* Perhaps...you should worry less about money and capitalizing off the death of your son.

MAMIE: *(Long pause. Astonished.)* What did you say?

WILKINS: *(Slow. Measured.)* I'm afraid you've allowed this *cult of celebrity* thing to get the best of you. The NAACP is not in the business of making movie stars, Mrs. Bradley. We're in the Civil Rights business. Nothing more, nothing less.

MAMIE: *(Slow burn. In disbelief.)* Shame on you Mr. Wilkins...and the *entire* NAACP. *Shame.*

WILKINS: Good day...Mrs. Bradley.

(Lights fade on scene. End scene.)

SCENE 2

Billie Holiday's "Strange Fruit" swells in the distance. Lights crossfade to Mamie standing in an isolated spot. Emmett's voice wafts through the darkness.

EMMETT: *(Voice-over.)* Mama? Help me!

(Mamie stands silent. Lights fade on her in the spot and crossfade to Alma, listening attentively, sitting in the family room area. Mamie is still lost in the moment.)

ALMA: Mamie? *Mamie Lizzie?*

MAMIE: *(Still somewhat disoriented.)* What?

ALMA: You were telling me about your dreams, then you stopped talking.

MAMIE: I'm sorry. *(Pause.)* Like I was saying. Emmett screams, then his screams go away. But the nightmare always comes back. The very next night. Sometimes, that same night. *(Beat.)* Mama, I feel like I'm going crazy.

ALMA: It's a wonder we all ain't lost our minds over this thing.

MAMIE: The thing is, I get up every morning. I brush my teeth, wash my face. I fix my hair and dress. And then...I could just kill myself for not protecting him better. For not...being the kind of mother who would always keep her child safe. *(Beat.)* When I found out I was pregnant...I dreamed of graduations, a wedding, someone to take care of me when I got old. Even grandchildren. Now...*(Brief pause.)* I keep thinking about all the things he'll *miss*. All the things...*I'll* miss. *(Beat.)* He'll never graduate from high school. *(Beat.)* He'll never drive a car...or go to prom. *(Beat.)* He'll never fall in love...or get his heart broken. *(Beat.)* My little boy...will never even have children of his own. To raise in his image. *(Beat.)* I heard one time....that when a child dies...he disappears into the blank pages of his potential. All they could have become. Everything they might have accomplished.

ALMA: I just...can't believe he's gone.

MAMIE: The other day, I saw an ad in the newspaper talking about this new movie... I can't remember the name of it right now. Something with Humphrey Bogart in it, I think. And... the first thing I thought was...I've got to make sure I tell Emmett about this movie. He always loved *Bogie. (Long pause.)* I suppose, when you lose a child...everything stirs up old memories. *(Beat.)* I'm just 33 years old, Mama. And I'm coming to the realization...that this is something... I'll have to live with for the rest of my life. *(Beat.)* Emmett...is not coming back to me. I realize that... *right* now. An hour from now, I might have a harder time accepting it. But his death...and the *way that he died*...it's...oh...how can I explain it...*(Pause.)* It's *mine now*. It's...a part of me. It's inside...of me. (Pause. Fighting back tears.) I miss me, Mama. *I miss me.* I miss the way I was...the way...*we were. (Beat.)* Everybody keeps tellin' me that everything is going to be all right. But...I'm...I'm just not whole anymore. I am not...*Mamie* any-more. And sometimes...sometimes, Mama...I just miss *me. (Long pause.)* I'm going to the trial.

ALMA: *What?! (Shock. Terror.)* Oh, child no! You can't go down there. After what just happened?!

MAMIE: When I first heard that they had arrested the two men who kidnapped Emmett... I knew then what I was going to do. I have business in Mississippi. *(Beat.)* Can't think of any other reason to go down *there*.

(They both laugh. Laughing through the tears. Mamie almost immediately drifts from gut busting laughter to a painful crying fit.)

ALMA: Baby, you just laughed. It doesn't mean that you care about Emmett any less. Or that you done forgot about him. Just because you laughed.

MAMIE: How can I ever enjoy anything again...when Emmett enjoys *nothing*?

ALMA: If you want to take this thing on, you've got to be strong. You've got to survive.

MAMIE: I guess that's what I'm saying, Mama. I'm not so sure I want to *survive*. It's like...I'm standing on a high wire...in a circus...with no net below. And...if I move too far in one direction...I'll fall. That's why, I don't dare think about him for too long. *(Beat.)* One inch, and I'll fall. *(Beat.)* One inch.

ALMA: So what if you fall? We'll always be here to catch you. A lot of people cared about that boy. And a lot of people care about *you*. I know you think you're a terrible mother…that somehow this is all your fault. But the world doesn't feel that way. And neither do I.

(The Mississippi parade march, folk song "Hen Duck" swells in the distance. They embrace. Lights fade on scene. End scene.)

SCENE 3

It is the Tallahatchie County Courthouse. Sumner, Mississippi. September 1955. When the song ends, raucous shouts, uneasy rustling, and low muffled jeers are heard. Eastland enters as Judge Swango.)

SWANGO: "I hereby call this court of the Seventeenth Judicial District of Mississippi to order. I'd like to welcome the members of the press here to Sumner. At this time, I will ask all photographers to take your pictures now…before opening remarks and testimony begins."

(Camera flashes cascade across the stage as Wright enters. The cast converts the stage into the shape of a makeshift courtroom. Wright takes a seat in the witness box.)

SWANGO: Now Uncle Mose, can you tell this court, what happened on the mornin' of August 28th, 1955.

WRIGHT: *(Slowly.)* Well…it was hot and still that night. And the moon was shining as bright as day. Me and my family was sleepin'. It was about two...three in the mornin'...when I heard somebody knocking on our front door.

(Loud door knocks are heard. Roy Bryant and J. W. Milam enter. Milam has a flashlight in one hand and a holstered pistol on his hip.)

BRYANT: *Preacher?!!! Preacher?!!!!* Get out here, nigger.

WRIGHT: Who's there?

BRYANT: This is Mr. Bryant.

WRIGHT: Mr. Bryant? What can I do for you, sir?

BRYANT: You got boys in there from Chicago?

WRIGHT: *(Confused. Frightened.)* Yass sir, I have. They in some kinda trouble, sir?

BRYANT: We want to see the boy what done all the talkin'.

WRIGHT: I'm beggin' your pardon, sir?

MILAM: *Come on preacher!!!!* Y'all better drag that Chicago boy out here fast ifffen you know what's good for ya. He ain't gonna get away with talkin' dirty to *our* women.

WRIGHT: I…I don't understand.

MILAM: *(Removing his pistol and holds his pistol down by his side.)* You wanna die, boy?!!!!

WRIGHT: Naw.

MILAM: DO YOU WANNA DIE, NIGGER?!!!!!!

WRIGHT: No!!!! No!!!! I...I mean...*NAW SAH!!!!*

MILAM: Then you better trot that fresh talkin', little nigger retard out here...'fore I burn your house down...and lynch every goddamn one of ya!!!

BRYANT: We want the one what talks funny. He's the one with all the sass.

WRIGHT: *(Beat.)* You talkin' 'bout Emmett? *Fresh talkin'?* *(Beat.)* Naw, sir. None of these boys would do somethin' fool like that. I know them children. They good boys, sir.

BRYANT: We just want the lady outside to take a look at him. If he ain't the one, we'll let 'em loose.

WRIGHT: Please, Mr. Bryant, sir. Please don't take him. *(Beat.)* Take me instead. I'm the one responsible for 'em. Take me!!! *(Beat.)* Emmett's a good boy, sir. But he ain't got good sense sometimes. I'll...I'll whupp him good...for whatever y'all say he's done...if y'all wants me to. I'll do it!!! *(Beat.)* He was raised up North. He don't know nuthin' 'bout our ways down here. *(Frantically searching through his pants pockets.)* I'll pay you gentlemen for the damages. I got some money. I'll pay y'all iffen...

MILAM: *(Pointed.)* Get the fuck outta the way...*boy.*

(Lights fade on Milam, soften on Wright and intensify on Emmett sleeping peacefully on a pallet. Bryant creeps into his room and stands over Emmett for what seems an eternity. Bryant, still holding a flashlight and clutching a pistol, suddenly pulls the covers off Emmett.)

BRYANT: *(Softly. Slowly.)* Wake up...boy.

EMMETT: *(Still asleep. Slowly waking.)* Huh? *(Beat.)* What?

BRYANT: I said...*wake up, nigger.*

EMMETT: Poppa Mose?

BRYANT: Naw. It ain't your *Poppa Mose.* I'm the husband of that White woman you sassed down in Money. You remember that little thing?

EMMETT: Huh? What's that ya sayin'?

BRYANT: Oh...you a smart ass littler nigger boy, ain't ya?! Well we gonna see how smart you are.

EMMETT: What?

BRYANT: Sassed my wife, boy. Now you gonna pay for it.

EMMETT: *Sassed?* Mister, I ain't sassed nnnnnobody. I ain't ddddone nnnnnuthin' like that.

BRYANT: *(Bryant violently grabs Emmett in his nightshirt collar. His tight grip is literally choking the life out of Emmett. He puts a pistol to Emmett's head and cocks the hammer.)* Goddamn it, nigger!!! You better say…*Yes, sir!!*…and *No, sir!!*…when you speak to me or I'mma blow your fuckin' head off…and splattter your colored brains all over that pillow! You hear me, boy?!!!!

EMMETT: *(Petrified. Emmett can barely breathe or speak.)* YYYYesssss. I…I…I mean…YES, SIR!

BRYANT: That's better. *(Mockingly, he continues.)* You from Chicago…ain't ya boy?!

EMMETT: *(Nervously.)* YYYYes…sir.

BRYANT: And you don't remember talkin' with no White lady…what owns a store in Money? Last Wednesday?

EMMETT: Whaaa…Yes. I…I mmmmmmean…NNNNNO...Sir. NNNO.

BRYANT: You…a little nervous 'bout somethin', nigger? Huh? Do ya…or don't ya remember talkin' wit' a White lady down in Money?!!! *(Beat.)* She sittin' right outside. So don't you lie to me.

EMMETT: *(Confused.)* I…I think I rrrrrrrrremember. BBBBBBut it won't nnnnnnnothin' like ya sayin' it was mmmmmmmister. I ain't ddddo nnnnnothin' to that lady… bbbbbut…

BRYANT: BBBBBBut what, nigger? *(Half-beat.)* BUT WHAT?!!!!!!!!!!!

EMMETT: I…I… jjjjjjjust asked her….for tttttwo cents of bbbbbuggle ggggum. *(Half-beat.)* Thasssss all.

BRYANT: *Like Hell you did!!!!* That was *my wife* you were talkin' fresh to…NIGGER! *(Beat.)* My WIFE!!!!! *(Beat.)* Folks laughin'… callin' me a godddamned fool! The whole town is talkin'. All because a your fresh ass mouth. Well we ain't gonna have it down here, boy. Naw, sir. *(Bryant violently jerks Emmett to his feet. He's got his man.)* Let's go, boy. I got somebody in the truck that wants to take a look at you.

(Emmett reluctantly rises from his bed and slowly starts putting on clothes.)

BRYANT: *(Impatiently.)* Hurry up, boy! *(Beat.)* What the Hell are you doin'?

EMMETT: I always put on my sssssocks and ssssssshoes bbbbbefore I go outside.

BRYANT: Boy, where you goin'…you ain't gonna need no ssssocks or no ssssshoes.

(Bryant drags Emmett from the room.)

WRIGHT: *(In tears…shaking like a leaf on a tree, he unashamedly begins to beg.)* Mr. Bryant, sir? Please, don't take that boy outta this house. He ain't done nothin' wrong.

I know'd it.

BRYANT: How old are you, Preacher?

WRIGHT: *(Fear almost stifling his answer.)* Sixty-four. I'm...64-years-old, sir.

BRYANT: Well...if you say anything about this to anybody or cause any trouble, you'll never live to see 65.

(Lights fade on Bryant. Lights restore on Wright seated in the witness box; petrified ...but not broken. Milam morphs into Gerald Chatham, Tallahatchie District Attorney, and enters.)

WRIGHT: Then I saw Mr. Bryant and his brother...Mr. Milam...drag the boy outside to their flat bed truck. *(Beat.)* We got a kerosene lamp...sittin' on our front porch. I could see the outline of Emmett's body...when they took him away. As they were carryin' him toward that truck... I saw Emmett look back toward the house...and to me. *(Pause.)* But I couldn't do nothin' to help him.

CHATHAM: Did you see your nephew alive after that night?

WRIGHT: Naw, sir.

CHATHAM: Do you see either of the men who came to your home that morning in this courtroom?

WRIGHT: *(Hesitates at first...then he straightens.)* Yas sir.

CHATHAM: Please stand and point them out to us.

WRIGHT: *(Slowly stands and points toward the audience.)* Tharr he.

CHATHAM: Let the record show that Mose Wright has identified Roy Bryant as one of the men who came to his house that evening and took the Till boy away. Do you see anyone else in this courtroom who was with Roy Bryant that night?

WRIGHT: *(Again he points outward.)* Tharr he.

CHATHAM: *(Half-beat.)* Let the record show that Mose Wright has identified J.W. Milam as the second man who came to his house with Roy Bryant on the morning of August 28, 1955. *(Beat. Lights fade on Bryant.)* Now...Uncle Mose...aren't you afraid of what your testimony might mean for your family...and yourself.

WRIGHT: *(Pause.)* Yes, sir. I truly am. But then...I just think about...*his face. Emmett's face. (Pause.)* When we drug him out of that river...I didn't want to look at him. But I *had* to. I was responsible for 'em. *Me.* I didn't look for his face...when his eyes found *me*. When I first looked at the body...I had to turn away. But I had seen enough to make out something *awful*...laying in the mud of that river bed. He was my nephew...and I loved him. I loved him...but I failed him. Now I've got to live with that thing. This is my nightmare. *(Pause.)* I'm sorry, Mamie. I'm so sorry.

(Lights fade on scene. End scene.)

SCENE 4

A fearful Willie Reed enters. At first Willie Reed mumbles, in low whispers. Head bowed. Eyes lowered.

REED: My name is Willie...Willie Reed. *(Beat.)* It was about six in the mornin'. My granddaddy had sent me to the store to buy some meat for dinner...when I seen 'em. I...I seen four White men and two other colored mens in the truck. They had him...they had him...in the back of that pick up. A '54 or '55 Chevrolet, I think it was. The truck had a green body and a white top. The colored mens in the back looked like they was kinda holdin' this colored boy down. Then the truck passed me and stopped at this barn. Just a few houses down from my Aunt Mandy. Amanda Bradley, I mean. Then...they took the colored boy inside a the barn. And they...

(Lights slowly up on Milam and Bryant, standing in the barn, glaring directly back at Willie seated in the witness box, grinning at him. Willie starts shrinking.)

SWANGO: Willie...you're gonna have to speak up now...so the court reporter can hear you.

(Taking deep breaths. Reed descends back into that night. Lights start to soften around him. He nervously mumbles in an even lower tone.)

REED: Then they took him inside.

(Beat.)

SWANGO: Now Willie, I told you to speak louder.

REED: They took him inside the barn. I had never seen his face until I saw his picture in one them...them newspapers. I didn't pay it no mind, I swear I didn't until I heard...I heard...

SWANGO: You heard what, *son*?

BRYANT: *(Grinning at Willie petrified in the witness box.)* Yeah, boy! What did you hear?!!

REED: *I heard his screams!!!*

(Lights soften on Reed and cross to Bryant and Milam beating Emmett. The beating should be portrayed as realistically and as brutally as physically possible. Two Black men stand around the edges of the scene, shadowing Emmett making sure that he can't escape. As he tries to crawl away, Emmett is grabbed by the Black men in the background and thrown back into the clutches of Milam and Bryant.)

EMMETT: *MMMMama!!! Mama!!!!* Mama! Lord...have mercy. *Lord have mmmmmercy!!!!! PPPlease...I didn't do nnnnuthin' wrong. I didn't do nnnnuthin'!!!!!*

MILAM: Shut up, boy.

EMMETT: PPPPPPPlease. I dddddidn't mean nnnuthin...

MILAM: I said...SHUT UP...NIGGER!!!!!

(Bryant gives Emmett a swift kick to the ribs.)

MILAM: Chicago boy.

(Bryant spits in Emmett's face.)

MILAM: I'm tired of 'em sending your kind down here to stir up trouble. I'm gonna make an example out of you. *(Milam pulls out a hunting knife and waves it in front of Emmett's face.)*

EMMETT: *DDDDon't...Please...*

(Bryant violently jabs Emmett in the side with the knife.

EMMETT: *AAAAAAHHHHHHHHH!!!!!!!*

(After the stabbing, Bryant wipes the blood on the knife off on Emmett's shirt.)

MILAM: You still got all them White girlfriends? Huh?

EMMETT: They jjjjjjjust ffffffriends. I dddone told ya...I ddddone told ya...

BRYANT: Ain't got all that sass now, do you boy?!!! Ya ain't so goddamned tough!!! *(Bryant smacks Emmett.)*

EMMETT: PPPPPlease mister...please...ddddon't.

BRYANT: Struttin' round with pictures of White women in your wallet like you some goddamn *movie star*. That what you think you are, nigger?!! A goddamned movie star?!!!!

EMMETT: It's a new wallet...they always put pictures of mmovie stars like that in nnnnew wallets, mmmister. I dddon't even kkkknow who them ladies are, mister. I sssswear ...I dddon't.

MILAM: A nigger like *you*? Bragging 'bout havin' White girlfriends? Carryin' 'round pictures of White women in his wallet? Boy, you ain't never gonna see the sun come up, again. *(Milam removes a pistol and points it at Emmett's head.)*

EMMETT: *No mmmmmmmister...pppppplease...PLEASE!!!!!!*

BRYANT: You still as good as I am? You done it to White girls, and you gonna keep on doin' it...ain't ya?! *Aint ya?!*

(A deafening gunshot is heard. Lights crossfade back to Reed.)

REED: Hearin' that thing...well...I could feel my whole body...just go numb. Like it was encased in one of them ice suits. I was just cold all over. *(Pause.)* I cried for that boy. I cried 'til no more tears would come. But I just can't wish away Emmett Till's voice. It was a...a... horrible... twisted up mess of a sound. *(Beat.)* After a while, everything was quiet. *(Half-beat.)* I didn't hear him no more. Then...I saw that big one come out of the shed with a gun . He was carrying it in a holster...that was kinda hangin' at his side...like he was John Wayne or somethin'. He come down to get some water from the well out front. Then I saw three other White men join him. They was tryin' to wash somethin' off a their hands. *(Beat.)* I seen 'em... back the truck up into Mister Milam's shed and the two Black mens helped 'em roll somethin' or other into the back of the truck. It was wrapped in a white canvas bag. *(Long pause. Fighting tears.)* There won't no reason...just no reason to beat on that boy like that. *(Pause. Breaking down on the stand but trying to hold his composure.)* I can still hear him. I can still hear him beg for mercy. No one answers. *(Half-beat.)* Not even *me. (Beat.)* When I seen his face in that *Chicago Defender*...at the funeral...an' I heard what them mens done to him... I swore that I'd never speak to GOD again...because I'd been praying for that boy. Praying for Emmett. *Did GOD just...ignore my prayers? (Pause.)* I remember...my mama always taught us...to pray to GOD. In times of great joy...and in times of great troubles. *(Beat.) That mornin'... (Beat.)* I prayed for Emmett Till.

(Lights fade on scene. End scene.)

SCENE 5

Lights fade on scene. Angry murmurs and unrest are heard in the darkness. Lights crossfade to Mamie seated in the witness box of the courtroom. Chatham enters.

MAMIE: Emmett was a good boy. But he was raised in Chicago, sir. He didn't know *how* to be humble to White people. *(Beat.)* I...warned him about the way things are for Negroes in Mississippi. I told him...to be very careful how he spoke to people while he was down here. I told him to say "Yes, sir"...and..."No, sir"...and "Yes, mam" and..."No, mam." I even told him to get down on his knees and humble himself if need be. I thought it would keep him safe in Mississippi. I was wrong.

CHATHAM: You sound like you blame yourself for what happened.

MAMIE: *(Long pause.)* Yes, sir. *(Beat.)* I was his mother. Mothers are supposed to protect their children. I couldn't do that. I failed him.

CHATHAM: What do you think happened in Bryant's store that day?

MAMIE: Emmett had been stricken with polio as a child. The illness effected his speech. He particularly had trouble with B's and M's. I imagine how he tried to say something like *bubble gum* and his words getting stuck. When he got nervous his stutter became worse. So I taught him, whenever he had trouble speaking...not to get frustrated ...but to just blow it out... in a *whistle*. In no way...will I ever believe that he was trying to flirt, or that he was being disrespectful. *(Half-beat.)* He probably was trying to stop a *stutter*. That's all. Now I realize the thing I thought would keep Emmett safe...may have cost him his life.

(Beat.)

CHATHAM: At Emmett's funeral, you decided to have an open casket. Why?

MAMIE: When I first looked at Emmett...I was so full of...of shock...and grief ...and...well, *anger.* I was so full of disgust that a human being could do something like this to another human being. Words...cannot describe my initial reaction. I'm telling you...the impact of seeing his body...in that condition was almost as if somebody had hit me in the stomach with a sledge hammer. But my only concern was that the world had to see what was taking place in the state of Mississippi. What one man is doing to another man. If people had not seen this with their own eyes they wouldn't have believed me. And if I had not kept my wits, I'd still be wondering to this day...*Could I have made a mistake? (Beat.)* But I now know for sure...it was my Emmett.

CHATHAM: How can you be so sure? *(Lights soften on Chatham.)*

MAMIE: Because I made an item analysis of my son's body. *(Half-beat.)* But I can't honestly say that I was prepared for what I saw. *(Beat.)* When we got the body...Emmett's body...to the funeral home...they removed it from this huge, oversized brown box. Probably the biggest box I had ever seen in my life. They took his body out...and placed it on an examination table. I forced myself...to examine it...*him*...from head to foot. *(Mamie is momentarily transported back to that night in the A.A. Rayner funeral home. Trying to maintain her composure.)* When the body...*his* body...arrived in Chicago...it was very decomposed. The smell was incredibly nauseating. It was sickening. The funeral home director had to open the windows and then shoot off something...some kind of powerful ammonia just to keep us from becoming ill. You could actually smell my son's body two or three blocks away from the funeral home. The body...*Emmett*...when it...*he* arrived in Chicago...was stripped naked. He was just covered up with a whole lot of white powder. Mr. Rayner said...the white powder on Emmett...was *lime*, to make his body decompose faster, you see. *(Beat.)* What I first noticed...was that...there was a *hole*...in my son's head...that was big enough to stick your hands through. I saw...that his mouth...was just laying there ...wide open. The wire from that...that gin fan those men tied around his neck to weigh him down in the water had left his mouth jammed open. And his tongue...had been choked out of his mouth. His tongue was so swollen...about ten times its normal size. *(Half-beat.)* This eye...over here...was laying down...dangling on his cheek... dangling... and the other one...the other eye...was almost completely gone. It seemed like it had been plucked out with a nut picker. The nose...his nose looked like someone had taken a chopper and sliced it up. *(Beat.)* The teeth...I was always so proud of his beautiful teeth. *(Beat.)* I only saw two...but I could recognize those that were left. When I looked at his ear, that's when I really got a shock. There's a little curl in Emmett's ear...I've got the same thing in mine. I found it, but that's where I noticed...I noticed that the head...his head...was actually in *two pieces*. I mean...the entire back of his head had been knocked off. *(Beat.)* This makes sense. Because when I arrived in Mississippi...I heard a rumor that one of the kidnappers had taken an axe and chopped straight down on Emmett's head. I looked at...what was left of my son's skull, and I remember asking myself...*Was that bullet necessary?* Because surely he was dead before they shot him. *(Beat.)* When I first saw that hole in Emmett's head, I noticed that I could actually see light...shining through to the other side of the room. *(Long pause.)* The funeral home director asked if I wanted to have Emmett's head fixed up for the service. I said...you can't fix that. Let the people see what I saw. *(Beat.)* So...when I saw what Mr. Rayner had done to his body for the funeral. When I saw the picture that *Jet Magazine* had published...I told Mr. Rayner that he had done a wonderful job on Emmett. You could actually see where my son's head had been sown together. How he pushed it back into place. And where he had removed the one remaining eye...and wired the mouth shut. *(Half-beat.)* What everyone saw was so much better than what I had seen until it just...well...we admired what Mr. Rayner had done. *(Beat.)* The entire time I was examining that body...looking at that sight...I kept telling myself...*I've got to look down here and really look good to see if I can find Emmett.* *(Half-beat.)* After looking...and searching...I finally found my boy. I found Emmett.

CHATHAM: No further questions. *(Grinning at Whitten.)* Your witness.

(Whitten begins his cross like a ravenous Bengal tiger ready to pounce.)

WHITTEN: *(Disgustingly apologetic.)* Now...Ms. Bradford...I'd like to know...

MAMIE: *Bradley.*

WHITTEN: Wha...what?

MAMIE: *Bradley.* My name...is Mamie Till *Bradley...sir.*

WHITTEN: Oh...I'm sorry. My apologies. Mrs. *Bradley. (Pouncing. Sarcasm.)* Now Mrs. Bradley...did your boy have a fondness for White women?

MAMIE: Excuse me, sir?

CHATHAM: Objection your honor. Emmett Till is not on trial here. J.W. Milam and Roy Bryant are.

SWANGO: Get to your point, Mr. Whitten. The witness will answer the question.

MAMIE: Emmett liked *everybody.* He was only 14. He wasn't old enough to have a *fondness* for anyone.

WHITTEN: So...when his own cousin says that he was bragging about all the White girl-friends he had...that same night he *accosted* Mrs. Bryant...that would be a lie?

CHATHAM: Objection your honor. There's no proof the Till boy accosted anyone.

SWANGO: Sustained. Wrap this up, Mr. Whitten.

WHITTEN: Now Mamie...we've heard you claim the body found in the Tallahatchie River on September 1st, 1955 is that of your son. Is that right?

MAMIE: Yes, sir.

WHITTEN: Have you ever identified a decomposed body before?

MAMIE: No, sir.

WHITTEN: Have you ever conducted an autopsy before?

MAMIE: No, sir.

WHITTEN: Are you trained in the practices of forensic medicine?

MAMIE: No, sir.

WHITTEN: Then you cannot possibly say...with absolute certainty...the body recovered from that river is that of your son...Emmett Louis Till?

MAMIE: Yes, sir, I can.

WHITTEN: How much life insurance do you have on your son, Mrs. Baxter?

CHATHAM: Objection your honor. Emmett Till is not on trial here. And Mamie *Bradley* is not on trial here, either.

SWANGO: I'm going to allow a little more of this. This better be good, Mr. Whitten. The witness will answer.

MAMIE: We have a nickel policy on Emmett that pays five hundred dollars...I think. And we have a dime policy that pays a thousand dollars. In case of accidental death...they doubled, sir.

WHITTEN: *Doubled?* So, you're saying that you could stand to make around three thousand dollars...*cash money*...if your boy is pronounced dead and these men are convicted?

MAMIE: I believe so, sir.

WHITTEN: But you agree that someone who held a policy like that would stand to make a lot of money if they would simply arrange for somebody to kill a loved one.

MAMIE: I suppose *someone* could, sir. But I wouldn't do that.

WHITTEN: *(Dripping sarcasm.)* This thing has made you a celebrity, hasn't it?

MAMIE: I suppose so.

WHITTEN: Oh...*come on now*, Mamie. You've been traveling 'round the country making speeches for that N.A.A.C.P. Raisin' money for 'em, talkin' to all kinds of colored newspapers. I even saw you on television one night. Hell, I don't know whether to cross examine you or ask for your autograph.

(Canned laughter in the courtroom.)

CHATHAM: Objection, your honor.

SWANGO: Sustained.

WHITTEN: Just a few more questions. Must be a lot of fun...havin' these people... fawning all over you?

MAMIE: Their prayers have been a great comfort to me, yes, sir.

WHITTEN: You like all that attention...don't you?

MAMIE: Not really, sir.

WHITTEN: Not even just a *little* bit? *(Beat.)* I bet you love that N.A.A.C.P. *money*, too. I mean...they've been paying you since this business started. Isn't that right?

MAMIE: No. I mean...no, sir.

WHITTEN: *Really?* According to one of your own colored magazines...the one called *JET*. In the last few weeks you helped raise almost $250,000 for the N.A.A.C.P. Sure sounds like you're working for 'em to me.

MAMIE: They've sponsored my appearances at times, sir.

WHITTEN: *(Bully boy mockery.)* But you have received money directly from this N.A.A.C.P.? Haven't you, Mamie?

MAMIE: Yes.

WHITTEN: How much?

MAMIE: *(Pause.)* I signed a contract where I would receive between $150 and $200 dollars per speech.

WHITTEN: Two hundred dollars per speech?! *Man alive*...where do *I* sign up!

CHATHAM: Objection, your honor.

SWANGO: Sustained. Mr. Whitten, I believe you've made your point.

WHITTEN: You and the entire N.A.A.C.P. concocted this whole mess...isn't that right?

MAMIE: No, sir.

WHITTEN: You all dug this body up from somewhere....

MAMIE: No, sir.

WHITTEN: ...stripped it naked....

MAMIE: No, sir.

WHITTEN: ...draped that cotton gin fan around its neck....

MAMIE: No, sir.

WHITTEN: ...put that ring on it's finger....

MAMIE: No, sir.

WHITTEN: ...and dumped the body in the river where you and your Communist N.A.A.C.P. buddies knew it would turn up sooner or later.

MAMIE: *No!* I...I would never...

WHITTEN: This entire thing has been nothing but a lie. A hoax! You know that your son...Emmett Louis Till...is alive and well...living with your father in Detroit even as we speak!!

MAMIE: That's not true. My father is sitting right over there at our table. And my son...is buried in Northland Cemetery...back in Chicago.

(Long pause. Score one for Mamie.)

WHITTEN: *(Whitten off balance. Trying to regain his composure.)* No further questions.

(Courtroom murmurs. Lights fade on Mamie and scene. End scene.)

SCENE 6

Lights up on Eastland in mid-conversation with Whitten. Eastland is sipping whiskey, but appears somewhat irritated. Whitten is slightly nervous, but reassuring.

EASTLAND: I don't like the way it's going.

WHITTEN: It's just the first day. We'll be fine.

EASTLAND: Damn Yankee newsboys are killin' us. Done made that Till boy out to be some kinda a nigra Jesus. And done wrapped his daddy up in the goddamn American flag.

WHITTEN: Well gimme somethin' we can use.

EASTLAND: *(Pause.)* What do we know about that boy's real daddy?

WHITTEN: He died in the war. That's about all. The newspapers up North are sayin' he was some kind of *hero*.

EASTLAND: Yeah? Well...them Yankee newspapers don't know everything.

(Lights crossfade to Eastland standing on the steps of the Tallahatchie Courthouse. Reporter, played by Carolyn Bryant, is overly sympathetic to the Senator. Lights crossfade to Mamie observing scene.)

EASTLAND: Gentlemen...I hold in my hands irrefutable proof that one Private Louis Till, the *real* father of Emmett Till, was convicted of raping three young girls while stationed in Italy. That's *convicted* mind you, not accused. He was also convicted of killing one of the women he raped. In accordance with Article of War #92, Private Louis Till was summarily court-martialed and hanged in July of 1945.

REPORTER: *(Voice-over.)* Senator Eastland, what bearing do you think this new evidence will have on the Till case?

EASTLAND: I can't say. I'm not involved in the trial. All I can say is what most right thinking, logical people will probably say.

REPORTER: *(Voice-over.)* And what is that, Senator?

EASTLAND: *(Slight chuckle to himself.)* That the apple don't fall too far from the tree.

(Lights fade on scene. End scene.)

SCENE 7

Lights cross to Chatham and Mamie in mid conversation. Heated and pointed.

CHATHAM: Why didn't you tell me?

MAMIE: *(Somewhat evasive.)* I just found out, myself.

CHATHAM: Oh come on, Mamie!

MAMIE: It's the truth.

CHATHAM: You expect me to believe that you didn't know anything about how your own husband died?

MAMIE: *(Beat.)* I was never told...*officially* what happened. I tried to find out...for years. But the government said everything surrounding his death was classified. *(Beat.)* Besides...Senator Eastland *conveniently* forgot to tell everyone that during World War II, ninety-five US soldiers were hanged for the crimes of rape and murder...and 85 of them were Negroes. You think that's a coincidence?

CHATHAM: *(Sarcasm.)* You got that little piece of information from your N.A.A.C.P. buddies?

MAMIE: What difference does it make?

CHATHAM: *(Incredulous. In disbelief.)* Do you know what this little *revelation* does to our case? These Southern press boys are having a field day. One newspaper even has a quote from *J. Edgar Hoover* of all people. He says that you always seemed a little *pink* to him anyway. My God, Mamie.

MAMIE: I don't understand.

CHATHAM: The fact that your boy's father was killed by our own government for rape and murder poisons this jury pool. Probably more than they already are. Damn! *(Beat.)* Anymore little *surprises* like that I should know about? *(Mamie shakes her "no.")* Good.

MAMIE: Is there anything else *I* can do? Anything specific...that would help my son's case?

CHATHAM: *Specific* like what, Mrs. Bradley?

MAMIE: Like...do you need to know what kind of *person* my son really was.

CHATHAM: I think we already know the answer to that.

MAMIE: I beg your pardon.

CHATHAM: You've done enough. I'll do my best when the Defense presents its case.

MAMIE: You mean...there's nothing else I can do?

CHATHAM: I only invited you down here to view these proceedings to play on the court's sympathy. To hopefully make a few of those jurors feel sorry for you and your boy. But now...I'm afraid we've lost that hold card.

MAMIE: So...there's nothing?

CHATHAM: *(Half-beat.)* On second thought...

MAMIE: Yes?

CHATHAM: If anyone in the press asks you a question...especially the Southern reporters, always end your answers with a "yes, sir" or a "no, sir."

(Mamie stares at Chatham in disbelief.)

CHATHAM: Do you want these men convicted?

MAMIE: Yes...*sir.*

CHATHAM: Perfect.

(Lights fade on scene. End scene.)

SCENE 8

Lights fade up on Whitten and Carolyn.

WHITTEN: Would you please state your name for the record?

CAROLYN: Carolyn Bryant. Mrs...Carolyn Bryant. *(Beat.)* Roy...Roy Bryant. He's my husband.

WHITTEN: Can you tell us about the Wednesday night the Till boy came into your store?

CAROLYN: *(Slowly. Feigned pain.)* Well, sir, I remember it was gettin' late. Things were kinda slow, so I was up at the front of the store by myself. My sister-in-law Juanita was out back, I think. Roy and J.W. was in Texas...on *business* they said. But I won't afraid to be in the store by myself. I mean...nothin' *bad* ever happens 'round here. *(Beat.)* I first noticed him when I heard two...or three others standing around outside a the front door. Sort of milling around. Giggling and gawkin'. *(Beat.)* That boy wasn't really lookin' to *buy* anything. Just lookin'. Every now and then he'd take a peek toward the door where them other nigras was standin'. But I didn't pay it no mind...really. *(Pause.)* I remember...that Chicago boy came up to the counter. He asked for two cents worth of bubble gum...I think it was. Then he...he...

WHITTEN: Take your time, Mr. Bryant. What did the Till boy do then?

CAROLYN: *(Half-beat. Gearing up for the show.)* He...He...*He grabbed me! Hard. He was sorta twistin' my wrist. And he was hurtin' me!* And he was holdin' me. Real...real tight. He was strong, too. Not like no little boy I ever seen. *(Pause.)* And he touched me...here? *(Carolyn strokes her neck and her exposed shoulder blade...softly...ala Soap Opera drama queens.)* And...here. *(Carolyn runs her hands sensually along the curves of her waist and then slowly places her own hands in suggestive positioning...toward her nipple areas.)* And then he placed his filthy hands...here...right in our store. I told him to let me go. He just smiled and kept holdin' my wrists... runnin' his, *Black* hands ...across my arms. *(Pause.)* I was scared. I was more scared than I ever been. Then he said..."How about a date, baby? Don't worry. There ain't no reason to be afraid. I ain't gonna hurt you. I been with *plenty* White girls before." *(Beat.)* I tried to scream...but I couldn't. Then he...he ran his hands down...along my arms and my waist. I couldn't believe this was happenin' to me. *(Beat.)* Then that boy looked right at me and said... *(Beat.)* He said..."I'm gonna make it real good for you. I done told ya. I knows what y'alls like." *(Beat.)* I tried to move away from him...to the back of the store...where my sister-in-law was. But he jumped between the two counters and blocked my way. Then...then he kinda raised his hands up...and put 'em around my waist...like... *like this.* All the time he kept sayin'..."Don't worry baby. I ain't gonna hurt ya." *(Beat.)* He must have heard Juanita come in...'cause he let go just enough for me to pull away. He started walking out the front door, but then he looked back at me and said..."Bye baby." All I could feel was *shame. Defiled.* He would've raped me right there if he thought he coulda got away with it.

(Lights fade on scene. End scene.)

SCENE 9

Lights up on Whitten and Chatham giving summations.

WHITTEN: I was born in Mississippi. This very county...is *my* home county. *(Beat.)* So I think I can speak for most of the White people round here when I say...without question...that we hate that this thing happened in our county.

CHATHAM: I too was born and bred in Mississippi. So I deeply understand the complexities associated with this case.

WHITTEN: Nobody 'round here, White or Colored, approves of this kind of thing. Gentlemen of the jury, I don't say that you all shouldn't have compassion for Mamie Bradley and her boy...if that really was her boy they pulled out of the Tallahatchie. But the prosecution hasn't even proved beyond a shadow of a doubt that this boy is even dead. Are you willing to convict these two, GOD fearing men...two of your own neighbors...on hearsay evidence?

CHATHAM: Gentlemen...even if we accept the testimony of the defendant's wife as the gospel itself, the very worst punishment to Emmett Till that should have occurred was to take a razor strap, turn him over a barrel and whip him. *(Beat.)* But Emmett was a Negro boy. And, in the view of the Southerner, he had violated a racial taboo. So Roy Bryant and J.W. Milam resolved in their minds to exact a warped sense of justice on this defenseless, little child. That was wrong.

WHITTEN: I know them both. *You*...know 'em both. They are outstanding men. *(Beat.)* You know your duty. If J.W. and Roy are convicted of this supposed *crime*...our forefathers would turn over in their graves. If you convict these men...where under the shining sun is the land of the free and the home of the brave!

CHATHAM: I know...that what I ask of you takes great courage....more courage than anything you'll ever do in this lifetime. I won't deny this. But you must do the right thing in this case for all of our sakes. For the sake of your children and every Mississippian that comes after them.

WHITTEN: Gentlemen, your duty is clear. Everybody in this courtroom knows that truth. Everybody in this state, knows the truth. And I'm sure every last Anglo Saxon one of you has the courage to do the right thing.

CHATHAM: Your verdict will make history...whatever it may be. But keep in mind, Mississippi will never be allowed to reach its full potential unless we show that we are more than capable of *fairly* governing our own. And we can only hope to maintain our way of life, our *true* heritage, when we support the constitutional guarantees of life, liberty, and the pursuit of happiness...for every citizen. Gentlemen of the jury...Emmett Till was entitled to his life.

(Lights fade on Chatham and Whitten and crossfade to Mamie, Alma, and Spearman.)

MAMIE: *(To Spearman. Mamie gathering her things.)* Let's go.

ALMA: *Go?* But...what about the verdict?

MAMIE: Oh, I already know what the verdict is. It's *not guilty*.

SPEARMAN: *(Slight chuckle. But still in disbelief at her statement.)* Not guilty? You heard all that evidence. Even down here...the case against those two men is just too strong for the jurors to do anything but convict 'em.

MAMIE: I can't explain it...but it's just a feeling that I have. And if I am right...nothing *Black* in this town is safe. It'll be open season on Negroes in Mississippi.

(Lights soften on Alma, Spearman, and Mamie. They stand under a soft spotlight and quietly observe the following scene. The following voice-over should be that of a radio announcer delivering the news, vis a vis 1950s vintage newsreel.)

SWANGO: *(Voice-over.)* Ladies and gentlemen of the jury, have you arrived at a verdict?

MILAM: *(Voice-over.)* "We find the defendants, Roy Bryant and J.W. Milam not guilty."

CAROLYN: *(Voice-over.)* Not Guilty!!!!!! Not Guilty!!!! Praise be to GOD!!! Roy and J.W.

are free! There is still justice in America!!! Whoopeeee!!!!

(Deafening cheers and raucous celebration swells around Carolyn, Milam, and Bryant. For the first time, Mamie, Milam, and Bryant meet face to face. Bryant lights a victory cigar and grabs Carolyn by the waist. It is all Spearman can do to keep his temper. But Mamie places her hand on Spearman's shoulder to keep him at bay.)

MILAM: *(Smugly.)* So long…niggers.

(Milam spits on the ground. Bryant and Milam laugh. Spearman turns in anger and advances on the men. But Mamie places herself between them. Milam braces, undaunted by Spearman's threatening advance.)

MAMIE: *(Holding onto Spearman for dear life.)* No daddy!!! *(Pause.)* Let's just go home.

(Lights soften on Milam, Bryant, and Carolyn.)

ALMA: *(Trembling with anger and grief.)* Mamie Lizzie? Now you listen to me. You can't let it end like this. You got to do all you can to make sure this kinda thing never happens again. Promise me, Mamie.

(Spearman and Alma exit. Lights soften on Mamie.)

MAMIE: I promise.

(Lights intensify on Bryant, Milam, and Carolyn.)

BRYANT: After their murder trial, Roy Bryant and J.W. Milam were forced to sell their homes and their stores. Blacks, who had once comprised 90% of their customers refused to shop there. Shortly there after, both families moved out of Mississippi.

CAROLYN: Carolyn Bryant divorced Roy Bryant in 1979. She later remarried and refused to ever publicly discuss her part in the Emmett Till case.

BRYANT: Roy Bryant spent the last years of his life steeped in debt. He died in 1994 and never publicly expressed remorse for his responsibility in the death of Emmett Till.

MILAM: J.W. Milam became a full-time farmer after the collapse of his business. Nearly broke and penniless, he died of spine cancer in 1981.

(Lights fade on Bryant, Milam, and Carolyn and crossfade to Whisperer #1.)

WHISPERER #1: *(Half-beat.)* When I was a child, I had known fear of hunger, pain, and the Devil. But after Emmett Till's murder…seeing his mangled face in those photos …there was a new fear instilled in me. It was a not so secret *secret* sealed in silence between my generation…and every generation of Black person after mine. The secret was my *fear*…that I could be taken from the safety of my home and killed…at any moment…just because I was a Negro.

WILKINS: *(Beat.)* It was also a call to awareness. That the world was ugly. And beautiful. And dangerous. And complicated. That it was an ever-changing thing…not to be passively admired from afar…but lived in…at your own risk.

WRIGHT: *(Half-beat.)* Emmett Till changed us. *All* of us. We vowed never to let something like this happen again. But it has happened. That's why we have to keep telling his story. To keep his sacrifice alive.

(Lights fade on the three men and crossfade to Mamie in isolated spots. Emmett enters.)

EMMETT: Mamie Till Bradley enrolled in the Chicago Teachers College in 1956 and earned a Bachelor's degree. In 1957 she married Gene Mobley. She served as an elementary school teacher in the Chicago public school system from 1960 to 1983. Mother Mobley died on the morning of January 6, 2003. To this date, no one has ever been punished for the kidnapping and subsequent death of Emmett Louis Till.

(Emmett moves to Mamie and embraces her warmly. Emmett exits. Cast sings a verse of the hymn "We'll Never Turn Back.")

CAST: *"We've been buked and we've been torn*

"We've been taught that, sure as you're born

"But we'll never...turn back

"No we'll never... turn back

"Until we all...live in peace...

"And we have equality."

(Lights up on Dees and Mamie. Again we are in November 1989. It is moments before her historic moment. We enter back into the point where we last saw Dees.)

DEES: Mrs. Mobley? *(Beat.)* Mrs. Mobley?

MAMIE: *(Emerging from the daydream.)* I'm sorry. What did you say?

DEES: I said...they're ready for your speech.

MAMIE: Oh yes. Thank you.

DEES: Good Luck.

(Dees exits. Lights intensify on Mamie in an isolated pool of light. A voice over is heard in the darkness.)

DEES: *(Voice-over.)* "Ladies and Gentlemen! The mother of Emmett Till, Mamie Till Mobley."

MAMIE: "Thank you. Before I begin, I'd like to say to Mr. Morris Dees, his staff, and all of the members of the Southern Poverty Law Center...that we love you, and we thank you for this touching memorial. This monument will serve as a constant reminder to the world that our loved ones are not gone...and that they will never be forgotten. *(Beat.)* We know...that the historic events which brought us all here today have chosen us to be the burden bearers. But the one who chose us for this task...gave us that special strength to bear these burdens. *(Beat.)* When it seemed that nothing would help...when the blackness of a hundred midnights surrounded my days...and when my eyes were a fountain of tears, the realization came to me that Emmett's death was not a personal experience for me to hug myself and weep. It was a worldwide awakening. With these hurts come additional responsibilities. None of us can afford the luxury of self-pity. We must always remember...that freedom is not free. Someone always has to pay a price for someone else to enjoy the liberty of freedom. *(Beat.)* The Lord told me that the world would weep for my son. And that no one would ever forget the name...*Emmett Louis Till*. Emmett...and the others we honor here today...paid the ultimate price...for the freedoms we enjoy."

(Lights soften on Mamie and crossfade to the Civil Rights Memorial table and wall. The engraved words of Dr. King "Until justice rolls down like waters and righteousness like a mighty stream" shine out over the darkening stage. After a beat, lights up on the entire cast entering, singing...a rendition of "Woke Up This Morning With My Mind On Freedom." Audience participation encouraged.)

CAST: *"I woke up this morning with my mind...*

"Set on freedom

"I woke up this morning with my mind...

"Set on freedom

"I woke up this morning with my mind...

"Set on freedom

"Hallelu...

"Hallelu...

"Hallelujah!!!!"

(Repeat. Slow fade to black.)

END OF PLAY

Arrangement for Two Violas

by Susan Lieberman

ALL INQUIRIES CONCERNING RIGHTS, INCLUDING AMATEUR RIGHTS, SHOULD BE ADDRESSED TO:
Russ Tutterow, Artistic Director, Chicago Dramatists, 1105 W. Chicago Avenue, Chicago, IL, 60622
Email: rtutterow@chicagodramatists.org; Phone (312) 633-0630

ORIGINALLY PRODUCED by Vision & Voices Theatre Co.

For theatre profile and information on Vision & Voices Theatre Co., see page 46.

* * *

Literary Manager David Scott Hay and I have long been proponents of a simple formula when it comes to plays: story, characters, and language. It seems simplistic, perhaps elementary, but you would be surprised how many scripts I have read that use remarkable language but don't have a through line to hang it on. We have also long been opponents of political or "agenda" plays. So, when Dave told me about *Arrangement for Two Violas* and its subject matter, I must confess I figured this was not a show for us. Two men in 1930s Wisconsin who fall in love? No. I plotted how the story was going to go, the speeches. Dave read it. And then I read it. After that, we began making plans to produce it.

Susan has crafted a heartbreaking, sweet, love story with compelling, well-drawn characters, and cradled it with language that sings. The show is not about an agenda and because of that I was afforded the opportunity to reexamine my own views on what constitutes a loving relationship, and what constitutes friendship and faith. That's the residual of any great play: the power to affect change—one audience member at a time.

Brian Alan Hill,
Artistic Director, Visions & Voices Theatre Co.

BIOGRAPHY

Susan Lieberman is co-author of the musical *Prairie Lights* (Jeff-nominated for New Work) produced by Stage Left Theatre at Theatre Building Chicago for two consecutive holiday seasons and now licensed by Dramatic Publishing Company. Other plays include *Marek's Monkey*, produced by Chicago Dramatists and *Steamship Quanza* (with Stephen Morewitz), produced in Chicago and upstate New York. She received regional Emmy nominations for her children's television scripts, *Sandy and Sam* (WGN-TV) and *Prairie Latkes* (WBBM-TV). Her other teleplays include *Charlie's Risk* and *A Hill of Beans*, which also aired on WBBM-TV. A graduate of Duke  University, she worked in London as a production assistant at Charles Marowitz's Open Space Theatre and later for producer Thelma Holt at The Round House. She was the Associate Editor of Theatre Crafts Magazine in New York for four years before returning to Chicago, where she has been a Resident Playwright at Chicago Dramatists for many years. She lives in suburban Chicago with her husband, Jim Stoller, and their three children–Gabrielle, Julia, and Joshua.

DEVELOPMENTAL HISTORY

Arrangement for Two Violas received a public staged reading at Chicago Dramatists in May 2003 and was then presented in a workshop production during Stage Left Theatre's LeapFest in May 2004, directed by Ann Filmer and featuring John Sanders, Keith Eric Davis, Vincent P. Mahler, and Laurie Larson.

ORIGINAL PRODUCTION

Arrangement for Two Violas premiered at Chicago Dramatists in a Visions & Voices Theatre Co. production on November 6, 2004.
It was directed by Ann Filmer with the following cast:

PETER CHASE . . . . .John Sanders
HENRY MEEGAN. . . . . .Stephen Rader
KARL SCHULER. . . . . .Gene Cordon
NAN SCHULER . . . . .Marssie Mencotti

and the following production staff:

Set Designer. . . . . .Susan Kaip
Lighting Designer. . . . . .Phoebe Daurio
Composer. . . . . .Joshua Horvath
Sound Designer . . . . .Nick Keenan
Costume Designer . . . . .Lisa Stevens
Stage Manager . . . . .Michael T. Maloney
Viola Consultant . . . . .Elizabeth Cohen

CHARACTERS

PETER CHASE: Mid-30s, country doctor

HENRY MEEGAN: Late 30s, medical specialist

KARL SCHULER: Mid-50s, editor of a county paper

NAN SCHULER: Mid-50s, Karl's wife, newspaper publisher

TIME & PLACE

Arrangement for Two Violas takes place during 1938 in a small Wisconsin town called Rocklin, with scenes in Milwaukee and elsewhere. The staging should indicate the various locations—from Peter's rustic clinic in Rocklin to Chicago's Orchestra Hall—with minimal furniture and props. Sound effects, lighting and music should be key elements in establishing scenes.

AUTHOR'S NOTE

Arrangement for Two Violas is a memory play, narrated by Peter Chase, who is present throughout the telling of his own story. That story should retain the dreamlike quality of a thought process, rather than proceed merely as a succession of events. For example, the viola playing should be stylized—touching the bow to the instrument as music spills out. Characters may enter and exit during Peter's monologues. Henry's collection of framed music manuscripts should be suggested, not seen. All that can be done to evoke the mood of Peter's recollections as the tale unfolds will best serve the script.

John Sanders (left) as Peter and Stephen Rader as Henry in Vision & Voices Theatre Co.'s 2004 production of *Arrangement for Two Violas* by Susan Lieberman, directed by Ann Filmer.   Photo by Brian Alan Hill

Arrangement for Two Violas

ACT I

SCENE 1

Music at rise. Peter enters and picks up a viola. He plays dreamily, then stops, although the music continues. He speaks directly to the audience as the music underscores softly.

PETER: I never kept a diary or wrote personal letters. It was too dangerous. My honest confessions could have robbed me of my medical practice and even perhaps of my beloved house. It was on a side street off the main road of Rocklin, a block from the pharmacy, two blocks from the telegraph office and three doors down from the Schulers, my friends. What I relished most about the house was its proximity to all that mattered—my friends, my patients, my viola, my car, and the road that led to the surrounding dairy farms. I wasn't a remarkable intellect or particularly good-looking or even worth much as an amateur musician. If I hadn't been the only doctor for miles around, I'd have scarcely been noticed at all. But I was the only doctor. There was hardly a child under the age of ten who didn't come into the world without my help, and hardly a recent tombstone in the cemetery for anyone who didn't have my signature on the death certificate. And in between, it was me who set the broken legs, diagnosed consumption, wove stitches into foreheads, eased whooping cough, and always—always—maintained the privacy of my patients. My hours were long and my income was small. But I was cherished and respected in this little Wisconsin town— a situation that never ceased to amaze me.

(Lights up on Karl and Peter at the Schulers' dining room table. Empty dessert plates and cards from a recent bridge game are scattered on the table.)

KARL: Are you going to finish up this pie?

PETER: Oh no. I'm fine.

KARL: I'm never fine enough.

(Karl takes more pie. Nan enters.)

NAN: Where'd they go?

KARL: Escaped while you were digging in the icebox.

NAN: Everyone just left?

KARL: The Gorings had to catch the early train to Madison, Lucy was tired—

NAN: What about the Learys?

KARL: Babysitter business.

NAN: Barb's mother was spending the night.

KARL: Well then, she lied to be polite.

NAN: You scared them off with your talk.

KARL: If they can't take the heat of the discussion, get out of our dining room and stop eating our pie.

NAN: The Learys brought it themselves.

KARL: It was given as a gift so it's ours.

NAN: Karl, you're impossible.

KARL: If I've got an opinion—

NAN: You don't need to jam it into everyone's face!

KARL: Of all people, Barb shouldn't be scared off by a column on birth control. She's the one needling me to write about shipyard workers and hobos and civil rights for Negroes.

PETER: Yes, but she's not a worker or a hobo or a Negro.

NAN: Well said, Peter. The subject's personal.

KARL: Everything's personal.

NAN: We're just a county paper, not the New York Herald Tribune.

KARL: That doesn't mean we don't take on the issues of the day.

NAN: The Learys are the most open-minded people around, but birth control might not be—

KARL: All talk and no action.

NAN: Sometimes I'd swear The Dispatch editorial policy is based on what'll most annoy our friends.

KARL: It's my heartfelt belief that women should not be enslaved to childbearing.

NAN: It's not a topic for Sunday bridge.

KARL: Margaret Sanger is a leading social force. I'm putting her in the paper!

NAN: One controversy should be enough for a lifetime. You remember the Soviet series, don't you, Peter?

PETER: No...

KARL: Before your time. I wrote about the benefits of the Soviet system. Best work I've ever done.

NAN: *(To Peter.)* We nearly folded from lost advertising.

KARL: That's just plain overstatement. The Dispatch is still here...and I'm writing what I'm writing. *(To Peter.)* How many times have you delivered a sixth or seventh baby just because some wilted farm wife didn't know about contraception?

PETER: More than I can count.

KARL: So what do you do about it?

PETER: If they ask, I give them some information.

KARL: "If they ask." Pretty weak brew.

PETER: I'm not trying to change the world, Karl.

KARL: Well, I am.

NAN: We don't have as many advertisers to lose this time around.

KARL: No, but we also don't have competition, besides Bobby's paper—

(Karl coughs and gasps for air.)

PETER: Deep and slow.

KARL: —and Bobby being in the next county, I'm not too worried that someone's going to—

PETER: Slow breaths.

(Karl takes a moment to breathe properly.)

KARL: —someone's going to pull their tractor classified and give it to—

(Karl coughs and gasps helplessly. Peter goes to him and gets him to sit up straight.)

PETER: Deep and slow.

NAN: Tell your patient to keep his hands off the cigar box.

KARL: I only had one this week.

NAN: There's five missing from the box since last Sunday.

PETER: You need to see that pulmonary specialist in Milwaukee.

KARL: You look after me just fine.

NAN: The emphysema's getting worse, Peter. He can hardly catch his breath at night.

PETER: I'll call Dr. Meegan's office tomorrow morning.

KARL: I'm not driving to Milwaukee.

NAN: Then I'll drive. I won't have you suffocating right under my nose!

(Nan picks up plates and leaves.)

KARL: Nan's a terrible driver.

PETER: What about the train?

KARL: The train, humph!

PETER: I'll make the appointment and you two figure out how to get there.

KARL: Big city specialist...he'll charge an arm and a leg.

PETER: I can't do a whole lot more for you here, Karl. *(Gets up to leave.)* Thanks for dinner.

KARL: Better than your pork and beans.

PETER: It keeps me going. Good night.

KARL: Get yourself a wife.

PETER: Why? I get to eat dinner from a can and play my viola at 3 in the morning.

KARL: Wait till you're old and sick and need help getting up from a chair. I'd be good for the trash bin if I didn't have Nan and the kids. Think of what I've got—Bobby starting a paper on his own, no help from me, Clara and Phil bringing me beautiful grandchildren. Get yourself a family, Peter. No reason to get out of bed otherwise.

(Karl tries to heave himself up. Peter helps him.)

PETER: If you don't see Dr. Meegan, you won't be able to get out of bed at all. Lay off the cigars—and birth control columns, too. Nan's going to have her hands full taking care of you.

KARL: If I hold off on Margaret Sanger for now, will you back me up later?

PETER: If anyone asks, you know where I stand.

KARL: I do. *(Pause.)* Peter.

PETER: What?

KARL: You'll be 40 before you know it. Stop waiting for the angel of mercy or Gloria Swanson or whoever the hell you think is going to throw herself at your feet.

PETER: Oh, I don't expect anything like that.

KARL: You live like a monk.

PETER: I'm one of the most content people around. Goodnight, Karl.

(Lights down on Karl. Lights shift to Peter addressing audience.)

PETER: It's true. I was content without a wife. I had one once, briefly. Her name was Mabel and she was from my home town in Iowa. We were married when I finished my medical training. She had auburn hair and hazel eyes and covered her mouth when she laughed or cried. Though I enjoyed her company during our chaste courtship, I couldn't quite muster passion for her. I assumed wedding night, for which we both fastidiously saved ourselves, would change all that. Mabel's sister had warned her that on wedding night, she'd receive what felt like a big carrot. Mabel prepared herself for the invasion. But I couldn't produce a carrot for her, only limp lettuce. Oh, she was sympathetic, convinced that I was so overwhelmed by love, I couldn't get it up. That went on for six months. Overwhelming love and a battle-ready new bride who was getting impatient. Summer came and Mabel's brother and his friends took us swimming one afternoon. He and his friends ran past us in their swim suits, their bare tanned shoulders for all the world to see, and leaped into the pond. In an instant, I had a carrot—and I lost a wife. Mabel, a virgin against her will, looked down at me, saw and understood, and went to confide in her sister. The sister then confided in their mother. And Mama discreetly confided in no one except her best friend. Then her best friend thought it was her duty to confide in the minister. He shared it with no one except his wife. Soon it was common knowledge that Peter Chase had married Mabel simply to be close to her brother—a man I'd barely made eye contact with—and that the marriage was never consummated. So it was annulled. Thereafter, no male would ever remove his shirt for an examination. The women followed the men's example and thus my brand new office stood empty of patients. Forced to leave my home, I packed up my medical certificates and my viola music, bought an old jalopy, and drove from state to state until I found an elderly doctor in an isolated town who was desperate for a young replacement. Rocklin welcomed me with open arms and easy terms on a run-down house. Ripping up old flooring and scraping off wallpaper, I turned the place into a serviceable clinic and a modest home as the town watched in gratitude. When I took a break and played my viola, they sometimes stopped by the window to listen despite my mediocrity. In this remote place, no one had even seen a viola. The Schulers, the Learys, and a half dozen other "enlightened" types made up the nest of my social life. We listened to the rare orchestral broadcasts on a Madison radio station, read Hemingway, and debated FDR, Hitler, and the Spanish Civil War. I belonged. I was content.

SCENE 2

A few weeks later in the Schulers' dining room.

NAN: Of all things, Dr. Meegan plays the viola. He's got one that's a hundred years old.

KARL: Handcrafted in Italy.

PETER: A hundred years old? Are you sure?

NAN: That's what he said.

KARL: He has a separate insurance policy for it.

NAN: Dr. Meegan plays with a community orchestra—they rehearse every Tuesday and give three concerts a year. I told him we'd drive in for one sometime.

KARL: Only if I can do the driving.

NAN: Oh, hush! I didn't go off the road or get a flat from a broken bottle.

KARL: You drive too slow.

NAN: We got there on time. Oh, Peter, afterwards we had lunch at a restaurant that had a view of Lake Michigan.

KARL: The martinis were something, too.

PETER: Martinis?

NAN: We haven't had so much excitement in years. You should go yourself.

PETER: I'm not crazy about big cities.

NAN: Oh, but you should get a tour of that pulmonary institute. I've never seen such a place. The janitorial staff alone is bigger than the whole staff at the county hospital.

KARL: Including the patients. It's a city unto itself.

(Karl gasps for breath.)

PETER: Slow breaths, Karl.

KARL: I'm slow enough already. Let me show you that brochure.

(Karl, with great difficulty, gets up and exits.)

NAN: Once he has the treatment, Peter, will he be normal again?

PETER: We probably should hope for "improved."

NAN: But what about...what about being a, uh, husband again?

PETER: Well, that'll depend on how he's feeling.

(Karl returns and shows brochure to Peter.)

KARL: Isn't that something?

PETER: It looks more like a palace than a hospital.

KARL: Peter, you must go to Milwaukee and meet Dr. Meegan. He's a Democrat too. You'll have so much in common.

PETER: He's a famous pulmonary man, I'm a country G.P.

NAN: Wouldn't you like to find another violist? Why, maybe you could join his community orchestra.

KARL: Don't jump ahead, Nan.

NAN: At the very least, you and Dr. Meegan could be colleagues.

KARL: Go see this man. His institute is full of young nurses-better looking than that nurse who works for you.

PETER: Lorna is my Rock of Gibraltar.

KARL: She looks like it too.

NAN: Oh Peter! Get into that old car of yours and go someplace besides a dairy farm!

PETER: All right, all right. I'll call Dr. Meegan.

(Lights shift to Peter addressing audience.)

PETER: Nan held me to that call. If she and Karl could venture beyond Rocklin, why shouldn't I, among their closest friends? Intrigued by a viola-playing liberal-leaning doctor, I called to arrange for a tour of his pulmonary institute. It wasn't difficult. Meegan was a rising medical star, a man experimenting with curare in the treatment of emphysema and TB. Despite the Depression, he'd recently been awarded a massive foundation grant to build another wing to his facility.

(Music in. Henry enters. Peter looks to him and continues speaking.)

PETER: So a call from an admirer in the hinterlands was not out of the ordinary. It was just a matter of finding time in his overbooked day to see me.

SCENE 3

Henry's apartment. Henry shows Peter around.

HENRY: Brahms.

PETER: Are those really his notations?

HENRY: From the man's very own pen. I picked it up in New York. Here's the Tchaikovsky I told you about.

PETER: The frame is beautiful.

HENRY: If you had a scrap of score by Tchaikovsky, wouldn't you frame it auspiciously?

PETER: I'm sure I would.

HENRY: Is this getting boring?

PETER: Oh no. I like museums.

HENRY: I live in a museum?

PETER: Compared to my home, yes. It's pretty...basic.

HENRY: Why is that?

PETER: I bought an old house awhile back and turned it into a clinic. It's much cheaper than renting a separate office. By the time I put in a waiting room and a lab and a couple of examining rooms, I didn't have much space left for me.

HENRY: Time to buy a new house.

PETER: Oh, I do all right. There's a kitchen and a bedroom in the back. My patients made curtains and rugs and blankets—

HENRY: God, you sound like a charity.

PETER: A lot of patients are behind on their bills. They try to make it up as best they can.

(Henry takes out his viola.)

PETER: Nan and Karl told me all about your viola.

HENRY: That's what makes a good lung man-possession of a rare musical instrument.

PETER: Look, it impressed them and that's good. I tried for two years to get Karl to see you.

HENRY: And not a minute too soon.

PETER: I know. I mean, I don't know—that's why I sent him to you. But he's got to have respiratory relaxation quickly or—

(Henry hands the viola to Peter.)

HENRY: You may play the damn thing.

PETER: That's all right. I'm not very good.

HENRY: Spoken like a true violist. What's the difference between a viola and an onion? *(Peter shrugs.)* Nobody cries when they chop up a viola.

(Peter looks blank.)

HENRY: I thought every violist knew the repertoire of insults.

PETER: You play with an orchestra. I haven't been around other musicians since college.

HENRY: You really don't get out much, do you?

PETER: I go to Madison every month or so.

HENRY: To use the university library? Stay current with medical journals? Stop at a second-hand bookstore or a music shop on your way home?

PETER: How did you know?

HENRY: I'm just imagining. Can I get you a drink?

PETER: Thanks.

HENRY: What would you like?

PETER: Anything.

HENRY: Could you be more specific? Wine? Brandy? Port? Ovaltine?

PETER: I've never had port.

(*Henry pours them each a drink.*)

HENRY: A confirmed bachelor, young Peter?

PETER: I'm not that young.

HENRY: But you are a bachelor, aren't you?

PETER: I was married once. It didn't last.

HENRY: I've never been married and never will be.

PETER: You sound so sure.

HENRY: Aren't you?

PETER: What do you mean?

HENRY: Aren't you very sure you will never marry again?

PETER: I probably should be by now. Girls in Rocklin seem to end up married and pregnant before I even notice they're around.

HENRY: Could it be you're just not watching them?

PETER: Well, I'm so busy most of the time...

HENRY: You need someone to talk to about music and medicine.

PETER: I'll talk to anyone about that.

HENRY: Is that why you were willing to come home with me?

PETER: Huh? Well, yes. Thank you, Dr. Meegan—

HENRY: I thought I was Henry by now. You're Peter, after all.

PETER: But I'm...Peter to everyone.

HENRY: I'm Henry to you.

PETER: Henry.

HENRY: I'm not interested in women.

PETER: Oh.

HENRY: It's men.

PETER: Oh.

HENRY: I'm a homosexual.

PETER: Oh.

HENRY: You can tell that's what I am.

PETER: I can't. I mean, I didn't. It's not like...like you have a scented handkerchief.

HENRY: I'm not a fairy, you mean?

PETER: Well...yes.

HENRY: You should know we're not all that way.

PETER: Of course, I didn't mean to say...uh...uh...

HENRY: Your handkerchief is hardly scented, Peter.

PETER: I'm kind of lost right now. What are we talking about?

HENRY: You.

(Peter finishes his drink.)

PETER: Port...I feel like a professor. Thanks.

HENRY: Have another.

PETER: I should get going. The guest house locks its doors soon.

HENRY: Where are you staying?

PETER: A place on Wesley near Harper Street. Really, I need to go.

(Henry refills their glasses and holds out Peter's.)

HENRY: If you want to get away from me, go right ahead.

PETER: Do you do this a lot—invite other doctors home, give them port, and hope they'll stay?

HENRY: The doctors I meet usually prefer women.

PETER: Then how did you get so...so...good at this kind of conversation?

HENRY: Are you asking, where do I go to talk to men like myself?

PETER: Yes.

HENRY: Percy's place.

PETER: Where's that?

HENRY: Not too far from your guest house. Do you really earn so little that you can't do better?

PETER: What's Percy's place?

HENRY: Just what you'd think—where men go to meet men. A homo house. You can stop by on your way back to the guest house. It's a few blocks away. You go down Harper Street till you get to 145—

PETER: I don't need to know.

HENRY: You can probably find a place like that near Rocklin.

PETER: Oh, come on!

HENRY: We're everywhere. You just haven't been looking in the right barns and taverns.

PETER: Well, that's true.

HENRY: What do you do for sex?

PETER: I...

HENRY: Yes?

PETER: I don't.

HENRY: Even with women, just to keep up appearances?

PETER: No.

HENRY: Then...you've done nothing since your marriage ended?

PETER: It ended because...well...I wasn't able to, uh, do my job.

HENRY: Are you saying you have absolutely no experience?

PETER: Yes.

HENRY: None?

PETER: I tried my best for six months.

HENRY: I'd take a rifle to my head if I were you.

PETER: Oh Lord, don't say that!

HENRY: You can't possibly be happy.

PETER: I'm content.

HENRY: Content to be impotent? (Peter is silent.) Does the word scare you?

PETER: I'm not...exactly.

HENRY: Ah...your equipment works then.

PETER: Just not at the right time.

HENRY: People like us run into that problem.

PETER: Do they?

HENRY: Yes, Peter. There are all kinds of humiliation out there for us.

PETER: But there must be good things too.

HENRY: Such as...?

PETER: What about friendship? Can't men spend time together?

HENRY: The way the scented handkerchief types do? Those effete half-men who do little dinner parties for each other and squire around widows, offering their elbows like chicken wings? "Shall we go into the dining room, dear?" New York's full of them. It's not for me. I'd rather throw money at a sturdy dock worker.

PETER: Pay a prostitute, you mean.

HENRY: Well, it keeps me in charge, doesn't it?

PETER: I don't know.

HENRY: It does...it does.

PETER: Can a person just go to Percy's place for a drink?

HENRY: Could you? Is that what you're asking? Yes, go in for a drink. 145 Harper Street. There's a fish market in front.

PETER: Would you come with?

HENRY: No.

PETER: But you're not doing anything tonight.

HENRY: I'd rather not go.

PETER: Oh. You sounded so anxious to tell me about it.

HENRY: Yes, but...

PETER: Come on, take me over there.

HENRY: Peter, are you serious?

PETER: Yes.

HENRY: Well...

PETER: Is there really a Percy's place—or were you just making it up?

HENRY: Oh, it's real.

PETER: Then what it is? Why shouldn't we go?

(Henry looks him over.)

HENRY: I should never have told you.

PETER: Of course you should.

HENRY: No. You're a virgin.

PETER: Let's not go back to that.

HENRY: But it matters. You know nothing!

PETER: I don't live in a cave! I've had to push my way into bars full of drunks to stitch up knife wounds. Have you?

HENRY: No.

PETER: I can hold my own.

HENRY: Not there!

PETER: If you won't come with, I'll go myself. 145 Harper Street?

HENRY: It's not good, Peter.

PETER: I have the stomach for an awful lot.

HENRY: For a bar where men fornicate in the back?

PETER: Oh.

HENRY: That's what it is. Nothing more.

PETER: Then it's not really a place where men can go to talk to other men.

HENRY: Well...it can be...I used to...

PETER: What?

HENRY: It's a long boring story.

PETER: Coming from you, it can't be.

(Peter pours Henry a drink.)

HENRY: Last year I got a grant from the Fleming Foundation.

PETER: A hundred thousand dollars—I read about it in the paper.

HENRY: Did you? It was such a feat to get that money. I was on trains back and forth to New York so many times I'd look out the window and forget whether I was going to or coming from. No one was about to give me money, a guy from Milwaukee, stock market in the hole. But I won the foundation people over. When I got the telegram giving me approval, I could hardly speak. My brother and his wife took me out that night for dinner. My mother was there, my nephews, my assistants, other doctors. A photographer interrupted our meal to take my picture, he was so anxious to get it off to the Chicago papers...My brother Eddie ordered so much champagne, we got about as raucous as that kind of group could ever get. The waiter didn't try to stop us—I was far too important. Finally, at ten or so we went our separate ways. I came home...

PETER: And?

HENRY: It was so quiet. I wanted to keep talking...I still had the telegram in my pocket. So I went over to Percy's place for a drink. Someone new was there—

PETER: A sturdy dockworker?

HENRY: No, a man around my age. He wasn't married—

PETER: Married men go there?

HENRY: Peter, don't keep embarrassing yourself. Most of them are married. This is Milwaukee, after all-not New York or London.

PETER: Oh.

HENRY: He was an office manager at a brewery. He started to make conversation, ask me questions about myself and had me read him the telegram-twice, three times. He just hung by my side, listening and grinning like he had all the time in the world to hear my tale. Turns out he had a small house a few miles outside of town. Would I go there with him? Would I do him the favor of telling him more stories of my grant success, my teaching, music, hunting deer with my nephews? I bought bottles of champagne and off we went...It was a strange house for a man, very fussy like an old grandma's. But we shut the door and closed the shutters and had ourselves quite a time. He wasn't the handsomest man I'd been with but he had the most stamina. We drank and drank and went at it until we were weak. He never took his eyes off me. He heard every word I said. I'd never been with anyone so...attentive. Then he asked the question...

PETER: What?

HENRY: Would I get him an apartment in Milwaukee?

PETER: But he had a house.

HENRY: It belonged to his aunt. When she came back at the end of the month, he'd have nowhere to live.

PETER: You said he had a job.

HENRY: He'd been fired. But he was absolutely certain I could fix things for him. After all, I had a hundred thousand dollars in my pocket.

PETER: No, you didn't. It was a grant.

HENRY: Do you think he understood the difference?

PETER: Well, if he'd been listening to you all night—

HENRY: He heard nothing past the telegram. The money. His head was busy spending it while I talked on and on about myself. But now he broke into a rage...he shoved me to the floor...

PETER: He shoved you?

HENRY: I don't load cargo—I play the viola. He pinned me down and pummeled me. Then he dumped champagne down my throat and took the empty bottle...took the empty bottle...and jammed it into me until I began to bleed from one end and vomit from the other....He got scared—thought I might die on him and then what? He pushed me and my clothes outside into the mud and locked the door...I couldn't get up for awhile...I just lay on the ground trying to figure out how I got there...Dr. Meegan, professor of medicine-I'm a full professor, did you know that? The youngest doctor in Wisconsin ever to be a full professor. A month before I was dining at the Waldorf-Astoria in a tuxedo...

PETER: Go on.

HENRY: ...I found the car key in my coat and managed to get myself behind the wheel...I tried hard to skid off the road and slam into a tree.

PETER: Kill yourself?

HENRY: Full professor, foundation darling-covered in vomit just because I thought someone was listening to me. When the car accident didn't do it, I took my hunting rifle out of the trunk...

PETER: No.

HENRY: Don't you ever think of killing yourself?

PETER: Never.

HENRY: We can't live on this earth, Peter! We're beasts! Everyone thinks so—even the other homos. I'm the head of a clinic that people travel cross country to go to...but to have what other men have after a night of celebration...I'm not entitled. I get shoved in the mud. I have to crawl on my knees...I can't go back to Percy's place—what if that man comes back? I have nowhere to go anymore...no one to be with. I should have done myself in with the rifle...I was going to, but some farm hands came along wanting a ride to the next town...

PETER: Thank God for them.

HENRY: No, no, no! I'd be so much better off. Why bother to keep going?

PETER: For your patients.

HENRY: They don't care about me, just my medicine.

PETER: What about your brother?

HENRY: Eddie's got his own family. I'm dispensable by bedtime.

PETER: All right, for God's sake, your mother.

HENRY: She'll die one day.

PETER: We all will. That's no reason to do yourself in. My mother won't even speak to me.

HENRY: Your own mother?

PETER: I disgraced her.

HENRY: But you're a virgin.

PETER: Well, I'm a disgrace and a virgin.

HENRY: I wouldn't mind being one now. Either dead or...or clean.

PETER: If a young girl who'd been raped came to you for treatment, would you tell her she's dirty?

HENRY: I'm a lung specialist.

PETER: All I'm saying is, the rape doesn't make you unclean.

HENRY: Stop being such a psychiatrist!

PETER: Don't ever consider killing yourself. You matter too much.

HENRY: To whom?

PETER: Everyone.

HENRY: Everyone is nothing. It's the one.

PETER: I know.

HENRY: Do you?

PETER: Yes, Henry. I'm alone too.

(Henry touches Peter's face. After a moment, Peter backs away.)

PETER: It's getting close to ten.

HENRY: So?

PETER: The front door of the guest house will be locked...I don't want to wake up the woman who runs it.

HENRY: Well, you better be on your way.

PETER: Good night.

(Peter exits, leaving Henry by himself. Lights shift to Peter addressing audience.)

PETER: I fled in terror—sweating and shivering, dizzy and clumsy, roaring down vacant Milwaukee streets to the guest house. For hours in my room I tried to sleep and couldn't. Finally, I dressed and went out to find 145 Harper Street. The stench of dead fish in garbage cans nearly bowled me over as I heard faint sounds coming from a dark passage between the fish market and the building next door. Instead of going in, I crossed to the other side of the street and just watched from a doorway. Occasionally, a light flickered when a door opened at the end of the passage...noise and movement and footsteps and then everything was silent again. How the men came and went like shadows, I didn't quite grasp. I stared and stared at this Sodom and Gomorrah of Milwaukee, waiting to turn into a pillar of salt. But the longer I stayed, the more my body roiled inside my clothes the way it should have on my wedding night. I wanted no part of Percy's place, the sum of all my fears about where I'd end up if I ever admitted who I really was. I desired only to be with one person in the entire world, the man who'd touched me with such hope that for once, he was being heard. The sun rose full of city smoke and morning noise, and in the light, Percy's place seemed to vanish. I had not turned into a pillar of salt. I was in love.

(Lights shift to Henry's apartment.)

SCENE 4

Knocking on the door. Henry in pajamas and robe lets Peter in.

HENRY: It's not even six.

PETER: I didn't mean to wake you.

HENRY: I was up already. I have patients starting at eight. What are you doing here?

PETER: I thought I'd say goodbye.

HENRY: You did that last night.

PETER: Before I leave to drive back to Rocklin.

HENRY: Goodbye, Peter.

PETER: Goodbye.

(Peter seizes Henry's hand and kisses his palm.)

HENRY: No one's ever done that.

PETER: Kissed your hand?

HENRY: Not just because they really wanted to. Only because we'd made some kind of arrangement.

(Henry draws Peter into a kiss. As it becomes more passionate, Henry pulls off his pajama top.)

PETER: Oh, Lord.

HENRY: Should I stop?

PETER: No.

(Henry takes off his pajama bottoms.)

HENRY: You ought to undress. It's going to take both of us.

(Lights out as Peter begins to unbutton his shirt. Lights up on Henry writing a letter.)

HENRY: Dear Peter, This is the letter I promised I'd write. Don't panic—I will follow your instructions faithfully. Sitting here alone, I think of you and not much else. I think of the chicken we shared last weekend. I had instructed my Italian housekeeper to make it on Friday so I could heat it up for a little dinner party on Saturday night. No one around here cooks like her, bathing chicken in garlic and oregano and olive oil. It was something to see your face unfold into utter euphoria when you took a taste. Peter, your pleasure in devouring the meal can't possibly equal the pleasure I had in watching you. I thought love was something more complicated than this...but it's not. It is this. There you have it—my love letter for the day. Now I will do as you ask and burn it in the sink and wash the ashes down the drain. Love, Henry.

(Henry takes out a lighter and burns the letter.)

SCENE 5

Six months later. Sunday, late morning. Henry's apartment. Peter sleeps on the sofa, snoring loudly as Henry reads the Sunday newspaper.

HENRY: Rimbaldo's coming. Peter, Alphonse Rimbaldo is coming to Chicago. *(Nudges him.)* Peter. *(No response.)* Peter?

(Peter snores on. Henry nudges him sharply.)

PETER: Mmm?

HENRY: Why is playing a viola solo like wetting your pants?

PETER: Hmm?

HENRY: Both give you a nice warm feeling while everybody else moves away. Rimbaldo's conducting at Orchestra Hall in a few months. Read here.

PETER: Oh...He's doing Handel's Concerti Grossi.

HENRY: Let's get tickets and go to Chicago.

PETER: How could we do that?

HENRY: Well, first send away for concert tickets, then check train schedules—

PETER: But we can't go together. You might run into someone from your orchestra.

HENRY: You and I should sit in different sections.

PETER: What if we turned up at the same restaurant afterwards?

HENRY: You'd let go of a few dollars for a restaurant meal?

PETER: Henry, if I'm paying for train fare and a ticket, I'll pay for food.

HENRY: Mine, too?

PETER: Yes. I'll take you to dinner.

HENRY: But only if I insist.

PETER: I don't earn as much as you.

HENRY: Tightwad.

PETER: I'd like to take you to dinner very much. Six month anniversary.

HENRY: Anniversary...Orchestra Hall...Rimbaldo....Handel...violas...violas...and more violas.

PETER: There's not much just for us, is there? I mean viola duets. It's all for violins or cellos.

HENRY: You've got some Handel—

PETER: That Telemann sonata.

HENRY: Brandenburg six.

PETER: Professor Birkhardt has me working on that now.

HENRY: I know. I told him to give it to you, then we can play together.

(Peter and Henry start to hum Bach's Brandenburg Concerto No. 6. They build to a pitch. Henry picks up his viola. Peter takes his. They begin to play a section of the music but break down laughing when Peter fumbles some notes.)

PETER: I've only had the piece a month.

HENRY: It's not the bum notes. The problem is you're like a deaf man. You don't hear a thing-you play without dynamics.

PETER: I do not!

HENRY: You sound like a sewing machine.

PETER: What?

HENRY: Music is the emotional abandonment of common sense.

PETER: Oh, listen to yourself!

HENRY: I do all the time. It's very satisfying.

PETER: You can't play music without common sense.

HENRY: That's why you sound like a tailor stitching a shirt. Come on, try it again.

(Peter repeats a few bars of the music.)

HENRY: More rubato, better accents...

PETER: Anything else, Maestro?

HENRY: Look, if you don't want to be held to standards—

PETER: In medicine—yes. But this is my hobby. I'm satisfied without being first chair at Orchestra Hall.

HENRY: "Content" again?

PETER: What's wrong with that?

HENRY: It's an opiate.

PETER: I think it's good to be satisfied sometimes. You should be—you don't have a bad life. You get to do work that you love.

HENRY: I don't "love" being a doctor.

PETER: Are you serious?

HENRY: It's a job my brother pushed me into after my father died. I wanted to be a conductor, but the best music schools wouldn't take me. So Eddie insisted on medical college in Boston. He doesn't know that my patients wear me down.

PETER: I don't believe that.

HENRY: They do.

PETER: But all your breakthroughs with curare—

HENRY: I achieved a goal. But I'm not like you, reborn every time you piece someone back together. You give to your patients like a French horn shitting sulfonamide.

PETER: I can't even get sulfonamide in Rocklin.

HENRY: Call me on Monday and I'll give you a name.

PETER: That would be wonderful.

HENRY: You see? You're reborn just by the thought of it.

PETER: Every doctor wants to get his hands on antibiotics.

HENRY: Not me!

PETER: Because you already have them.

HENRY: Another goal achieved.

PETER: You should be satisfied.

HENRY: No—I want to be Rimbaldo!

(Church bells ring.)

PETER: 12 o'clock!

HENRY: Get a move on it, or you'll run into Mrs. Keifer.

(Peter dashes off. He clamors around offstage, then suddenly screams in pain.)

HENRY: What is it?

PETER: Oh, damn it, damn it!

(Peter hops back into the room.)

PETER: I got a sliver.

HENRY: Let me look.

PETER: No. I'll take care of it.

(Peter sits down on the sofa, still howling, trying to examine the sole of his foot.)

HENRY: Don't be an idiot. Let me look.

(Henry tries to grasp Peter's foot.)

PETER: Aghh!

HENRY: Hold still. That woman will roll in from church any minute. *(Inspects Peter's foot.)* It's huge. I'll get some iodine.

(Henry brings out first aid supplies.)

PETER: Don't touch me with that stuff.

HENRY: For Christ sake, my nephew's better behaved.

(Henry dabs the spot with iodine as Peter tries to twist away.)

PETER: Not so hard!

HENRY: If you don't shut up and let me do this fast, Mrs. Keifer will figure out our Saturday music lasts into Sunday.

PETER: Awww!

HENRY: It's out.

(Henry tapes up Peter's foot.)

PETER: I'll bring slippers next month.

HENRY: Next month...next month...insane to wait so long, isn't it?

PETER: I could come more often.

HENRY: No. Mrs. Keifer might start taking notes. You know her son works—

PETER: For your brother. You've told me 12 times.

HENRY: Can't I come to see you?

PETER: Stop asking! I can't pass gas in Rocklin without everyone knowing.

HENRY: Write me?

PETER: It makes me too nervous.

HENRY: I burn letters to you all the time.

PETER: I'm just not a writer.

HENRY: Then call.

PETER: Remember, it's all party lines.

HENRY: We'll talk about Handel and Karl Schuler.

PETER: I'll call you tomorrow to talk about Handel and Karl Schuler.

HENRY: I'll be home around eight.

PETER: What if we met somewhere in between Rocklin and Milwaukee in a week or so?

HENRY: What's there besides roadside taverns?

PETER: Me.

HENRY: Find a town and send me directions.

PETER: All right. We'll meet at a roadside tavern to discuss Handel...and Karl Schuler.

HENRY: Tomorrow, on the phone, I'll tell you my sulfonamide source, and give you a list of nights I'm free for consultation.

PETER: I'll be ready.

(Peter grabs his viola case, kisses Henry goodbye, and is about to dash out when Henry pulls him back into a furious embrace.)

PETER: Not so tight.

HENRY: Drop the damn case.

(Peter sets his viola case down.)

HENRY: I am not content, Peter. We have to say goodbye too much.

PETER: We'll see each other in less than two weeks.

HENRY: So? It'll be the same misery, just chopped into smaller pieces.

PETER: We used to be alone, Henry. Think about that. We didn't even have goodbyes to say.

HENRY: Oh Peter...

PETER: Shh...

(Peter comforts him a moment, extricates himself, and leaves quickly. Henry finds his own viola on a chair and cradles it in his arms desperately. Lights shift to Peter addressing audience.)

PETER: Everything was new—making music as two instead of one, making second pots of coffee, making carrots—carrots. Making plans. We always had to plan carefully: one night every four weeks at Henry's, then the mid-month rendezvous whereby Henry and I would drive to one obscure town or another on a weeknight. First we'd find each other's cars, park where no one could see us, and in cold weather retreat to the backseat or in warm weather spread a blanket on the ground. Later, grumbling about bad bratwurst and rank farmers, Henry would join me at a dark tavern. And I, weary from a day's work and soft from sex, talked little during those meals. I just listened as Henry filled in the gaps since we'd last seen each other. I learned to freeze my face as he talked so that no one could detect the rapture sweeping through me. Twice a month we met, three times a month we phoned, and never did we exchange letters, much to Henry's dismay. I let the affection between us billow invisibly in the air. To put it down on paper for someone else to see was too great a risk.

(Lights shift to:)

SCENE 6

A few months later. Sunday evening. The Schulers' dining room.

KARL: "Give us God, not the Devil, in the Dispatch."

PETER: Say that again.

NAN: "Give us God, not the Devil, in the Dispatch."

PETER: Margaret Sanger as the Devil.

KARL: No, I'm the Devil.

NAN: So am I—Bobby and Clara are getting hate mail too.

PETER: Your kids?

KARL: You missed a lot this weekend.

PETER: Which church was it?

NAN: Not anyplace I've heard of. It's one of those hellfire and brimstone groups that meets in someone's home. I didn't recognize most of those people.

KARL: They had to be shipped in from elsewhere. "Give us God, not the Devil!"

NAN: Miller's garage pulled their display ad. So did Nemrod's pharmacy.

PETER: Nemrod's?

KARL: To hell with them. Those two have been playing poker and cursing the Dispatch ever since my Socialism series.

NAN: Our children didn't get threats to their personal safety back then.

PETER: Oh, Lord.

KARL: What do you think hate mail is? Those loo-loos set fire to our bushes too.

NAN: One of them threw a cigarette in the bush.

KARL: They want to smoke us out and make us go to their birdbrain church. I'd rather fry—

NAN: Karl, shush. They might come back next week.

KARL: I hope they do because I'll be ready for them with the Sheriff. Trespassing, vandalizing property, harassing citizens—

NAN: Clara's supposed to visit with the children. I won't have them here with picketers and police cars.

KARL: Oh, we'll have good stories for the bridge crowd.

NAN: We're losing revenue—and you're thinking about entertaining anecdotes?

KARL: We haven't lost that much.

NAN: It's enough for me to lose sleep! I'm the one who keeps the books, not you. You toy with our finances, your health, our personal safety—

KARL: You're not in any danger.

NAN: Clara shouldn't come. I'm going to call her.

KARL: No one's going to set fire to the house, Nan.

PETER: What if you just weren't home next Sunday?

KARL: Well, that would take the fun out of the protest, now wouldn't it?

NAN: You talk like this is some sort of game!

PETER: Here's an idea. Turn a few lights on and maybe the radio too, and before that church service lets out, you'll come to my house.

NAN: Are you saying fool them?

PETER: Yes, let them rant and rave to an empty house.

NAN: Maybe we should just drive to Clara's.

KARL: I'm not leaving Rocklin.

PETER: I'll make Sunday dinner for all of you. Get Bobby to come too.

KARL: You?

PETER: Don't I owe you 10 years worth of dinners?

KARL: Yeah, but I won't eat pork and beans on Sunday.

PETER: I'll make chicken. We could even have martinis.

KARL: I may need them to swallow your chicken.

PETER: What do you say, Nan?

NAN: No one's likely to guess we're at your place.

KARL: Call Clara and tell her the plan.

NAN: If we lose another advertiser—just one more—

KARL: We won't.

NAN: If we do, I want your word you'll cancel the rest of the series.

KARL: It's an unrung bell, Nan. The county knows our views.

NAN: Your views.

KARL: Now don't give me that.

NAN: I'm not saying I disagree—but no one in the county knows my personal views, or Peter's. Isn't that right?

PETER: Privacy is important for a doctor.

KARL: You said you'd stand behind me on this.

PETER: I said, "If anyone asks, you know where I stand." And I meant it. But I won't go out of my way to make public announcements. Women are willing to ask me for help because they know their question stays in my office.

NAN: Well said, Peter.

KARL: Pretty weak brew.

PETER: Will you still come on Sunday?

KARL: I really shouldn't. Not after you—

NAN: Yes, we will.

KARL: Nan—

NAN: You can count on us.

PETER: If you're sure...?

NAN: We are.

PETER: Good. I'll see you later.

(Peter leaves.)

KARL: He is a damn coward. He won't practice what he preaches.

NAN: You've got that wrong! He practices discreetly in his office while you're out tooting your own horn just to hear the noise. Peter's in a very delicate position. Behind closed doors, I bet he's told Barb Leary where to get a pessary—

KARL: She's got one?

NAN: I'm just guessing. Another pregnancy would be a fiasco. You can't call Peter a coward for doing what's best for that family. If I needed birth control, I wouldn't want to make it a public forum that incites people to set our bushes on fire. I don't even want to be part of that now. I'm sick of you putting a stick in a hornet's nest.

KARL: Nan...

NAN: Yes?

KARL: I'm not the Devil.

NAN: That's not what I'm saying.

KARL: Remember when I was starting the Socialism series? You were excited by it. You were proud. Remember?

(Nan doesn't answer for a long time.)

NAN: I do.

KARL: What happened?

NAN: We got stung.

KARL: If we don't get a sting every once in a while, how will we know we're alive?

NAN: None of those issues ever makes a difference in what goes on in our own home.

KARL: Not true. One day Clara may want to stop having more babies.

NAN: Then she can go to Peter and we'll never know about it.

KARL: Time was, a doctor could get arrested for prescribing birth control. But Margaret Sanger and some others were willing to put a stick in a hornet's nest to change that. Our little Dispatch might be a county paper, but the big social reformers count on all of our small voices.

NAN: Well said, Karl.

KARL: Takes a lot these days to get that out of you.

NAN: I was very, very proud of your Socialism series. But to have people we considered old friends pull their ads...I don't want that kind of trouble anymore. We're a decade older. With your health this way, it's not like we have forever.

KARL: I'm a hell of a lot of better than a year ago.

NAN: Then let's enjoy life. Let's enjoy each other.

KARL: But we do.

NAN: Not in some ways...like we used to.

KARL: Well, as you say, we're decades older.

(Lights shift to:)

SCENE 7

A street in downtown Chicago. The following Saturday afternoon. Peter waits. Henry approaches him.

HENRY: Dr. Chase?

PETER: Dr. Meegan! Nice to see you.

HENRY: I'm on my way to Orchestra Hall. And you?

PETER: Orchestra Hall.

HENRY: Are you a fan of Rimbaldo?

PETER: Yes. Where are you sitting?

(Henry pulls out a ticket.)

HENRY: Main floor, row K...seat 16.

PETER: Main floor, hmm. I'm up in the gallery. Row C, seat 26.

HENRY: The acoustics are terrific up there.

PETER: That's what I've heard.

HENRY: Are you catching a train after the concert?

PETER: Not till 8:00.

HENRY: Mine's at 8:30. Let's have dinner first. There's a restaurant in the Palmer House.

PETER: I've never been there.

HENRY: You'll get a good meal, Dr. Chase.

PETER: I look forward to it.

HENRY: See you at the Palmer House.

PETER: Before you go...

(Peter hands Henry a box.)

HENRY: What's this?

PETER: A present from your tightwad.

HENRY: Peter, don't.

PETER: I'll walk ahead. You open it.

(Peter leaves. Henry waits till he's gone, then opens the box. He takes out a white silk scarf.)

HENRY: Silk...

(Henry drapes the scarf around his neck, strokes its smoothness and strolls away whistling joyfully. Lights shift to: Orchestra Hall. Henry is seated on one side of the stage, Peter on the other. Henry looks up as Peter searches below him.)

HENRY: A...B...C...one two three...

PETER: Row A...B...C...D...

HENRY: ...four five six...

PETER: H...I...J...

HENRY: Twenty-six-must be all the way...oh no, those clods from Milwaukee. They'll glue themselves to me at intermission...what the hell are their names? Ruth and Ralph? Rita and Robert?

PETER: 14, 15, 16-there he is. Wearing the scarf. He looks like a concertmaster on tour.

HENRY: ...C or E 26...What did he say? C or was it E? The "R"s see me. *(Waves.)* Hello, Rowena and Randall.

PETER: Who's he waving to?

HENRY: ...C, it was C...don't dim the lights yet, I didn't find him...

PETER: He's looking the wrong way...

HENRY: Oh yes! At the very end! How happy he seems.

(Henry looks up and Peter looks down.)

PETER: He looks...content.

(They give slight waves to each other as the lights dim and the music starts.)

END OF ACT I

Act II

Scene 1

Peter addresses the audience.

PETER: When my parents told me I needed to leave town following my annulment from Mabel, they did so at my office. Not in my childhood home after a Sunday dinner but in my examining room on a Tuesday. "It's best," they explained. Best that I disappear before I could inflict further pain on the family. Ever the dutiful son, I vanished quickly and quietly and lived very much as a shadow. Then after a few busy years in Rocklin, I felt myself begin to reappear. But not till that afternoon at Orchestra Hall did I fully return, rounded and pulsating like any other human being: Henry below me, absorbing the same concerti and stockpiling discussion for our dinner at the Palmer House, friends and patients and neighbors awaiting me back home. Music may transport some to the heavens, but in my case it gives me weight and heft for my life on earth.

(Sunday afternoon, the day following the Chicago concert. Waiting room of Peter's clinic. Karl and Nan sit on wooden chairs and drink martinis.)

KARL: We'll never eat at this rate.

NAN: Shh.

KARL: It's two o'clock. I don't see hide nor hair of any protesters. Let's go home and eat your leftover meatloaf. It's got to be better than whatever smelly thing Peter's cooking up—

PETER: *(From offstage.)* Dammit!

NAN: Need some help?

PETER: No, everything's under control.

KARL: It's a good thing Clara didn't bring the children.

NAN: No, it's not.

(More clatter and cursing from the kitchen.)

KARL: You can't feed little kids this late...and why do we have to sit in the waiting room?

NAN: I think Peter's embarrassed to let us see how clumsy he is in the kitchen.

(Peter comes out with a plate of saltine crackers.)

PETER: I brought you something to snack on.

KARL: Crackers?

PETER: I might have some olives to go with the martinis.

KARL: How old are these crackers anyway?

PETER: I'm sorry I'm not more prepared.

NAN: You got home late last night, didn't you?

PETER: Close to midnight.

KARL: Where in God's name were you?

PETER: In Chicago at Orchestra Hall for a concert.

NAN: Orchestra Hall!

KARL: You went all the way to Chicago for a concert?

PETER: Rimbaldo was conducting.

NAN: And you got to hear him!

PETER: Yes. It was...something.

KARL: Living high off the hog, aren't you?

PETER: Music is my one indulgence. I've always wanted to go to Orchestra Hall.

NAN: So have I.

PETER: We should drive down some weekend for the Saturday afternoon concert. The tickets are cheaper than the evening performance.

NAN: Why don't we do that, Karl?

KARL: Is that chicken coming along?

PETER: I'll check.

(Peter exits.)

NAN: If Peter can hear Rimbaldo, why can't we?

KARL: He's responsible to no one but himself.

NAN: What's that got to do with anything?

KARL: He doesn't have to save for his future the same way.

NAN: Oh, a lot of good it's doing our future to hole up here. It's terrible the children canceled on us.

KARL: Clara and Phil have always been skittish.

NAN: What about Bobby? What's his excuse other than outright fear?

KARL: Lots to be scared of. Look at those protesters setting fire to the house...

NAN: He's lost advertisers, too. First Community Bank pulled out after last week's column.

KARL: First Community?

NAN: Yes, Karl. They're punishing Bobby because of you. People don't want to read about coils and pessaries in the paper! And here we are, hiding from lunatics and bereft of our grandchildren on a Sunday, while the rest of the world gets to hear Rimbaldo.

KARL: Only Peter.

NAN: I'm certain Orchestra Hall had more than one person in the audience. They can't all be millionaires either. For years I've read about the marvelous acoustics in the gallery, and before I'm too old to—

KARL: No.

NAN: Karl!

KARL: I'm not driving all the way to Chicago.

NAN: I'll go myself.

KARL: Come on, you can't go gallivanting off to Chicago.

NAN: Are you going to stop me?

KARL: Fine. Go to Chicago. You'd rather not have me around anyway.

NAN: Don't just say things.

KARL: Wouldn't you?

NAN: I would very much like to hear a concert with you.

KARL: What's wrong with the music in Milwaukee?

NAN: Nothing, if we went to hear it.

KARL: We could get tickets to Dr. Meegan's orchestra.

NAN: You'll do that?

KARL: Just to please you. See, I'm not all bad.

NAN: You might even enjoy yourself for a change, like Peter does.

(*More clatter and cursing from the kitchen.*)

KARL: Oh, yes. He's having a great time.

NAN: I bet he is. He's never made anything that didn't come from a can till now. Indulging in music is doing him a lot of good.

KARL: I wonder if he isn't indulging in something else—like a lady friend in Milwaukee.

NAN: Don't you think he'd tell us?

KARL: The man who swears by everyone's privacy?

NAN: Well, he certainly deserves a good woman.

KARL: We don't know if she's good—or even if she is.

NAN: Wouldn't that be something?

KARL: Better company at night than his viola.

NAN: Oh, I hope he met a nice girl.

KARL: And he's not too cheap to buy her an ice cream sundae and movie tickets.

NAN: He really does watch his pennies, doesn't he? Look at this place! A woman would have a fit.

KARL: She'd make his patients pay up for once and go buy a couple of easy chairs.

NAN: We have to get to Milwaukee and find out who she is. Peter?

(Peter enters.)

NAN: When is Dr. Meegan's next concert?

PETER: The community symphony, you mean?

NAN: Yes, we're going to go. When is it?

PETER: Next month.

NAN: What's the date?

PETER: I'll have to check.

NAN: We'll all buy tickets and make it an outing.

PETER: All right.

NAN: Is something wrong?

PETER: Uh...no.

KARL: How's that chicken coming along?

PETER: It still seems awfully pink and raw.

KARL: Smells peculiar too.

PETER: That's the garlic.

NAN: Garlic?

PETER: Uh...yes.

NAN: Should I go home and get the meatloaf? There's also mashed potatoes.

KARL: Say yes.

PETER: Okay, yes.

NAN: I'll be right back. I can't wait to hear Dr. Meegan's orchestra.

(Nan exits.)

KARL: You can mix us another round of martinis. That you do pretty well. Where'd you learn?

PETER: From someone in my music group.

KARL: So that's why you dash out of here so fast every month. And I thought it was to study with that music professor.

PETER: I do. But then I get together with other musicians afterwards.

KARL: For martinis?

PETER: We play music for a while and then have dinner.

KARL: Any unattached women in the group?

PETER: A few.

KARL: Ah-hah! I can't wait to get to that concert and check them out myself. (Holds out his glass.) Join me for a second round?

PETER: All right.

(Lights shift to:)

SCENE 2

Several months later. A warm night. Wooded area somewhere between Rocklin and Milwaukee. Peter and Henry lounge on a blanket on the ground. Their shirts are off. Peter lies on his stomach as Henry massages his back.

PETER: ...The first twin was fine but the second was stillborn...the father was so upset, he sat in a chair and cried all night. Meanwhile, the mother's grandmother—her grandmother, not mother, she had to be 80—wouldn't stay in the kitchen and watch her great grandchildren. They all kept going in and out and getting in the way. Then Granny insisted I needed more boiling water—she knew more about delivering babies than I did, she said—so she picked up a huge kettle and collapsed from cardiac arrest.

HENRY: Scalded the children with the boiling water?

PETER: She missed them by a foot. I sent the oldest girl to the neighbor's to call the ambulance, but that took forever, which meant I was pumping Granny's heart for close to an hour while the father cursed at me for keeping the old lady going while his newborn was dying—

HENRY: It was dead already.

PETER: He didn't understand. I couldn't wait to get out of there. When I got back to the clinic, I had sixteen patients falling out of the doorway and my nurse was home with a cold.

HENRY: You need a knight in shining armor to carry you away.

PETER: Like in a fairy tale?

HENRY: Listen. Five years ago, I had a conversation with my brother. We don't usually talk about personal things. No, that's wrong. We talk about them constantly—his wife, the kids, our mother. But never heart to heart. Just...activities. Eddie and I were hunting with his boys and out of the blue he asked, "I should stop waiting for you to get married, shouldn't I?" I said yes.

PETER: He was telling you...he knew.

HENRY: Yes. He knew. Somehow.

PETER: What happened after that?

HENRY: Absolutely nothing. I keep my private life private, be the bachelor brother and spoil his kids as much as possible. I'll buy them double ice cream cones even if they get a bad report card. They're crazy about me...Uncle Henry. Then just this last week, Eddie asked did I want to go hunting on the 25th.

PETER: That's our weekend.

HENRY: I told him I was busy. He said, "You'll be with your viola group, won't you?" I said yes. He said, "I'm glad you found someone to share your music." Someone. You.

PETER: Do you think Mrs. Keifer told him?

HENRY: I have no idea. But however he put the pieces together, he's accepting the fact. He appreciates how careful I've been. He's thanking me...and you too.

PETER: But I don't exist for him.

HENRY: Only because he hasn't met you.

PETER: How can he?

HENRY: You'll move to Milwaukee.

PETER: I'll do what?

HENRY: Get an apartment in town so you don't have to drive two hours to see me.

PETER: I can't run my practice from Milwaukee.

HENRY: You'll give it up.

PETER: Give it up?

HENRY: I'll get another job for you—a medical position. Anything's got to be better than pumping hearts for old ladies who aren't likely to pay their bills.

PETER: These are my patients.

HENRY: You'll have new ones.

PETER: I don't want new ones.

HENRY: Do you think a single one of them would bail you out if you were really in trouble?

PETER: Yes. You don't realize how dependent people are on each other in a small town.

HENRY: What if they knew about us?

PETER: They don't—and they won't.

HENRY: Do they mean more to you than me?

PETER: Henry, that's a foolish question. Would you trade the Institute and Eddie and your friends—

HENRY: I have no real friends. I have colleagues...acquaintances.

PETER: Well, you've got a brother who loves you. My family won't have me home for Thanksgiving.

HENRY: I would give it all up for you.

PETER: You shouldn't.

HENRY: You're the only one who cares whether I live or die.

PETER: That's not true.

HENRY: You don't know how other people regard me. No one pays attention like you do.

PETER: Do you pay attention to them? I don't mean order them around because they work for you, or charm them because you want them to fund the Institute, or buy them double ice cream cones so they'll call you "Uncle Henry." I mean really pay attention to someone as a human being.

HENRY: I try, but I always get off track somehow. You know that Yeats poem, "The Second Coming"?

PETER: No.

HENRY: "Turning and turning in the widening gyre..."

PETER: Oh, that one. Barb Leary teaches it to her students. "...The falcon cannot hear the falconer..."

HENRY: "Things fall apart, the center cannot hold..." That's me. My center falls apart without you. It's always been a mess, I just didn't know it before. You are my peace. I love you.

PETER: The poem is about destruction in order to allow the rebirth of Ireland. That's how Barb explains it.

HENRY: To hell with Barb! I'm telling you what you mean to me. Can't you say anything significant? What am I to you but a bare ass in the backseat of a car?

PETER: Lord, Henry, the things you say...

HENRY: What am I to you?

PETER: You are...my music.

HENRY: Are the Schulers and the Learys and everyone else in Rocklin your music too?

PETER: I keep a calendar in the kitchen and every morning, I mark off the days till we're going to be together in pinpricks.

HENRY: What's wrong with an "x"?

PETER: Too noticeable. The nurse uses the kitchen. Every night, I run my hand along the backside of the calendar page and feel how many pinpricks there are. The more pinpricks—the closer I am to being with you—the more I feel your music. You're the only one who's ever given me that.

HENRY: Move to Milwaukee and get yourself a place where we don't know the neighbors. Then you won't need that calendar. I could drop by at night or meet you for lunch.

PETER: But what about Eddie accepting you as long as everything stays private?

HENRY: All right, we can't all go hunting together. We'll be discreet.

PETER: Invisible?

HENRY: Yes.

PETER: That means I will be invisible. I'll have no friends.

HENRY: But I'm your knight in shining armor. I'll take care of you.

PETER: Take care of me?

HENRY: Yes.

PETER: Sort of like what the man you met at Percy's place wanted.

HENRY: I didn't say that.

PETER: I'll be your boy in a back street apartment-on call when I'm needed.

HENRY: No!

PETER: That's not a life-that's an arrangement.

HENRY: I just want us to be together more. Eddie doesn't have to cut corners to be with Vera. Why does he get her all the time but you and I have to break our backs keeping to the shadows? It's not fair. I'm sick of having what amounts to an illicit affair when there's nothing illicit about us.

PETER: Well, that's our opinion.

HENRY: There's nothing wrong with us, Peter! We're not any less than Eddie and Vera. I'd like to have sons—daughters—offspring—a legacy. I don't want to be alone so much. I don't understand why they get to have a family and we get nothing.

PETER: But that's how it is.

HENRY: It's criminal!

PETER: No, Henry, we're considered the criminals.

HENRY: Is that what you think?

PETER: It's in the goddamn Bible!

HENRY: Yes! We've been around for millennia. It's time people figured out we're not going away and just let us into their world. You and I could do as well as any couple.

PETER: Society's not going to change just to please us.

HENRY: Then we should.

PETER: Henry, I'm really tired...

HENRY: Aren't you miserable?

PETER: Right now I am. My arms are sore and my head is swimming. I haven't eaten a thing all day except a candy bar—

HENRY: Peter!

PETER: What do you want me to do?

HENRY: Something has to change!`

PETER: Should I turn into a woman and have your child?

HENRY: How can you keep going like this?

PETER: It's better than nothing.

HENRY: That's not good enough. Something has to change.

PETER: I heard you the first time.

HENRY: Something has to change. Something has to change. Something has to change—

PETER: I won't be invisible!

HENRY: Something has to change or—or—or....

PETER: It's not a fairy tale, Henry. In your dream world, you might think you could give up your career and your family, but down on earth you've never had to do it. I did, and I'm not willing to do it again.

HENRY: What are you willing to do?

PETER: Tonight? Not much. I'm very, very tired. I want to eat dinner and drive home without falling asleep at the wheel.

HENRY: And after tonight?

PETER: Come on—meet me at the tavern. Henry?

(Henry doesn't answer.)

PETER: No? I'll have dinner alone? Is that what you mean? If I don't do what you want, it's over and we go our separate ways?

(Henry still doesn't answer.)

PETER: I'm sorry I can't remake the world for you tonight.

(Peter puts his shirt on and starts to leave. Henry holds out his hand to him. Peter goes over and takes it. He kisses the palm.)

PETER: Come talk to me while I eat.

(Lights shift to:)

SCENE 3

Several months later. An outdoor garden behind a university concert hall in Milwaukee. Karl, Peter, and Nan gather around Henry who is dressed in concert black. He wears his white silk scarf.

NAN: You're just shy.

HENRY: That's not something I've ever been accused of.

NAN: Self-effacing.

HENRY: That either.

NAN: It was a beautiful concert.

HENRY: The brass section was a little off.

NAN: I only had ears for the strings.

HENRY: Our orchestra improved drastically when we moved from a high school auditorium into a real concert hall.

NAN: Were the musicians inspired?

HENRY: No, the acoustics are better. It covers a multitude of sins.

NAN: No more excuses, Dr. Meegan, your community orchestra is really quite talented.

HENRY: Let me introduce you to our conductor.

NAN: You don't have to.

HENRY: Don't be shy and self-effacing. Come with me.

NAN: What an honor. Karl?

KARL: You go ahead.

HENRY: We'll be back in a minute.

KARL: Take your time. Peter's going to introduce me to some of those women.

NAN: Keep an eye him.

PETER: I will.

(Henry and Nan exit.)

KARL: Is that a coffee cart over there?

PETER: Yes, help yourself.

KARL: Want a cup?

PETER: No, not for me. But get one for Henry. Two and a half sugars, no cream.

KARL: Two and a half sugars, no cream...all right.

(Karl goes off for the coffee as Peter gazes in Henry's direction. Karl comes back quickly with two cups of coffee and watches Peter looking towards Henry.)

KARL: Here we go.

PETER: I'll hold it for him.

KARL: What good service.

PETER: Henry's my mentor. I never had a real teacher till he set up lessons for me with Professor Birkhardt. I never heard a viola joke till him. What do a viola and a lawsuit have in common?

KARL: What?

PETER: Everyone is happy when the case is closed.

KARL: That's a joke?

PETER: Well you see, compared to violinists, violists are considered second rate, so—

KARL: Tell me about that blonde over there.

PETER: I don't really know her.

KARL: What about the one next to her?

PETER: She's in the orchestra. Henry knows her name.

(Henry and Nan return. Peter hands Henry his cup of coffee.)

NAN: You must meet him, Peter. He's a stitch.

HENRY: Do as the lady says.

PETER: Have your coffee first.

HENRY: No, I'll have it during. Come on.

(Henry and Peter go off.)

NAN: What a day, isn't it? It's so rejuvenating to get out of Rocklin.

KARL: Don't expect to do it all the time.

NAN: Why shouldn't we? The tickets didn't cost much.

KARL: Everything adds up.

NAN: You agreed to this trip. Try to enjoy yourself. We're away from the mess with the Dispatch.

KARL: Don't call it that.

NAN: Bobby did. "Dad's making a mess of the paper again..."

KARL: He's entitled to his views. We're not one and the same. But if Bobby doesn't care for my columns, he's not going to like this.

NAN: "This?"

KARL: Those two.

NAN: What are you talking about?

KARL: Peter knew that Dr. Meegan took two and a half sugars in his coffee.

NAN: That's a lot of sugar.

KARL: Who knows what a man takes in his coffee? His wife, that's who. Other men pay no attention—unless they're acting like a wife.

NAN: What are you saying, Karl?

KARL: Peter isn't seeing a woman. He's seeing Dr. Meegan. They're queer.

NAN: You're out of your mind.

KARL: Look at them! Watch that conductor too...He moves like a butterfly.

NAN: Shh.

KARL: Peter's queer. You need to admit that much.

NAN: Oh, Karl...

KARL: You brought it on yourself, pushing him to go meet Dr. Meegan in the first place.

NAN: I thought they'd strike up a friendship.

KARL: Since when do women introduce men to each other?

NAN: When they're lonely and isolated. When there's a chance they could reach out to someone who shares their interests. Anyway, you pushed Peter to meet Dr. Meegan yourself.

KARL: Only so he could meet those nurses at the Institute.

NAN: Poor Peter...

KARL: You feel sorry for him?

NAN: He has so much to hide. *(After a moment.)* But he does look happy.

KARL: Nan!

NAN: If Peter cares for Dr. Meegan—

KARL: Don't talk that way.

NAN: I don't know how else to say it.

KARL: Then don't.

NAN: I'm admitting he's...queer.

KARL: Don't say he "cares" for someone. A man can't care for another man.

NAN: Well, this one does. You can see it in his face.

KARL: But two men...

NAN: Two men what?

KARL: Two men...

NAN: Yes?

KARL: It's against the law.

NAN: Funny, isn't it? Margaret Sanger gets herself into trouble for advocating birth control and you think she's a great hero.

KARL: But I...it's...you can't...

NAN: Explain yourself, Karl. Margaret Sanger and I would like to know.

KARL: Men and women producing more children than they can raise right-it's a natural phenomenon. But men and men-well, they produce nothing. Their bodies aren't arranged that way.

NAN: Whatever you say, if it weren't for those two doctors, your own body might not even be here.

KARL: They could damage their careers. Ours too. All we need is for word to get out—

NAN: So now it's finally personal—a hornet's nest with your own dear friend, not a bum on the railroad track.

KARL: Stop this, Nan.

NAN: Peter is in love—

KARL: Don't use that word!

NAN: Happy and in love with Dr. Meegan the way you used to be with me. Years ago, before that Socialism series, the biggest pleasure in your life was the children and me.

KARL: Nan!

NAN: You looked at me the way Dr. Meegan is looking at Peter. I thought once your health improved, you'd remember how you felt. But you haven't.

(Peter and Henry return.)

PETER: Everyone's going for dinner at the University Steak House. Why don't we go along?

KARL: Another time.

HENRY: Don't be frightened—the restaurant's got nothing to do with the university's lousy food.

KARL: We're heading back to Rocklin.

PETER: But you're driving with me.

KARL: We'll take the train.

NAN: We will not!

PETER: I can leave now.

NAN: We'll stay for dinner, Peter.

KARL: No, Nan.

PETER: I'll bring the car over and—

KARL: We'll get a taxi to the station.

NAN: Karl!

KARL: Then I'll take myself.

NAN: You can't go alone!

KARL: Go and have your steak. I can get myself home.

NAN: You'll do no such thing!

(Karl exits.)

NAN: You're not really—Karl!

PETER: Karl! *(To Nan.)* Come on.

NAN: No, Peter. Stay. I'll handle him.

PETER: I can't let you two leave.

NAN: I'm going to give that man a piece of my mind. I don't want you around to hear it.

(Nan exits. Peter starts to follow.)

HENRY: Don't move.

PETER: But—

HENRY: They know.

PETER: Know...know?

HENRY: Without a doubt. Why else would they run so fast from us?

PETER: Karl and Nan aren't like that.

HENRY: Oh, so you've discussed homosexuality around the bridge table. They're open minded and comfortable—

PETER: We've never talked about it.

HENRY: They know.

PETER: Lord...

HENRY: Karl doesn't like it.

PETER: He's always treated me as family...

HENRY: Not anymore.

PETER: Nan wouldn't throw me out...

HENRY: She went with her husband, Peter. That should tell you the depth of your friendship. It was a mistake to let them come. I told you that in the first place.

PETER: I didn't know how to keep them away.

HENRY: It's getting harder and harder to pretend we're not together.

PETER: Go talk to someone in the orchestra. I'll leave on my own.

HENRY: I didn't mean you should go.

PETER: I should. The "R"s are over there watching.

HENRY: Don't leave.

PETER: Your orchestra friends will keep you company.

HENRY: They aren't my friends.

PETER: They could be if you'd let them.

HENRY: You're my only friend!

PETER: Henry, stay calm.

HENRY: The Schulers aren't your friends anymore. Karl won't play cards with a sodomist.

PETER: Shh. The "R"s are watching us.

HENRY: We're both sodomists.

PETER: Not so loud! Someone might hear us!

HENRY: So's the conductor and the second violinist...Don't even ask about the French horn, a Catholic with five children...wonder what he has to say in confession. Holy Father, I have sinned, I have impaled the red-haired clarinetist—

PETER: I'm going.

HENRY: Don't leave me alone.

PETER: You're embarrassing me.

HENRY: It's good for you.

PETER: I'll never come to another concert of yours.

HENRY: That's all right. I'll come to Rocklin—

PETER: No, you won't.

HENRY: Yes, I will.

PETER: I'll meet you anywhere you want but—

HENRY: Rocklin.

PETER: You just can't.

HENRY: Everything's different now. The Schulers won't have the time of day for you.

PETER: You must not come to Rocklin.

HENRY: I told you something had to change.

PETER: Don't wreck a good thing.

HENRY: Something had to change and it did. Karl left and Nan followed. They've made their choice, Peter. It's time for you to make yours. Now, I'm going to the University Steak House. You can come with me so everyone knows who Peter is, the one who keeps me from spinning out of control—

PETER: I'm not doing a very good job of that right now.

HENRY: Or you can leave, and I'll talk about you so much, they'll all know anyway.

PETER: Don't make it so black and white.

HENRY: But I am black...and you are white.

PETER: I should have bought a gray scarf. Here come the "R"s.

(Henry waves his scarf coquettishly.)

HENRY: Come chat with the homos.

PETER: Stop it!

HENRY: Hello, Raoul and Roxanne or is it Rasputin and Rochelle? Rusty and Renee? This is my lover and—

(Peter leaves.)

HENRY: —we commit illegal sex acts when no one's looking—*(Notices Peter is gone.)* Peter! Peter! *(Henry searches for Peter but can't find him.)* What have I done...oh God, what have I done?

(Henry panics as the unseen "R"s close in on him and the music rises. He desperately tries to compose himself, smoothing out the scarf and doing his best to smile as fear spreads across his face. Lights shift to:)

SCENE 4

Peter's clinic. Evening. A month later. Peter pores over his ledger book and a pile of bills. He hears a knock.

PETER: It's open.

(More knocking.)

PETER: Open!

(Peter continues to work as Henry enters.)

HENRY: A conductor and a violist are standing in the middle of the road.

PETER: Henry! Jesus Christ!

HENRY: Which one do you run over first?

PETER: You can't stay.

HENRY: The conductor. Why?

PETER: I said, you can't stay.

HENRY: Business before pleasure.

PETER: Henry, what's going on? You show up unannounced—

HENRY: A month of letters and calls didn't give you a hint? How long were you going to play hard to get?

PETER: You know I have no privacy. The postmaster has a mouth the size of Lake Michigan.

HENRY: Excuses, excuses—

PETER: If my neighbors see so much as a strange car outside, they'll stop in to find out who it is.

HENRY: So get the hell out of this Godforsaken place. In one glance, I can tell that whatever job you get elsewhere, it'll pay more and provide more resources than here. You might actually be able to do something worthwhile.

PETER: I'm doing that already.

HENRY: In your little country medical center with the homemade curtains?

PETER: Don't you make fun of my clinic. Get out!

HENRY: Wait!

PETER: I own it—I can throw you out.

HENRY: Peter, wait. I didn't mean—

PETER: Out!

HENRY: I didn't mean it. I said it without thinking.

PETER: The way you didn't mean to say "my lover and I commit illegal sex acts" in front of dozens of people last month?

HENRY: That I meant.

PETER: How could you?

HENRY: We are homosexuals. You, me—

PETER: Yes, I am one. I'm also right-handed...a physician...a Democrat...a Presbyterian. But I'm not an exhibitionist. I will not tolerate you forcing me to be one.

HENRY: But...

PETER: No, Henry. You can't step on our dignity.

HENRY: I won't do it again.

PETER: Ever?

HENRY: Ever.

PETER: This is very important to me, Henry. You need to understand.

HENRY: I do.

PETER: All right then.

(Peter exits.)

HENRY: Where are you going?

PETER: I'm closing the curtains and locking the door.

(Peter returns.)

PETER: We'll say you came here to tour the county health facilities. You had no choice but to spend the night at Dr. Chase's.

HENRY: Then...I can stay?

PETER: I've missed you so much.

(Peter and Henry kiss. There is a knock at the door. They push apart.)

KARL: *(From offstage.)* Peter? Peter, are you all right?

PETER: Fine.

(Peter goes off to let Karl in.)

KARL: I saw that car outside and—oh, Dr. Meegan.

HENRY: Hello, Karl. Staying off the cigars?

KARL: I'm trying to.

HENRY: Good. Peter's been showing me around. I get the grand county tour in the morning.

KARL: Well, I won't disturb you. Just wanted to make sure everything was okay.

PETER: Thank you, Karl.

(Karl looks them up and down.)

KARL: You need to keep this out of Rocklin.

PETER: We will. *(To Henry.)* Won't we?

HENRY: Yes.

KARL: Goodnight.

PETER: Goodnight.

(Karl exits. Peter locks up after him.)

HENRY: Well, I can see you don't make a fourth for bridge anymore.

PETER: We played together an hour ago.

HENRY: That man had you in his home?

PETER: Yes.

HENRY: What kind of blackmail do you think Nan used on him?

PETER: It doesn't really matter.

HENRY: Just as long as the game goes on?

PETER: Is that so different than hunting with Eddie?

HENRY: Eddie acknowledged us. Voluntarily.

PETER: He's never met me, doesn't know my name—

HENRY: He gave his approval nonetheless.

PETER: Don't be so sure. Karl's had to be with us together, when we stupidly let our guard down.

HENRY: Maybe it's time for Eddie—

PETER: Oh, no.

HENRY: He's my brother, not yours.

PETER: Don't test him.

HENRY: I should.

PETER: Let the man be, Henry! Doesn't it ever occur to you that he has his dignity too?

HENRY: Yes.

PETER: Then don't rub us in his face.

HENRY: What about getting out of his way altogether? Let's leave Wisconsin. I can't stand living in a backwards brewing town anyway.

PETER: Oh, now what's the plan? Move to Chicago and sell shirts at Marshall Field's?

HENRY: We can do better than that.

(Henry hands Peter a pair of train tickets.)

PETER: Train tickets to New York?

HENRY: I'm not unknown there.

PETER: You bought us train tickets?

HENRY: Yes.

PETER: Henry.

HENRY: Well?

PETER: New York...

HENRY: It's a different universe. We could be together without neighbors knocking if they see an unfamiliar car. New York's so big, all the cars are unfamiliar.

PETER: So are the people.

HENRY: It's better than a tiny town where everyone's so nosy you have to mark your calendar in pinpricks. Let's get out of here!

PETER: And do what?

HENRY: Everything we do now-but side by side, not fifty miles apart.

PETER: We can't have any kind of medical practice and live openly. It's unheard of.

HENRY: Someone needs to start sometime.

PETER: Not us!

HENRY: Peter, I went to New York as a Wisconsin hick five years ago and sold high society on the notion that my institute was the best place to put their money. If I can do that, we can do this.

PETER: As long as we live in a boarding house and sell shirts in a department store.

HENRY: We won't have to do that-not with my national reputation.

PETER: I wouldn't count on that if I were you.

HENRY: All right. We'll take our chances. It'll be an adventure, an experiment.

PETER: Since when am I your guinea pig?

HENRY: It's both of us!

PETER: Two guinea pigs then!

HENRY: I'm not doing this as a social experiment. It's to get something more than table scraps!

PETER: Wait'll you see what it's like to be a nobody—not the guy in charge but the one who gets pushed around and then ignored.

HENRY: I won't let that happen.

PETER: Oh, you're sure of that, are you? Well, I have news for you—you can't be on the edge and still be the boss.

HENRY: We won't be on the edge!

PETER: I was once publicly acknowledged as a homosexual. Trust me, it's the edge. You, on the other hand, have never been anyplace but front and center. Eddie got you started that way and you've hung on.

HENRY: I'll let it go.

PETER: You won't like it.

HENRY: I'm ready to try. Now will you pack a bag? It's me or those bridge players.

PETER: No, it's not!

HENRY: Come to New York. We'll go to Carnegie Hall and sit next to each other!

PETER: Oh, give up the fantasy.

HENRY: I have real train tickets, Peter!

PETER: We'll sleep on it and talk in the morning.

HENRY: There's nothing to discuss. It's very simple.

PETER: It's more like magic: We suddenly ditch our lives without anyone noticing, then go to New York where we set up medical practices with no trouble—because you're so famous—and sit next to each other at Carnegie Hall because nobody cares about our private lives.

HENRY: You have no imagination.

PETER: I'm a plain person.

HENRY: I am always alone...

PETER: In your fantasies, you are—we're always alone when we dream. But here on earth, I'm with you. So are Eddie and Vera and those nephews—

HENRY: Wrong! I'm nothing but the bachelor brother—the sixth finger on his family hand. I just don't fit! I'm alone! It's always just me, by myself, pushing to change the world.

PETER: The world can't be changed.

HENRY: You won't even try, will you? You'll stay in your comfortable lair here, lying to yourself and everyone around you, playing your goddamn viola like it's a sewing machine instead of an instrument of beauty and passion—

PETER: Henry, please!

HENRY: That's how you play!

PETER: Still, you are my music.

HENRY: Go play your sewing machine, Peter. You hear nothing when you play anyway. When we're on the ground, you have the ears of a hunting dog—

PETER: Henry—

HENRY: —but if we try to rise above this lousy planet—play Bach, have an adventure, go someplace new, take a risk—

PETER: Henry, I—

HENRY: —you can't hear a thing. The truth is, I may be your music but you don't know how to listen!

PETER: I love you.

HENRY: You love me?

PETER: Yes.

HENRY: Then you'll come with me.

PETER: No. I can't be in your dream, Henry. I'm here on earth. That's the only place I can love you.

(Peter takes Henry's hand and tries to kiss it. Henry pulls it away and storms out. Peter paces awhile, then picks up the train tickets. Lights suddenly shift. Sounds indicating a car crash are heard. Lights shift as Henry appears like a ghost. Peter reaches for him but Henry collapses slowly to the ground. Peter runs to Henry's fallen body as Nan and Karl enter.)

KARL: Did you see what he did? Drove head on into the tree! I was sitting on the porch when he—

NAN: Shh, Karl! *(To Peter.)* We called the ambulance. Are you all right? Peter?

(Nan and Karl watch as Peter feels for a pulse at Henry's neck. Peter turns to them and shakes his head, conveying that Henry is dead. He collapses onto Henry, sobbing and kissing him.)

KARL: Don't do that.

NAN: *(Very gently.)* Why don't you come inside?

(Peter presses Henry's hand against his mouth and begins to sob.)

PETER: My music...

KARL: Listen to Nan.

PETER: My love...

NAN: Peter?

KARL: You should get away from the body. The Learys will be out here any minute.

NAN: So will the whole town.

(Nan kneels beside Peter.)

PETER: My music...

(Nan puts her arm gently around Peter's shoulders.)

NAN: For your own good...

KARL: It'll ruin you.

NAN: Come on, Peter.

KARL: Stand up like a man.

PETER: I am a man!

(Karl leads Nan away as Peter continues to cling to Henry. Peter releases Henry, who then rises and exits slowly. Lights shift as Peter addresses the audience.)

PETER: Once the ambulance finally arrived, I of course had to follow it to the county hospital, sign the death certificate, and telephone Henry's brother in Milwaukee. I stayed through the night to handle the details. By morning, the entire county knew of Henry's suicide and once again, I was regarded as a shadow. No one made small talk with me in my office and after hours I was ignored altogether. At first Nan came at night, bringing me food as she checked over her shoulder to make sure no one saw. But eventually that too stopped. The hole in my heart where Henry had been was far too big for her compromised casseroles and conversation to fill. Nothing could fill it. I couldn't bear to pick up my viola. That was a bigger loss than my friends, as throughout everything else in my life, the viola had steadied my course. Days, weeks, months passed since Henry's death and then it turned into a year. Almost on the anniversary, a box turned up for me at the post office. In the privacy of my home I opened it to find Henry's viola and a note from his brother Eddie. He wrote, "Dear Dr. Chase, It has taken a year to settle my brother's estate and dispose of his possessions. Now I am in the final stages and would like you to have his viola. I know what you meant to him and what music meant to you both. His death has been a great loss to us all. Best wishes, Edward Meegan." Lord. He said it. "I know what you meant to him." He put it down on paper for anyone to read. What a foolhardy risk for a man like him to take, what a leap not to blame me for his family's tragedy. I went to the stationery shop and bought paper, the kind for personal correspondence, and wrote a reply. "Dear Mr. Meegan, Thank you for the kind gesture of sending me Henry's viola. I know what you meant to him as a brother. And he did mean everything to me. Best wishes, Peter Chase." Now I too put it down on paper for anyone to read. After I mailed the note, what else could I do but learn the viola all over again, filling my house with sound that told the town I was more than a shadow? I'm so much better these days. I play Henry's music.

(Peter picks up Henry's viola and begins to play. The music rises as the lights go down.)

END OF PLAY

RESIDENT PLAYWRIGHT BIOGRAPHIES
Chicago Dramatists' Resident Playwrights, 2005

ALICE AUSTEN's *Foul* was performed in London in June, 2005. *Fire* was produced by Prop Thtr in 2005. Her screenplay adaptation of *Sex, Surrealism, Dali and Me* has been optioned by Fate Productions. *The Match Box* was produced by the Irish Theatre Company in Brussels, Belgium, where she lived for a number of years. Ms. Austen's plays have been developed in Chicago through Women at the Door, Stage Left Theatre, the New Plays Festival, and Chicago Dramatists.

DAVID BARR III's plays include *The Face of Emmett Till* (published in this anthology), *Ev'ry Time I Feel The Spirit*, and *My Soul Is A Witness*, which just completed a 60-city tour of the U.S.A. He has received a myriad of awards, including three Illinois Arts Council Playwriting Fellowships and the Goodman Theatre's first Ofner Prize, which he shared with Carson Becker in 2000. His most recent play, *The Upper Room*, premiered at Pegasus Players in Chicago, receiving a 2004-2005 Joseph Jefferson Citation Nomination for New Work.

CARSON GRACE BECKER earned her MFA in Playwriting from the University of Iowa. She has been commissioned by the Goodman, Nebraska Repertory, and Riverside Theater, and won two Illinois Arts Council Playwriting Fellowships and a Jeff Award for New Work. Her musical, *Africa & Pumbridge*, for which she wrote the book, was featured at the annual New Tuners showcase in Chicago and The International New York Fringe Festival. She just finished an artist's residency at the William Inge House in Kansas.

DERRELL CAPES has been a Resident Playwright at Chicago Dramatists since 1998 and has had his plays produced from San Diego to Washington, D.C. Most recently, his play *A West Texas 2-Step* was selected for the Saturday afternoon reading series at Chicago Dramatists. Mr. Capes is a vested member of Actor's Equity Association and an associate member of The Dramatists Guild.

LYDIA R. DIAMOND Chicago's Steppenwolf Theatre commissioned *Voyeurs de Venus* (to premiere in 2006 at Chicago Dramatists) and her adaptation of Toni Morrison's *The Bluest Eye* (which Steppenwolf produced in 2005). The recipient of an Illinois Arts Council Playwriting Fellowship, Ms. Diamond's other plays include: *Stage Black* (2003 Going To The River Festival at Ensemble Studio Theatre, NYC) and *The Gift Horse* (Goodman Theatre premiere 2002, Women at the Door Festival, Theodore Ward Award 1st Place, Kesselring Prize 2nd Prize, and anthologized in "7 Black Plays").

MARSHA ESTELL's plays have received readings at the Goodman Theatre, Chicago Theater Company, ETA Creative Arts Foundation, the Dayton Playhouse, New Perspectives Theatre (NYC), and Famous Door Theater. She was awarded a 2001 Illinois Arts Council Fellowship for Playwriting. *Mama Said There'll be Days Like This* was commissioned and produced by Chicago's Black Ensemble Theatre. She is currently working on a musical about the life of Etta James and *Before I Wake*, a post Vietnam War play. Her play, *Heat*, is featured in this anthology.

JOSEPH FEDORKO has been a Resident Playwright at Chicago Dramatists since 1987. He has worked with Bailiwick Repertory, Circle Theatre, Stage Left Theatre, Prop Thtr., and Terrapin Theatre in Chicago, as well as New York's Greenwich House Theatre. His plays *Scrimmages* and *Rebuttals*, published under the title *Extracurriculars* by Bakers Plays, have been produced in high schools across the country. He teaches Playwriting in the Creative Writing MFA Program at Roosevelt University in Chicago.

JOHN GREEN, a Resident Playwright with Chicago Dramatists, has had dozens of plays produced in Chicago, across the country, and in Paris. He won Chicago's Jeff and After Dark Awards for Best New Work for *The Liquid Moon* (published in this anthology). His short play, *Twilight Serenade*, was published by Dramatic Publishing. *Hiding* was a finalist in The Tennessee Williams One-Act Contest. Mr. Green won a Jeff Award for Best Actor for his portrayal of George in Robert Fall's production of *Of Mice and Men*.

MARK GUARINO has had seven plays produced in Chicago at theatres including Zebra Crossing, Curious Theatre Branch, and Chicago Dramatists, where he is a Resident Playwright. In 2001, he was awarded the Tennessee Williams Scholarship from the University of the South. He is also the recipient of the 2003 New Play Prize from Prop Thtr in Chicago. In 2005, his play, *Partial Post*, will be published in the anthology, "35 in 10: Thirty-Five Ten-Minute Plays" by Dramatic Publishing.

JIM HENRY is an actor, playwright and screenwriter who currently lives in LA. His play, *The Angels of Lemnos*, premiered at Chicago Dramatists, winning a Jeff Award for New Work. *The Angels of Lemnos* has been produced in the U.S. and Australia, and ran for five months in L.A., where it received the L.A. Times Critic's Choice and rave reviews from Variety. His other plays include *When We Were Alive*, *The Seventh Monarch*, *Widower's Poker*, and *A Worthy Choice*.

KEITH HUFF's plays have been produced regionally and Off-Broadway. His most recently produced works include *The Age of Cynicism or Karaoke Night at the Hog* (at Chicago Dramatists), *Prosperity* (commissioned by Riverside Theater), *Leon and Joey, Dog Stories*, and a new musical originally commissioned by Noble Fool Theater, *Ebenezer: Return of the Scrooge*, (with composer and co-lyricist Adryan Russ), which was recently developed at the Disney/ASCAP Music Theater Workshop.

JOEL DRAKE JOHNSON got his start as a writer with Chicago's critically acclaimed EconoArt Theatre. In Chicago, Victory Gardens Theater produced the 2003 Jeff nominated *The End of the Tour* (published in this anthology), and the Jeff Award winning production of *The Fall to Earth* was produced by Steppenwolf Theatre in 2004. His latest plays, *A Blameless Life* and *Final Days*, are commissioned by Steppenwolf Theatre, which will workshop the former in its 2005 "First Look Series."

McKINLEY JOHNSON's *Georgia Tom* premiered in Chicago in a 2003 Jeff Recommended production at the Bailiwick Arts Center. *Being Beautiful* (co-authored with Stephanie Newsom) premiered at Chicago Theatre Company in 2001 and was nominated for Jeff Awards and Black Theatre Alliance Awards. Mr. Johnson has received two Pilgrim Project Grants, for *Georgia Tom* (2002) and *Train Is Comin'* (1992), which was produced twice at Chicago Theatre Company and at St. Louis Black Repertory, Black Theatre Troupe of Phoenix, and Paul Robeson Theatre of New York.

GENE JONES has had two plays produced by Chicago Dramatists, *Much Ado About Murder* in 1984 and Emil in 1987. Emil earned Jeff Citations for its two leading actors. He has three current works-in-progress: *Angel Kisses*, a drama about incest, *Stay With Me*, a comedy about a grieving father who expects his daughter to replace his deceased wife, and *Family Matters*, a comedy about faith and love overcoming life's hardships. Twelve of his musicals were marketed in 2004.

NAMBI E. KELLEY *Bus Boyz* premiered in Chicago in 2005 in a joint production between MPAACT and Prop Thtr. She is a playwright-in-residence with MPAACT, which has also produced her play *Chris T. How Kintu Became a Man* was nominated for several Ovation Awards in its Los Angeles premiere. Ms. Kelley's work has been commissioned and produced by HealthWorks Theatre in Chicago. *Bus Boyz* and *He, She and My White Mama* were both developed in Prop Thtr's New Plays Festivals.

ROBERT KOON became a Resident Playwright at Chicago Dramatists in 2001. His plays include *St. Colm's Inch* (which Chicago Dramatists will produce in the fall of 2005), *Inpainting, The Leverage of Affection, Changing Attire, The Point of Honor*, and *Looking West from Firá*. Mr. Koon has received praise as an actor, director and designer; and now teaches playwriting at Chicago Dramatists, where he is on staff. His play, *Vintage Red and the Dust of the Road*, is featured in this anthology.

ALINE LATHROP is an award winning playwright whose work has been seen at the Abingdon Theatre Company, American Theater Company, Boarshead Theater, Centre Stage South Carolina!, Chicago Dramatists, Circle Theater of Forest Park, Famous Door Theatre Company, and Stage Left Theatre, among others. Monologues from her plays will appear in upcoming Smith & Kraus anthologies. Ms. Lathrop's work has been supported, in part, by the Illinois Arts Council and a Dr. Donahue Tremaine grant.

DONALD LEWIS is a published playwright and produced screenwriter. The Chicago native's plays have been produced and awarded by theatres nationwide, including West Coast Ensemble, Bailiwick Repertory, Phoenix Theatre, Bloomington Playwrights Project, Trustus Theatre, City Playhouse, Beverly Hills Theatre Guild, Asylum Theatre, and in Australia by the Mackay Festival of Arts. Most recently, Mr. Lewis collaborated on a baseball-themed play, *High and Inside*, with former Chicago Cubs/White Sox lefty ace Steve Trout.

SUSAN LIEBERMAN, whose plays and musicals have been seen in Chicago, New York, Boston and elsewhere, is the recipient of two Jeff nominations for her playwriting and two regional Emmy nominations for her children's teleplays. She began her career in London, working at Open Space Theatre for producer Thelma Holt. She then spent four years in New York writing for TheatreCrafts, before returning to her native Chicago, where she has been an active scriptwriter ever since. Her play, *Arrangement for Two Violas*, is featured in this anthology.

MIA McCULLOUGH's plays have been produced at theatres around the country, including Chicago Dramatists, Steppenwolf Theatre Company, Stage Left Theatre (all in Chicago); Actors' Express (Atlanta); and the Cincinnati Shakespeare Festival. Her play *Chagrin Falls* garnered several awards including the ATCA Elizabeth M. Osborn Award, a Jeff Citation, and an After Dark Award. Her play *Since Africa* was a finalist for the 2005 Susan Smith Blackburn Prize. Ms. McCullough lives just outside Chicago with her husband and young son. Her play, *Taking Care*, is featured in this anthology.

ROBERT McEWEN is a winner of two of the nation's top awards for dramatists, including first prize in the 21st Century Playwrights Festival for his play *Cholo!* in judging chaired by Edward Albee. During the 2004 election season, Bob published an acclaimed collection of short satires entitled "Tales Of The Pea Sea," a pun on the excesses of political correctness.

BRETT NEVEU Productions include *4 Murders* with A Red Orchid Theatre (Chicago), *Eric LaRue* with Royal Shakespeare Company (Stratford), *American Dead* with American Theatre Company (Chicago), *Empty* with Stage Left Theatre (Chicago) and *Eagle Hills, Eagle Ridge, Eagle Landing* and *twentyone* with Spring Theatreworks (New York City). Mr. Neveu has been commissioned twice by Steppenwolf Theatre Company and was awarded the Goodman Theatre's Ofner Prize for New Work, as well as The League of Chicago Theatre's 2005 Emerging Artist Award. His play, *Drawing War*, is featured in this anthology.

TOM PATRICK's play *Descent (A Darwinian Comedy)* was produced by The Aardvark in Chicago, Next Act in Milwaukee, and Stage Door Acting Ensemble in New York City. *Middleman* was produced by Milwaukee's Cedar Creek Repertory, *Soft Target* by Chicago Dramatists, and *The Vow* by Stage Left Theatre of Chicago. *Wildwood* will be produced by The Road Theatre of Los Angeles in 2006. *MisAmerica* was published in the 2004 writer's issue of Performink.

ROGER RUEFF's award-winning stage plays *Hospitality Suite* and *So Many Words* have been produced in the U.S. and internationally. His works for the screen include the teleplay *God Lives* and the screenplay *The Big Kahuna*, starring Kevin Spacey and Danny DeVito. Mr. Rueff has also authored a collection of poetic proverbs written for his son, titled "Fifty Things I Want My Son to Know" (Andrews-McMeel, publisher). He is represented by Anonymous Content, Los Angeles.

TANYA SARACHO is cofounder of Chicago's Teatro Luna and has written for all of its ensemble works, including *Generic Latina, Dejame Contarte, Kita y Fernanda, The Maria Chronicles, S-e-x-Oh!* and *SÓLO Latinas.* Her plays *La Dueña, Kita y Fernanda* and *Adnakiel* have received readings at Victory Gardens, Chicago Dramatists, Teatro Luna, Songs Of Coconut Hill Festival, Repertorio Español, and Teatro Vista. She is the recipient of the Ofner Prize from the Goodman Theatre.

MARK YOUNG's plays have appeared in Chicago, New York and Washington, DC. In 2002, he received the Source Theatre's H. D. Lewis New Play Award for his plays *They All Fall Down* and *New Orleans*, which were produced in the Washington Theatre Festival. He has twice been a finalist for the Heideman Award at the Actors Theatre of Louisville for his plays *Night* (2004) and *Black & White* (2002).

CHICAGO
DRAMATISTS

THE PLAYWRIGHTS'THEATRE

RUSS TUTTEROW . . . . .Artistic Director
BRIAN LOEVNER . . . . .Managing Director
DOMENICK DANZA. . . . . .Outreach Director
ROBERT KOON . . . . .Director of The Playwrights' Network

RESIDENT PLAYWRIGHTS
Alice Austen, David Barr III, Carson Grace Becker, Derrell Capes, Lydia R. Diamond, Marsha Estell, Joseph Fedorko, John Green, Mark Guarino, Jim Henry, Keith Huff, Joel Drake Johnson, McKinley Johnson, Gene Jones, Nambi E. Kelley, Robert Koon, Aline Lathrop, Donald Lewis, Susan Lieberman, Mia McCullough, Robert McEwen, Brett Neveu, Tom Patrick, Roger Rueff, Tanya Saracho, Mark Young

BOARD OF DIRECTORS
Teresa L. Powell, *President*; Sandra Blau, Patrice Fletcher, *Vice Presidents*; Brian Loevner, *Secretary*; Jeff Mier, *Treasurer*; Alice Austen, Patricia Heimann, McKinley Johnson, Michael J. Keating, Ellen J. Krasnow, Dianne S. Rossell, Neill E. Shanahan, Nancy P. Taylor, Russ Tutterow, Elizabeth Urech

ADVISORY BOARD
Michael Cullen, Ann Filmer, Rebecca Gilman*, Evan Guilford-Blake*, Rondi Reed, David Rush*, Bruce Sagan, Steve Scott, Dana Singer, Chuck Smith, Edward Sobel, Michele Volansky

* Resident Playwright Alumnus

CHICAGO DRAMATISTS is supported in part by The Shubert Foundation, The Sara Lee Foundation, The Illinois Arts Council, a state agency, Starbucks Foundation, The Gaylord and Dorothy Donnelley Foundation, The MacArthur Fund for Arts & Culture at The Richard H. Driehaus Foundation, Prince Charitable Trusts, Polk Bros. Foundation, The Mayer & Morris Kaplan Family Foundation, BlueCross BlueShield of Illinois, a CityArts Program 3 Grant from the City of Chicago Department of Cultural Affairs, Northern Trust Company, Kraft Foods, Chicago Tribune Foundation, The Dramatists' Guild Fund, Dr. Donahue Tremaine Trust, The Chicago Drama League, Altria Group, Inc., The Saints—Volunteers for the Arts, and numerous individual donors. Major in-kind support is provided by The Arts & Business Council of Chicago and the Chicago Community Trust.

CHICAGO DRAMATISTS is a professional theatre producing in accordance with Actors' Equity Association, Chicago Area Theatres Contract; and is a Constituent of Theatre Communications Group (TCG), the national organization for the American theatre; and a member of the League of Chicago Theatres and the Producers Association of Chicago Theater (PACT).

FOR INFORMATION ON CHICAGO DRAMATISTS AND ITS PLAYWRITING PROGRAMS, CALL OR WRITE:
Chicago Dramatists, 1105 W. Chicago Avenue, Chicago, IL 60622
E-mail: newplays@chicagodramatists.org; Phone: (312) 633-0630
Or visit our web site at **www.chicagodramatists.org**